The Red Man's West

Medicine Crow

The Red Man's West

True Stories of the Frontier Indians
from *MONTANA,*
The Magazine of Western History

Selected and Edited by
MICHAEL S. KENNEDY

HASTINGS HOUSE, PUBLISHERS • NEW YORK

Published simultaneously in Canada
by Saunders, of Toronto, Ltd., Toronto 2B.

Library of Congress Catalog Card Number: 65-26672

Printed in the United States of America

Contents

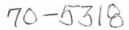

Introduction

WE AMERICANS are a strange people . . .

When, almost two centuries ago, we threw off the yoke of despotism ours was a society of immigrants and minority groups of different nationalities, creeds and colors. Then, while we matured as a nation, we established a reputation as champions of human rights throughout the world, with a fine display of humanitarianism and tolerance. We even staged international crusades for the securing of rights for others. Over the years, we have contributed billions of dollars, publicly and privately, in combating poverty, oppression, disease and other evils that beset nations and peoples.

And yet with two of our own minority peoples — the Indians and the Negroes — we have negated much of that essential nobility, tarnishing our shining armor. After more than a century we have solved neither the Negro "problem" nor the Indian "problem," although the forces for the amelioration of the former are now strongly in motion.

Expressing the basic problem from the Indian's point of view (call it the white-man problem), Alvin Josephy has said:

> From the first coming of the Europeans to America, the Indians were faced by the gravest threats that men face: challenges to freedom, right of conscience, personal security, the means of existence and life itself. In each crisis the [Indian] people acted and reacted as other persons under similar circumstances would have acted anywhere in the world.

The conquest of the Americas by the whites was not a pretty process. Sometimes brutally, sometimes almost casually, the conquerors wrenched the land away from its inhabitants. As the invaders saw it, the conquest was natural and inevitable: the Indians had no option — if they couldn't or wouldn't bow meekly to fate, they would have to be exterminated. As Senator Pendleton of Ohio put it in the 1880's:

"They must either change their mode of life or they must die."

By then the Indians were a minority in a realm they once had ruled. "Strangers in their own land," outnumbered and defeated, they faced the second phase of a conflict that had started with the white man's drive to take that land from them. Now the objective was to rob them of their traditions, to force them to forsake their way of life and fit into the white man's world.

Driven to desperation, threatened with starvation, the Indians had joined battle and carried on a hopeless fight with magnificent courage. It was bound to end in tragedy for them, but fortunately their extermination, so callously called for, was not realized. Indian history did not end at Wounded Knee; it has not ended today. Our Indian population (full and part blood) now stands at more than half a million. Many of them have accepted the white man's culture, either completely or in part. Many others have accepted none of it. Again, as Alvin Josephy has so well put it:

> On the whole the Indians are still a proud and dignified people. But they are still a conquered people, who continue to stand in confusion and helplessness between two worlds. Their old standards and ways of life are smashed and gone, but it is not easy — even a hundred years later — for a once independent people to abandon and forget what was.

This, in brief, sets the stage for *Red Man's West*. Without some understanding of this bitter background, one cannot fully appreciate the contents of this book. Yet the selections here were not made from any desire to amplify the tragedy. There are some excellent books on that phase of our history and there will undoubtedly be more.

My purpose in *Red Man's West* was to select a well-rounded, interesting and entertaining group of authoritative narratives which together would make a broad panorama. It would portray the First Americans from pre-historic times to the present day. They would be seen as human beings, wonderfully adapted to their natural environment, with well established standards of morality, philosophy and religion.

Because the whole wide West is too broad a focus and because *Montana, The Magazine of Western History*, from which these articles were selected, is essentially oriented to the Northern Plains and Rocky Mountains, our lens narrows to the Indians of this remote region — the Blackfeet and Assiniboins on the north, the Flatheads and the Nez Percés to the west, the Shoshones, Crows and Northern Cheyennes to the south, and the Mandans and Sioux to the east. Their legends and lore, family and tribal life, moments of glory and of tragedy, pathos, humor, heroism, cowardice, adventure and routine have been blended herein. This anthology represents a broad concensus, as well as the weighted contradictions of many observers. It reveals almost as many viewpoints as there are authors. Some of these essays are classics of their kind; some are scholarly and some are exceptional literature. All of them are by people who knew their subject well, observed keenly and had something to say. The photographs and illustrative matter, culled from thousands, are among the rarest and the best in existence. My guideline in editing and selection was based on a brief passage by the brilliant George Bird Grinnell, who dedicated sixty-five scholarly years to learning everything he could about the Indians:

> These primitive people in certain ways lived more in accordance with form and custom than we do, and a comprehension of the motives which govern their acts cannot be had without these details. I have never been able to regard the Indian as a mere object for study — a museum specimen. A half-century spent in rubbing shoulders with them, during which I have had a share in almost every phase of their old-time life, forbids me to think of them except as acquaintances, comrades and friends. While their culture differs from ours . . . fundamentally they are like ourselves, except insofar as their environment has obliged them to adopt a mode of life and of reasoning that is not quite our own, and which, without experience, we do not readily understand.

Here, then, is your opportunity to know and understand better the Indians of the Northern Plains. We have tried to provide the answers to many questions, as well as an extended tour of vicarious re-examination. But above all, I hope you will find in *Red Man's West* a rich feast, blended between the delicate savoring of sage tea to the full satisfaction of pounds of prime roast buffalo hump slowly cooked over aspen coals.

MICHAEL KENNEDY

Montana Historical Society
August, 1965.

Picture Credits

Bureau of American Ethnology, pp. 179, 294

E. S. Curtis, frontispiece; pp. 22, 25, 31, 32, 35, 61, 86, 87, 88, 149, 150, 151, 152, 153, 154, 165, 169, 170, 220, 221, 241, 290, 320

Montana Historical Society, pp. 2, 8, 9, 10, 11, 17, 27, 31, 32, 35, 36, 37, 40, 48, 53, 57, 66, 70, 71, 77, 79, 80, 83, 93, 95, 97, 102, 105, 108, 113, 115, 120, 123, 124, 127, 131, 132, 134, 139, 159, 168, 169, 173, 180, 181, 185, 192, 193, 197, 202, 205, 211, 215, 225, 235, 262, 267, 269, 273, 276, 278, 281, 283, 286, 294, 302, 305, 308, 309, 313, 316, 317, 324, 330, 331

Nebraska State Historical Society, pp. 225, 226

O'Neil Jones, p. 229

Ruth Koerner Oliver, pp. 20, 107, 155, 191, 236, 263, 269, 311

Ernst Peterson, p. 156

Smithsonian Institution, pp. 142, 327

Norma Linderman Waller, pp. 245, 247, 254

ARTISTS AND PHOTOGRAPHERS

George Catlin, pp. 131, 142

Edward S. Curtis, frontispiece; pp. 22, 25, 31, 32, 35, 61, 86, 87, 88, 149, 150, 151, 152, 153, 154, 165, 169, 170, 220, 221, 241, 290, 320

Fire Bear, pp. 70, 71, 77, 79, 80

W. A. Huffman, pp. 10, 17, 181, 185, 278, 317

Paul Kane, p. 131

W. H. D. Koerner, pp. 20, 107, 155, 191, 236, 263, 269, 311

Henry Lion, p. 120

Charlie Russell, pp. 40, 108, 123, 168, 169, 192, 197

Olaf Seltzer, pp. 132, 134

Harold Von Schmidt, p. 115

CHILDREN OF NATURE

Crow Indians: a very early photo. *Below:* Crow Indians

Prehistoric Man in the Yellowstone Valley

By STUART W. CONNER

THIS IS THE story of Prehistoric Man in the west — more precisely in the Yellowstone Valley. The story goes back through eons of time, through centuries and millenia, through periods of climatic change (each almost as long as the period of recorded history of mankind), back to the Ice Age. The present state of our knowledge is minimal. As one of the outstanding American archaeologists, Waldo Wedel, puts it, we are looking through a glass, darkly. But recently we are getting new glimpses of our Stone Age predecessors.

Let us look through the dark glass, past the time when the Plains Indians had horses and were nomads afoot; further back before any European had ever tainted America; back into the Stone Age.

Look further back before the Indians had bows and arrows to the time when Christ was on earth, then still further to the time of the Sumerians and the beginnings of recorded history in Europe, to the time of Abraham, 4000 years ago. Man was then beginning his third great stage in the famed valley of the Yellowstone, in what is now Montana.

Then the earth was beginning to bloom again after nearly three millenia of desert or near-desert conditions, for there had been a drouth that lasted 3000 interminable years.

But before the great drouth (which is known as the *altithermal* climatic period), the climate was moist and the countryside verdant. During that time a hardy brand of men hunted on the Yellowstone.

Man did not originate in the Americas. The view accepted by nearly all present-day scholars is that he migrated from Asia during the latter part of the last Ice Age. During that time the ocean level was considerably lower, and it is assumed the Bering Strait was a grass land. The prehistoric horses and camels crossed the land bridge from North America to Asia, and the now-extinct mastodons, mammoths and giant prehistoric bisons with six-foot horn spreads migrated from Asia to North America.

The Ice Age was probably characterized by interminable rains and snows more than by unendurable cold. Most of Alaska was free of glaciation, and at

3

different times there were mountain valleys free from ice, down which man could have come. It is this period of about 10,000 to 15,000 years ago that probably saw much of the human migration from Asia. But there is some evidence that man was in North America uncounted generations before that, perhaps in excess of 30,000 years ago.

Anthropologists often wonder whether man consciously migrated to America, or whether the populating of the continents was an infinitely slow progression resulting from people following game. An inference is sometimes made (because of the lack of sound evidence) that man's coming was not a deliberate migration. While evidence of man in the American continents in excess of 12,000 years ago is meager, archaeological sites which date between 8000 and 12,000 years ago now number in the dozens on the two continents. This appears to indicate a substantial increase in population, beginning about 12,000 years ago.

It might be inferred that such an increase resulted from repetitious migrations, and that at least the later emigrants intentionally left their homeland in Siberia for the new country this side of the lush Bering plains. Even in aboriginal times the word got around!

As the great American ice cap receded, the climate became more temperate, but damp. This climatic period, known as the *anathermal,* produced lush vegetation. There were many great beasts to try the skill and courage of the Early Hunters.

When the Early Hunters are first known on the Montana plains, between 10,000 and 12,000 years ago, the continental ice sheet covered much of North America north of Montana. The more adventurous of the early Yellowstone people may have seen the vast fields of towering, but crumbling ice.

The Early Hunters came to America in small bands, bringing with them either fire or fire-making implements. They hunted mammoths and the giant prehistoric bison with short spears propelled by three-foot spear-throwers we now call atlatls. The animals were trapped in bogs and box canyons. The people made functional tools of stone and bone. They painted their spears with the many pigments offered by nature. Their economy was primarily based on hunting, but their diet no doubt included plants as well.

In the sites on the plains where the stone tools of the Early Hunters are found in association with the skeletons of the ancient bison, the tail bones are missing. Archaeologists noticed the same phenomenon in the bone deposits of the buffalo jumps of the much later Plains Indian. Ethnological research reveals that in skinning bison, Indians took the tail with the hide. This indicates that the Early Hunters also made use of the hides, probably for clothing and shelter.

Early Hunters did not bury their dead near the camps. We know nothing of their habitations, except that rock overhangs were occasionally utilized. Principal dwellings may have been temporary shelters suited to nomadic life. Their wooden darts, or short spears, thrown with the help of atlatls, were tipped with stone points of distinctive patterns, the better known being the now famous and well docu-

A Crow lodge with decoration

Crow Indians

mented Folsom point. In 12,000 years no one ever exceeded the exquisite workmanship employed on Folsom points. But why were their stone knives, hide scrapers and butchering tools so indifferently manufactured? Could the people have had a rudimentary religion based on the "magic of the hunt" requiring sacred hunting weapons? Surely the sustenance of life depended on their effectiveness.

And as the giant ground sloths, camels and elephants disappeared from the Americas, man concentrated more on bison, the principal source of his food, shelter and raiment for the next 100 centuries. And then for three or four millenia, 200 successive grandfathers of these Early Hunters knew the region. Their camps have been found at Red Lodge and Helena, their tools at Glendive, and also scattered, here and there, over the vast prairies. All, of course, were not Folsom projectile points, because through the centuries styles changed. And about sixty-five or seventy centuries ago, the climate also changed.

About 6500 or 7000 years ago, humidity gave way to drouth. Our smaller streams probably turned to dust, while the larger ones became mere channels in the stream beds. The prairie was nearly denuded, or perhaps it was in fact a desert. The valley and the country north of the Yellowstone may have been less devastated than the Wyoming Basin to the south.

Throughout the Great Plains there seems to have been pronounced local variations of climate and vegetation. Yet wherever people could sustain life, they had to forage for subsistence, except possibly at higher altitudes. Man was reduced to eating plants and roots, augmented by any unwary animal that walked, crawled or flew; but they were few. He ground berries and seeds, for his household utensils included various large stone implements used in grinding. The Plainsmen during this period no doubt moved constantly, always searching hungrily for bushes, roots and small animals. Since few bones of large animals are found at the skimpy habitation sites of these people, they have become known as The Foragers.

We know exceedingly little of our inhabitants during the altithermal drouth. It is possible man and animals may have virtually abandoned the area. There is increasing evidence that the mountain tops near the Yellowstone Valley enjoyed a more temperate climate during the altithermal drouth than they do now or than the valley did then. Peat bogs and the trunks and stumps of great trees (above the present timber line in the Beartooth Mountains) speak eloquently of growing seasons in excess of two or three months in times past. The alpine glaciers would have provided water for a considerable period, possibly throughout the altithermal, for glaciers are here yet in the rugged country south of Red Lodge.

Recent discoveries in the upper Yellowstone Valley reveal that during the altithermal period a "quake lake" was formed by a landslide blocking the river valley. Archaeological remains from the site include bison bones. Noticeable by their absence are the characteristic grinding tools of the typical Foragers. Perhaps here, some 5000 years ago, life was more endurable than elsewhere on the plains. What big game animals survived in the region must have congregated near the lake and in the neighboring Yellowstone Park and Beartooth Plateau. It is beginning to appear that the upper Yellowstone Valley was an oasis in the altithermal desert.

Then as the climate moderated and vegetation returned, man again returned to the valley of the Yellowstone.

About 4500 years ago men were trapping rather imposing bison in a blind coulee in Powder River County, on a southern tributary of the Yellowstone, still killing them with the venerable weapon of their ancestors, the spear thrower or atlatl. Bison no longer carried the immense straight horns. But even so, they probably dwarfed the modern buffalo of Old West history. Now man could look forward to forty-five centuries of increasing bison herds.

In all probability, by the time of Abraham man was enjoying a new security in our valley. The generations would come and go and the hard days of the Foragers would slowly disappear from the word-of-mouth legends of the ancient story-tellers. As bison herds increased, the human population flourished and grew. Bands of Yellowstone hunters now followed great herds to the Musselshell and the Big Horn. But they were never happier than when in the valley of clear water, grass and firewood, the mild, pleasant, provident Yellowstone.

About 200 generations ago, when the first civilization of man was flourishing unsuspected between the Tigris and the Euphrates half a world away, a band of hunters camped in a rincon on Bitter Creek, only some five miles from the site of the present city of Billings.

A great rock shelter over 100 feet long and forty-five feet deep attracted these people. It offered protection from storms, yet permitted the late afternoon sun to warm and cheer them. Here they stayed for many years in Pictograph Cave, although if they painted pictures on the walls (as others did many centuries later) not a trace remains. Perhaps these were descendants of the Powder River folk. Some of their stone atlatl points were much like those discovered at the coulee in the Powder River country.

More centuries came and went. Grass grew abundantly each spring and the bison covered the land. The families grew into bands and the bands, imperceptibly, into tribes. On the other side of the world the great civilizations of ancient Greece and Rome rose and fell, and a man splintered the faith of Abraham and Moses. People followed the bison with their atlatls and lived in the great cavern on Bitter Creek from time to time.

Finally one day a man with foresight thought how well it would be for his people if a bison herd could be intentionally forced over a cliff to its mass death. Before this, man had relied on isolated kills in stealth, but once in a lifetime lightning stampeded a herd to its destruction in the night.

It was about the time of Christ that these Indians learned to stampede bison over cliffs. It carried great economic impact. From that time until the coming of the white men, hunger seldom stalked the people. Great communal drives were organized. Herds were enticed between lines of rock and brush piles and then stampeded over cutbanks or cliffs. If the prairie did not offer rocks or brush, buffalo chips, piled high, made an adequate hiding place for a man to lie motionless until the herd was abreast. Then the hunter made his movement to further frighten the leaders of the herd. A rock or brush corral was sometimes built below the cliff to contain those animals which survived the fall.

After adoption of the bow and arrow 1500 years ago, a few arrows may have helped spook the herd along, particularly if the leaders tried to turn through the line of hunters to avoid the cliff. But not every buffalo run was successful. Sometimes the herd did turn. Then there was wailing in the camp, both for the trampled fathers and sons and for the lost meat and empty bellies.

With the coming of new arrows, man found the old stone points were too large. So hunters chipped smaller ones, with thin, sharp edges and notches on each side through which sinew could be tied. Man used the small arrow points for many centuries until eventually the white man's "barrel hoops" provided an even better source. A few small bone points were used, however, up to the last of the era.

Neighboring tribes often caused trouble, killing small hunting parties or kidnaping women; but not many men were killed in battle. If things became intolerable, a tribe was forced to stop such enemy depredations. The men then went forth with their big shields, decorated with their favored medicine sign. When men from the neighboring tribe spied them approaching and ran forth to do battle, both sides lined up, facing each other, in a line of skirmishers. They hid

Crow Indians

behind their shields, loosing barrages of arrows at the opponents. Not many were injured because a shield offered almost complete protection when one crouched behind it. Only the most daring or improvident died.

And so another millenium passed. Then 3500 miles away, on an ocean not mentioned by even the oldest storyteller in the tribe, a great ship landed men with black beards and pale skins. But many generations would pass and many buffalo would be driven over many cliffs before the word of the pale faces reached the valley.

We do not know when the prehistoric Indians of the Yellowstone first adopted skin tipis for habitations. These symmetrical, roomy lodges were, however, in use before the coming of the first white man. The tipi covers were held down on the prairie with rocks. The "tipi rings" of stone (some with fireplaces) are still to be found on the Montana prairies, mute evidence of the homes of nomadic plainsmen.

One group which had lived in what we now call North Dakota became engaged in a bitter family disagreement with the rest of their tribesmen and departed westward. They may have come up the Yellowstone River by slow stages. These people, not primarily hunters in their old home lands, had lived in huts covered with mud, and had cultivated corn, squash and other vegetables. They made pottery, too, and decorated it with designs pressed into it before the clay was fired. For several years they camped at the site of the present city of Glendive. But the summer heat was less severe nearer the mountains upstream, so the people continued on. Pottery, too heavy for dogs and women, had to be left behind.

The new people broke into smaller units as they followed the herds. Some went west to the mountains, where 5000 years before people had camped on an old lake shore that had long ago given way to the erosion of the Yellowstone River. Others moved south on the Big Horn River where buffalo were numerous. Finally the tribe had two main bands, the River Crows and Mountain Crows. As one group passed the great rimrocks we suspect that they, too, camped for a while at Pictograph Cave and made pottery again, although not as well as their grandmothers. They painted pictures on the roof of themselves and their great shields. But rock shelters were not for these people, for they were now plainsmen who followed the buffalo and lived in skin tipis.

Then came the fateful eighteenth century of the white man. The Crows' old tribe in North Dakota with whom they occasionally visited and traded (the Hidatsa) had beads, hard metal pots and knives and axes traded from their eastern neighbors, the Mandans. And they had heard of the "great dogs" the white men rode, called "horses."

The Flatheads and Nez Percés from further west, as well as the Shoshones from the south, momentarily had the edge on the hostile Blackfeet in the first half of the 1700's. For a short time the new horses gave the mountain tribes easy access to the buffalo plains of the Crows. The Crows were astonished and envious of the bravery and dexterity of the western Indians riding these big animals. Sometime between 1730 and 1750 the Crows acquired their first horses; but whether in stealth or by trade has been lost in time.

The glorious day of the mounted Plains Indian had arrived. Now man could travel great distances and strike devastating blows at enemy tribes, although receiving retribution in kind. But the culture flourished, even if smaller tribes were caught in a bloody vise between more powerful neighbors. Ultimately the more numerous Sioux were forced into the Lower Yellowstone by pressure of the white advance. For fifteen years, beginning about 1860, the Crows, forced west and south up the river, were never safe below the site of the present city of Billings. Between the depredations of the Sioux from the south and east and the Blackfeet from the north and west, the Crows were fighting for survival when the demise of the immeasurable buffalo herds and the conquest of the white horse-soldiers spelled the end of the glorious days.

Group of Crow chiefs; left to right, White Bear, Wet, Covers Up His Feet, Bell Rock, Medicine Crow, Pretty Eagle, Four Balls, Old Dog

A postscript to prehistory was discovered in 1937, between Billings and Roundup. On a sandstone cliff, carved into the rock, appears a drawing of two white men in a boat, along with horses and guns. Perhaps it was intended to depict Lewis and Clark, Francois Larocque, Colter and Potts, or some other early white explorers. One might almost say it was a prehistoric record of an important historical event, the end of prehistory and the beginning of history.

If civilization was not always charitable in its relations with the native American, at least the Yellowstone Valley had been his friend. As the great Crow chief, Arapooish, so eloquently put it:

The Crow country is a good country. The Great Spirit has put it exactly in the right place; when you are in it you fare well; Whenever you go out of it, whichever way you travel, you fare worse ... The Crow country is exactly in the right place. It has snowy mountains and sunny plains; all kinds of climates, and good things for every season. When the summer heat scorches the prairies, you can draw up under the mountains, where the air is sweet and cool, the grass fresh, and the bright streams come tumbling out of the snowbanks. There you can hunt the elk, the deer, and the antelope, when their skins are fit for dressing; there you will find plenty of white bears and mountain sheep.

In the autumn when your horses are fat and strong from the mountain pastures, you can go down into the plains and hunt the buffalo or trap beaver on the streams. And when winter comes on, you can take shelter in the woody bottoms along the rivers; there you will find buffalo meat for yourself, and cottonwood bark for your horses; or you may winter in the Wind River Valley, where there is salt weed in abundance. The Crow country is exactly in the right place. Everything good is to be found there. There is no country like the Crow country.

Buffalo grazing, northern Montana, 1880

Horn in the Ice

AN INTRODUCTION TO THE EARLIEST CHEYENNES

By VERNE DUSENBERRY

WATER. WATER AND SKY. NOTHING MORE.

No grass, no trees, nothing but water and sky. No animals, no people.

Suddenly, a Person appears floating on the water. Around him are birds, swans, geese, ducks and all the birds that swim. The Person becomes tired of water and calls the birds to him and asks them to look for some earth. The larger birds dive down, only to return with nothing. One by one they try it. Nothing happens. Finally, a small duck dives down and returns with a bit of mud on its bill. He swims happily to the Person and gives him the mud. The Person takes the mud in his hands and works it with his fingers until it is dry. The mud grows in quantity as the Person works it. Soon he has a large handful of it. This he sprinkles over the water and makes little piles of it here and there on the water. The dust forms land, and the Person leans back and watches it grow and grow and grow until it spreads as far as he can see. Suddenly, all is land, solid land. And the earth is created.

Heamma Wihio — the Person, the Creator — is lonesome as he looks at all the endless land he has just made. He creates two people — a man and a woman — and stands between them with his back toward the rising sun. The woman is to his right, the North, and the man stands to his left, the South.

"Where the woman is," he said, "it will be cold. You will freeze. Only a few animals will live there and the grass and the trees will not grow. You, Woman, will control *Hoimaha*, the winter man or storm — the power that brings the cold and the snow. He will bring sickness and death, yet he will obey you. Your hair, Woman, will always be gray, yet you will never grow old.

"Man," *Heamma Wihio* continued, "you will represent the Sun and typify Summer. Where you live, everything will be good. All kinds of birds and animals will live there plentifully. And the bushes and the grasses and the timbers will be many. You are young and you will never grow older. But you will never have the power the Woman does. *Hoimaha* will obey her and will control you, too, for every year the Sun will be defeated. Winter will drive you away."

Man and Woman moved to their respective lodgings. *Heamma Wihio* was

11

left alone again. So, out of his loneliness, he created other people. And these people multiplied and became the *Tsi-Tsi-Tsas*,[1] those related to one another, those similarly bred. *Our People. Us.*[2] And some day the Dakotas would call them *Sha-Hi-'Ye-Na*, people of alien speech; and the white man would corrupt that name and call them Cheyenne.

Where or when all of this happened the Cheyennes do not know. Emerging from the cloudy mist of another legend is the story of their having lived in a land that was perpetually covered with ice and snow. Trying to escape the continual rule of *Hoimaha*, they started eastward toward the sun. After many years, they came to a narrow neck of sea at a time when the water was frozen. As the people were about halfway across the frozen water, one of the young women discovered a horn sticking out of the ice.

The horn took her fancy. Even in these difficult times of moving, the women and the children made sliding sticks from horns and managed to enjoy life a little more. The girl wanted this horn, for it was large and long, and would make a splendid sliding stick. She tried to pull the horn out of the ice; but the harder she pulled, the tighter the horn seemed to be imbedded. Finally, she called to her relatives for assistance. Some of the men came and helped her. But, like her, they were unable to pull the horn out. Then, they began to cut the horn, for they liked the girl and wanted to make her happy. As they cut deeper into the horn, blood spurted out in great gushes.

The people were frightened and grouped together on both sides of the men who had been cutting the horn. Just as they realized that the horn must be that of a monster, they felt a great tremor and knew that the monster must be struggling below the frozen water. Before anyone could move away, the ice suddenly broke, the horn disappeared, and a great chasm appeared. Some of the people were drowned. Many of them found themselves before an ever-widening channel of water, so they had to retreat to the land from which they had come. Those on the side toward the Sun watched their friends retreat; then, saddened by the inseparable gulf between them, they took flight onward in pursuit of the Sun and moved into the East and the New Land. Never have these people — the *Tsi-Tsi-Tsas* — forgotten this story. Their descendants, telling the story today,[3] are puzzled by the implications of this division. These people today know that the Cheyenne tribe is the result of the absorption of a kindred-speaking group, the Sutaio; they also know that their own tribe has been divided — the Northern Cheyenne in Montana and the Southern Cheyenne in Oklahoma.

Tradition and legend continue. Without any explanation of how they reached there, the Cheyennes tell another story of another time when they lived near a big lake far to the North, yet in a place less cold than their former habitat. Men constructed seines from willows to catch fish, and women pounded the fish bones and made oil. Fish and oil were the main sources of food.[4] Then another legend. The tribe had moved southwesterly and the men were hunters. Aside from fish, they lived on rabbits, wild fowl and eggs, and especially, in the autumn, fat skunks.

Cheyenne village, drying buffalo meat and hides   Young Cheyenne mother and child

For a long time they seemed to have lived in this country where maple-sugar trees grew, and they had learned the secret of extracting the sirup from the trees. Even in much later times, they alone of the Plains Indians knew how to tap a box-elder tree and to boil the sap and use it — even to sweeten coffee after the introduction of that commodity.[5]

From these intangibles we may assume (and the assumption is based on vague references) that the Cheyennes may have lived somewhere in the region of the North Atlantic or Hudson's Bay. If we can make that assumption, we can surmise a series of movements that eventually led them to the mid-central region of what is now the United States at the point where historical references begin. Mooney advances the theory[6] that the prime cause for their upheaval and south-western migration could be attributed to the increasing pressure of the Crees after the establishment of the English trading posts on Hudson's Bay, beginning about 1668. With the establishment of the Hudson's Bay Company in 1670, intertribal warfare began on a large scale, and the advantage rested with the Crees, who had the wealth of the newly formed company behind them. The Assiniboins, driven into an alliance with the Crees in 1679, became implacable foes of their relatives, the Dakotas. That alliance, plus their normal enemies — the Objibways — forced the Dakotas northwestward, and in all likelihood caused the Cheyennes to move — perhaps in the vanguard.

All writers who study these earliest historical movements of the Cheyennes are dependent upon practically the same sources, and this one will be no exception. Jablow[7] relates how La Salle reported the arrival of a group of Indians at Fort Crevecoeur (near present-day Peoria, Illinois) in February, 1680. These Indians known as the *Chaa*, came purportedly to seek trade relations with him. La Salle does not mention who called these Indians *Chaa*, but according to Jablow, it could be a shortened corruption of Sha-Hi'-Ye-Na — the Dakota word for the Cheyennes. If that hypothesis is correct, and the *Chaa* who visited La Salle are the Cheyennes, they are only several miles away from the first geographical area actually recorded for them. As *Chaiena*, the name of the tribe appears on a map made by Joliet and Franquelin prior to 1673, and the location is on the east side of the Mississippi above the mouth of the Wisconsin River.[8] Prior to 1700, the date generally assigned as the time the Cheyennes moved westward into what is now North Dakota, they were reputedly living along the Minnesota River.[9]

Archaeological research has cleared away much of the confusion about the early movement of the Cheyennes by establishing their residence at the big bend of the Sheyenne River in what is now North Dakota during the eighteenth century. And, not only the fact that they were living there but that they existed as sedentary horticulturists has been well established. In 1930, the Columbia University-North Dakota Historical Society expedition under the direction of Dr. W. D. Strong of Columbia University began its series of excavations of a site in east-central North Dakota about twelve miles southeast of the present town of Lisbon and on the Sheyenne River where it makes its big bend. Dr. Strong's report is most inclusive:[10]

> The site is located on a river terrace with a steep bank on the north facing the former channel of the Sheyenne River. There are the rings of about seventy houses surrounded by a deep ditch or moat which surrounds the village except along the steep river bank. Our excavations tested the ditch, seven houses, and numerous cache pits. The ditch proved to have a width of almost ten feet and a depth of almost five feet. There were no bastions . . . and no positive evidence of a stockade. . . . The houses . . . were all circular earth lodges with four central posts set in an almost exact square and a central fireplace. . . . Many of the post molds contained wood in good condition and were tamped in place with bison or other large bones. Charred beams were particularly abundant. All houses . . . had been burned.
>
> Contact materials from this site include a few glass beads (most of which were inset in pottery as a decoration!), one piece of glass, a trigger guard ornament from a British or a French gun of early eighteenth-century manufacture and thirteen lance, arrow, and knife blades made of brass and iron. . . . The one gunpart . . . was drilled to be worn as a decoration, and the finding of only one dubious gun flint suggest that the Cheyenne were either without or were weak in regard to firearms at this time.
>
> Pottery was fairly abundant at the site . . . 3767 sherds being removed. No complete or restorable vessels were found. Cheyenne pottery is predominantly of a light one, passing through various shades of buff and tan to mottled gray-black and black. . . . The great majority of the sherds indicate vertical grass wiping of the necks and horizontal paddle markings on the body. . . . Cheyenne pottery (in surface treatment) resembles the later sedentary Plains treatment but in decoration it seems more Woodland.

Summarizing his report on the Cheyenne village, Dr. Strong continues:

In brief, the Cheyenne at this period were both agriculturists and hunters. They lived in fixed fortified villages, used a four-post earth lodge, and possessed a culture very similar to that of the semi-sedentary Caddoan and Siouan peoples of the eastern Plains. Their ceramics are of a northeastern type and, in their use of birchbark, shell knives or scrapers, stemmed arrow points, and a few other traits, they also differed from their sedentary Missouri River neighbors. However, their earth and basic culture were so similar to the latter that contacts must have been close.

Long before these scientific observations of Strong's were reported, other writers mentioned the location of the site. Hayden, writing in 1863, spoke of the Sheyenne River as being one of the most important branches of the Missouri, for that river seems to be the starting point of our knowledge of the Cheyenne Indians.[11] Grinnell points out that Dakota and Cheyenne tradition places at least twelve villages along the Missouri River and its tributaries in North Dakota.[12] He further states that as late as 1850 the Dakota called the site along the Sheyenne River *Sha-Hï-e-Na-Woj-Upi*, "Where the Cheyenne plant corn."[13] Mooney, whose acquaintanceship with the Cheyennes extended for nearly twenty years (1885-1905), likewise mentioned the Sheyenne River site and added that during the time they lived in permanent villages, they subsisted chiefly on corn of their own planting, and on fish and ducks from the lakes.[14]

It is Grinnell, perhaps, who has explored the habits of the Cheyennes more thoroughly than anyone else. During his many years of close association with them, he found old women who still remembered how their mothers had made pots during the years of residence along the Missouri River. One of the last of these pots was buried with an old woman on the Northern Cheyenne Reservation in 1896.[15] Likewise, Grinnell quotes the testimony of informants who told him of how they had farmed regularly at various spots along the Missouri, the Grand, the Little Missouri, the North Platte and the Laramie rivers. These old men and women (who died between 1900 and 1915) were explicit in telling how the crops were planted — one grain at each corner of a square with one grain in the center, and that the grains were all planted with the soft end up. He also received information that as late as 1850 the Cheyennes put in crops of corn along a broad flat on the Platte River in the general vicinity of Fort Laramie. Another evidence of their corn culture appeared in the Corn Dance, which was participated in by young men and women carrying a sacred ear of corn on a stick. Grinnell discovered that the dance was continued until 1876.[16]

When the Cheyennes left their sedentary life and their village homes to adopt the wandering nomadic life of buffalo hunters is both speculative and argumentative. Strong believes that 1750 might be the approximate date of the abandonment of the Sheyenne site that he had excavated.[17] Other writers, particularly Grinnell, state that the end of the eighteenth century is a more nearly accurate time. That they were living in villages at the time of the Lewis and Clark Expedition (1804-

1806) is also reflected in Grinnell when he says, "It was perhaps a mere accident that Lewis and Clark did not come upon an occupied Cheyenne village."[18]

Grinnell and Mooney both attribute the departure of the Cheyennes to the Assiniboins. Swanton, however, writes ". . . the Cheyenne town was . . . destroyed by a body of Chippewa Indians led by Sheshepaskut, head chief of those bands of Chippewa which were forcing their way southwest at the end of the eighteenth century."[19] Swanton's authority is David Thompson, who in his *Narrative of His Exploration in Western America, 1784-1812* relates a story told him by Jean Baptiste Cadotte, a young half-breed trapper who was with the Chippewa at the time of the destruction of the Sheyenne-Cheyenne village.

According to Cadotte — as told to Thompson and quoted by Swanton — the Chippewas did not like the Cheyennes but badly needed their corn and vegetables as trade items. Several of the Chippewas were killed and at first the Chippewas blamed the Dakotas; but during one of their regular trading periods, some of the Chippewas saw fresh scalps that they recognized as belonging to their own people hanging in the Cheyenne village. A council of the Chippewas followed and their decision was to destroy the Cheyenne village. The following spring, when the Cheyenne men were hunting, the Chippewas swooped down and killed everyone in the village except three women. Likewise, they looted everything in the village that appealed to them before setting fire to it. This incident, according to these sources, took place about 1790.[20]

Too much significance should not be placed on the exact timing of the departure of the Cheyennes from their village homes, however, for evidence shows that there was no mass migration westward. Following the advent of the horse and the supply of trade goods, various groups left at irregular intervals. Perhaps the movement started with one band from a village going out on the plains to hunt and then returning to their village with a meat supply for their relatives. Undoubtedly, these hunting trips became longer and longer, and gradually, as the hunters wandered westward, they reached the Black Hills. Abounding with a fabulous supply of game, liberally sprinkled with flowing streams of good, clear water, comfortably protected from the winds of the Plains and from the watchful eyes of roaming enemies, and no doubt appealing to the spiritual nature of the Cheyenne as well, the Black Hills unquestionably provided an enticing picture to the villagers as the hunters told tales about it. Thus, perhaps, another group would leave to seek its riches in that strangely provident land.

Grinnell has given us the clearest picture of the probable movement of the Cheyennes westward when he wrote:[21]

> The tribal movement in fact may almost be compared to the familiar actions of a flock of feeding blackbirds . . . walking over a field in a broad front. The birds in the rear ranks constantly rise on the wing and fly over their fellows to alight just in front of them, where the ground has not been passed over and the food has not been consumed, while the whole front walks forward. In the same way — though slowly — the rearmost camps of the migrating Cheyenne were constantly moving onward and passing those in advance of them in the hope of finding new regions where food might easily be had.

Pretty Bird in uncovered Cheyenne sweat lodge

Cheyenne family on the move

That they were not early weaned from their former diet is evidenced by the report of Loisel, who stated that they "roam over the prairies west of the Missouri in this side of the Black Hills from which they come regularly to visit their old and faithful friends at the beginning of August, the Ricaras."

He also states that while the trade goods of the "Ricaras" attract the Cheyennes, they are more interested in the maize, tobacco, beans and pumpkins that the Arikaras could provide them. The prairie turnip, cut in pieces, dried and pounded into flour by the Cheyenne women, was bartered to the Arikaras for vegetables at a profit of three to four measures for one, according to Loisel, who also pointed out that the Cheyennes were difficult traders. These "savages" were disdainful of his wares and prided themselves on being ignorant. Loisel's irritation shows most clearly that the Cheyennes' attitude ". . . has been conducive to my detriment in the slight trade with the Caninanbiches (Arapaho) and others who obstinately defer to their [the Cheyennes'] judgement."[22]

Loisel's years on the Plains covered events beginning in 1795, so we have a picture of the Cheyennes, or at least some bands of them, fairly well established west of the Missouri. We see that they were dependent in part upon the food of their sedentary former neighbors, the Arikaras; we also can see that a friendship had been established with the Arapahoes, a tribe with whom the Cheyennes maintained a close relationship throughout the buffalo period. Even today, the Southern branches of the two tribes are together in Oklahoma; the Northern Cheyennes maintain a closer relationship with the Northern Arapahoes of the Wind River Reservation in Wyoming than with any other tribe of Indians.

Some time after the Cheyennes reached the Plains and occupied the territory between the Missouri River and the Black Hills, their numbers were increased by the addition of another tribe, the Sutaio. Again, one must depend upon legend for the story of the union of the two tribes. Rufus Wallowing of Lame Deer, Montana, a well informed member of the tribe and past president of the Northern Cheyenne Tribal Council, tells the following story about the Sutaio:[23]

> A long time ago at some place east of the Black Hills, the Cheyennes were fighting another tribe of Indians when suddenly the other Indians let out a whoop and started yelling at each other. The Cheyennes recognized that their enemies were speaking the same language, so they stopped fighting and got acquainted. So, from that time on, the Sutaios traveled with the Cheyennes and camped close by. They always remained a little separate but they finally intermarried with the Cheyennes and the Sutaios died out.

Mooney believed that the Sutaio were identical with the "Staetan" described by Lewis and Clark, who mentioned them as a "small tribe of 100 men and 400 souls" living along the Missouri,[24] and indicated that it was not until approximately 1833 that the two tribes united.[25] He added further that the Sutaio retained their distinctive dialect, dress and ceremonies, and camped apart until about 1851. This information parallels that of Grinnell, who describes the Sutaio language as being "rougher, harsher and more guttural" than the Cheyenne.[26] Grinnell was also able to secure a description of the clothing worn by the Sutaio at the time of the union of the two tribes. According to his findings, the Sutaio clothes were made much more crudely. The men did not wear a breachcloth, as did all of the Cheyennes as far back as memory extends, but rather wore flaps that hung down from the belt in front. Moccasins came from one piece of buckskin with a parfleche sole fastened to it. The traditional pattern for the Cheyenne moccasin utilized two pieces. Sutaio women dressed in hides that were tied together at the sides rather than being sewed. His date of the union of the tribes — "after 1832" — coincided almost exactly with the one being given by Mooney.

The meaning of the name *Sutaio* is obscured, and the original connotation seems to be forgotten. Dr. Rodolphe Petter, whose work with the Cheyenne language was extensive, believed that the word probably indicated "people left behind."[27] Others have thought that it came from the same root as *is-suht* which means ridge or hill. Willis Rowland, official interpreter for the Cheyennes for many years, felt that it carried the implication of "backward" or "behind."[28]

The Sutaio's richest contribution to the Cheyenne, however, is in the religious life, for two of their greatest ceremonies became associated with those of the Cheyennes. Best known is that of the Medicine Lodge, the Cheyenne counterpart of the Sun Dance. As elaborate as this ceremony became and as integral a part of the Cheyenne life as it was at the time of the white contact, the knowledge of the Medicine Lodge came from the Sutaio. It had been taught to them by their cultural hero, Standing on the Ground, who is sometimes referred to as Red Tassel of Corn or Straight Horns.[29]

Ranking almost in significance with the Medicine Lodge is the Sacred Hat, the *Is'se-Wun*. Old-time Sutaio claimed that the extinction of their tribe resulted as a punishment to them for having once abandoned a priest of the Sacred Hat in his old age.[30]

Be that as it may, the Sacred Hat has occupied a conspicuous place in the life of the Cheyennes, especially the Northern Cheyennes. It was reposing in its tipi within the camp circle along the Little Big Horn that day in June, 1876, when the Seventh Cavalry disturbed the peace and contentment of the Cheyenne people[31] and changed forever their way of life. It remained in the north, carefully guarded at Fort Keogh,[32] during the days of exile of the Northern Cheyennes in the years that followed that Custer fight. Today, it is kept in a special tipi at Birney, Montana, guarded by Josie Headswift, herself of Sutaio descent.

Thus, during the dawning years of the nineteenth century, the Cheyennes left their permanent villages along the Missouri and its tributaries and become nomadic hunters. They enriched their spiritual life by adopting the ceremonial of the Medicine Lodge and the Sacred Hat through the absorption of a cognate tribe, and emerged upon the Plains fortified for their sobriquet, "The Fighting Cheyennes."

NOTES

1 George Bird Grinnell, "Some Early Cheyenne Tales," *Journal of American Folklore*, XX, 170-172.

2 George Bird Grinnell, *The Cheyenne Indians*, New Haven, 1923, I, 2-3.

3 Personal interview, Rufus Wallowing, Lame Deer, Mont., Aug. 30, 1955. Mr. Wallowing gave credit to Frank Old Bird, a member of the Southern Cheyenne tribe who at the approximate age of 80 visited his northern brethren in 1951 and related the story.

4 George F. Will, "The Cheyenne Indians in North Dakota," *Proceedings of the Mississippi Valley Historical Association*, VII (1914). Mr. Will expresses his gratitude to George E. Hyde of Omaha, Nebraska, for the use of many of the traditions that Hyde had secured from older Cheyenne people. Grinnell states that in their buffalo-hunting days, the Cheyennes — unlike other Plains Indians — caught fish and enjoyed eating them. He wonders if their liking for fish might be traceable to their earlier Northeastern home. Grinnell, *The Cheyenne Indians, op. cit.*, I, 149.

5 Joseph John, "The Cheyenne in Plains Indian Trade," *Memoirs of the American Anthropological Association*, I, 1907.

6 James Mooney, "The Cheyenne Indians," *ibid.*

7 Joseph Jablow, "The Cheyenne in Plains Indian Trade Relations, 1795-1844," *Monographs of the American Ethnological Society*, XIX, 2.

8 Will, *op. cit.* Mr. Will states the Franquelin's map of 1688 places the Cheyennes on the Minnesota River.

9 E. D. Neill, *The History of Minnesota: From the Earliest Explorations to the Present Time*, Minneapolis, 1883; 154.

10 William Duncan Strong, "From History to Prehistory in the Northern Great Plains," *Smithsonian Miscellaneous Collections, 100*, Washington, 1940; 371-374.

11 F. V. Hayden, "Contributions to the Ethnography and Philology of the Indian Tribes of the Missouri Valley," *Transactions of the American Philosophical Society*, XII, 274-320.

12 George Bird Grinnell, "Early Cheyenne Villages," *American Anthropologist*, n.s. XX, 379.

13 *Ibid.*, 365.

14 Mooney, *op. cit.*, 368.

15 Grinnell "The Cheyenne Indians," *op. cit.*, I, 368.

16 *Ibid.*, 252-254.

17 Strong, *op. cit.*, 375.

18 Grinnell, "Early Cheyenne Villages," *op. cit.*, 379.

19 J. R. Swanton, "Some Neglected Data Bearing on Cheyenne, Chippewa, and Dakota History," *American Anthropologist, n.s.* XXXIII, 157.

20 *Ibid.*, 158.

21 Grinnell, "Early Cheyenne Villages" *op. cit.*, 379.

22 E. H. Abel (ed.) *Tabeau's Narrative of Loisel's Expedition to the Upper Missouri*, Norman, 1939; 153.

23 Personal interview, August 28, 1955.

24 R. G. Thwaite (ed.), *Original Journals of the Lewis and Clark Expedition*, New York, 1905; VI, 101-102.

25 Mooney, *op. cit.*, 370.

26 Grinnell, *The Cheyenne Indians, op. cit.*, I, 170.

27 Personal interview, Mrs. Rudolph Petter, Lame Deer, Mont., Aug. 29, 1955.

28 Grinnell, *The Cheyenne Indians, op. cit.*, I, 95.

29 Grinnell, "Some Early Cheyenne Tales," *op. cit.*, 170.

30 Mooney, *op. cit.*, 370.

31 T. B. Marquis, *A Warrior Who Fought Custer*, Minneapolis, 1931; 198.

32 Personal interview, John Stands-in-Timber, Lame Deer, Mont., Sept. 11, 1954.

PEOPLE OF THE
MOUNTAINS AND PLAINS

Piegan painted lodges

Piegan encampment

The Blackfeet: Barrier to the Best Beaver Bonanza

By RALPH L. BEALS

THE BLACKFEET AREA now generally known as Glacier and Waterton National Parks, and their immediate surroundings, was for almost a century one of the least known regions of the Far West. Supposed to be (as it, in fact, was) one of the richest beaver regions of the Rockies, it long remained an El Dorado from which the fur traders and trappers were barred by the persistent hostility of the fierce Blackfeet Indians. Although some daring parties may have penetrated the region at an early date, no record survives. It is possible that none of those who attempted an entry ever returned to tell of it.

Yet, the earliest history of the region is primarily the history of fur-trade expansion and efforts to tap this rich source of beaver — obtuse as it may seem. East, north, west and finally, south, the tide of western expansion swirled up to the borders of Blackfeet Indian territory, comprised of the Blood, Piegan and Blackfeet branches, but left it an island of unknown lands until mid-nineteenth century explorers visited it. French traders, the Hudson's Bay Company, the North-West Company, American Fur Company and Rocky Mountain Fur Company, to mention only the better known and best organized efforts, all came near these "Shining Mountains." Yet throughout the major fur-trade period none entered or knew their Alplike, pristine character — although they knew and respected the resistance of the original inhabitants, who remained a constant source of successful defiance for more than a century.

The rise and growth of the early fur trade and the formation of the great companies, therefore, are of significance. The events and policies of fur companies affected the explorations and efforts to penetrate the area commercially. All this is vital in understanding the Blackfeet Nation. For example, when the Hudson's Bay Company was formed in 1670, the charter gave it title to all land drained by waters flowing into Hudson's Bay and Hudson Strait. Thus, at a pen stroke by the dissolute Charles II, in 1670 the story of the Hudson's Bay Company is first distantly linked to the history of the Blackfeet, for the northern streams flow into Hudson's Bay and are hence within the area granted to the company.

The desire of Pierre Radisson, the French adventurer who had turned to the

English, to penetrate and explore the interior was in large measure thwarted by the initial and long-enduring policy of the Hudson's Bay Company to restrict its posts to the shoreline and wait for the Indians to bring in furs. It remained for a London gutter urchin, Henry Kelsey, who knew and perhaps was inspired by Radisson, to be the first Englishman to reach the plains, the time being 1691 and 1692. His journey was for many years in doubt, and only the later discovery and publication of his journals make it clear that he was also the first Englishman to see and shoot the buffalo and grizzly bear. Even yet it remains obscure whether Kelsey was sent by the Company or took "French leave," but the probabilities appear to favor the first theory.

Kelsey, in his journey, was far from reaching the Blackfeet domain. He did not even see the Rocky Mountains. But for over half a century he was the only known Englishman to reach as far as the plains east of the Rockies.[1] The area was respected for good reason.

The first known visitors to actually approach the region were all representatives of the Hudson's Bay Company. In 1754-5, Anthony Hendry wintered with Blackfeet and Bloods, probably wandering the region of the Bow River in Alberta and passing down the Red Deer and South Forks of the Saskatchewan in the spring. From them he learned something of the area to the south. He found a French post near the Grand Forks of the Saskatchewan. His journey brought no results, for his stories of Indians on horseback were not believed and his whole account was discredited.

In 1772 the competition from Montreal stirred the Hudson's Bay Company into activity and Mathew Cocking was sent to the Saskatchewan. Crossing the South Fork, he met some Blackfeet at the Eagle Hills and spent the winter with them, confirming Henry's account. He found French traders who had married into the tribe and adopted native life. Some of these nameless personages were probably the first whites to visit the confines of the present Glacier National Park, but their doings remain unknown to history. Cocking returned to the Bay in 1773. That same year the council of the Hudson's Bay Company had ordered establishments to be made on the Saskatchewan, and Cumberland House was built at Sturgeon Lake. From this time on "patroons of the woods" were engaged to live inland with the Indians. A staff of fifty-one men was kept regularly at Cumberland House. There is no record of how far west or south some of these men may have gone.[2]

While there is ample published material on the entry of the North-West Fur Company into the region north of the Saskatchewan, their activities in the direction south can only be inferred from the movement of the Hudson's Bay Company there. Of the independents and free traders we likewise have little data. In 1780 a free trader's post is mentioned at the Eagle Hills near Battleford, Canada. A curious note from the *Manuscript Journal of a Gentleman Belonging to the Army of General St. Clair* remarks on meeting a Mr. M_____, who, about five years before (which would place the date as 1786) had visited the

A Piegan camp-moving

Three Piegan chiefs

Bringing the
sweat-lodge willows

headwaters of the Missouri with a fur-trading party from Montreal. The party consisted of 100 men and had come in contact with the "Great Belly, Blood, Blackfoot, Snake, Ossnobians (Assiniboins?), Shiveytoon, Mandon, Paunee, and others." An attempt by his party to cross the "Shining Mountains" was frustrated by hostile Indians. Apparently no other record of this trip is known. The geographical and tribal information given is far beyond what one would expect at the time. Whether this particular expedition occurred or not, it is evident that there had been an expedition (or expeditions) to the headwaters of the Missouri before Lewis and Clark came close to Blackfeet country[3] by way of Maria's River.

About 1786 David Thompson, most able of all the early fur-trade explorers, was at Manchester House, forty miles up the North Saskatchewan from Battleford, wintering with the Piegans in the neighborhood of modern Calgary.[4] This marked the approach of the fur trade to the Rockies on a permanent basis. By 1790 the Hudson's Bay Company had established South Branch House on the South Saskatchewan. Two years later Peter Fidler left the Hudson's Bay post of Fort George on the North Saskatchewan, and wandered over the Bow and Little Bow rivers. The following year, 1793, he crossed the Red Deer at the mouth of the Rosebud, reached the Bow, and followed it to Chesterfield House at the South Saskatchewan and Red Deer rivers. Thompson, the same year, found both a Hudson's Bay and a North-West Company post at the site of South Branch House, close to Blood country.

But in 1794 an important event occurred. Thompson left the Hudson's Bay Company and joined the North-Westers. By winter of that year he had run a survey from Lake Superior to the Mandan villages on the Missouri. Here he found that free traders, outfitted by the Hudson's Bay Company, had been trading for several years. Insignificant bits such as this are the only hints we have that whites penetrated beyond the established fur company posts and had been nearer the Blackfeet region than any established record shows.

In 1800 Thompson went to the Upper Saskatchewan, spending two years wandering the country between the North and South Forks. Four men sent by him were probably the first whites to paddle down the South Fork of the Saskatchewan from near its headwaters. In 1807 Thompson passed over Howse Pass, discovered by Duncan McGillivray in 1800, before reaching the headwaters of the Columbia. Some of these parties must have been in contact with Blackfeet tribes. In 1805 West Chesterfield House was built by John McDonald of Garth near the mouth of Red Deer River. It was abandoned the following year and for 17 years there were no further efforts to penetrate the area with permanent establishments until the new Hudson's Bay Company re-established the post in 1822, a venture continued only for a few years.

In the meantime David Thompson had been exploring in the more peaceful region of the upper Columbia, evidently utilizing Howse Pass. In 1809 Joseph Howse (not Jasper Howse for whom the Pass was named) followed Thompson over the Pass, and in 1810 he took a Hudson's Bay party onto the Pacific slope. He

Tribal leaders at Blackfeet agency — Stabs-by-Mistake, White Antelope, Neck, White Calf, Moves Out, Rides-at-the-Door

was followed by James McMillan of the North-West Company to see that he was not successful.

Thompson built posts among the friendly Kalispell, Couer d'Alene and Salish Indians, but all respected the Blackfeet's resistance to whites — which would continue for almost another half century. Thompson's men at these posts were the first white men to go over Marias Pass into the heart of Piegan land. In 1810, Finan McDonald, Michael Bordeaux and Baptiste Buche accompanied 150 Flathead Indians on a buffalo hunt. They bravely and defiantly crossed the mountains by a "wide defile of easy passage eastward of Selish [Flathead] Lake," (undoubtedly Marias Pass). At a spot believed to be just below the old railroad siding of Skyland, on Bear Creek, the party was attacked by 170 Piegans. A fierce battle ensued; and uncharacteristically it was won by the Flatheads, aided by their white companions. In August 1812, the Flatheads, accompanied by Bordeaux and Michael Kinville, again invaded Blackfeet territory. This time they used Cutbank Pass. The Piegans now were guarding the eastern approaches and a terrific running battle ensued. Both white men and many Indians on both sides were killed. The Flatheads were forced to withdraw. They had more than met their master!

In 1810, Thompson was prevented from using Howse Pass by the Piegan tribe of the Blackfeet Confederacy, who objected to Thompson's furnishing arms to the Kutenais. Thompson then discovered and crossed the mountains by Athabasca Pass. This became the main route over the Rockies. But for the never-yielding Blackfeet obstacle, the main routes would have been further south and closer to present Glacier, perhaps within its borders.

For the next few years the North-West Company was occupied in developing the rich beaver country west of the Rockies, building posts, and sending out trapping companies which frequently reached far south of Glacier Park. They do not appear, however, to have worked back toward the region because of Blackfeet enmity, and perhaps partly because of the difficult nature of the country. The Hudson's Bay Company is not mentioned in this vicinity at all after 1810, until the merger was made with North-West Company in 1821, when, as noted above, an old North-Wester re-established Chesterfield House for a short time.

In the meantime, on the east side of the mountains, things were different. Thanks to the research of James Willard Schultz, we know of the first positive visitation by a white man on the southern Blackfeet soil. This was the adventuresome Hugh Monroe, whose later life is deeply mingled in much legend and lore of the Blackfeet. As a green recruit of the Hudson's Bay Mountain Fort Post on the North Fork of the Saskatchewan, he traveled through the east side of what is now the Glacier National Park region, in 1816, with a trapping party of Blackfeet headed for the Yellowstone area. Monroe later spent much of his colorful, rich life in the blue shadows of the Glacier peaks and undoubtedly was the first permanent white resident of this portion of Blackfeet country.

In 1832 the Hudson's Bay council ordered the abandonment of Rocky Mountain House, "because of the defection of the Piegans." They also ordered the building of a post to be called Piegan House somewhere near the 49th parallel, with the object of intercepting Blackfeet Indians who might be going across the border to trade with Americans. This is the first reference to American competition in the Plains region. In 1833, Piegan House was established on the Bow River in what is now the Stony Indian Reserve. But after five months it was abandoned and Rocky Mountain House restored. The same year the council of the Hudson's Bay Company, alarmed by the dimunition of the beaver, forbade the issuance of traps to any but the Piegan Indians. In 1848 the artist Paul Kane passed through Rocky Mountain House and noted it to be of unusually strong construction because of danger from the Blackfeet.[5]

Nine years later, in 1857, Father La Combe paid his first visit to Blackfeet Indian territory. (In 1865 he took up permanent residence there).

In the years 1857 and 1858 the Imperial Palliser Expedition reached Glacier Park. In 1857 Palliser went up the South Saskatchewan to within sight of Chief Mountain, the earliest mention of the peak in standard British sources (which missed Hugh Monroe's much earlier visit). Palliser crossed the Kananaskis to the Kootenay River, and the following year crossed Kootenay or Blakiston Pass. The expedition named Waterton Lake.

The Palliser Expedition marks the end of the period of the fur trade in this area from a Canadian viewpoint, although it lingered on for many years. The monopoly of the Hudson's Bay Company was beginning to crumble. Settlers had been moving into the Red River Valley over whom the Company could exercise no control. In 1866 American traders began to pour over the border from Fort

Benton, establishing trading posts near Blackfeet territory. The most famous of these were Fort Whoop-up at the junction of the Belly and the St. Mary's rivers, Fort Stand-off on the Belly River, and Pincher Creek.

Although there were exceptions, most of these men were whisky traders, of a very low class. Liquor flowed freely and the Indians were hopelessly debauched. Gambling and lawlessness reached a true "Wild West" pitch. Another class of raw Americans, the wolfers, who made their living by poisoning wolves, bitterly opposed the fur traders, who were encouraging the hunting of the buffalo for their hides. This added a further disordered element to a situation which endured for some years.

The approach to the region from the south lagged far behind that from the north. Early traders from St. Louis under Spanish control never entered any distance up the Missouri, although they were gaining experience nearer home which was eventually to take them, at one bound, to the headwaters of the great river. All had heard of, and heeded, the Blackfeet reputation.

In Canada, a government expedition marked the closing period of the Rocky Mountain fur-trade era. In the United States it was a government expedition which initiated it. Lewis and Clark went into a country, which beyond the Mandan villages had never been visited by American traders. On their return in 1806, Lewis made his overland trip from the Missouri along the base of the Rockies as far as Maria's River, and named Chief Mountain. A question is raised as to whether he would have discovered Marias Pass had he not been threatened with Blackfeet troubles. In any case this is the earliest historical mention of a natural feature connected with the present Blackfeet Reservation.

In 1811 all posts of the Missouri Fur Company above the Mandan villages were abandoned. The Astorians in this year went overland from Arikara rather than risk ascending the river through Blackfeet territory. No recorded efforts to make establishments above the Mandans are known for some years. The abortive Yellowstone Expedition of 1819 seriously injured American prestige. Yet, two years later, in 1821, another effort was made and the first Fort Benton was built at the junction of the Big Horn and Yellowstone rivers; while the Rocky Mountain Fur Company established a post the following year at the mouth of the Yellowstone — that was a long distance away from the Piegan home camps. Disaster still attended all efforts to push into Blackfeet country proper. The Rocky Mountain Fur Company was attacked at the Great Falls of the Missouri and driven back. Blackfeet stole so many horses from the Rocky Mountain Fur Company post at the mouth of the Yellowstone — 400 miles away from the home base — that it was abandoned and moved up to the Big Horn River. The following year the Missouri Fur Company found this upriver trade so unprofitable and dangerous that it withdrew all the way downriver to the Omaha.[7]

A second and more successful Yellowstone expedition, in 1825, made a change for the better in the American fur trade. The expedition moved some distance up the Yellowstone, where it met General Ashley, moving spirit at the time in the

Rocky Mountain Fur Company, and made treaties with all the tribes of the River except the Blackfeet, with whom it was unable to establish contracts. In 1827 Ashley projected a post at the mouth of Maria's River for Blackfeet trade, but his interest was diverted and no attempt was made to carry out the plan.

The year 1828 saw the entry of the powerful American Fur Company on the upper river, with posts at the mouth of the Yellowstone and further up the Yellowstone. The Company was determined to finally open trade with the Blackfeet Nation at any cost. An old trapper by the name of Berger, formerly with the Hudson's Bay Company, who had lived among these Indians and spoke the language, appeared at Fort Union. He offered to lead a party into the country and set off with three companions, returning with forty Blackfeet braves, many of whom had never before visited this far down the Missouri. So suspicious were the Blackfeet that Berger told them the distance was less than it actually was. One day's journey from the fort, they refused to travel further. Berger courageously offered his life as forfeit if they did not reach the fort the following day.

To this old mountain man must go the credit for bold handling of a dangerous enterprise which resulted in the establishment of American relations with the wary Blackfeet Indians for the first time.

The immediate result of Berger's success was the establishment of Fort Piegan, at the mouth of the Maria's, which had a successful season except for one abortive attack. The Blackfeet wished the post kept open in the summer. When the founder, James Kipp, left it according to his instructions, they burned the first fort. The same fall it was rebuilt by D. D. Mitchell in what is now known as Brule Bottom and renamed Fort McKenzie after the energetic director of the Missouri River operations of the American Fur Company. From this time on the American Fur Company maintained almost peaceable relations with the Blackfeet. But all was not real peace. This same year Bridger and Fitzpatrick of the Rocky Mountain Fur Company had one of their many encounters with these Indians, miles away.

On the United States' side the year 1831 was epoch-making in another respect. That year, steamboat navigation began on the Upper Missouri and the first steamboat reached Fort Union at the mouth of the Yellowstone. This was destined to revolutionize the fur trade from the South.

The American Fur Company built Fort Cass at the mouth of the Big Horn in 1832, the year of the building of Fort McKenzie and also notable for the visit of Catlin to Fort Union. The following year came Maximilian, Prince of Wied. Both men were famous chroniclers of Indian customs. In 1834 Thomas Nuttall and J. K. Townsend, English scientists, crossed the continent by way of the fur posts on the Missouri. In 1836 Larpenteur speaks of some Blackfeet trading at Fort Union, and of traders being to the Blackfeet country, as though it were a regular thing.[8] Father de Smet began his famous missionary labors among the Flatheads in 1840. The usefulness of Fort McKenzie came to a close in 1842-3 when F. A. Chardon, post manager, attempted to massacre a group of Bloods in revenge for

A Grizzly-Bear Brave

Upper right:
Putting up a tipi — medicine pipe on tripod

Lower right:
Framework of Blackfeet sacred sweat lodge

the killing of a favorite Negro servant, reviving Blackfeet animosity. Fort Benton, which had much indirect influence on the Indians, was built in 1846, slightly above the Maria's mouth of the Missouri. It was destined to become a famous commercial center because of its situation at the head of steamboat navigation. But the day of the fur trade was about to wane, and here the earliest story of the belligerent Blackfeet is taken over by engineer, explorer, cowboy, scientist, miner, railroad builder and settler. They would record and report on the remarkable beauty of this area that had so long escaped recording by the Mountain Men and fur traders. The Blackfeet were the last tribe to resist their persuasive efforts — guarding their Beaver Bonanza even beyond the period when such trapping was a major enterprise elsewhere.

NOTES

[1] Source of most of the preceding material is from Burpee, *Search for the Western Sea*, N. Y.: Appleton, 1908; Pinkerton, *Hudson's Bay Company*, N. Y.: Holt, 1951; Laut, *The Conquest of the Great Northwest*, 2 vols. Outing Pub. Co. 1908 & 1917; and the Henry Kelsey papers, Ottawa, Archives of Canada, 1929.

[2] Hendry Journals, edited by L. Burpee, Canada, 1907; and Cocking Journals, Royal Society of Canada, Series 3, Vol. 2.

[3] Massachusetts Historical Society, Series 1, Vol. 3, p. 24.

[4] Best readily available source: the *David Thompson Journals*, edited by M. Catherine White, Montana State University Press, Missoula; also *David Thompson's Narrative*, edited by J. B. Tyrell, Toronto, 1916.

[5] *In the Shadows of the Rockies*, MacInness; *Hudson's Bay Company*, Pinkerton.

[6] Principal sources for the above: Laut, Burpee and *The Fur Trade in Canada*, by Harold A. Innes, 1929.

[7] The classic fund of fur-trade information is the three-volume work of Hiram Martin Chittenden, *The American Fur Trade of the Far West*, New York, Harper, 1902. The best pin-pointing of the Montana scene was done by Paul C. Phillips: see his *Life in the Rocky Mountains*, Denver, Old West Pub. Co. 1940; and many articles and monographs on the Montana fur trade.

[8] *Forty Years a Fur Trader on the Upper Missouri*, edited by Elliot Coues, New York, Harper, 1904.

Weasel Tail

Group of Blackfeet

The Flatheads

By ALBERT J. PARTOLL

IN THE HISTORY of Far Western exploration and fur-trade days, and continuing to the present time, the name "Flathead" as identifying a certain tribe of Indians has often led to misunderstanding and misinterpretation. The name as applied to the Flathead-Salish Indians of present-day Western Montana is frequently mistaken to imply an origin of ethnic head deformation; while in reality the tribe officially bearing this name did not deform their heads. A study in nomenclature reveals that the Flatheads were also known as the *Salish* and *Tushepaw*, and that each appellation was well grounded in tribal significance of long ago.

Within the journals of early-day explorers, fur traders, travelers and visitors in the Pacific Northwest appears the name of "Flathead," as applied to Indians of the interior Rocky Mountains. This reference is directly to the Flathead-Salish of Western Montana. The name also appears when designating certain Indians along the Pacific Coast, who were incorrectly so-called because of some ethnic feature or characteristic. Along the Pacific coast the Chinook and Clatsop Indians did practice mutilation upon the foreheads of their infants, resulting in "peaked heads." The effect of placing an infant in a frame which induced such a malformation later gave the tribal adults a distinct appearance, which, for want of better terminology, led to a generalized designation of Flathead. In reality "peaked head" was the proper term.

Flathead as applied to this practice among the Chinooks and Clatsops meant head deformation. The reason for this ethnic mutilation was that it set the practitioners apart in a supposed class of aristocracy and distinguished them from other Indians, especially those whom they had enslaved from other tribes. Picturesque and descriptive illustrations by early explorers of this aboriginal technique, of alleged beautification, tended toward popular misinterpretation of the "Flathead" term. Illustrations of heads in process of "peaking" not "flattening" as well as the erroneous attachment of the label of "Flatheads" led to widespread and strongly entrenched conceptions that Flathead was synonymous with head deformity.[1]

One of the most widely circulated accounts describing this unique idea of

33

attractiveness is contained in Washington Irving's *Astoria*, Chapter 10, of the Philadelphia edition of 1836. The account reads: "A singular custom prevails, not merely among the Chinooks, but among most of the tribes about this part of the coast, which is flattening of the forehead. The process by which this deformity is affected commences immediately after birth. The infant is laid in a wooden trough, by way of cradle. The end on which the head reposes is higher than the rest. A paddling is placed on the head of the infant, with a piece of bark above it, and is pressed down by cords, which pass through holes on each side of the trough. As the tightening of the paddling and pressing of the head is gradual, the process is said not to be attended with much pain. The appearance of the infant, however, while in this state of compression, is whimsically hideous, and 'its little black eyes,' we are told, 'being forced out by the tightness of the bandages, resemble those of a mouse choked in a trap.'

"About a year's pressure is sufficient to produce the desired effect, at the end of which time the child emerges from the bandage a complete flathead, and continues so for life. It must be noted, however, that this flattening of the head has something in its aristocratical significance, like the crippling of the feet of the Chinese ladies of quality. At any rate it is a sign of freedom. No slave is permitted to bestow this enviable deformity upon his child; all slaves therefore are round heads."

Since in literature the implication of ethnic mutilation was associated with the name of "Flathead," it is not surprising that the one tribe bearing the title of Flathead as a proper name should have their name misunderstood, since they did not deform their heads. Washington Irving, in Chapter 3 of the edition cited, was aware of the tribe of Flatheads proper and states: "The Flatheads in question are not to be confounded with those of the name who dwell on the lower waters of the Columbia; neither do they flatten their heads as the others do. They inhabit the banks of a river on the west side of the mountains, and are described as simple, honest and hospitable."

That the name of Flathead was subject to speculation as to its meaning is evidenced by the notation made by John K. Townsend, who in 1832 met these Indians. He noted in his observations on Western Indians that "The tribe called Flatheads, or Salish, who reside near the sources of the Oregon have long abolished this custom." Another observer, W. A. Ferris, who resided with these Indians at various times between 1830 and 1835, states in his account: "The Flatheads probably derive their name from an ancient practice of shaping or deforming their head during infancy, by compressing it between boards placed on the forehead and back part, though not one living proof of the existence at any time of that practice can now be found among them. They call themselves ... 'Salish' ..." Neither Townsend nor Ferris found justification for the name, hence concluded that these Indians had ceased head deformation, although there was no evidence to show that they ever practiced this custom.[2]

Uncertainty if not confusion persisted in explaining the term Flathead as

Flathead Indians of western Montana: Joe LaMoose, Chief Charlot, Chief Moies. *Right:* Big Knife

used in identifying the Salish and resulted in theories worthy of mention. The Reverend Samuel Parker who met the Flathead-Salish at the fur-trade rendezvous at Green River (in present Wyoming) August 12, 1835, noted in his account: "I was disappointed to see nothing peculiar in the shape of the head of the Flathead Indians to give them their name. Who gave them this name, or for what reason, is not known. Some suppose it was given them in derision for not flattening their heads, as the Chinooks and some other nations do, near the shores of the Pacific." Further in his account he describes the Chinook process of head deformation. A similar opinion is expressed by James Mooney in later years, and in effect states that the Flatheads were so called in derision of the fact that they did not deform their heads, in contrast to those who did, since the heads of the Flathead-Salish were left natural.[3]

Another theory, traceable to the writing of George M. Dawson in "Notes on the Shuswap People of British Columbia," states: "The Salish proper, as is well known, were originally designated the 'Flatheads', though not in the habit of artificially deforming the cranium. When first discovered by the Canadian voyageurs, slaves from tribes of the coast, where the head was usually deformed, were found among them." This information was supplied to Dawson by J. W. MacKay, Indian Agent at Kamloops, and later incorporated into the *Handbook of American Indians* (B.A.E. Bulletin 30) under the Dawson citation.[4]

In the light of historical evidence the opinions of Reverend Parker and Mr. Mooney are worthy of consideration: yet further investigation of this interesting subject appears to be warranted. The Dawson version offers a theory not to be regarded as factually conclusive. The designation of Flathead as applied to the

White Castles on the Missouri, painted in 1833 by Karl Bodmer

Salish antedates the coming of the voyageurs to the region, and hence was not based upon the presence of the "peak heads" among them as discovered by the voyageurs; and further the Flatheads did not customarily (if ever) take slaves. It would appear that the origin of Dawson's explanation was largely influenced by hearsay testimony, requiring additional clarification.

Ross Cox, who visited the homeland of the Flatheads or Salish in 1813, records in his adventures on the Columbia: "I could not discover why the Blackfeet and the Flatheads received their respective designations; for the feet of the former are no more inclined to be sable than any other part of the body, while the heads of the latter possess their share proportion of rotundity. Indeed it is only below the falls that the real flat-heads appear, and at the mouth of the Columbia that they flourish supernaturally." It is evident that Cox expected to see some physical justification for the respective Indian names.

Long before the advent of the white man into the Rocky Mountains of the Pacific Northwest, it was customary for the various Indian tribes to engage in sign language pantomime in exchanging information with other Indians, whose language they did not understand. Sign language, while limited in many ways for extensive "conversation," was sufficient for tribal identification and the conveyance of essential facts. Tribes like the Blackfeet, Crows, Gros Ventres and others had a sign which identified them; this was their tribal signature. So also the Flatheads or Salish had a tribal sign, the translation of which meant "Flat Head" or natural head. As a rule the tribal sign portrayed some special tribal attribute, physical characteristic, ornamentation or individuality. The name of Blackfeet was not due to the discoloration of the feet but was rather a translation of black moccasin, their identity in the sign language, made by touching the foot and

Ft. Owen, western Montana, sketched in 1853 by John Mix Stanley

giving the sign for black, or with the finger and thumb encircle the ankle. The Gros Ventres had a sign, made with appropriate movement, allegedly meaning Big Belly. The Crows identified themselves by waving the hands to show a bird in flight; the Flathead-Salish designated themselves by patting the head with their right hand to show that the head was natural.[6]

The journal of Antoine F. Lorocque for 1805 is enlightening as to the use of tribal signs, and their interpretations. The passage reads in reference to the sign language employed by the Crows: "They represent a Sioux by passing the edge of their hand across their neck, a Panis (Pawnee) by showing large ears; a Flathead by pressing with both hands on each side of the head."[7]

As to the habitat of the Indians he calls Flathead, he states: "The Flatheads inhabit the western side of the Rocky Mountains at the heads of the rivers that have a southerly course and flow into the western ocean. The ridge of mountains that parts these waters from the Missouri can be crossed in two days and no more mountains are found to the coast. They come every fall to the fort of the Missouri or thereabouts to kill buffaloes, of which there are none on across the range of mountains, dress robes and dry meat with which they return as soon as winter sets in. They have deers of various kinds on their lands and beaver with which they make themselves robes, but they prefer buffaloes. They have a great many horses which they sell for a trifle and give many for nothing."

At the time of making his observations in the summer of 1805, Larocque was on the eastern side of the Rocky Mountains in the Yellowstone River district. His statement has significance in that it identifies the residence of the Flatheads and gives a variation of their tribal sign by the Crow Indians, which translated meant Flathead. The journal, being in French, has the "Tetes Plates" for Flatheads.

In historical significance the Lewis and Clark expedition was beyond parallel in revealing the hidden wonders of the great unknown region beyond the Rocky Mountains. The expedition took special cognizance of the Indians, and in the course of travel reached the ancestral home of the Flathead-Salish in the Bitter Root valley. Of this notable highlight in the history of this Indian nation — the Journals of Lewis and Clark proper, and the respective Journals of Patrick Gass and John Ordway offer contemporary and comparative recording. The journals for September 4, 1805 mention no head deformation among these Indians, whom they call *Flathead, Salees and Tushepaw*. By some strange interpretation, the word *"Eoot-last-schute"* also crept into the journals of Lewis and Clark proper, and of Gass.[8]

The difficulty of conversing with the Flathead-Salish is revealed in the Ordway Journal, which records that speech with them had to go through several vocal languages, and the sign language as a supplement. Also noted is that they appeared to have an impediment of speech, or brogue on their tongue. George Drouillard, interpreter and master of the sign language, and Sacajawea, a Shoshone Indian woman, who knew the Rocky Mountain territory and much about the Indians enroute, were entrusted with the task of supplying varied information on tribes met. An interesting account of how these explorers carried on conversation with Indians is related by Charles MacKenzie of the Northwest Company, who met the Lewis and Clark expedition in the Mandan country, to the east, in the spring of 1805. He narrates that "the woman (Sacajawea) who answered the purpose of wife to Charbonneau, was of the Serpent (Shoshone) nation and lately taken a prisoner by a war party. She understood a little Gros Ventres, in which she had to converse with her husband, who was a Canadian and did not understand English. A mulatto (York) who spoke French and worse English, served as interpreter to the Captains, so that a single word to be understood by the party required to pass from the natives to the woman, from the woman to the husband, and from the husband to the mulatto, from the mulatto to the captains."[9]

The appellation of "Flathead" for these Indians resulted from translation of their identification in the sign language, and appears in each of the respective journals of the expedition. Descriptions by the explorers nowhere mention these Indians as being in any way different from others in physical perfection, since no head deformation is noted. Later when the expedition reached the coastal region, observations and recordings were made of the Chinooks and Clatsops who deformed the heads of their young. These Indians, the "peaked heads," were in a broad sense designated as Flatheads of the coast, by the explorers. When portions of the journals were published, in both authentic editions and the spurious or unauthorized editions, great confusion resulted in a misunderstanding of nomenclature.

"Salish" has been variously spelled in the early writings and has its origin in the name of the Flatheads for themselves. Its appearance in the journals of the Lewis and Clark expedition is given as synonymous with Flatheads. In the immediate years after the expedition visited the home of the Flatheads, David Thompson, another explorer of note, made an extended sojourn among these same people and recorded their name as Flathead and "Saleesh." Respective journals and historical writings through the decades of the fur trade and later, make similar recordings as to the name of these Indians. Its pronunciation is "say-lish," although the spelling may vary. Originally the names Salish and Salishan were limited to the Flatheads here under consideration; however, the name Salishan as applied to linguistics, has been expanded to embrace those tribes speaking a language similar to that of the Flatheads or Salish.[10]

The name "Tushe-paw" is of Shoshone Indian origin, and is unquestionably the name given to the Flathead-Salish by Sacajawea, the Shoshone Indian woman guide and interpreter with the Lewis and Clark expedition. The word is derived from "Tush" or "Tushe" with the variation "Tats" meaning summer, and "paw" or "pah" meaning water — the combination resulting in "summer water." This was the Shoshone or Snake Indian name for the Flathead-Salish, since these Indians lived in the Bitter Root valley which was noted for its mild climate in the winter, and numerous hot-water springs, which were ideal for bathing. The Bitter Root valley was along the route traveled by the Shoshones from the west to the eastern buffalo plains and was along an old Indian trail worn from time immemorial by moccasined feet, and later by the hoofs of Indians ponies when the tribes ceased to be afoot. Tushepaw, appropriately descriptive of this haven of rest and its natural resources, became the Shoshone name for the tribe residing there.[11]

"Eoot-lash-Schute" and the variation Ootlashoot, as recorded in the respective journals of Lewis and Clark proper, and of Patrick Gass, for September, 1805, was another name originating with the explorers, who used it as synonymous with the Flatheads or Salish of the Bitter Root valley. In the tribal lore of the Flatheads the Bitter Root River was called "In-schu-te-schu," meaning red willow. Phonetic misrepresentation and limited interpretation may have changed "In-schu-te-schu" to "Eoot-lash-Schute." The red willow grew in such abundance along the river that the Kutenai, the neighbors and allies of the Flatheads, nicknamed these Indians Mukwohenik in the Kutenai language, meaning Red Willow People. It is not an unfair assumption that the name "Eoot-lash-Schute" may have been intended to identify some feature of the environment or of the terrain, and that its real meaning and association was lost through faulty translation. The name is peculiar to the writings of the Lewis and Clark expedition alone, and does not appear as tribal identification thereafter, unless borrowed from this source.[12]

Memories of the historic meeting of the Flatheads or Salish Indians and the Lewis and Clark expedition in 1805 in the Bitter Root valley of later western Montana have been perpetuated by the Salish. Into their tribal traditions "witnesses" to the coming of the white man have interwoven connecting threads of history. Among those remembered by posterity as present were Chief Three Eagles and his son, a lad of fifteen, later known as Chief Victor; Agnes or Mother Victor, later the second wife of Chief Victor, and at the time a girl in her early

Lewis and Clark Meeting the Flatheads (Charles M. Russell)

years; Chief Insula or Red Feather, also known as the Little Chief; Moise, later a second chief of the Flatheads, and Eugenie, who was in her early teens. In future decades, these survivors with others who witnessed the advent of the white man recounted this memorable event, which heralded the end of their unknown existence in the wilderness. The written chronicles of history thereafter added their tribal names of Flathead and Salish to the roster of mankind.[13]

Following the explorations of Lewis and Clark there began a gradual influx of explorers, trappers, traders, missionaries and the trimmings of frontier civilization to the homeland of the Salish of the Rocky Mountains. The fur trade penetrated their unplundered empire in its quest for furs, and their name was used to designate the "Saleesh" House of David Thompson of the Northwest Company in 1809, and later the Flathead Post of the Hudson's Bay Company in the early 1820's. Thus identification of these trading centers gave geographic recognition, and affixed their name to Flathead lake and the river that drains it.[14]

In the annals of Western history the Flathead or Salish Indians attained early distinction as a friendly people. Their name, often misunderstood, is an interesting reminder of the frontier era and a link in the chain of our Western heritage.

NOTES

[1] For graphic illustrations and descriptions see: George Catlin, *Illustrations of the Manners and Customs and Conditions of the North American Indians,* (2 vols., London, 1841). Same author, *Letters and Notes on the Manners, Customs and Conditions of the North American Indian,* (2 vols. New York and London, 1844); Paul Kane, *Wanderings of an Artist among the Indians of North America,* (London, 1859); Otis T. Mason, *Cradles of American Aborigines,* in the Report of the National Museum for 1887, (Washington, D. C. 1888); Charles Wilkes, *Narrative of the U. S. Exploring Expedition during the Years 1838-1842,* (5 vols. Philadelphia, 1844), IV, p. 388.

[2] John K. Townsend, *Journey Across the Rocky Mountains to the Columbia River* (Philadelphia, 1839), reproduced in *Early Western Travels; 1748-1846,* edited by Reuben Gold Thwaites, (33 vols. Cleveland, 1904-1907) XXI, pp. 303-304; W. A. Ferris, *Life in the Rocky Mountains . . . 1830-1835,* edited by Paul C. Phillips, (Denver 1940) p. 88. This volume has copious material on the Flatheads or Salish proper.

[3] Samuel Parker, *Journal of an Exploring Tour Beyond the Rocky Mountains . . . 1835-37,* (Ithaca, N. Y. 1838), p. 75. For notation on Mooney see next footnote.

[4] George M. Dawson, *Notes on the Shuswap People of British Columbia,* Proc. and Trans. Royal Soc. of Canada, IX, Sec. II (Montreal, 1892) p. 6; James Mooney, in The American Anthropologist, July, 1889, (New York, 1899) New Series, 1, p. 140; Frederick W. Hodges, *Handbook of American Indians North of Mexico,* (2 vols. Bulletin 30, Bureau of American Ethnology), (Washington, D. C., 1910) Part 1, p. 465.

[5] Ross Cox, *Adventures on the Columbia Including the Narrative of Six Years on the Rocky Mountains, 1811-17,* (2 vols. London, 1831) I, p. 128. Another contemporary source of information is contained in Gabriel Franchere, *Narrative of a Voyage to York, 1854,* reprinted in Thwaites Edition of Early Western Travels, VI, (Cleveland 1904). Franchere calls the tribe here considered "Flathead" and "Salish" and mentions that along the lower Columbia slavery exists and that the slaves of the Indians practicing head deformation are not permitted to deform their heads. Alexander Ross, *Adventures of the First Settlers on the Oregon or Columbia River, 1810-1813* (London, 1849), and by the same author, *Fur Hunters of the Far West,* (2 vols. London, 1855), calls these Indians the Salish or Flathead.

[6] W. P. Clark, *The Indian Sign Language,* (Philadelphia, 1885) pp. 174-179, gives this sign for the Flatheads or Salish and quotes Father Anthony Ravalli, S.J. from whom he personally obtained the information. Father Ravalli came to the Flatheads in 1842, and stated to Clark that the Flatheads never deformed their heads. Chief Michelle of the Pend d'Orielles gave like testimony to Clark regarding the Flatheads. Garrick Mallery, *Sign Language among North American Indians,* in First Ann. Report of the Bureau of American Ethnology, (Washington, 1881), has this tribal sign demonstrated (Figure 291, page 468) by Tendoy, a Shoshone Indian, who came to Washington, D. C. in 1880; Mallery also cites a letter from J. W. Powell, Indian Superintendent of British Columbia, giving this as the Kutine (Kutenai) sign for the Flatheads.

Worthy of mention in connection with the sign language is the observation that "peaked heads" (Chinook and Clatsop), might be mis-identified by the uninformed from misunderstanding of the tribal sign given by other Indians, who designated them by "one hand placed on top of the head, and the other on back of the head," suggesting a peaked head as distinguished from a natural head.

The tribal sign here is definitely for the "peaked heads." It is reported in the notes of Major S. H. Long, and was erroneously included with those for the Flathead-Salish in the compilation by Garrick Mallery. Failure to distinguish between the "peaked heads" and the Flatheads or Salish also appears in the narrative of James O. Pattie for June, 1926. Mallery, opus citra, p. 468; Edwin James, *Expedition from Pittsburg to the Rocky Mountains, 1819-1820* . . . from the Notes of Major S. H. Long, and Others, (London, 1823), reprinted in Early Western Travels, Thwaites Edition, cited, XV, p. 336; James O. Pattie, *Personal Narrative During an Expedition from St. Louis, . . . 1824-1827*, (Cincinnati, 1831), reprinted in Early Western Travels, Route Across the Rocky Mountains, annotated by Carl L. Cannon, (Reprint of the Lafayette, Ind., edition of 1486, by Princeton University Press, Princeton, N. J., 1932), p. 63-64.

[7] Antoine Francois Larocque, *Journal de Larocque, 1805*, edited by Lawrence J. Burpee, (Ottawa, 1911), pp. 75-76. The journal is in French.

[8] Lewis and Clark, *Original Journals of the Lewis and Clark Expedition, 1804-1806*, edited by Reuben Gold Thwaites, (8 vols. New York, 1904-5); Patrick Gass, *Journal of the Lewis and Clark Expedition* (reprint of the edition of 1811), (Chicago, 1904); John Ordway, *Journals of Captain Meriwether Lewis and Sergeant John Ordway, Kept on the Western Exploration, 1803-1806*, edited by M. M. Quaife (Wisconsin Historical Society Collection, XXII, Madison, 1916). Entries in the respective journals for Sept. 4 are: Lewis and Clark (Thwaites Ed.) vol. 3, p. 53; Gass Journal, p. 137; Ordway Journal, p. 281. Additional entries in the respective journals are also pertinent to nomenclature. For characteristics of the Flathead-Salish Indian language see Footnote 10.

[9] The MacKenzie statement is published in L. R. Mason, *Les Bourgeois de la Campagnie du Nord-Quest*, (2 vols. Quebec, 1889), I, p. 336. Father Lawrence B. Palladino, S. J., who came to the land of the Salish in 1867 and was fluent with this Indian language notes: "Among the many Indian tribes of the Rocky Mountains there is none more renowned than the Salish . . . commonly called Flat-Heads." Elsewhere he notes: "Their language is in many points original and difficult to master. Its utterance is slow, tolerably clear and distinct, though some of its sounds are aspirated and others intensely guttural. Five of the consonants commonly heard in other tongues, that is, b, d, f, r and v, are wanting in theirs, and are supplied by p, t, l and m. Thus Adolph with them is Ato; Ambrose, Amelo; Raphael, Apel; Mary, Malee; Rosalie, Usalee; Victor, Mitt'to etc., the accent in all these names falling on the last syllable and "ee" sounding as the Italian "i" in Forli." This note on the language is of interest in considering the Lewis and Clark difficulty of interpretation. L. B. Palladino, S. J., *Indian and White in the Northwest* . . . (Baltimore, 1894), p. 1 and 6.

[10] An interesting linguistic work by the missionary priests records Salish as identifying the Flathead Indians, and vice versa under "Flathead" gives "Indian tribe, Selish," or themselves. *A Dictionary of the Kalispell or Flathead Indian Language*, Joseph Giorda, S. J. (2 vols., St. Ignatius, Montana, 1877-79). The Nez Perce Indian name for the Flatheads is given as "Selig" in *A Dictionary of the Numipu or Nez Perce Language*, (by Rev. A. Morvillo, S. J.) Part I, English-Nez Perce, St. Ignatius, Montana, 1895). Additional data is contained in Mengarini's *Narrative of the Rockies, Memoirs of Old Oregon, 1841-1850*, and *St. Mary's Mission*, edited by Albert J. Partoll, (Reprinted from the *Frontier and Midland*, Vol. XVIII, No. 3 and 4, 1948), (Missoula, Montana. 1938).

[11] A variation of the word "Tushepaw" was first recorded by Lewis in a letter dated April 17, 1805, from Fort Mandan, when he mentions he expected to meet the Flatheads or "Tut-see-was" Indians as the explorers traveled westward across the Rocky Mountains. Sacajawea, as an interpreter, would appear to have supplied the term as it is of Shoshone derivation. The Lewis letter was part of the Message to the Senate and House of Representatives of the United States, February 19, 1806, and appeared as part of "Travels in the Interior Parts of America; Communicating Discoveries made in Exploring the Missouri, Red River and Washita, by Captains Lewis and Clark, Dr. Sibley and Mr. Dunbar," in vol. VI, of *A Collection of Modern and Contemporary Voyages and Travels*, (London, 1807), printed for Richard Phillips, p. 35. Shoshone or Snake Indian vocabulary in reference to Tushepaw is given by Granville Stuart, *Montana As It Is*, (New York, 1865), p. 29. George W. Hill, *Vocabulary of the Shoshone Language* (Salt Lake, 1877); John E. Rees, *Idaho Chronology and Nomenclature: Bibliography*, (Chi-

cago, 1918) p. 117. The word is given in the Journals of Lewis and Clark (Thwaites Edition), and also in the Ordway Journal, as identifying the Flatheads or Salish. The biography of the Shoshone interpreter is given by Grace Raymond Hebard, *Sacajawea, Guide of Lewis and Clark*, (Glendale, 1933). Shoshone Indians were named Snake and Serpent Indians in translation of their tribal sign, which was the dart or movement of a snake.

[12] The Salish themselves had no such word in their vocabulary, and did not consider this their name. The appellation was an incorrect designation. The word "In-schu-te-schu" was recorded by the writer in an interview with Duncan McDonald (1849-1937), in 1929; Al Partoll, "Historical Sketches-Duncan McDonald," supplement to *The Montana Kaimin*, March 12, 1929. The Kutenai term appears in the vocabulary recorded by Edward S. Curtis, *The North American Indians*, edited by Frederick W. Hodges, VII (Norwood, Mass., 1911), p. 179.

[13] Three Eagles is mentioned in the recollection of Agnes as stated in a letter of Sept. 5, 1899, by J. D'Aste, S. J., and published by Olin D. Wheeler, *The Trail of Lewis and Clark, 1804-1904*, (2 vols. New York, 1904) II, p. 65. Similar facts are narrated by Agnes or Mother Victor, as she was sometimes known, in an article "When the Flatheads First Saw White Men," in the *Anaconda Standard*, (Montana), December 20, 1903, part 3 p. 2. Although unsigned, the article was written by Arthur L. Stone, later dean of the Montana School of Journalism. Chief Victor was a good sized boy when Lewis and Clark came, as he recounted to Major John Owen, in 1867. When Victor died in 1870 he was eighty, hence was born about 1790, and would have been 15 in 1805. *The Journals and Letters of Major John Owen; Pioneer of the Northwest 1805-1871*, edited by Seymour Dunbar and Paul C. Phillips, (2 vols., New York, 1927), II, p. 42; *Life, Letters and Travels of Father Pierre-Jean DeSmet, S. J. 1801-1873*, edited by H. M. Chittenden and A. T. Richardson, (4 vols. New York, 1905), IV p. 1338, notes the death of Victor. The "Liber Mortuorum, St. Mary's Mission" 1866 et. seq., (Manuscript record) states that on July 14, 1870, Victor the head of the Flatheads died while on a hunt, and that he was about 80 years old.

[14] Eugenie, a Flathead girl in her early teens, was also present as recorded in Palladino, opus citra, p. 3. William Marshall Anderson tells of Little Chief or Insula relating his boyhood recollections of Lewis and Clark to him in June, 1834. Anderson's *Narrative of a Ride to the Rocky Mountains in 1834*, edited by Albert J. Partoll (Missoula, Montana, 1938), (reprinted from the *Frontier and Midland*, XIX, No. 1, 1938). Moise, a second chief of the Flatheads, as a boy witnessed the advent of these explorers, as is mentioned respectively by Captain John Mullan and Frank H. Woody. Mullan's statement is in the compilation by Isaac I. Stevens, *Report of Exploration for a Route for the Pacific Railroad, Washington, 1855*, I, p. 325. F. H. Woody, "A sketch of the Early History of Western Montana," (written in 1876 and 1877), published in *Montana Historical Contributions*, II, (Helena 1896) p. 89.

[14] The writings of David Thompson and Alexander Henry are most interesting and historically valuable. They were the original followers of Lewis and Clark into the region. Both journals note that the Flatheads called themselves the Salish. Thompson used "Saleesh" for the main part, and Henry "Saleeish."

David Thompson's *Narrative of his Explorations in Western America, 1784-1812*, (pub. by the Champlain Society, XII), edited by J. B. Tyrell, (Toronto, 1916); Alexander Henry and David Thompson, *New Light on the Early History of the Greater Northwest, 1799-1814*, edited by Elliot Coues, (3 vols. New York, 1897).

The Assiniboins

MIGHTY MEAT BOILERS OF THE NORTHERN PLAINS

By MICHAEL KENNEDY

In the rolling rangeland, south of the sluggish Milk River and reaching to the gentle aspen slopes of the Little Rockies, lies the present Fort Belknap Reservation, home of some 3000 Indians whom the world has gently passed by. Some two automobile hours east, just beyond the largest earth-filled dam in the world on the mighty Missouri, one passes through the adjoining towns of Wolf Point and Poplar. These are the principal trade centers of the larger Fort Peck Indian Reservation. Around these towns, from the barren gumbo breaks of the Big Muddy, north toward the Canadian line across mostly uninspiring prairie and dry-land farming strips, on more than two million acres are located the cabin-clusters of another 4000 Indians.

On these two lonely northern federal-government land areas of almost 2,700,000 acres live almost all of the American-based remnants of what once was one of the boldest, handsomest, most able buffalo-hunting, gregarious, pictur-esque, peripatetic, individualistic and iron-willed of all of the Northern Great Plains Indian tribes — the Assiniboin.

Like their well-adjusted natural culture as well as their once unchallenged freedom, their physical domain has shriveled drastically. Within the early fleeting seconds of the white man's span of recorded history in northern North America, the Assiniboin — once lords and masters of the most prodigious kingdom on the continent — now possess a pittance. Their historic realm, less than three centuries ago, was tremendous. To the north, they dominated the sweep of wilderness from Hudson's Bay westward across the present huge provinces of Saskatchewan and Manitoba to the eye-filling scenic approaches of the Canadian Rockies in Alberta. On the broad southern perimeter the Assiniboin had been noted by the earliest Jesuits, explorers, voyageurs and fur traders wandering the interminable stretches of lakeland, forest and prairie starting from north of Lake Superior, thence west-ward across the northern areas presently occupied by the large states of Min-nesota, North Dakota and much of Montana, until they collided with the Black-feet in the west.

It is characteristic of the regimentation and decimation that has been the

Assiniboin's lot since the white man adopted him, that only a third remnant now resides on the ancestral soil of Canada. At the beginning of this century when the majority of all existing Assiniboins were wards of the two Montana reservations, in Canada, (where they were now known by bands — not in the correct ancestral terms, but simply by the possessive of their chief's or sub-chief's name) they were widely scattered: The Mosquito's, Bear Head's and Lean Man's bands, all small, were at the Battleford Agency; Joseph's and Paul's bands (plus a few orphans) were at Edmonton Agency; Carry-the-Kettle's band was at Assiniboin Agency; Ocean Man's and Rump's bands were at Moose Mountain; and all others, numbering half of all those then in Canada (1400) were on the Stoney Reservation out of Morley, Alberta.

More recently they have grouped largely on this reservation. Here, oddly enough, the Assiniboins now live much more in the proximity of their hereditary enemies, the Blackfeet, than they ever lived in historic or prehistoric times. And most distressing of all, because of the name of their principal reservation, they are almost universally known as "Stonies" or "Stoneys" in Canadian literature and to most people it is not now recognized that they are actually Assiniboin.

There is a dearth of information concerning these people, even in the fine archival collections of the English, French and Spanish-speaking world. Aside from *Land of Nakoda* (1939) and its sequel, *The Assiniboines,* which deal exclusively with the U. S. Assiniboins, the only other book-length study of this tribe was written by the eminent American anthropologist, Robert H. Lowie, more than half a century ago. It treats almost entirely of the Morley, Alberta, Canada, Assiniboins on the Stoney Reservation, slightly about the Fort Belknap but not at all about the Fort Peck Assiniboins.

Through the inexplicable whims of Indian Service bureaucracy the Assiniboins at Fort Belknap (almost since the agency's establishment in 1888) have shared their reservation with the Gros Ventres or *Atsinas,* their bitter enemies for many centuries. In fairness it must be stated that this reservation was originally established for the Gros Ventres. The reverse is true on the Fort Peck Reservation. Initially it was to house only Assiniboins, but various bands of Sioux were moved in until the Sioux now numerically dominate the reservation. Needless to say, none of the tribes concerned is happy about the arrangements. Even today century-old enmities are likely to burst into flame. On the reservation initially established only for the Assiniboins — Fort Peck — Assiniboins number less than half of the present 4000 enrollment. At Fort Belknap less than 800 of the reservation's 2500 occupants are Assiniboins.

The Indians themselves have done far more to cling to their tattered heritage and preserve traditional blood lines and naturalistic culture than has the Indian Service. Despite some four generations of co-existence, intermarriage between the Gros Ventres and Assiniboins has been astonishingly low on the Fort Belknap reserve. Full-bloods make up forty-three per cent of the present population. There are only a handful of high-school graduates and virtually no college graduates on the whole reservation.

Because of much closer proximity to public schools in the nearby towns, the literacy situation on the Fort Peck Reservation is much better; intermarriage, both with whites and intertribal, is also considerably greater. Less than thirty per cent of the Fort Peck enrollees are full-bloods, and this percentage now drops with increased rapidity due to the advanced age of most of the present full-bloods, both Assiniboin and Sioux.

Enough of the twentieth-century scene: these unsung Noblemen of the Plains can best be appreciated in the context of what the artistically able articulate George Catlin had to say about them (along with Blackfeet, Sarcees and a branch of the Crees) during his exciting visit to old Fort Union in 1832. Being one of the most informed men of his day on this subject and aided in vantage as a guest of the American Fur Company, he participated fully. Catlin wrote:

"The several tribes of Indians inhabiting the regions of the Upper Missouri . . . are undoubtedly the finest looking, best equipped, and most beautifully costumed of any on the Continent. They live in a country well-stocked with buffaloes and wild horses, which furnish them an excellent and easy living; their atmosphere is pure, which produces good health and long life; and they are the most independent and the happiest race of Indians I have met with: they are all entirely in a state of primitive rudeness and wildness, and consequently are picturesque and handsome almost beyond description. Nothing in the world, of its kind, can possibly surpass in beauty and grace, some of their games and amusements — their gambols and parades . . ."

Having spent six previous years as one of the leading Indian students of his day, Catlin knew. He had painted the Seneca, Oneida, Tuscarora, Ottawa and Mohegan tribes of the East. In company with the eminently qualified General William Clark of Lewis and Clark-expedition fame (but then U. S. Superintendent of Indian Affairs for all Western Indians) he had studied and painted such tribes as the Iowa, Sioux, Omaha, Sauk, Fox, Missouri, Delaware, Kaskaskia, Kickapoo, Peoria, Potawatomi, Shawnee and Weah. Traveling with Indian Agent Major John Dougherty, Catlin had also become familiar with the Pawnees and Otoes, and had revisited the Omaha and Missouri people.

So, when Catlin spoke glowingly of these Northern Great Plains Indians — Assiniboins, Blackfeet, Crows, Crees and Gros Ventres — it was neither idle nor impetuous; although admittedly Catlin, as a true creative genius, was also a romanticist. Catlin also stated:

"As far as my travels have yet led me into the Indian country, I have more than realized my former predictions; that those Indians who could be found most entirely in a state of nature, with the least knowledge of civilized society, will be found to be the most cleanly in their persons, elegant in their dress and manners, and enjoying life to the greatest perfection. Every one of these red sons . . . of the prairie is a knight and a lord . . . his squaws are his slaves; the only things which

Assiniboin and Gros Ventre village near Ft. Belknap. *Below:* Sun dance, Ft. Belknap

he deems worthy of his exertions are to mount his snorting steed, with his bow and quiver slung, his arrow shield upon his arm, and his long lance glistening in the war parade; or divested of all his plumes and trappings, armed with a simple bow and quiver, to plunge his steed amongst the flying herds of buffaloes, and with his sinewy bow, which he seldom bends in vain, to drive deep to life's fount the whizzing arrow . . ."

True, this was flowery language, but time and the spirited paintings of Catlin attest to his sincerity. He was deeply in love with the Upper Missouri Indians.

Except for the Lewis and Clark expedition of a little more than a quarter century earlier, Catlin remains among the first white Americans who reported at length on the Assiniboins. Part of the reason for this was the extreme sparsity of whites in the region; but even more so, the fact was geographic, for only at this time (except for a pre-white historic time to be mentioned later) were the Assiniboins, now superbly horse mounted, inclined to drift so far south of their beloved woodlands and lake domain in Canada.

This brings us to their earliest known origin. Ethnologically it is generally believed that these people came from Siouan stock. This is agreed upon by such authorities as Frederick Webb Hodge, Robert H. Lowie, John C. Ewers of the Smithsonian Institution, William Jones of the Field Museum of Natural History, Diamond Jenness and Clark Wissler. Lowie is the most cautious. He merely says: "Linguistically they form a member of the Dakota branch of the Siouan stock."

Hodge describes the Assiniboins as a large Siouan tribe, originally Yanktanai, who separated from the parent stem only shortly before the coming of the white man, as judged by the slight dialectical difference in their language. Jenness sets the period of separation from Siouan parentage and their coming in from the south to Canadian soil as no later than 1600. Most ethnologists believe that prior to the time of Columbus' visit to the New World there had been an eastward Siouan invasion from the west through to the Atlantic Coast. Later the tenuous lines were severed and there remained only isolated pockets of the fierce invaders along the Atlantic Coast. It is possible, but improbable, that some of these might have been driven on to the north finally to emerge as the Assiniboins.

The first recorded white man's mention of Assiniboins appears in the *Jesuit Relations* of 1640, which places them as a distinct group in the vicinity of Lake Winnipeg. The *Relations* of eighteen years later mentions them as occupying the territory between Lake Superior and Hudson's Bay. It appears almost certain that the Siouan separation occurred in the vicinity of the headwaters of the Mississippi (in present Minnesota) and that their movement thereafter was north and east, rather than westerly, from the eastern seaboard.

Since the derivation of the name comes from the Chippewa tongue and means "stone cooker," or more literally, "one who cooks by the use of stones," and since this was the name applied by the earliest Canadian Jesuits, it is obvious that the Assiniboins had for a considerable time been in contact with Chippewas. The Chippewas, in the earliest part of the seventeenth century, were the most northerly of all mid-Canadian non-Eskimo tribes. The same Jesuits who placed the

Assiniboins in the vicinity of Lake Winnipeg found the Chippewas much further north and west: principally in the area around Lakes Athabaska and Great Slave, across the mountains from Yukon country and not too far south of the Arctic Circle.

From the oldest traditions passed down by the oldest living members of the tribe in the 1930's — recollections passed down over the centuries — the Assiniboins lived "in a land always covered with snow." Granted that this may have been modified from "land mostly covered with snow," logic would place them in such a northerly region in the mid-1600's, in the central basin of mid-America, but not along the Atlantic Seaboard. And although Hodge believes that their separation from the parent stem only slightly predated the coming of the whites, because of the slight dialectical difference, it should be pointed out how little a language changes even after centuries of usage.

Regardless of what further study adds to the little-known pre-history, it is abundantly clear from the sparse but reliable records which do exist that they were a superior tribe, exceptionally strong in character as well as physically and mentally strong; adventuresome, and unusually adaptable. When they broke away from their Siouan ancestors, from a semi-horticultural existence in a sub-humid, moderate climate, the easy move would have been somewhat south and east. But they chose the hard, more adventuresome northlands. Rather than taking the easier life — in the lush lakes and woods region just beyond the present Canadian border — they moved to the rigorous regions where their life depended every day on great skill as hunters, the warmth of their fur clothing, bravery, fortitude and quick wit.

Regardless of their reason — and certainly it was not escape — the Assiniboins, after having lived for an indeterminate period in the vicinity south of the Arctic Circle, had reversed their northward trend by the time they were first noted by the Jesuits. They had not only survived but they had thrived in the cold climes. In the 1600's they probably numbered upward of 12,000. Yet despite this extremely large population (for an Indian tribe) they rattled like peas in a giant pod, living almost in a vacuum in their prodigious realm. Far to the east were the Iroquois, seen only rarely by a far-ranging war party. Far west were the Blackfeet — so distant that probably even their most adventuresome respective war parties had not yet made contact. Only the peaceful, orderly Crees and Chippewas lived within the vast circle. Since their neighbors' campsites were very stable the Assiniboins lived in and around them, like a giant grizzly who roams undisturbed among the other wildlife, small and large, in a vast wilderness. I would judge that during this period the word *Dakota,* their earlier ancestral identification, gradually became corrupted to *Nakoda,* meaning, broadly, "People Not at War." With the pressure of the French and British moving in from the east, and with the coming of the horse, the Assiniboins edged more and more westerly. The Assiniboins after the mid-seventeenth century may be accurately documented from the written record, supported by their own word-of-mouth traditions and recollections.

Henry Kelsy is the first white man known to have made a record of Indians on the Northern Plains prior to 1691. The tribes that he saw were Assiniboin and Cree. Judging from De l'Isle's map of 1703 and the reference by Jesuits, traders and others who kept written records, they were most numerous in the vicinity of Lake Nipigon (or Rainy Lake) and they were seen from Lake Winnipeg on the west to the southern reaches of Hudson's Bay on the east. They are mentioned as living around Lake Winnipeg as early as 1670 and are thus located on Lahontan's map of 1691.

Chauvignerie in 1736 placed them in the same region. Dobbs of the Hudson's Bay Company in 1744 located one division some distance northwest of Lake Winnipeg and the other west of an unidentified lake somewhat north of there. Dobbs called these groups "Assiniboin of the Meadows" and "Assiniboin of the Woods," but gave no reason for this. In 1775, Henry found the tribe scattered along both the Saskatchewan and Assiniboin rivers; from the forest meanderings and well up to the headwaters of the Saskatchewan. Hayden in 1862 limited their restricted and changed range during the previous century as follows: "The Northern Assiniboins roam over the country from the w. banks of the Saskatchewan and Assiniboin rs., in a w. direction to the woody mts., n. and w. amongst some of the small antliers of the Rocky Mts. e. of the Missouri, and on the banks of the small lakes frequently met with on the plains in that district. They consist of 250 or 300 lodges. The remainder of the tribe, now reduced to 250 lodges, occupy the district defined as follows: Commencing at the mouth of the White Earth r. on the e., extending up that river to and as far beyond its source as the Grand Coulee and the head of La Riviere aux Souris, thence n.w. along the Coteau de Prairie, or divide, as far as the beginning of the Cypress mts., on the n. fork of the Milk r., down that river to its junction with the Missouri, thence down the Missouri to White Earth r., the starting point. Until the year 1838 the tribe still numbered from 1000 to 1200 lodges, trading on the Missouri, when the smallpox reduced them to less than 400 lodges. They were also surrounded by large and hostile tribes, who continually made war upon them, and in this way their number was diminished, though at the present time they are slowly on the increase."

From the time they separated from the parent stem and joined the Crees until brought under white control, the Assiniboins were almost constantly at war with the Sioux.

But continuing the chronology, and getting back momentarily to the 1700's, one finds an interesting observation by Diamond Jenness, not generally noted elsewhere. In *Indians of Canada,* he observes that during this century, although the Assiniboins were (as during the centuries before and after) dependent on the chase, they also gathered large quantities of wild rice which they cooked "like their neighbors the Ojibwa, in clay pots and vessels of birch bark. . . ."

Most observers of the period note two distinct groups of Assiniboins. These do not always jibe. But somewhere and some time after the seventeenth century there was a noticeable division. Probably it consisted of a more vigorous western group of buffalo hunters who ranged more and further afield and were more warlike. Then there were those who chose to remain in the lake and woods regions, living on moose and deer, cooking their wild rice, and generally neighborly with the Chippewas and Crees, more eager to trap and trade with the French and Englishmen.

On one of his great treks, in 1737, the doughty French adventurer Sieur de la Verendrye also recorded his belief that they were divided. The woodlands tribe to the north, he believed, hunted fur-bearing animals for trade with the French. The Plains tribes further south and west, less affected by contact with the whites were, therefore, more savage and independent. The eastern branch constituted the middlemen. They bought corn, squash, colored buffalo robes, furs, feathers and many unorthodox items from tribes in all directions, even in some cases through trade with the Mandan villages far away on the muddy Missouri. And these items, along with their own furs and produce were traded to the French and English for metal axes, knives and arrowheads, guns, bullets and powder, woolen cloth and trinkets. It is difficult to ascertain if the traditions and legends passed down for centuries pertain to this division or to the earlier Siouan one. One of these, mentioned by De Smet, is a quarrel between two women over the apportionment of a buffalo; another pertains to the seduction of a woman. Without taking anything from their fascinating legends, I am inclined to believe that both divisions were prompted by more logical and more important reasons than these.

With the acquisition of horses and firearms about the middle of the eighteenth century, the Assiniboins increased their range and shifted further west. With their Cree allies they fought bitterly against the Blackfeet for the control of the western Canadian prairies. They also waged war, not only on the Sioux, Mandan, and other Missouri River tribes, but even with the Kutenai and Salish tribes across the Rocky Mountains. Their hunting grounds (about 1750) now embraced all the prairies of Canada. The unending buffalo provided them well with sturdy tipis and substantial food. As the greatest of all buffalo hunters, in the world's richest buffalo pasture, they slaughtered entire herds by driving them into pounds. They roasted the meat on spits, or boiled it in hide bags by means of hot stones — for they had now abandoned the clay pots and birchbark vessels that had served well in the lakelands.

After 1750 the Assiniboins may be regarded as an almost typical Plains tribe. Living in their large buffalo-hide tipis, they moved camp from place to place, more frequently than when they lived in the woodlands. In the earlier years, through their proximity to the forests, they had a variety of game: moose, beaver, bear, birds, porcupine and many other animals. The existence of the tribe now depended solely on the migratory buffalo. Long after other Plains tribes had abandoned them, each Assiniboin family owned several dogs, which, hitched to the poles of the travois, dragged their household possessions in summer and winter

Assiniboin women and children, probably about 1880. *Right:* Assiniboin council near Ft. Walsh, 1878

alike. Rivers that they encountered in their wanderings were generally forded or swum; but not infrequently they ferried themselves across in bullboats, which were tublike vessels covered with buffalo or moose hide and paddled from the front. Thus they followed the wanderings of the buffalo herds, dispersing into small bands during the winter months when the buffalo were more scattered and hunting difficult, and reuniting in spring for the great sun-dance festival and the driving of the herds into pounds.

Foot-wanderers whose only transport animals are dogs must necessarily be slow of movement and circumscribed in their range. Hence, the contacts of the Assiniboins with hostile Blackfeet were comparatively slight until they acquired the horse. The weapons of most Plains tribes were similar. Besides the ubiquitous bow and arrow, they used a long-handled spear for close fighting and three or four types of stone-headed clubs, as well as a wooden knobkerrie. Some men wore "Jackets of Moose leather six fold, quilted and without sleeves" as a protection against arrows, others carried shields of painted buffalo hide, decorated on its outer surface with painted scenes or figures derived from the vision in which the warrior had received his supernatural blessing. Whatever blessing this afforded him then attached itself in part to the shield, which guarded its owner in battle and rested beside him in his grave. Whether he carried a shield or not, every warrior had a war charm especially made for him by some old medicine man. Individual warriors sported special skin shirts and elaborate warbonnets that were thought to aid their wearers in battle. The right to wear them came either from a vision, or by purchase from a man who himself had received "permission" through a vision.

The introduction of horses and firearms gave the same stimulus to Assiniboin warfare that it gave to buffalo hunting, materially widening their field. Enemies hundreds of miles away, who previously could be reached on foot only after many days of hard traveling, were now within measurable distance for a raid; and firearms were more accurate and deadly than arrows that could not even penetrate a shield. The Assiniboins, at this juncture, became infected with the war fever. They divided their great energies between the exciting buffalo hunt, raids and counter-raids against their ever-present Indian enemies. Flashes of sunlight from a mirror and columns of smoke dampened at intervals with a blanket passed the warning from camp to camp whenever foes were lurking in the neighborhood. A warrior who dreamed of killing an enemy regarded the dream as a prophecy, enlisted a band of volunteers, and (with the consent of the military society of soldiers' council) sallied out to capture scalps and horses. Paintings on the outside of his tipi portrayed his exploits. The eagle feathers in his warbonnet recorded the number of enemies he had slain. Women danced around the scalps that his party brought back to camp, and older warriors recited their own exploits to encourage the younger generation. In communities infected by such war passion and devoid of an hereditary class of chiefs and nobles, valor and success in battle offered the surest road to honor and high rank.

These people, however, did not devote themselves exclusively to war and hunting. There were many activities and events in their daily life representing social recognition and public ceremonies. The Assiniboins gave names to their children in a pleasing ceremony that closely resembled the Ojibwa custom. An old man, or a prominent warrior, took the infant in his arms and conferred on it a name usually derived from a propitious dream, or from a successful feat in battle; all the assembled relatives and friends then embraced the child in turn and added their benediction. Parents distributed gifts generously when their daughters reached maturity. At marriage they arranged formal processions of relatives to bear presents of food and clothing and to lead strings of horses between the tipis of the groom's parents and the bride's. In earlier days there had been no marriage ceremony. The suitor merely made his offer through the medium of an old man. The girl moved over to his lodge at night, if her parents accepted the bridal price.

Assiniboin funeral rites were more elaborate than marriage rites, as in nearly all Indian tribes. Occasionally the Assiniboin — unlike most — cremated their dead, or deposited their greatest warriors on the surface of the earth beneath cairns of logs and stones; but usually they followed the standard Plains procedure described by De Smet:

"They bind the bodies with thongs of rawhide between the branches of large trees, and, more frequently, place them on scaffolds, to protect them from the wolves and other wild animals. They are higher than a man can reach. The feet are always turned to the west. There they are left to decay. When the scaffolds or the trees to which the dead are attached fall, through old age, the relatives bury all the other bones, and place the skulls in a circle in the plain, with the faces turned toward the centre. They preserve these with care, and consider them objects of religious veneration. You will generally find there several bison skulls. In the center stands the medicine poke, about twenty feet high, to which Wah-Kons are hung, to guard and protect the sacred deposit. The Indians call the cemetery the village of the dead. They visit it at certain seasons of the year, to converse affectionately with their deceased relatives and friends, and always leave some present."

Principal gods were Sun and Thunder, which were regarded, at least in historic times, as direct manifestations of the Great Spirit, ruler of everything. Both deities received public worship at the sun-dance and the horse-dance festivals held during the summer months. On especially solemn occasions, individual Indians frequently made Sun and Thunder offerings of tobacco smoke; and prayed for long life, health, or success in some vital venture. But the Assiniboins placed less reliance on these "higher" powers than on the supernatural blessing supposedly bestowed in a vision (generally in answer to fasting and supplication). Such a vision brought only an indefinite assurance or conviction of some supernatural power who watched over every action, and stood ready to help in times of crisis. To others it had great powers or privileges — power to heal diseases with herbal remedies or else by supernatural means, authority to establish a dancing society or the privilege of painting on their lodge an episode of the dream itself. Assiniboin society recognized, besides a military society of noted warriors, four classes of men more or less distinguished from the rank and file, two orders of medicine men, the owners of painted tents, and the founders or leaders of various dancing societies.

Their medicine men and the owners of painted lodges enjoyed little prestige unless they also distinguished themselves in warfare. Their military society, comprising the bravest, most active men between the ages of twenty-five and thirty-five, controlled every large camp. The leader of the war society received orders only from the dominant chief; but since it was only through the military society that the chief could enforce his wishes, he dared not oppose its expressed opinion. The military society also policed camp and regulated the buffalo hunt. They received delegations from other tribes and authorized dangerous sporting raids for scalps and horses. On special occasions, warrior members dressed in brilliant battle array danced to the wild accompaniment of drums and fierce singing. They recounted individual exploits with the avowed purpose of impressing the laity with their strength and of even stimulating the ever-popular zeal for warfare.

The number of dancing societies increased and waned. Their usual purpose was social, although fellow members, like our Rotarians and Masons, aided one another in daily life, too. The religious aspect was prominent only in the "horse-dance," in which an "altar" was erected inside an enlarged tipi, incense and tobacco smoke was offered to *sun, thunder* and *earth*.

Nearly all Assiniboin dancing societies restricted membership to men. But at least as far back as 1820, women had a special society of their own. Candidates paid an initiation fee of varying amounts, and (in the second half of the nineteenth century) women's societies held annual dances when the bands united in early summer.

The most important religious event in the Assiniboin year was the Sun-dance. "They often speak of it in the course of the year, and look forward to its immediate arrival with joy, respect and veneration," said De Smet. The leader was always a prominent warrior who had inherited the privilege and received instruction from his father. After a ceremonial buffalo hunt (which also provided necessary food) a tribe moved to some previously chosen site. Here they erected the sacred pole (cut down after the manner of an enemy), dragged to the camp amid great rejoicing. To this pole, and to the rafters of the gigantic lodge, tribesmen lashed their offerings to Sun-God, and the leader gave a testimonial on behalf of the entire tribe. Sun-dance ceremonies lasted at least three days. On the first day the people danced; on the second day their medicine men displayed great tricks; and on the last day the whole camp banqueted, with dog's meat having a prominent place on the menu. Sometimes the feast period was prolonged, if times were good and food abundant.

The Blackfeet, Sioux and other Great Plains tribes' celebration of the Sun-dance centered about the voluntary torture endured by neophyte warriors. They allowed their breasts, or shoulders, to be pierced with sharp skewers and attached by stout thongs to either the sacred pole or a heavy buffalo skull. They strained at the pole or dragged the skull until these either broke loose or friends and relatives took pity on their sufferings and released them. The Assiniboins, however, did not associate self-torture with the Sun-dance. It was used only in preparation for war. Braves who aspired to lead a war party often lay out in the rain or snow for several nights, fasting and praying to the Great Spirit for visions, and some of them gashed their arms and breasts with knives, the more to excite his pity.

There may have been times in previous centuries when the Assiniboin nation was more populous, but I believe they hit their peak shortly before the time of the Lewis and Clark expedition. In 1823 Renville estimated their number at 28,000, which included upward of 7000 warriors and 3000 lodges. This was as large or larger than all other branches of the mighty Sioux combined. Almost without exception the Sioux are credited with greater numbers than any of the other Plains tribes, but historians should check their facts on this.

From the time that Lewis and Clark reached the Mandan villages, in the winter of 1804-5, and throughout most of the long trek as far westward as the great falls of the Missouri, their journals give periodic indication that they were in more frequent contact with the Assiniboins than with any other Indians. Yet despite the vital fact that this was the best game country which they passed through, even these contacts were infrequent. On the expedition's return trip, after leaving Blackfeet country — where their most dangerous human encounter was with the Gros Ventres at Maria's River — they encountered even fewer Indian signs throughout the long stretch of the winding Missouri all the way back to the Mandan villages; and the few aborigines seen were apparently Gros Ventres. Since this was during the heat of summer, it appears that the Assiniboins still remembered the cool lushness of their earlier habitats and their early-nineteenth-century summer buffalo range continued to be in the more pleasant climes far to the north.

Because the Lewis and Clark journals were among the first published American reports even to carry the name Assiniboin (although they butchered the spell-

Assiniboins and Gros Ventres at sun dance, Ft. Belknap

ing), and since they definitely constituted not only the most detailed but the closest thing to scientific fact as of then reported to the people of the U. S., it is pertinent that some of these sparse but significant mentions be provided:

October 25, 1804 (near present Washburn, N. D., the first citation):

". . . several parties of Mandins rode to the river to view us . . . we are told that the Sioux had recently stolen horses of the 'Big Bellies', on their way home they fell in with the Assiniboine who killed them and took the horses. A Frenchman has lately been killed by Indians on the Trak to the trading establishment on the Ossineboine R. in the North of this place (or British fort), . . ."

A few weeks later, Nov. 13, 1804, the entry reveals: ". . . A Chief & 7 men of note (visiting them at Fort Mandan) . . . the chief was one of 3 bands of Osiniboin who rove between the Missouri and Ossiniboine R., about 600 braves, who hunt on the plains and trade on the Ass. R. . . . They are the Descendants of the Seaux and speake their language . . . they come to the nations in this quarter to trade or make presents for horses . . ."

The winter months were dreary at Fort Mandan; and only once did Captain Clark make mention that a band of Assiniboins had camped during the later part of the winter at the mouth of the Little Missouri, in company with "The Mine-tarees"; and a little later (March 4, 1805) ". . . the Assiniboines returned & attempted to take horses of the Minetarees & and were fired on by them . . ."

After their hopeful departure from the winter camp, as they approached the area which later became Fort Berthold (built by the American Fur Company in 1845) on the edge of the Dakota badlands: ". . . at 1 pm. we overtook 3 french hunters who had set out a few days before us with a view of trapping beaver . . . they avail themselves of our protection against the Ossiniboins who sometimes hunt on the Missouri . . ."

April 14, 1805, above the mouth of the Little Missouri, the more literate Lewis wrote: ". . . Capt. Clark walked on shore this morning, and on his return informed me that . . . in the bottom lands he had met with several uninhabited Indian lodges built with the boughs of the Elm, and in the plains he met with the remains of two large encampments of a recent date, which from the appearance of some hoops of small kegs, seen near them we concluded that they must have been the camps of the Assiniboines, as no other nation who visit this part of the Missouri ever indulge themselves with spiritous liquor. of this the Assiniboines are passionately fond, and we are informed that it forms their principal inducement to furnish the British establishments on the Assiniboin river with the dryed and pounded meat and grease which they do. they also supply those establishments with a small quantity of fur, consisting principally of the large and small wolves and the small fox skins. these they barter for small kegs of rum which they generally transport to their camps at a distance from the establishments, where they revel with the friends and relations as long as they possess the means of intoxication, their women and children are equally indulged on those occations and are all seen drunk together. so far is a state of intoxication from being a cause of reproach among them, that with the men, it is a matter of exultation that their skill and industry as hunters has enabled them to get drunk frequently. in their customs, habits and dispositions these people very much resemble the Siouxs from whom they have descended. The principal inducement with the British fur companyies, for continuing their establishments on the Assiniboin river, is the Buffaloe meat and grease they procure from the Assiniboins, and Christanoes, by means of which, they are enabled to supply provision to their engages on their return from rainy Lake to the English river and the Athabaskey country where they winter; without such resource these voyagers would frequently be stratened for provision, as the country through which they pass is but scantily supplyed with game, and the rappidity with which they are compelled to travel in order to reach their winter stations, would leave them but little leisure to surch for food while on their voyage. The Assiniboins have so recently left this neighbourhood, that the game is scarce and very shy . . ."

The following day Lewis recorded: ". . . I saw the remains of several camps of the Assiniboins; near one of which in a small ravine, there was a park which they had formed of timber and brush, for the purpose of taking . . . Antelope. It was constructed in the following manner. a strong pound was first made of timbers, on one side of which there was a small apparture, sufficiently large to admit an Ante-lope; from each side of this apparture, a curtin was extended to a considerable dis-tance, widening as they receded from the pound . . ."

On the 17th of April, Captain Clark reported that he again had seen the re-mains of "Ossiniboinne" camps in every part of the woodland through which he passed, and the next day that he had seen fresh Indian tracks and four rafts on the opposite shore of the Missouri which he presumed were "Ossiniboine" who had been on a war party against the "Rockey Mountain Indians." (He also mentioned that here they saw the biggest and fattest beaver yet encountered, which may have been another reason for the Assiniboins' presence.)

And finally, as the last meaty reference in all of the vital expeditions' westward passage: in Captain Lewis' handwriting on May 2, 1805 as they approached the mouth of the Mussellshell:

". . . Joseph Fields one of the hunters who was out today found several yards of scarlet cloth which had been suspended on the bough of a tree near an old indian hunting camp, where it had been left as a sacrifice to the deity by the in-dians, probably of the Assiniboin nation, it being a custom with them as well as all the nations inhabiting the waters of the Missouri so far as they are known to us, to offer or sacrifice in this manner to the deity watever they may be possessed off which they think most acceptable to him, and very honestly making their own feel-ings the test of those of the deity offer him the article which they most prize them-selves. this being the most usual method of we[r]shiping the great sperit as they term the deity, is practiced on interesting occasions, or to produce the happy even-tuation of the important occurances incident to human nature, such as relief from hunger, or mallady, protection from their enemies or the delivering them into their hands, and with such cultivate, to prevent the river's overflowing and distroying their crops &c. s[a]crefices of a similar kind are also made to the deceased by their friends and relatives . . ."

Lewis and Clark noted that the Assiniboins physically resembled the Sioux, and later observers also mentioned the similarity. Catlin wrote: ". . . the stone-boilers are a fine and noble looking race . . . bearing both in looks and customs a striking resemblance to the Dahcotas or Sioux from whom they have undoubtedly sprung. The men are tall and graceful in the movements; and war their piactured robes of the buffalo hide with great skill and pleasing effect. They are good hunt-ers, tolerably supplied with horses . . . and in a country abounding with buffaloes . . . live well. Their dances, frequent and varied were generally exactly the same as those of the Sioux . . ."

Much of this physical resemblance was in size and conformation, but the most striking similarity was in the manner in which men wore their hair. What most of the frontiersmen missed (except the trader Denig at Fort Union) was the fact that some of the most vain Assiniboins actually were competing with the Crows in the great length of their hair, which sometimes reached the ground. During the past century and a half their clothing, tipis and customs were similar to those of the

Plains Crees, although they observed more decorum in camp and were among the most cleanly of all plains tribes. Assiniboin hospitality was noted by most traders who kept records during the fur-trading frontier period, as was the fact that polygamy seemed quite common.

As long as the buffalo lasted, because, as the old explorer Henry said, "they were the most expert buffalo hunters on the plains," they were also the West's greatest producers and traders of pemmican. Assiniboin dried buffalo meat had the best reputation in the Old West. They were the last of the plains tribes to use dogs extensively as beasts of burden, long after the introduction of the horse.

From the earliest days of the white men's contact, considerable ado was made about identification of the various bands or divisions. With few exceptions they are notoriously inaccurate. Some were so far-fetched that one today wonders how they were ever arrived at. Among the principal Assiniboin bands mentioned by Lewis and Clark — *Menatopa, Gens de Feuilles, Itscheabine, Watapachnato* and *Osseegah* — not one even comes close.

Maximilian made a better try but missed badly with his: *Itscheabine (gens des filles); Jatonabine (gens des roches); Otopachgnato (gens du large); Otaopabine (gens des canots); Tschantoga (gens des bois); Watapachnato (gens de l'age); Tanintauei (gens des osayes); Chabin (gens des montagnes).* A band mentioned by Hayden, *Minishinakato*, has not been identified with any named by Maximilian. Henry enumerated eleven bands in 1808, of which seven called *Red River, Rabbit, Eagle Hills, Saskatchewan, Foot,* and *Swampy Ground* Assiniboin, and *Those-who-have-water-for-themselves-only* cannot be identified. This last may be Hayden's erroneous *Minishinakoto*. Other divisions mentioned, chiefly geographical, by some of the historic reporters are: Assiniboin of the Meadows, Turtle Mountain Sioux, *Wawaseeasson*, and *Assabaock*. The only Assiniboin village mentioned in print is *Pasquayah*. None of these is correct.

With the country better understood because of the explorations of Captains Lewis and Clark, some of history's toughest competitors — the American Mountain Men — moved in to the Northern Rocky Mountain-Northern Great Plains region to compete with the long-experienced and astute French-Canadian trappers and traders for valued beaver plews. Much of the recorded contemporary history of the first half of the nineteenth century comes from this source, but it is lean, indeed. Mountain Men had neither time nor the inclination to record observations of even their most hair-raising adventures and escapes. Nevertheless, because of what they did record, much more became known of the Sioux, Cheyennes, Crows, Snakes, Flatheads, Shawnees, Pawnees and Arapahoes. The terrible Blackfeet — most geographically isolated of all — came in for the most mention of all the tribes because they set out to control and keep for themselves, not only the Sun, Marias and other great beaver streams within their realm, but the faraway beaver-rich waters of the Yellowstone, even the Snake and Green rivers, all the headwaters of the Missouri, and everything of value in between.

The Assiniboins were different: not only for geographic reasons (because their

Black Eagle (Assiniboin)

long stretch of the Missouri was not prime beaver country despite the large size of the flat-tails which the Lewis and Clark expedition noted) but also because they had long since exploited and wearied of beaver trapping and trading with the earlist French-English traders in Canada; and by the nineteenth century had moved into the more advanced, lucrative economy of the buffalo-pemmican trade.

In the epic period, therefore, when such stalwarts as Jim Bridger and Brokenhand Fitzpatrick were making blood-curdling history, the Assiniboins rate only one innocuous citation. This pertains to the peak period of the beaver trade in the region. It started in St. Louis, when Majors Andrew Henry and William H. Ashley issued their stirring call for "one hundred enterprising young men to ascend the Missouri to its source" in the early spring of 1822.

In less than a month the Ashley-Henry party of voyageurs, boatmen, hunters, trappers and all-purpose frontiersmen had been recruited, including such famed names as Bridger, Jedediah Smith, grizzly-resistant Hugh Glass and the "King of the keelboatmen," Mike Fink.

A score of voyageurs were required on each keelboat, marching along the runways with their poles or cordelling the boat through the swollen, muddy waters. The fierce river ever bristled with fierce snags; below the mouth of the Kansas, one plunged through a boat and a $10,000 cargo disappeared. The expedition pushed on past the camps of the Pawnees, Otoes, Sioux and a few crude cabins of trappers. Northwest of the Mandan village, a band of Assiniboins suddenly struck. No one was killed but the Indians stole fifty valuable horses.

The Assiniboins had gained this brief mention — the only one that can be located in some two exciting decades recorded on the American fur trade in the region.

The glorious days of the Assiniboins were soon to wane. The white man's whisky was not yet as dangerous as his virus. The Assiniboins fared no worse from alcohol than did their brethren; but smallpox, carried by some unknown trader probably not too long after the time of Lewis and Clark, struck the most terrible series of blows that they were ever to receive. It is well described by Maximilian, Prince of Wied (whose staff artist Karl Bodmer, like Catlin, did the best job of early paintings of the Assiniboins, and whose visit to old Fort Union was so significant) in his *Travels in the Interior of North America, 1832-1834:*

"The Prairie all around is a vast field of death, covered with unburied corpses, and spreading, for miles, pestilence and infection . . . The Assiniboines, 9000 in number, [actually about double this] roaming over a hunting territory to the north of the Missouri, as far as the trading posts of the Hudson's Bay Company, are, in the literal sense of the expression, nearly exterminated. They, as well as the Crows and the Blackfeet, endeavored to flee in all directions, but the disease [smallpox] everywhere pursued them. . . ."

After the first epidemics, Porter in 1829 estimated Assiniboin population as having dwindled to 8000. Drake said they were up again to 10,000 before the smallpox epidemic of 1836 struck, during which another 4000 of them perished. When Gallatin (1836) placed the number at 6000 it was probably after the epi-

demic. By the time of the first United States Indian report (1843) in which they figured, the Assiniboins numbered 7000; in 1890 they totaled only 3008 and in 1904
but 2600; and several hundred less than this when Curtis made his 1908 estimate.

When Prince Maximilian arrived at Fort Union in 1833, not only was the
American Fur Company steamer on which he had sailed from St. Louis named
Assiniboine, but his most exciting experience was this: At upriver Fort McKenzie
where he was visiting in the latter part of August, a trading party of Blackfeet
under Lame Bull were encamped under the protecting walls of the fort. They were
suddenly attacked at dawn by a war party of some 1500 Assiniboins. As the raiders
swarmed down the bluffs and over the valley toward the fort, it was supposed that
they were attacking McKenzie proper. The Prince, along with the entire garrison
of some seventy men, hurriedly opened fire. Maximilian's gun was already loaded
as he dashed to a porthole in the upper bastion, but in the excitement he rammed
down another charge. As described later in Lieutenant Bradley's journals, the
Prince, finally getting a good bead on a charging Assiniboin, "pulled the trigger
and proceeded to revolve with great rapidity across the bastion till he came in
severe contact with the opposite wall and fell stunned to the floor. . . ." Had not
the quality of Maximilian's weapon been superior to the cheap trade rifles, the
double charge undoubtedly would have done him in.

At any rate, the garrison speedily discovered that the Blackfeet were the real
object of attack. They stopped fire and directed their efforts toward getting the
Piegans into the opened gates of the fort. Bradley's account continues: ". . . about
twenty-five [Blackfeet] men, women and children were overtaken and killed at that
point. Major Culbertson stood at the gate endeavoring to facilitate the entrance of
the Piegans, when the Assiniboins came swarming around him. They might easily
have killed him but forebore to do so. 'Get out of the way! get out of the way!'
cried Lunica, or Longhair, pushing him to one side and dispatching a Piegan that
he [Culbertson] was helping in. This Lunica was afterwards . . . the principal chief
of the Upper Assiniboines and lived to a great age, dying in February 1874. Maj.
Culbertson was at that time interpreter at Fort Belknap Agency, when the Assiniboines received their annuities, and he and Lunica had many a laugh over the
comic incidents of this attack." Prince Maximilian did not find the incident laugh-
able, and his artist Bodmer, in reaction to the scene left one of the most vivid and
famous of all frontier drawings for posterity.

Major Culbertson in later years pointed out that after the worst smallpox epidemic (1837) there was "a marked decline in the physical condition of these tribes
[Assiniboin, Gros Ventre and Blackfeet] in respect to height, beauty of form,
strength and freedom from disease. This degeneration was not of immediate oc-
curence, but twenty-five or thirty years subsequent was plainly manifest to those
who had known the Indians prior to the ravages of the disease. The general dis-
persal of the several tribes, and the vast proportions of deaths consequent upon it
was followed by such a breaking up of families that all knowledge of relationship
to each other on the part of the young was lost; and therefore in later years when

grown to maturity and marrying it could not but result that marriages between first cousins and even of brothers and sisters should be frequent. . . ."

Aside from Lowie's anthropological study of the Canadian (Stoney Reservation) Assiniboins, only one other man ever wrote prolifically about these people. He was as odd and as remarkable a character as the Upper Missouri frontier was to produce, Edwin Thompson Denig. (See "A Literate Fur Trader . . ." by Ewers, *supra.*)

Space does not permit the recounting of facts compiled so articulately and minutely by this strange trader in all of his works. Suffice to say, some of his detailed observations on the Assiniboins do dovetail with facts revealed by Lowie. Some of them are supplementary; but the majority are at wide variance with the Assiniboins' own subjective beliefs and recollections. Much Denig material is extremely inaccurate but Denig had no access to the great scholarly tracts and accumulated knowledge and perspective gained during the past century. Considering the fact that he married an Assiniboin woman whom he treated with the fullest degree of love and respect, he was unbelievably biased regarding her people. It is almost paradoxical, when early in his meticulous 451-page report to Governor Stevens, he states: ". . . of all the Indians now residing on the Missouri River the Assiniboin appear to have made the least progress toward acquiring civilized ideas or knowledge of any kind. Superstitious, lazy and indisposed to thought, they make no attempt to improve themselves in any way."

Denig totally misunderstood the pride and centuries-old cultural heritage of the Assiniboins — their perfectly satisfactory culture (for them) which they were more reluctant to take part with for the white man's mess of proffered pottage than any other tribe which he observed. Denig contradicted himself without understanding the implications, as the few lines which follow will indicate: ". . . they do not think the Great Spirit created them on or for a particular portion of country, but that he made the whole prairie for the[ir] sole use . . . and the Indian to suit the prairie, giving them among other reasons the fact that the buffalo is so well adapted to their wants as to meat and clothing, even for their lodges and bowstrings. To the Indian is allotted legs to run, eyes to see far, bravery, instinct, watchfulness, and other capacities not developed in the same degree in the whites."

What else would any proud and adjusted people feel about their birthright and their rightful place in the sun? Denig saw only the fact that these "savages" were here to be conquered, exploited and enslaved by his "master race." Nevertheless anyone interested in learning about the Assiniboins must certainly read the contradictory Denig, their most prolific — and at times irascible — biographer.

Despite smallpox, whisky, the sharp practices and deceit of all too many whites, the decimated remnants of the Assiniboins carried on. They did it — for an exceedingly proud people — in a most humanitarian way. From the period before the coming of Lewis and Clark, during the entire period of Fort Union's prominence, throughout the terrible Indian wars and up to the time of their confinement on the two United States Reservations, they were not only the dominant Missouri River Indian tribe — acting as a buffer for the whites between the fierce Sioux on the east and the Blackfeet-Gros Ventre coalition on the west — but they were unusually friendly with all whites. History has given this accolade to the Crows and Flatheads. Considering their long heritage of savagery and warfare, this is all the more remarkable for the Assiniboins. No military post of United States troops was ever needed against them. They committed fewer depredations against whites from the entire period of exploration, through the fur-trade, gold-rush, cattle-trail, open-range and early homesteading and railroad-building periods (the first full century of Montana's frontier history) than did any other tribe, including the more sedentary Crows and Flatheads. History hereafter should give such long-neglected credit to the Assiniboins.

The only such compilation that I know of, covering a decade of Indian depredations after 1870 in Montana Territory, was assembled by Robert Vaughn, in his delightful pioneer reminiscences, *Then and Now*. Of the many killings of men, women and children by Indians during this period, only three are charged to Assiniboins: or less blood altogether than either the Sioux, Blackfeet or Nez Percés were reputed to have let on some of their single raids. The three last named tribes account for almost all of the killings cited by Vaughn.

As nearly as books can do it — particularly when they are introspective and in a sense biographical — the material in *Land of Nakoda* and *The Assiniboine* tells about all that is in print on the valiant Assiniboine and their way of life. It was a rare stroke of good fortune that enabled Indian researchers, particularly the dedicated James L. Long of the Federal Writers' Program, meticulously to interrogate, interview and record — almost always in the Assiniboin tongues — the facts, stories and recollections of the twenty-five oldest and most reliable members of the tribe in the 1930's. Many of these oldsters retold facts and incidents related to them by their parents, grandparents, great and even great-great-grandparents, which of course predated Lewis and Clark and almost any semblance of white influence on their primitive life and culture.

I have never changed my opinion that the Assiniboins once were one among the largest, most savage, yet most commendable and outstanding of all the Plains Indian Tribes. I hold great respect and affection for my friends the Assiniboins.

Naming the Nez Percés

By ALVIN M. JOSEPHY, JR.

IN 1965 THE PEOPLE of the U. S., and particularly of the Northwest, had special reason to remember the once-strong and proud Nez Percé Indians. It was 160 years ago, on Idaho's gentle Wieppe Prairie, that men and women of the tribe gave succor and friendly welcome to the starving members of the Lewis and Clark expedition, who had struggled across the Bitterroot Mountains and the Lolo Trail from what would become Montana. The occasion marked Americans' first acquaintance with the Nez Percés, a tribe whose history during the next century was intimately, and often dramatically, associated with some of the most important events of the Pacific Northwest's early development.

United States schoolboys in the nineteenth century read of the Nez Percés in the exciting Washington Irving histories of Astoria and Captain Bonneville. Mountain men spun the Nez Percés into their narratives of the fabled fur trade, and in the 1830's eastern pulpits rang loud with the inspiring account of a Nez Percé and Flathead delegation which trekked from the Rocky Mountains to St. Louis in search of a missionary for their peoples. The tribe's later welcome to the Whitmans and Spaldings, its roles during the Waiilatpu tragedy, the Indian wars of the 1850's and the Clearwater gold rush that led inevitably to the surge of miners across the Bitterroots into Montana Territory, all form colorful chapters in the Nez Percé story, a narrative that rises to thundering climax in the sad but valiant attempt by part of the tribe to escape their white tormentors in 1877.

Those who have been interested in the Nez Percés and their epic history have long wrestled with a small, but intriguing, riddle: How did the tribe get its present name? The question is particularly fascinating because its answer somehow became lost in the earliest and least-known years of Northwest history, and its pursuit takes one back among romantic names and events that are still heavily cloaked in obscurity.

The bone of contention has been: Did the Nez Percés ever pierce their noses, and, if not, how did such a misnomer come to settle upon them? For modern writers, the confusion was defined about sixty years ago in the monumental *Handbook of American Indians North of Mexico*, an authoritative encyclopedia and

65

Nez Percé Indians

bibliography prepared by the eminent Frederick Webb Hodge.[1] In describing the Nez Percés, Dr. Hodge wrote that the term was "applied by the French to a number of tribes which practiced or were supposed to practice the custom of piercing the nose for the insertion of a piece of dentalium. The term is now used exclusively to designate the main tribe of the Shahaptian family, who have not, however, so far as is known, ever been given to the practice."

Since then, almost everyone who has tackled this point of Nez Percé history has bobbled over the question, many of them finding only confusion and ambiguity in the earliest accounts and narratives of the tribe, and settling finally for Hodge's inconclusive lead. For instance, Phillip Ashton Rollins, in his notes to the *Discovery of the Oregon Trail*, a transcript of Robert Stuart's 1812-13 journal of his eastward trip from Astoria, wrote: "The name Nez Percé was given by French voyageurs, but the reason for doing so is now uncertain as these Indians seemingly neither wore nasal ornaments nor pierced their noses."[2] Oscar Osburn Winther, a respected historian, went further in *The Great Northwest*: "The Nez Percé were erroneously named by French explorers; there is no evidence that either Nez Percé men or women pierced their nasal septums for nose ornaments,"[3] while Fritz L. Kramer, in his *Origin of Idaho Town Names* followed suit with "There seems to be no evidence that these Indians ever pierced their noses, as the name would lead us to believe. It has been suggested that the name, as originally given by the French-Canadian trappers, may have been *Nez presse*, but this suggestion has not been substantiated."[4]

The roll of uncertainty and conjecture goes on. In *Hear Me, My Chiefs!* an enthralling Indian version of Nez Percé history, L. V. McWhorter wrote: "There is nothing in their tribal lore and traditions indicating that nose-piercing in any form was ever practiced among them,"[5] while Robert G. Bailey's *River of No Return*, a compendium of central Idaho history, legend and lore, termed the name a misnomer stemming from misunderstood sign language. Earlier writers on the Nez Percés, like Kate C. McBeth, H. J. Spinden and Edward S. Curtis, who thought the name was rightly applied, made little or no impression on these later commentators, and even those who presented the opinions of anthropologist Spinden or historian Curtis — like Helen A. Howard and Dan L. McGrath in their book *War Chief Joseph* — did it uncertainly, and without presenting evidence to convince the reader one way or the other.

Obviously, the heart of the puzzle lies in the question: Who first settled the name Nez Percé on this tribe, and why? Getting at the answers requires knowledge of the first whites to have contact with these Indians, for it is they who did the deed. By the time the earliest ones had passed away and a second generation of fur traders was on the scene, the answers were already shrouded in confusion and misinformation. Whatever documentation the first generation left disappeared (with the exception of Lewis and Clark's, whose role we shall discuss further on) and future writers were left with the hearsay and ambiguities of come-latelies, a situation responsible for modern conclusions wide of the mark, such as Fritz

Kramer's statement in *Idaho Town Names* that "The term Nez Percé does not seem to appear in literature earlier than 1840."

The first whites known to have met the Nez Percés were the members of the Lewis and Clark expedition, coming from the upper Missouri in 1805. The next outsiders were Iroquois, French-Canadian and half-breed trappers associated with explorer and trader David Thompson, one of the truly majestic figures of early Northwest history, who beginning in 1807, led the North West Company's westward push across the Canadian Rockies and down into the present U. S. Northwest. These are the two groups with whom our answers lie. Lewis and Clark's documentation has been available for a long time, but it is not the most important. The vital guidance comes from Thompson and his men, a shadowy group about whom absolutely nothing was known to historians throughout most of the nineteenth century, and whose activities still lie in the romantic realm of half-truth and half-mystery.

Although bits and pieces of Thompson's interesting journals began appearing about sixty years ago, the most important clue to the naming of the Nez Percés came to light only recently with the appearance of certain previously unpublished portions of the diaries in *David Thompson's Journals Relating to Montana and Adjacent Regions,* a wonderfully valuable, and rare, book edited and annotated by M. Catherine White and published by Montana State University in 1950. This book indicates, as we shall see, that the Nez Percés, usually identified with Idaho and Washington, actually received their name in Montana, where so much of their stirring history, before and afterward, occurred.

Thompson was one of the last, and possibly the greatest, of the northern explorer-traders whose drive after new and better fur territories carried them westward across the Canadian wilds into uncharted lands, and to knowledge of previously unknown tribes. The push commenced in earnest after the signing of peace between England and France in 1763, when Canadian traders out of Montreal (sneeringly called *Pedlars* by the Hudson's Bay Company employees who clung close to their northern forts around the Bay) began building posts along the Saskatchewan River. As the *Pedlars* cut off communications between the Hudson's Bay posts and the inland tribes with whom they had been trading, Hudson's Bay policy changed, and they too sent expeditions south and west to build competitive forts. By 1785, both groups had groped almost to the Rocky Mountains and knew the warlike and unpredictable Atsinas, Bloods, Blackfeet and Piegans. Through these tribes, they might have known vaguely of the Kutenais, who had been driven westward across the Rockies in the mid and latter eighteenth century by the newly armed Blackfeet. The whites had not yet, however, met the Kutenais.

There were two other nations with whom the Saskatchewan tribes warred and about whom they told the whites. They were two large, generally defined peoples, and the Canadians, who had not yet met either of them, thought of them as occupying great areas. One was the Snakes, the People of the Serpent, whom the Blackfeet had scattered south and west into the Rockies; and the other was the Flatheads, living somewhere between the Rockies and the Pacific Ocean in an area that now includes Washington, Oregon, Idaho and western Montana. The Canadians heard a lot about the Flatheads, and they referred nebulously to everyone who might be living in that area as Flatheads. An interesting map, presented to the American Congress in 1785 by Peter Pond, a United States Citizen of Connecticut, who had been one of the earliest and most aggressive explorer-traders in the high northern Athabasca country of Canada, bears this out. Pond's map, a copy of which is in the British Museum,[7] shows a river labeled *Naberkistagon R.* approximately in the position of the still undiscovered Columbia, flowing into the "South Sea," and underneath it the encompassing legend, *flat-head Indians country.*

It is unlikely that Pond at this early date — before any whites had crossed the mountains — had picked up the term from an account written by John Ledyard or another mariner who might have seen coastal Indians who really did flatten their heads. More probably, Pond and his colleagues got all the information they had about the trans-mountain area from the knowledge and hearsay of plains tribes whom they knew. The fact that these tribes referred to everyone living across the Rockies as Flatheads was later corroborated on several occasions in Lewis and Clark's journals. On March 19, 1806, for example, Lewis said that he had seen heads being flattened among all nations west of the Rockies, and commented that "it is why *nations east of Rockies call all the nations on this side,* except the Aliohtans or Snake Indians, by the generic term of *Flatheads.*" This is probably as good an explanation as any of how the name, Flathead, arose in the first place, though it has led to other puzzles, such as why it was fastened on the present Flathead tribe alone, and also to the confusion, by Americans during the early nineteenth century, between Flatheads and Nez Percés. We shall hear more of this later.

Until the time of Lewis and Clark, however, we have no documentation from the few Canadian half-breeds, and possibly whites, who had crossed the Canadian Rockies farther south than Mackenzie, indicating what they had learned about the Flatheads or other Columbia Basin tribes. During the winter of 1804-5, Lewis and Clark took shelter near the Mandan and Minnetaree Indians on the upper Missouri close to present-day Bismarck, North Dakota. In preparation for their spring jump-off to the unknown west, they gathered all the information they possibly could about geography and tribes along the route they hoped to follow. Their principal informants were the Minnetaree Indians who lived where the expedition was wintering, but who frequently went west on war parties against the Snakes, and who knew many of the strange plains tribes and something of the geography as far as the Bitterroot and Salmon River Mountains in Montana and Idaho. What the Minnetarees had to tell was interpreted for the Captains by Toussaint Charbonneau, who had been living and trading among the Minnetarees (he had purchased from them, as a wife, the famed Sacajawea, whom they had captured during a fight with the Snakes near the Missouri's Three Forks); and by René Jessaume, a not completely reliable French-Canadian freeman who had first come down from the Assiniboine River to the Mandans about 1790 and, off and on, had been living among them and the Minnetarees for almost ten years. Further infor-

mation was probably picked up from several Northwest traders who visited the Mandans while Lewis and Clark were there, and who might have contributed hearsay intelligence gathered from other Northwesters via the Blackfeet farther west.

All the information the explorers collected that winter was put in a detailed summary and sent back to President Jefferson from the Mandan villages in April, 1805, when the expedition took off for the Rockies. The Minnetarees told them about the Crows and the Snakes. Then, beyond the Snakes, were Flatheads — *Tut-see-was* to the Minnetarees, *Tate Platt* to Charbonneau — the broad "generic" term by which Plains Indians knew the people west of the Rockies. "The information I possess with respect to these people," Lewis wrote in the summary, "has been received from the Minitares, who have extended their war excursions as far westerly as that nation, of whom they have made several prisoners, and brought them with them to their villages on the Missouri; these prisoners have been seen by the Frenchmen residing in this neighborhood. The Minitares state, that this nation resides in one village on the west side of a large and rapid river, which runs from south to north, along the foot of the Rocky mountains on their west side; and that the river passes at a small distance from the three forks of the Missouri . . ." The tribe, in this case narrowed down to one known village, did not yet have a white trader, Lewis noted, and the river it lived on was supposed to be a branch of the Columbia.

The summary also referred vaguely to a previously unknown tribe living somewhere in the big domain long designated simply as "country of the flathead." They were the "Blue Mud Indians" who lived "In the Rock or Shineing mountains on the S. Side of a River Called *Great Lake* River, Supposed to run into the *Columbia* river, but little known."[8] This information possibly came from the North West traders, who might have picked it up from half-breeds or Blackfeet in or near the Canadian Rockies, for the name appears again only in the far western literature of the North West Company. In or about February, 1811, five years after Lewis and Clark first recorded the name, Northwest Trader Alexander Henry noted in his journal that Northwesters west of the mountains were now trading with Nez Percés "or as some call them, the Green Wood or Blue Earth Indians."[9] So the American Captains' reference in 1805 might possibly be the first recorded allusion to the tribe later called Nez Percé. There is no mention in their summary of any other tribe west of the Flatheads, of pierced-nosed Indians, or of anyone whom the French called Nez Percés, and it is not reasonable to assume that they knew anything about a pierced-nosed tribe at this time. Every scrap of information about the western tribes was eagerly collected and itemized for President Jefferson, and if anyone at the Mandan villages had mentioned pierced noses, or any name, Indian or otherwise, referring to pierced noses, the Captains would undoubtedly have made note of it.

After leaving the Mandans, the explorers saw no Indians until they met the

Shoshones on Idaho's Lemhi River, and here the record is clear that they heard, for the first time, about the Nez Percés. *How* they heard, however, is not clear, and we are not sure whether the information came by word or by sign language. Lewis, with his sign-language interpreter Drouillard, was across the Divide, a couple of days' journey ahead of Clark, with whom Charbonneau and the Shoshone woman Sacajawea were traveling. The date was August 13, 1805, when Lewis first met the Shoshones, and he wrote, "I enformed them by signs that I wished them to conduct us to their camp." On August 14, still without Sacajawea to translate for him, he wrote, "The means I had of communicating with these people was by way of Drewyer [Drouillard] who understood perfectly the common language of jesticulation or signs which seems to be universally understood by all the Nations we have yet seen. It is true that this language is imperfect and liable to error but is much less so than would be expected, the strong parts of the ideas are seldom mistaken."

Immediately after this sentence in the original manuscript comes an interlineal memorandum, possibly written in later by Clark: "This part to come in the 20th related to Captain C. thro' the interpreter," which apparently meant Charbonneau, who interpreted Sacajawea's Minnetaree version of what the Shoshones told her. After the interlineal memorandum, still in Lewis's hand under August 14th, comes: "The Chief further informed me that he had understood from the *persed nosed* Indians who inhabit this river below the rocky mountains that it ran a great way toward the setting sun and finally lost itself in a great lake of water which was illy taisted, and where the white men lived . . ." and further, in the same entry, "I now ask Cameahwait (the Shoshone chief) by what route the Pierced nosed Indians, who he informed me inhabited this river below the mountains, came over to the Missouri. . . ."

These are the first references by Lewis and Clark to the Nez Percés. If the interlineal memorandum is wrong, and Lewis was actually having the conversation on August 14 with the Shoshones, he was conducting it by sign language. The sign for the Nez Percés, used by almost all tribes met by Americans or British, was made by closing the fist of the right hand and, with forefinger extended to the left, passing it horizontally beneath the nose, as if indicating a pierced nose. The Shoshones of the Lemhi used it, and Drouillard would probably have interpreted it to Lewis as meaning pierced nose.

If, on the other hand, the conversation with Cameahwait occurred on August 20, after Clark had come up and was using Sacajawea and Charbonneau to interpret for him, then the Shoshone chief must have used a word to Sacajawea which referred directly to the Nez Percés as pierced-nosed Indians. This is rather unlikely. There is no evidence of such a Shoshone term for the Nez Percés, or that they ever again, on their own, made such a reference. In 1865, Granville Stuart noted that the Shoshones called the Nez Percés *Thoig a-rik-kah* (Kouse eaters), a much more likely appellation by a tribe that usually called everyone after the food they ate.

This is all conjecture, however, and, either from sign or word, Lewis and Clark, independently of anyone else, first referred knowingly to the Nez Percés as pierced noses. A month later, when the explorers met the Nez Percés, they saw enough reason for a sign that indicated a pierced nose. Clark was alone this time, ahead of the main party and without an interpreter, and he says, September 20, 1805: "They call themselves Cho punish or Pierced noses." Without an interpreter the implication must be that he both understood them to say the word "Cho punnish" and saw them make the pierced-nose sign, but, more important, the noses of some, if not many, of them *were* pierced. There is no reference to it in the journals at this point, but when Lewis and Clark later came to summing up their impressions of the Nez Percés, they said it plainly. On May 7, 1806, Lewis wrote: "The ornaments worn by the Chopunnish are, in their nose a single shell of Wampom . . ." And on May 13 the journal states: ". . . the ornament of the nose is a single shell of the wampum." One can only wonder what additional proof has been needed by all the writers who through the years have questioned whether they ever did pierce their noses. But we will have more to provide as we proceed.

It is questionable whether the name Chopunnish had anything to do with pierced noses. The word is believed by some to have resulted from a misunderstanding by Clark, and then Lewis, of a Nez Percé version of the term "Tsutpeli" or "Tsupnitpelun" (whose meaning we don't know) adopted possibly by some of the buffalo-hunting groups of Nez Percés, after hearing themselves called that — or a word of which that was their own translation — by some of the tribes out on the plains. The Crows knew the Nez Percés rather well at this time and frequently traveled with them, and though they apparently were not able to communicate knowledge of the Nez Percés to Lewis and Clark (via the Minnetarees at the Mandan villages) during the winter of 1804-5, there is an isolated and puzzling note made at the very same spot only a year later by the North West trader, Alexander Henry. On July 26, 1806, Henry entered in his journal that a party of Crow Indians "brought word [to the Mandan villages where he was visiting] that the American party of Captain Lewis and Clark had ascended the Missourie, crossed the Rocky Mountains, and fallen upon a large river which they supposed would conduct them to the ocean. They also informed us that these gentlemen had had trouble with the Snake, Flathead and Oreille Perce nations, who inhabit the Rocky Mountains."[10]

Who were the *Oreille Perce*? Pend Oreilles, whom Lewis and Clark had not met, or the Nez Percés, whom they had met? If the Crows meant the Nez Percé, their sign language for that tribe (which the Shoshones also used, and which we have already described) might have been misread, for if they were trying to indicate pierced noses, they were referring to a tribe of which the Northwesters, as far as we know, were still ignorant — and whom their people farther west would not meet and call Nez Percé for three or four more years, and then without the benefit of Crows or other plains tribes as intermediaries. For the same reason, any spoken name the plains tribes had for the Nez Percés — such as "Tsupnitpelun" —

is also a side issue to the main thread of our inquiry, as we have no evidence that those names were communicated to, or known by, the French-Canadians in the far Northwest who would meet the Nez Percés through tribes west of the Rockies. If there is a link between what the Crows, Minnetarees and other plains tribes called the Nez Percés, and the Northwesters who eventually settled the name "Nez Percé" on the tribe, it has not yet come to light. We have a stronger case, as we shall see, in the evidence contained in David Thompson's journals. It is also possible, moreover, that Chopunnish — speculation over the origin of which has carried us along this side road — was corrupted from the word Shahaptian (a term of location), which the Flathead and Salish tribes west of the Rockies called the Nez Percés, and which, according to David Thompson and the men associated with him, was pronounced both by the Salish and the Nez Percés in a variety of ways, including "Sawpatin."

At any rate, Lewis and Clark returned to the United States calling the Nez Percés *chopunnish,* or the pierced-nosed Indians — a definite step short of the precise name whose origin we are seeking. Eventually, the term "Chopunnish" was dropped and disappeared, but as late as 1855, Colonel Lawrence Kip, an observer of the great Walla Walla treaty council, reported that some of the Nez Percés are still calling themselves "Chipunish."[11]

After the American explorers, the first white man of record to reach the tribe was David Thompson, and to understand his role we must briefly narrate the process by which he came upon them. The relevant portion of his exciting story begins in October, 1800, when he started up the eastern slope of the Canadian Rockies for the first time, trying to find the Kutenais, about whom the Northwesters had been hearing for years from the Blackfeet. Accompanied by five half-breeds, a Cree and a Piegan guide, Thompson traveled up the mountains with trade goods worth 300 beaver skins. On October 13, he learned that the Kutenais would be on the Divide the next day, and on the 14th, after riding twenty-two miles, he finally met a Kutenai chief with twenty-six men, seven women and eleven horses at the foot of a high cliff. The next day, he followed the Indians to their encampment and remained with them, trading and watching their gambling and horse-racing, until the 17th. Then he prevailed on some of them to follow him back to the Rocky Mountain House on the Saskatchewan, which they reached on the 20th. He conversed with them on the geography of their country, asked them to come again to guide him to their lands west of the Divide, and then sent two of his men, LaGasse and LeBlanc, back with the Kutenais to help them evade their enemies, the Piegans, and to winter with them across the mountains. The year was 1800, and these two men were probably the first whites to cross the Rockies south of Mackenzie's route, and the first to absorb knowledge from the Kutenais of the tribes that lived to their south and west.

They left no record of what they learned, however, and Thompson tells us nothing of what they communicated to him. But following on their trail, from

1801 until 1807, it is apparent that a number of freemen — Iroquois, Crees, Nipissings, half-breeds, French-Canadians and their families — associated with the North West Company — drifted back and forth across the Divide, trapping and trading with the Kutenais, and picking up scattered bits of information about tribes beyond: the Flat Bows (Lower Kutenais), the Salish, including Flatheads, Earbobs (Pend Oreilles) and Pointed Hearts (Coeur d'Alenes) and, perhaps, the Nez Percés, who would have been called *Shahaptians*. None of this information got into any document that has come down to us, but it is clear from Thompson's later journals that French-speaking trappers had been out ahead of him at this time, gathering information about tribes in present-day Montana and Idaho.[12]

During 1801, Thompson made a fruitless attempt to cross the mountains himself, then turned back to explore and trade elsewhere in northern Canada for the next five years. In 1806, stirred to action by the American Lewis and Clark threat to outflank the British traders on the west, the North West Company ordered Thompson to attempt again to cross the Rockies and open trade with the tribes in the Columbia River country. He returned to the Rocky Mountain House — on the Saskatchewan River, east of the Rockies — in October and prepared to cross the Divide the next spring. A half-breed, Jacques Raphael "Jaco" Finlay, who was to figure in much of western Montana's earliest history (and who is the Jocko memorialized in that region's modern nomenclature), was sent ahead with several men to cut a trail across the Rockies and build canoes on the Columbia River for Thompson's use.

On May 10, 1807, Thompson set out with his family and three voyageurs. Near the foot of the mountains, he was joined by his clerk, the strapping Finan McDonald, and five other men, and together they topped Howse Pass on June 25, and reached the upper Columbia five days later. Thompson called it the Kootanae River, and on it he built the Kootanae House, where he traded with the Indians and wintered with McDonald. There were many freemen in the area, some of them apparently far-wanderers who might already have been in Montana, and they and the Kutenais provided him during the winter with interesting details about tribes and events farther south. Thompson heard much about the Flatheads, and their troubles with the Piegans, Bloods and Blackfeet, and on August 13, the Kutenais informed him "that about 3 weeks ago the Americans to the number of 42 arrived to settle a military Post, at the confluence of the two most southern & considerable Branches of the Columbia & that they were preparing to make a small advance Post lower down on the River. 2 of those who were with Capt. Lewis were also with them of whom the poor Kootenaes related several dreadful stories . . ."[13]

We can only speculate on who those Americans were, or what dreadful things happened to them, as the only known party from the States at that time, Manuel Lisa's, was still far away, down the Missouri River, in July, 1807, bound for the Yellowstone. The period and the possibilities, however, are still wrapped in tantalizing mystery, and future research may reveal surprises. It does appear that

somebody, unknown to present historians, was actually on the upper Missouri or the upper waters of the Columbia at this time and, in the context of our subject, may have had contact with the Nez Percés. During this same winter, for instance, Thompson also received letters at the Kootanae House from an American military group somewhere in the Northwest (and apparently led by a man by the name of Jeremy Pinch), warning him as a British subject to get out of the area. There has been much guessing about Pinch, but he is still unidentified. Then, in February, 1810, Thompson records too fully to dismiss, the murder, by the Piegans, of a man named Courter, "a trader and Hunter from the U States," apparently on the present Clark Fork River, above Hell Gate. We don't know who Courter was, how long he was there or how widely he and his men had traveled among the western Indians. But his presence made an impression: on his maps, Thompson named that portion of the Clark Fork "Courter's River," and years later, Finan McDonald, leading the 1823 Hudson's Bay Snake Country Expedition, referred in a letter to the site of "Corta's old Fort."[14]

Whoever the mysterious figures were, the various letters, messages, rumors and hearsay of the winter of 1807-8 helped to broaden Thompson's awareness of new territories and new tribes farther south. On September 16, for instance, thirteen Flat Bow Indians arrived and told him that they lived in a country adjoining the Pend Oreilles, or "Ear Pendants." They "drew a Chart of their Country as far as the Sea, describing the Nations along the River," Thompson noted, adding that he was very anxious to go down and visit the Flat Bows and Ear Pendants, but had to wait for Ugly Head, the big chief of the Flat Bows.

Thompson failed to record mention of the various tribes the Flat Bows told him about who lived "along the River," and if he learned this winter of the Nez Percés, he omitted that fact from his journal. In April, 1808, he portaged from the head of the Columbia to the Kootenai and descended that river to the site of Bonner's Ferry, Idaho, where he dispatched a Kutenai Indian with tobacco to the Flatheads, who were still farther south and whom he had not yet met. Without waiting for a reply, he explored farther along the Kootenai River, then returned by canoe and horseback to the Kootanae House (note the absurd difference in spelling the same word occasioned by Canadians and Americans who were unaware of Thompson's versions, and who stamped approval on a number of later local preferences). He crossed the Divide with furs and returned to winter again on the Columbia, this time sending Finan McDonald and several companions down the Kootenai River with trade goods to build a post and traffic during the winter with the Indians at the falls. McDonald pitched two skin tents and built a long storehouse almost opposite present-day Libby, Montana. During the winter (1808-9), he sent two of his men, Boisvert and Boulard, to explore Lake Pend Oreille in Idaho. Near the end of the season, James McMillan came down from the Kootanae House to join him, and it is believed the two men visited Pend Oreille and possibly also Flathead Lake.

Again, we have no documentary evidence of all the tribes these men and their companions met, or heard about, during this first historic winter in Montana and Idaho. There might have been some Nez Percés in the Pend Oreille country, but more likely the whites would have become aware of them in Montana, as they were in the habit of crossing eastward on the Lolo Trail to the Bitterroot and Clark Fork Rivers. Even if McDonald's men on the Kootenai didn't meet them, they might have heard of them, either from the Indians at the falls, or from some of the French-speaking freemen — eastern Indians, half-breeds and whites — who were beginning to circulate through the country, living and trading with the Kutenais and their friends the Flatheads. The documentary record this early, however, is bare of knowledge of the Nez Percés.

In the spring of 1809, Thompson again went east with furs, but was back on the Columbia in July. He descended the Kootenai River again to Bonner's Ferry and this time portaged his trade goods across country on an old Indian trail called the "Great Road of the Flatheads" to a point on Lake Pend Oreille just east of Sandpoint, Idaho. The occasion marked the first time Thompson had met the Flatheads, though they must have been pretty well known by this date to some of his men and to the free-wheeling freemen.

On the shores of the lake, he built his Kullyspel House, the first trading post in Idaho, and on September 24, 1809, while working in the warehouse, noted: "2 Green Wood Indians arrived, they made me a present of a Bear skin, 1 Beaver do & 5 Rats with 2 parcels of dried fish and 2 Mares for which I shall pay them." According to Alexander Henry's journal of 1811, which we have already cited, these "Green Wood Indians," apparently named by sign, since no other Indians

were present this day to interpret for Thompson, were none other than Nez Percés, the first Thompson had seen. The next day, Thompson wrote of them: "The lower Indians went away, gave each a bit of Tob. [acco] & an awl, showed them how to stretch the different Skins & they promised to be here by the time the Snow whitens the ground."

Near the end of September, Thompson explored down the Pend Oreille River with one man and an Indian boy to a point near Cusick, Washington. During his return, he was irritated one day to find that "our Lad had gone off with one of my Horses to the Green Wood Indians we were therefore obliged to wait at 4 PM he arrived." It was Thompson's last mention of the "Green Woods" and, with the exception of Henry's reference in 1811 to the fact that the Nez Percés were also called the Green Wood or Blue Earth Indians, there is no further known use of the term.

October, 1809, was a busy month for Thompson. He rode sixty miles up the Clark Fork from Pend Oreille Lake, crossed to the Kootenai, joined James McMillan, bringing new trade goods down from the Columbia, and descending the Kootenai to Bonner's Ferry, portaged back to the Kullyspel House. On November 1 he was off again, up the Clark Fork to a point near Thompson Falls, Montana, where on November 9 he commenced building the Saleesh House, a trading post for traffic with the Flatheads. Leaving Finan McDonald in charge at Kullyspel, Thompson wintered with James McMillan at the Saleesh House, making several trips in early 1810 farther up the Clark Fork with some of his voyageurs, freemen and Indians.

This part of the country seemed now very much alive with French-speaking trappers who had drifted over the Canadian Rockies and down from the Columbia before and after Thompson. They and Thompson's voyageurs swarmed around the Saleesh House and provided contact between the North West Company trader and the Indians along the Clark Fork. In Thompson's journals, edited by Miss White and published for the first time in 1950, we find their names — important to us, because as a group they already knew the Nez Percés and were telling Thompson about them: Etienne Forcier, Crepeau, Beaulieu, Roberge, LaGasse, François Methot, Boulard, Mercier, Mousseau, Register Bellaire, Bostonnais, François Rivet, François Sans Facon, Baptiste Buche, François Gregoire, Jacques, Martin, Pierre, Ignace and Joseph (all Iroquois), Joseph and Baptiste Delcour, Vaudette, LeBarbier, Michel Bourdeaux, LeMuet, Pierre Ginon, LeBon Vieux, Lolo (was the famous trail named for him?), Charles Loyers, Jaco Finlay and Jacques Hoole (eighty-eight years old, a fabulous veteran of the battle on the Plains of Abraham and of the Quebec siege during the American Revolution).

From the Flatheads and other Salish tribes, these men learned to call the Nez Percés something that sounded like *Sa-ah-pe-tinne*, which referred to the country in which the Nez Percés lived, south and west across the Lolo Trail, and that is the term by which Thompson also first referred to them in his 1809-10 journals at the Saleesh House. On December 16, 1809, he wrote: "Sent Beaulieu with an assortment of Goods & 2 Horses to the Sap me ap e tin Indians."

But to the French-Canadians, the word must have been unmelodious and tedious, if not difficult, to use. They coined their own term, and on March 11, 1810, it appeared for the first time in Thompson's journal and, as far as we know,

for the very first time anywhere: "Traded a very trifle of provisions from the Nez Perce . . ." Thompson, irritated by something, added the uncomplimentary reference, "a parcel of lazy, thievish people," a judgment with which few others in the future would have reason to agree, and in which Thompson soon reversed himself.

It is plain that these Indians were the Nez Percés of today, and not Yakima or Cayuse or any other tribe along the Columbia in the vicinity of the Nez Percés whom Thompson later described as also having pierced noses. It was the Nez Percés of the Clearwater and Snake country alone who trekked over the Lolo Pass to visit with the Flatheads in Montana. Moreover, we must assume that the French-speaking trappers called them Nez Percés because they, or some of them, *did* pierce their noses. Furthermore, although Lewis and Clark had heard them called pierced noses and had seen them wearing small pieces of dentalium in their noses, and had so reported, their testimony had not yet appeared to influence Thompson, or his men. Later, in September of 1810, Thompson might have seen a copy of Sergeant Patrick Gass's journal (published in 1807), which Alexander Henry had at the White Earth House of the North West Company on the Saskatchewan River, and Thompson is believed to have had one with him on his 1811 trip down the Columbia,[15] but Gass made no reference in his book to "the pierced noses," as Lewis and Clark did in their journals, which were finally published in 1814.

Since this is the first known use of the term for this tribe (thus entering literature thirty years earlier than previously acknowledged), it is fitting to inquire how the French-Canadians associated with Thompson probably arrived at it. During the early years of the twentieth century, the anthropologist James A. Teit made a study of "The Salishan Tribes of the Western Plateaus," including the Coeur d'Alene, Okanogan and the Flathead group. Most of his work was done with the assistance of Indian informants many decades after the fact, but the accumulated material, edited by the famed anthropologist Franz Boas, and published in 1930 as the forty-fifth annual report of the Bureau of American Ethnology, manages to throw convincing light on the early relations between these tribes and the Nez Percés.

With reference to the Coeur d'Alene, Teit discussed the use of nose ornaments, as follows: "Nose pins were used by many women and by some men. . . . After the tribe began to go to the Plains for buffalo hunting, nose pins rapidly went out of style. The Nez Percé and the tribes to the south used them, but none of the tribes to the east."[16] Later, discussing the Flatheads, he comments: "No nose ornaments or nose pins were used by the Flatheads and Pend d'Oreilles, and they were rare among the Kalispel and Spokan. It is said that they were common among the Nez Percé and all the more western Shahaptian and Salishan tribes."[17] And, finally, describing the Salish sign language, he explains the sign for the Nez Percés: "Forefinger or right hand pointed across the nostrils or point of nose. Sometimes the forefinger was simply held for a moment horizontally across in front of the nose. The meanings of the signs are 'Pierced noses.' They were so named because long ago nearly all the Nez Percés had their noses pierced, and they wore nose-pins of shell and bone to a greater extent than any other tribe."[18]

If this testimony can be believed, we must imagine that the French-Canadians on Clark Fork River saw Nez Percés with pierced noses, saw the sign language for them (which Lewis possibly also saw among the Shoshones on the Lemhi River), and easily took to calling them Nez Percés, which Thompson first recorded in his journal on March 11, 1810.

Thompson traveled back and forth between the Saskatchewan River posts and the Columbia River country for two more years, the advance leader of the Northwesters who by 1812 were ready to move into the region in full force and monopolize the area's trade. His journal shows repeated contacts with the Nez Percés both along the Clark Fork River in Montana and in the area surrounding the confluence of the Snake and Columbia rivers in present-day Washington. There is no further use of the term "Nez Perce" in his journals, as he seemed gradually to become aware that one large family, which the Salish called the Shahaptian, and which apparently stretched from the Columbia to the Bitterroots, was composed of many different tribes, or bands, each with its own name. On his historic trip of 1811 down the Columbia to its mouth, he began to find all the tribes south of Wenatchee using the Shahaptian language, and most of them wearing "shells in their nostrils." As he progressed, the pierced noses among the Shahaptians became fewer and near present-day Pasco, where he met Yakimas and Palouse, he reported, "Many of the women had not a shell in their nostril."[19]

The term "Nez Percé," however, continued to be used by the French-speaking Iroquois, Crees, half-breeds and French-Canadians who, as Northwest voyageurs or freemen, swarmed in increasing numbers into the Columbia River country from across the Canadian Rockies and down along the routes surveyed by Thompson. In western Montana, the term settled on the Nez Percés who came across the Lolo Trail to visit and go buffalo hunting with the Flatheads. Along the Columbia, it was generally used to designate the tribes about the confluence of the Snake and the Columbia, but because the tribe presently known as Nez Percé was by far the strongest, most powerful, best known and most widely spread of all these tribes, the title settled hardest on them, and, even though they very early abandoned altogether the habit of piercing their noses, they became in the popular mind of the French-Canadian trappers the Nez Percés, and their river, the Snake, was often called the Nez Percé.

When Donald McKenzie came to build a North West post several miles below the junction of the Snake and Columbia rivers in 1818, it seemed natural to call it Fort Nez Perces. In 1855, Alexander Ross, who had had charge of the Fort in its first days, explained why McKenzie so named it: "When the first traders arrived in the country, they generally distinguished all the natives along this part of the communication indiscriminately by the appellation of 'Nez Perce' or pierced noses, from the custom practised by these people of having their noses bored, to hold a certain white shell like the fluke of an anchor. The appellation was used until we

Donald MacKenzie

had an opportunity of becoming better acquainted with their respective names. It was, therefore, from this cause that the present establishment derived its name."

And so the term "Nez Percé" settled on a tribe whose early abandonment of nose-piercing caused confusion among later fur traders, missionaries and emigrants, and resulted in a literature full of such observations as that of Overton Johnson and William H. Winter, members of the 1843 overland emigration, who noted in their journal that the custom of piercing noses for the purpose of wearing shells, quills, rings, etc., has been "almost universal and is still so with some" among "tribes inhabiting the shores of the Pacific, but not among the Nez Perces."[20]

The nose-piercing custom was undoubtedly a reflection of the fact that, early in their history, prior to their possession of the horse, the Nez Percé culture was closely identified with that of the tribes along the Columbia River who not only highly valued the haiqua shell, gathered mostly north of Nootka and traded inland from tribe to tribe as an ornament for the nose, but also practiced head-flattening. The Nez Percés intermingled with the Columbia tribes at the Dalles and other river trading areas, and the river tribes exerted strong influence on the Nez Percés who copied their nose-piercing and, to some extent, the flattening of their children's heads.

When these Indians got the horse from the Cayuse and Snakes about 1730, their culture took a turn, becoming less influenced by the river tribes and more by the Flatheads, with whom they now went buffalo hunting east of the Bitterroots. This tribe, to whom both nose-piercing and head-flattening were alien, used the pierced-nose sign for Nez Percé. It appears possible, however, that in traveling over the plains with the Nez Percés, the Flatheads were given their own present name by other tribes who were struck by the few flattened Nez Percé heads among the group. This is pure speculation, and without direct relevancy to our subject, but for many years the two tribes were confused by both Indians and whites, and most Americans inevitably called the Nez Percés "Flatheads," until the 1830's after Jedediah Smith had broken into the Northwest, and United States trappers were able to learn more about the individual tribes in the area. Clark repeatedly referred to the Nez Percés as Flatheads in his 1805-6 journals, and Patrick Gass used no other name for them, save near the very point of leave-taking when he finally said, "The nation here the Cha-no-nish." In 1808, John Colter told of a battle on the Gallatin River, a day's journey from Three Forks, in which he joined a large party of Crows and "Flatheads" in beating off a vicious attack by Blackfeet. Three years later, Wilson Price Hunt, leading the Astorians in the first overland crossing of the United States since Lewis and Clark, met a band of Snakes and "Flatheads" in Wyoming's Big Horn mountains. These "Flatheads" may really have been in part, or in toto, Nez Percés. In the journal of his eastward crossing of 1812-13, Astorian Robert Stuart says, on August 12, 1812: "This tribe (Cayuses) as well as the Flatheads (who are reputed to be excellent Indians, about 1,800 warriors and inhabit that tract of country situate between Lewis' River (the Snake) and the northwest branch, or main Columbia, bounded in the rear by the rocky mountains,) own immense numbers of horses . . ."[21] From Stuart's context, and the geographical description, these "Flatheads" can only be the Nez Percés. Moreover, for almost thirty years, many maps of the region, including some of the best and most influential, such as Brue's of 1833, showed the Chopunnish and Salish as two tribes of a parent Flathead nation which stretched from the Columbia River to the area of the Continental Divide, indicating the continuing influence of the plains tribes' reference to all people west of the Rockies as "Flatheads."

After 1821, the British of the Hudson's Bay Company learned to call the tribe Nez Percés from the French-Canadians of the old North West Company, and in time the American trappers, missionaries and settlers of the 1830s and 1840s, learned the name from the Hudson's Bay men. They called them N'parsies, Nay-peersays, Neckperces, and a hundred variants, finally settling for the present spelling and the pronunciation *Nezz Purses.*

It is perhaps inappropriate to conclude without attempting to lay to rest, for all time, one hopes, an exaggeration in the opposite direction, which a number of writers have repeated without examination. While in the East, pleading for his people after the 1877 War, Chief Joseph gave an interview which appeared, written as if in his own words, in the *North American Review* of April, 1879, under the title, "An Indian's Views of Indian Affairs by Young Joseph." Joseph, who knew little English, and leaned heavily on the Chinook jargon when conversing with whites, certainly couldn't write English fluently, yet in the article he is made to say, "These men [the first whites in the Northwest] were Frenchmen, and they called our people Nez Perces, because they wore rings in their noses for ornaments. Although very few of our people wear them now, we are still called by the same name."

Portions of this article have been used again and again to quote Chief Joseph's "own words" on the war and on other subjects. But the Nez Percés never wore rings in their noses, wore nothing in their nostrils in 1879, and Chief Joseph never would have said they did. The article, in truth, was written by an imaginative Eastern journalist, after the interview in which most of the talking was done by Arthur W. Chapman, an interpreter who had served General O. O. Howard during the wartime pursuit of Chief Joseph, and who was assigned as interpreter to Joseph during the Indian statesman's visit to the East.[22]

It is a small point, but to the admirable Nez Percés, and students of history, an important one.

NOTES

[1] Published by the Bureau of American Ethnology, Washington, D. C. as Bulletin No. 30. The reference is from Vol. 2 (1910) p. 65.

[2] Edward Eberstadt & Sons, New York, 1935, pp. 347-348.

[3] Knopf, New York, 1947, p. 7.

[4] Idaho State Historical Dept., 23rd Biennial Report, Boise, 1951-52 p. 86.

[5] Caxton, Caldwell, Idaho, 1952, p. 9.

[6] Lewiston, Idaho, 1947, p. 224.

[7] Add. MSS. 15332D. It is reproduced, rather indistinctly, in "The Northwest Company" by Gordon Davidson, Univ. of Calif. Press, Berkeley, 1918.

[8] Original Journals of the Lewis and Clark Expedition, edited by Reuben Gold Thwaites, New York, 1904, Vol. VI, p. 106.

[9] New Light on the Early History of the Greater Northwest, Elliot Coues, New York, 1897, Vol. II, p. 716.

[10] New Light on the Early History of the Greater Northwest, Vol. I, p. 398. See The Nez Perce Indians by H. J. Spinden, in Memoirs of the American Anthropological Association, Lancaster, Pa. 1908, II, Pt. 3, p. 171-2, for comment on Indian names for the Nez Perces.

[11] The Indian Council at Walla Walla by Col. Lawrence Kip, U. S. A., Eugene, Ore. 1897, p. 11.

[12] Reports of the experiences of some of these men, perhaps forwarded East by Thompson or other Northwest traders on the Saskatchewan, may yet be found someday in Canada, or in the Hudson's Bay archives in London.

[13] Thompson's Journal, May 10-Sept. 22, 1807, in Oregon Historical Quarterly, Vol. XXVI (1925), p. 43.

[14] See Jedediah Smith by Dale L. Morgan, Indianapolis, 1953, p. 123.

[15] Thompson's Journal, July 3-15, 1811, Oregon Historical Quarterly, Vol. XV (1914), p. 60.

[16] Teit, p. 82.

[17] Teit, p. 340.

[18] Teit, p. 147.

[19] David Thompson's Narrative, ed. by J. B. Tyrrell, Toronto, 1916, pp. 486-8.

[20] "Route Across the Rocky Mountains with a Description of Oregon and California, Etc." by Overton Johnson and William H. Winter, Oregon Historical Quarterly, Vol. VII, p. 183.

[21] Stuart's journal in "The Discovery of the Oregon Trail," ed. by Philip Ashton Rollins, p. 82.

[22] McWhorter Archives NP 42, State College of Washington Library, Pullman, Wash. Also, see "Pays Tribute to the Famous Nez Perce Chief" in Spokane, Wash., Spokesman-Review, Nov. 4, 1906.

Spokan camp

Kalispel village

Dusty Dress (Kalispel)

Nespilim girl

Embarking (Kootenai)

Country of the Kootenai

On Spokane River

The Métis of Montana

By VERNE DUSENBERRY

SEVERAL YEARS AGO in the tiny gold-mining town of Zortman, there lived a quiet, scholarly, graying man. He was Joseph Dussome, for many years president of the Landless Indians of Montana. For nearly half a century Joe had been collecting data and assembling material pertinent to the bands of "wandering Cree and Chippewa" that too often, during the past eighty years, plagued the conscience of too many Americans and Canadians, as well. In his old age, Dussome sat in his small, neatly kept home and pored over his huge collection of evidence. He had documents, a vast file of letters; he had his memories! He knew better than any other person — for he was one of them — who these people are who now reside in the State of Montana and who number conservatively at least 4000 displaced, disenchanted individuals. While these people insist upon being called "Chippewa," perhaps to escape the scorn with which reservation Indians refer to them as "Cree," or as *"bon jours," or "bon hommes* from Lake LaBiche," Dussome was able to point out to an interested visitor that these people were part of the Métis, descendants of the Red River hunters who lived not only in Canada, but also across the border in what is now Michigan, Wisconsin, Minnesota, North Dakota and Montana. Joseph Dussome, born at Cree Crossing, M.T., on February 26, 1879, died at the Montana Tuberculosis Hospital in Galen on November 6, 1963. He was eighty-four. Most of his life had been spent fighting in a futile cause.

To understand those Indians who are unaffiliated with any established reservations, it is necessary to go back to the early French colonization of North America. For it is from these early explorers that one finds the progenitors of the landless Indians. Even the surnames are the same, since the French encouraged their men to marry Indian women. These mixed-blood descendants, at first concentrated along the Great Lakes, scattered throughout the Northwestern States and Canada, but maintained their greatest numbers along the Red River of the North, which has its source in what is now North Dakota and Minnesota, forming the boundary between much of those states before flowing north into Lake Winnipeg and ultimately into Hudson's Bay. And so it is that these 4000 people living in Montana today, whose ancestry was predominantly a non-native tribe — Chippewa — trace their ancestry back to the Red River settlements, especially to those on the American side of the now established forty-ninth parallel that forms the international boundary between Canada and the United States.

Now known generally as "The Landless Indians," they have had various names — half-breeds, *bois-brule*, and Métis. The frontier English and the Americans referred to them chiefly as "half-breeds," while the French occasionally designated them "*bois-brule*" (burnt wood) from the translation of the Chippewa apellation for them, *Wisahkotewan Niniwak*, meaning "men partly burned." This name had been given them by the Chippewas because of the color of their skin — dark, but not quite as dark as that of the pure Indian. More frequently, however, the early French referred to them as the Métis, a French adjective meaning cross-bred, a proud appellation without stigma.

Perhaps the word Métis is the best for them, for their degree of Indian blood was seldom fixed at exactly one-half. The child of an Indian mother and a French father would be a half-blood, but when that offspring reached maturity, he might marry either a fullblood Indian or a fullblood Caucasian. Thus as the years went by, and intermarrying continued, the individual could possibly become almost pure Indian or pure white. So, too, did the blood become mixed between Indians of various tribes. For while in Canada it was the Cree with whom the Frenchman usually married, in the United States it was the Chippewa. Thus there emerged, along the Red River particularly, a group of people who were neither Indian nor white, neither Chippewa nor Cree nor French, but a mixture of all three. They represented, as Joseph Kinsey Howard pointed out,[1] the emergence of a new race indigenous to this continent.

And in this emergence as a new people, they adapted various traits from their French fathers and their Indian mothers. For their livelihood they depended primarily upon the buffalo, as did their Indian forebears. But unlike their Indian grandparents, the hunt stemmed from the Red River settlements, where they returned each fall with pemmican (for which they became famous), to be sold or traded to the Hudson's Bay Company for other food items to be consumed during the winter months. Their transportation was not confined to the horse alone, as was the Indian's, for their distinguishing characteristic was the Half-Breed Cart, a unique invention of their own, made entirely of wood. Its wheels, oftentimes six feet in diameter, had very broad tires; while a small body rested on the axle and shafts. Each cart, drawn by a single pony, could carry from 600 to 800 pounds. Since no grease was used on the axle, the noise made by these carts was almost insufferable. Almost every Northern Plains historical writer has attempted to describe the horrible screeching that a train of such carts made; but probably none has presented it more graphically than did Joseph Kinsey Howard when he said, "it was as if a thousand fingernails were drawn across a thousand panes of glass." Later, when metal was used in their construction and the wheels could be greased, the Métis generally called their vehicles Red River Carts. In either case, however, the cart served a dual purpose. In the long winters, a man would lift the body easily from the wheels, hitch a horse to it, and have a *carriole* or sleigh.

The housing of the Métis was copied directly from their fathers. In the settlements, they lived in one-story houses, often gaudily painted. While on the plains hunting, they used tents. Frequently, however, their hunts took them far to the west, particularly along the Milk River in Montana, and since the distance was too great for them to return to the Red River but occasionally, the Métis built frontier cabins, generally of cottonwood, there. They plastered the interior with clay mixed with buffalo hair, and, in one end of the building, they always built a fireplace, likewise cemented with clay. Scraped skins of buffalo calves, carefully worked until they were translucent, covered the windows. Floors were left bare. Just as their Indian antecedents placed their tipis in a circle, so did the Métis build cabins, but in the center of the enclosure they built a large structure with puncheon floors.

These larger buildings were primarily used for dancing, since the Métis had inherited the Indian's love of the dance. But, instead of using the dance as a medium of religious expression, the Métis danced for sheer pleasure. Nor was the music that of the primitive drum; rather, it was the fiddle, sometimes a genuine one but more frequently one made from a hollow piece of wood with cat-gut strings attached. The tunes were generally adaptations of old French folk songs while the dance itself was a lively number which in time became known as the "Red River jig."[2]

The dress of the Métis, too, was a blend of Indian and French. The men usually wore an overcoat with a hood made from a blanket and adorned with brass buttons, scallops, fringes, and beads. Known as a *capote*, it combined the warmth of the heavy, all-wool blanket with the tailored quality of a coat. (Its present counterpart, but generally shorter in length, is the parka.) In warmer weather, the men wore fringed jackets made from buckskin but always they had leggings. These again were made from a blanket and were fringed with a seam of bead work embroidered along the outside.[3] The women wore black dresses, simply made. During their girlhood they had gaily colored shawls; in adult life the shawl was always black.

From the influence of their French fathers, the Métis devoutly followed the teachings of the Roman Catholic Church. So devoted to their church were they that as a matter of general practice they seldom embarked upon a hunt without having a priest accompany them. When they stayed away from the settlements over a long period of time, they observed Sunday with recitations of the rosary and with prayers. Wandering Jesuit and Oblate missionaries looked for them on the plains, and when finding them conducted open-air services, baptized infants and blessed marriages. In fact, the church adopted the policy of recognizing marriages as being legitimate when they were contracted away from the settlements, providing such marriages were later blessed by the priests. One of the best sources about the Métis may be found in the parish registers of the early missions in Montana, where, as early as the 1850's, Jesuit priests such as Fathers de Smet, Croke, Imoda and Hoeken recorded baptisms, marriages and deaths of the Métis.[4]

The Métis also developed a language of their own — a composite of Indian tongues, usually Cree and Chippewa, and French. Often a few English words were added. Yet, while most of them understood English, few of them ever used it. The French they spoke was an obsolete form drawn primarily from the *patois* of Normandy and Picardy.[5] A Frenchman usually could understand them; but the Métis, in turn, had difficulty understanding correct French. So it was with Indian languages such as the Cree. Mrs. Dussome, for example, nurtured on the Métis tongue, understood only isolated words of Cree as spoken on Rocky Boy's reservation today.

Their political structure was a blend, again, of Indian and French. Strictly democratic, like the Indian, restraint seemed needed principally when the Métis were on the hunt. Then, the entire group was under the control of the soldier society, known among themselves as *Les Soldats,* who executed the orders of the chief. Both the chief and the members of the soldier society were elected by the people themselves. Punishments, such as banishment from the hunt or the payment of fines, resulted if individuals refused to obey orders. Generally, the chief was known as *governor,* a title they borrowed from the French. Jean Baptiste Wilkie was an outstanding governor of the early-day Métis.[6]

While the geographical heart of this new race seems to have been along the Red River near present-day Winnipeg, Canada, and Pembina, North Dakota, not all of them, by any means, lived in Canada. True, the majority of the French-Cree descendants lived there. On the American side of the line a goodly number also lived — those who were related a little closer to the Chippewas. Their center was Pembina, established as a trading center in 1780, a factor which gives it the distinction of being the oldest settlement in the Northwest. Pembina exists now, a drab, tiny village at that spot on the map where North Dakota and Minnesota come together at the Canadian border. With Pembina as their headquarters, the southern Métis enjoyed, particularly, the hunting resources of the Turtle Mountains, some 100 miles to the west, in mid-North Dakota, just south of the Canadian line. For their long-range hunting activities, however, they moved constantly westward in their pursuit of the buffalo — along the Missouri River and its tributaries, particularly to the Milk, but often west and south again to the valleys of the Teton, the Dearborn, the Sun and the Marias rivers. In 1842, Alexander Ross, when he accompanied the hunters, tells of being at the mouth of the Yellowstone. In his record,[7] Ross mentions the names of several Métis who were in the party — Wilkie, Valle, Courchene and Parisien — all names familiar among these people in Montana today.

Individual members penetrated the now-Montana region, too, often serving as guides for the fur traders. One of them, Jacob Berger (often spelled Bergier or Bercier and always pronounced so by the Métis today) was in the employ of the American Fur Company in 1830. It was he whom Kenneth McKenzie, then in charge of Fort Union, sent into the Blackfeet country to induce the hostile tribe to trade with the American Fur Company. So successful was Berger (for he induced

Fort Union, painted in 1833 by Karl Bodmer

a number of the Blackfeet to accompany him to Fort Union) that the following year, McKenzie sent one of his most trustworthy men, James Kipp, to the Blackfeet country. Kipp established Fort Piegan at the mouth of the Marias River, near present-day Loma, Montana, to tap the rich resources of the Blackfeet trade. The largest and most influential fort operated on the Upper Missouri by the American Fur Company, Fort Union, was constructed by Métis laborers.[8] Louis Revis, sometimes spelled Revais or Rivets, Augustin "Frenchy" Hamell and Pierre Cadotte are other Métis names significant in the opening of the fur trade in what is now Montana.

But it was not only with the fur trade that the Métis came into Montana. As the years passed, more and more carts filled with Red River hunters came into the territory and settled in the regions where buffalo were always plentiful. In making this move, the Métis followed somewhat the pattern of their Indian heritage, a nomadic tendency to follow the source of their food. Unlike the Indian, they built cabins and stayed, sometimes for several years. Then, group by group, they returned to relatives and friends in the Pembina region, where after a succession of years of residence, they moved again to Montana. Thus it was that during the decades of the 1850's, 1860's and 1870's, the creaking carts groaned their way back and forth between the little settlement of Pembina and the unspoiled valleys of Montana.

From old parish registers one learns the names of some Métis who were in Montana during this early period. Many of them remained along the Milk River; others went farther west. Along the tributaries of the Marias River, especially near Dupuyer Creek, the records reveal the names of Guardipee, Morrin, Lespera, Larion, and Trembles. Somewhat southward, near present Choteau, the Champaignes, Vivies, Ducharmes, Cardinals and Moriceaus camped, while in the Sulli-

van Valley near St. Peter's Mission and not far from the Dearborn River, Gabriel
Azure, Modeste Gladeau and members of the LaSerte and Cadotte families lived.
When one of Montana's earliest cattlemen, R. S. Ford, established his holdings in
1872 on the upper reaches of the Sun River, near present Augusta, he employed
Métis families that included such names as Sangrey, Jarvais, Landre, LaRance,
Swan, Nomee and Paul.[9]

Perhaps one of the best known settlements (for it became more permanent
than did the others who so frequently left their cabins and returned to the Red
River) is the one at present Lewistown in central Montana. A group of Métis left
the Pembina district in 1870 and headed westward with no particular destination
in mind save that of trailing the buffalo. One of the members of the group described facets of that expedition well when she wrote, shortly before her death
in Lewistown in 1943, the following account:[10]

> While we roamed the prairies of western Minnesota and the Dakotas, we
> were always in the same company of people of part Indian blood, and travelled in
> many groups. We left Walhalla, North Dakota, in 1870 shortly after we were
> married, and set out travelling all over the Dakotas, just camping here and there
> without thought of settling permanently at any place, just following the buffalo
> trails. You might think we lived the life of the real Indians, but one thing we had
> always with us which they did not — religion. Every night we had prayer meeting
> and just before a buffalo hunt we would see our men on bended knee in prayer.
> Our men did all the hunting, and we women did all the tanning of the buffalo
> hides, jerky meat making, pemmican and moccasins. For other supplies, we gen-
> erally had some trader with us like Francis Janeaux who always had a supply of
> tea, sugar, tobacco and so on.

Leisurely, the party made its way across North Dakota and followed the Milk
River westward into Montana. For nearly seven years the group camped at the
big bend of the Milk, northeast of present Malta. In 1877, they were living at
Chinook when Joseph surrendered his army at the Bear Paw battlefield south of
that city. They assisted some Nez Percé stragglers who had eluded capture and
were making their way to Canada. Along the Milk River the men hunted, but
game became increasingly scarce until suddenly, in the spring of 1879, it seemed
to have disappeared completely. Pierre Berger, leader of the group, called the
members around him to discuss the situation. He recalled that previously a Cree
Indian had told him of a spot across the Missouri River where small game and
wild birds were abundant and where the grass grew high. The land sounded
promising, so in May, 1879, twenty-five families left the familiar Milk River area
in their squeaking carts and started for this new region. As it was necessary for
them to go by way of Fort Benton and then eastward until they came to the
Judith Mountains, it took most of the summer for the group to make the journey.

Here at their destination, the Judith Basin looked fertile and inviting. Berger
decided that this area would provide an excellent home site. The twenty-five
families built cabins and hurriedly made preparations for the approaching winter.

Plains Cree family   Louis Riel

True to the description given by the Crees, game was plentiful. So, during the
decade of the 1880's (and at a time when the Métis who remained behind in their
accustomed haunts around the Turtle Mountains were starving) the Spring Creek
colony flourished. Soon Janeaux established a trading post for them; in time other
establishments sprang up, and a colorful Montana frontier village, destined later
to become Lewistown, was born.[11] Early Métis occupancy is reflected in the names
of two Lewistown streets, Morasse and Oullette Avenues, while Janeaux Street
bears the name of their trader.

In 1869, while Montana Territory was being colonized by Red River hunters
— at least on a temporary basis — an historical incident occurred that left its mark
upon the landless Indians of Montana. It has been a prime cause of confusion
about them ever since. When the Hudson's Bay Company relinquished its charter
to Rupert's Land (which comprised all of the prairie provinces of Canada as well
as the Northwest territories) and the Dominion of Canada was formed, the Métis
in the Red River settlements became dissatisfied. Finally, in 1869, they established
a provisional government, a land they called Assiniboia — now Manitoba. Louis
Riel, that remarkable Métis, was their leader. When the British successfully overcame the Métis government, Riel and many of his mixed-blood followers went to
the United States. Riel himself eventually came to Montana Territory, becoming a
naturalized citizen of the United States, at Helena, in 1883.[12] A few years later, the
Métis who in the meantime had moved into Saskatchewan, became dissatisfied
with the land policy of the newly formed province and again revolted against the
Canadian government. Louis Riel was called upon to return to Canada and lead
them. Their military leader, Gabriel Dumont, came from Saskatchewan to St.
Peter's Mission, near Cascade, Montana, to convince Riel that he should leave his
teaching at the mission and return to Canada to head the revolt. The year was

1885. When the British army crushed this second rebellion, more Métis than ever came to the United States, particularly to Montana Territory. Riel, however, was captured by the British, tried for treason and subsequently hanged in Regina. Gabriel Dumont lived for many years in the Lewistown area, particularly near Grass Range where he brought several boys orphaned by the Rebellion to his childless home, but later he returned to Canada, where he died.

No one knows the exact number of the Canadian Métis who came to the United States following the two uprisings. They were of Cree extraction but reared in a cultural pattern much like the Chippewa Métis who had lived south of the international border for centuries. Their loyalties were with the Crees who had joined them in the 1885 rebellion. (Some of these Crees came to Montana, were granted political amnesty and ultimately were placed on Rocky Boy's reservation.)[13] These Canadian Métis, however, have been the cloud that has obscured the American Métis ever since, for it has been easy to dismiss any mixed-blood Indian, especially one with a French name, as being Canadian. Thus the fiction grew until all Métis were lumped together as Canadian Crees. True, the groups have intermarried, but available evidence indicates that the majority of the landless Indians of Montana today are from the Pembina region — an area which has belonged to the United States since 1818. Hence it is that one must go to Pembina to establish the actual citizenship of the American Métis.

The United States Census of 1850 for the Pembina district, Minnesota Territory, gives the names, ages, sexes, occupations and birthplaces of the 1116 residents of the area.[14] Reading the list today one recognizes the names of Montana citizenry. Only a random sampling of names indicate their familiarity — Azure, Batock, Beautinau, Belgarde, Bellgard, Berger, Bushman, Cadotte, Caplette, Cardinal, Collins, Delorme, Demon, Falcon, Filcon, Fion, Gardipin, Gingrais, Gladau, Grandbois, Houl, Jerome, LaPierre, Laframbois, Landrie, Landy, LaRock, LaRocque, Laurente, Laverdue, Lonais, Monisette, Montoir, Montreau, Morin, Morrin, Nedeau, Papin, Pappin, Paranteau, Parente, Parisen, Peltier, Plouffe, St. Pierre, Trottier, Valier, Valle, Vandall, Vivian, Wells, Wilkie.

Along with the Métis in the Pembina area, there lived a small group of Chippewas — probably the farthermost western Chippewa group. Many of them had probably intermarried with the Crees; some of them had French grandparents in their ancestry, while most of them had definite relatives among the American Métis. Like all the other Chippewas, they had at some time or other occupied regions on both sides of the international boundary. This small band, however, claimed for their area the land lying north of Devil's Lake in North Dakota, a region that included the Turtle Mountains. Their recognized chief and spokesman had been named Little Shell for three generations — grandfather, father and son. When the time came for the American Métis to face the reality that they were Indians, because of the growing demands of the white settlers, it was Little Shell's band to whom they went. By proximity and by marriage they were closely related. Furthermore, since the United States government consistently recognized the

Bob Tail, Plains Cree   Nah-pe-Se-O, Plains Cree

Chippewas as an American tribe and effected treaties with them, the Métis felt
that since they, too, were now considered Indians, their rights were as significant
as were those of their maternal ancestors.

The United States government designated this small Chippewa group in
North Dakota as the "Pembina band." The first treaty with them was made in 1863
when Alexander Ramsey went to Red Lake, in northern Minnesota, to meet a large
delegation in that area. Representatives from the Pembina band and Métis were
present, also, and while a right of way was ceded through their territory, Ramsey
wrote that "The Pembina Band, who subsist by buffalo hunting, also retain for
themselves a tract of country claimed by them, embracing some of the favorite
pastures of that animal north and northwest of Devil's Lake."[15] They were, moreover, to receive an annuity of $20,000 for twenty years, with one-fourth of it to be
applied to agricultural and other beneficial purposes.

During the next twenty years, irritations mounted. The Pembina band of
Chippewas seemed too far away to receive much supervision from the United
States Indian agents. The Métis straggled away into Montana, again, to follow the
buffalo or to find other subsistence as best they could. When, in the early 1880's,
the buffalo disappeared, the Pembina band of Chippewas and their mixed-blood
relatives began to press strongly their claims upon Washington. Despite the warning of the then Commissioner of Indian Affairs, H. Price, who maintained that the
group had as good a title to their land as had any Indians in North America, the

government, on October 4, 1882, officially opened 9,000,000 acres — the land claimed by the Pembina band — to white settlement. At the same time, two townships, in the southeastern part of the Turtle Mountains, were retained and by an executive order became a permanent reservation. Two years later, John W. Cramsie, Indian agent at Devil's Lake Agency, wrote the Commissioner and told him that thirty-one Chippewas and 1200 mixed-bloods were living on the newly created reservation. Prophetically, he added:[16]

> If poverty and ignorance in abject form is to be found in this world, I know of no better place to seek it than among the half breeds of the Turtle Mountains. With but few exceptions, the half breeds have lived on the buffalo all their lives, and now that their means of subsistence have all disappeared, I cannot tell how they are to make a living without assistance. Fifty thousand dollars worth of stock and farming implements would hardly supply their wants, and without it they will starve or be compelled to steal. Unless generous aid and instruction are furnished these people, the near future will see our jails and penitentiaries filled to overflowing with their prolific rising generation.

Despite their increasingly destitute condition, the Chippewas and the Métis remained relatively quiet during these years. A sub-agent, E. W. Brenner, reported in 1883 that they did not wish to do anything to endanger their friendship with the government while their affairs were pending. "A great danger," he wrote, "is from the mixed bloods living away from the reservation. Many are entitled by blood to the same treatment as those residing here, and in many cases have even better claims than many of the residents."[17] The question, however, of who was an Indian, especially a Turtle Mountain Indian — as the group was beginning to be known — was becoming more acute. It is the same question that has plagued the Métis continually — and unfortunately, still does.

Finally, on August 19, 1890, Congress authorized the President to appoint a commission of three persons to negotiate with these Indians for cessation and relinquishment of whatever right or interest they might have to their claim, and for their removal to a settlement upon lands to be selected subject to the approval of Congress. The commission was charged also to determine the number of Chippewas and the number of mixed-bloods that were entitled to the consideration of the government.

But the commission did not come to the Turtle Mountains at once. The then current chief, Little Shell, like his half-breed relatives, had been forced to wander westward in order to find subsistence. From Wolf Point, Montana, on August 28, 1891, Little Shell wrote to the Commissioner of Indian Affairs and proposed an agreement whereby he would vacate the Turtle Mountain area in exchange for a reservation on the north side of the Missouri River above the mouth of the Milk. Since the Turtle Mountain lands seemed much more valuable to the white men, Little Shell believed that a cash settlement should be made to his people in addition to their securing a strip of land lying adjacent to the Fort Peck reservation.

Commissioner Morgan disposed of the request with the statement that the land desired was part of the public domain and thus could not be given to Little Shell. Morgan did believe, however, that there was sufficient land on the Fort Peck reservation for the Little Shell group to live if they so desired.[18]

Perhaps in anticipation of the day that the commission would arrive, the United States Indian Agent, John Waugh, appointed a committee of thirty-two men made up of sixteen full-blood Chippewa and sixteen Métis to represent the interest of their people in any transaction with the government in the adjustment of their claims. This committee was appointed in August, 1891, over a year and a half after the establishment of the commission by Congress. Coincidentally, Waugh picked the committee during the same month that Little Shell and his party were on the Fort Peck reservation. To many of the Chippewa group, as well as to a goodly number of the Métis, the selection of a committee at this particular time indicated that Agent Waugh wanted a hand-picked group with whom he could work without interference. Furthermore, Waugh selected five members from his committee of thirty-two to go over the list of eligible names, both Chippewa and Métis, and to delete those families or individuals who were not entitled to participate. As a result, 112 families, comprising 525 individuals, were immediately stricken from the rolls.[19]

Finally, in September, 1892, the commission arrived. It was composed of three members, headed by P. J. McCumber. The commission met in session at the Turtle Mountain Indian Agency beginning September 21 and called for the standing committee's report. (This would be the report of the thirty-two men selected the year previous.) Since this report concerned itself primarily with eligible persons, Chief Little Shell and his assistant, Red Thunder, protested forcefully against the dropping of the names of many individuals. Little Shell first spoke to the commission and pled for the consideration of people who had moved away, particularly for those who had gone to Montana because of dire need for food. Red Thunder succinctly summed up the situation by saying: "When you [the white man] first put your foot upon this land of ours you found no one but the red man and the Indian woman, by whom you have begotten a large family." Pointing to the Métis present, he added, "These are the children and descendants of that woman; they must be recognized as members of this tribe."[20] Firmly, the commission chairman told Little Shell that only the committee appointed by Agent Waugh would be heard, but that once the rolls were established, Little Shell might receive a copy of it. In disgust, Little Shell replied that his group would leave and that he would place his authority in the hands of his attorney, John Bottineau, a member of the tribe and a Métis.

On September 24, the commission finished hearing the report of the committee and then published the roll of eligible members. Instead of giving a copy to Bottineau, the roll was posted on the doors of the church. When Bottineau saw it, he was astounded at the number of people who had been dropped from the accepted group; and more flabbergasted, yet, when he received the following letter:[21]

U. S. Indian Service
Turtle Mountain Agency
October 15, 1892

John B. Bottineau, Esq.
Belcourt, North Dakota
Sir:

As per the enclosed you will observe that all persons except those mentioned in said notice are directed to withdraw from the limits of the reservation. I am instructed by the commission that in the matter of treaty for which a meeting has been called that they are instructed to deal directly with the people and will not recognize an attorney. Trusting that you will govern yourself in accordance with the directions of said notice, I remain,

Yours truly,
John Waugh,
U. S. Indian Agent,
Per E. W. Brenner,
Farmer in Charge.

The enclosure received by Bottineau was the same one that went to all Métis whose names were not on the rolls:

To Whom It May Concern:

Notice is hereby given to all parties who are not residents of the Turtle Mountain Reservation, or enrolled as members of the Turtle Mountain Band and accepted by the Commission now present as entitled to participate in any proceedings with the said Commissioners having in view the making of arrangements for a treaty, are hereby directed to withdraw from within the limits of the Turtle Mountain Reservation at once or be arrested.

John Waugh,
U. S. Indian Agent,
Per E. W. Brenner,
Farmer in Charge.

The commission continued its deliberation with the committee and on October 22 announced its agreement. The Turtle Mountain band of Chippewas, including the Métis who were considered eligible members, agreed to withdraw all claim to the 9,500,000-acre tract of land in the region, except the two townships previously established as a reservation in 1882. For their withdrawal, the government promised to pay the tribe $1,000,000. (Here is the basis for the description of the treaty that is so often given by the Métis of Montana when they mention the incident. The term, "ten-cent treaty," refers to the government's action in taking 9,500,000 acres of land for the sum of $1,000,000.)

Little Shell was aghast. By this willful action his people's sole remaining resource was given away for a paltry sum. Moreover, he saw no logic, equity or reason in the arbitrary determination of persons "chosen" as constituted members of the Turtle Mountain band; eligible members often had full brothers or sisters denied membership. Furthermore, he was incensed with what he thought to be the generally high-handed tactics of the commission. Immediately he announced repudiation of the treaty and called his council, *La Loge de Soldat*, together. On October 24, Chief Little Shell mailed a protest to Washington listing grievances. He reviewed carefully the regular method by which the Chippewas reached an agreement through its Council, to which neither the appointment nor the action of this committee conformed. He protested against the manner in which his attorney had been ordered off the reservation. And finally, he made specific charges against the commission, the committee of thirty-two, and the Indian agent, accusing all of coercion.[22]

There is no evidence to indicate that Little Shell's protest was ever considered. A few weeks later, December 3, 1892, the Secretary of the Interior transmitted the agreement, as concluded by the commission, to President Harrison, who in turn sent it to Congress for ratification.

Then came long years of waiting. Congress failed to ratify the treaty. The years that followed were marked by unrest and acrimony, both by Indians and whites. At least one committee of white citizens appealed to Congress to settle the issue. More Indians had to move westward to try to find a livelihood in a land that was fast becoming settled; and even the government Indian agents were discouraged, frustrated and outraged by the long delay. Finally, on January 26, 1898, Chief Little Shell wrote to his attorney, John Bottineau, who was then in Washington trying to secure some kind of settlement, an impassioned letter:[23]

> Belcourt, N. D.
> January 26, 1898
>
> The chief, Little Shell here speaks: We are tired, fatigue since so long waiting for the settlement of our claims. Even though we are fatigue, we keep strong — firm — to stay by you and your efforts in our cause . . . In regard to the affairs and doings of the three commissioners — the ten-cent treaty commissioners — we are very much troubled in here about it; but I repeat to you here again . . . that I would never sign their affairs, the ten-cent treaty; I am all the same yet and now. My greatest fatigue is to see my people so poor and going hungry.
>
> Little Shell, Chief
> (his x mark)
> Sasswein, Henri Poitrat
> (his x mark)
> Gaurin, Baptiste Champagne
> (his x mark)
> Bay-riss, Cuthbert Grant
> (his x mark)

Written by John B. Reno, Secretary of the Council.

The years passed. More Métis moved west. Others came back to the Turtle Mountains to see what had happened during their absence. Despairingly, a sympathetic agent, F. O. Getchell, wrote to the Commissioner of Indian Affairs describing the reservation and its people:[24]

Such is the place and such are nearly 2000 of the people who are besieged in their mountain fastnesses by the peaceful army of the plow that has settled their erstwhile hunting grounds. Here they are held in worse than bondage while they are waiting, waiting, waiting for a settlement with the Government for the lands so settled by the plowman, *waiting for a day that never comes*, while their chances in the land that was their own is fading, fading away from them. God pity their patient waiting and appoint that it may not have been in vain.

At long last, on April 21, 1904, nearly twelve years after the McCumber Commission presented its report, Congress ratified the so-called treaty. In the final ratification, provision was made that all members of the Turtle Mountain band who were unable to secure land upon the reservation could take homesteads upon any vacant land in the public domain without charge and would still retain their rights to tribal funds, annuities or other property held by the Turtle Mountain group, provided that such right of alternate selection of homesteads should not be alienated.[25]

But this ratification did not even end the litigation, for on January 19, 1905, the Assistant United States Attorney General held that the document signed by the Indians did not give a general release of their claim to the lands in North

Cree camp, northern Montana

Dakota; and that ratification could not be complete until such release was obtained. Word was sent to the agreeable Indians, who called a meeting on February 15, 1905, and executed the necessary release. Little Shell and his followers refused to sign.

Now that the final legal entanglements seemed cleared, it appeared that some kind of settlement could be effected. But again, such was not the case. Once more the specter of the rolls confronted the Indian agents. One agent, Charles L. Davis, writing his report to the United States Indian Commissioner for the year 1906, mentioned the trouble by saying that he was attempting to follow the report of the 1892 commission and that he was adding only those names who had been born to families listed on thn original report. He also mentioned that he tried to eliminate such members who "seemed to have discontinued or forfeited their tribal rights by long abandonment."[26] Francis E. Leupp, Commissioner of Indian Affairs, listed the criteria in his report for 1906 by which Indians should be judged, and singled out, as well, those to whom no grants could be given. Those individuals, then, who should be excluded — aside from death — were to include:[27]

1. Applicants coming from Canada after the date of the McCumber treaty.
2. Persons receiving land script or other benefits as Canadian Indians.
3. Applicants not living on the nine-million-acre tract at the time of the Mc-Cumber treaty unless they can show they were born and raised there and were absent temporarily.
4. Those who may have been living on that tract at the time of the McCumber treaty and who have since permanently removed therefrom are debarred.

How, the Métis wondered, as they heard of the last provision, could they have existed during those fourteen years that had elapsed between the time of the McCumber treaty and its final execution?

One of the provisions of the treaty was that Indians unable to secure land on the reservation could file for homesteads on the public domain. During the year 1906, a total of 549 members of the Turtle Mountain band filed on public land. The land office at Devil's Lake, North Dakota, recorded ten such filings; the one at Minot, 390; the one at Great Falls, 142, and the one at Lewistown, seven. But, in his report for the following year, 1907, Commissioner Leupp stated that there were at least 1370 Indians for whom no provision had been made and that these included principally the wives and children of the reservation allottees. "If these Indians are to secure lands it must be from the public domain in North Dakota and Montana," he wrote. "But protests have been made against their taking so much of the public domain in these states, because the lands will remain untaxable as long as they are held in trust by the government."[28]

So the government concluded its responsibilities toward the Pembina band of Chippewas — full-bloods and Métis. What happened, then, to the Métis who straggled back to Montana?

The wild game was largely gone; their cabins burned; barbed wire greeted them at every turn, for their timing coincided with the homestead boom that had struck the high plains that once had been their home. A few, like Joseph Dussome, tried to homestead but encountered difficulties — were they or were they not Turtle Mountain Indians and hence qualified to take land on the public domain without payment of fees? Some of them intermarried with enrolled Indians on established reservations where their children at least would have the benefits accorded to them by the government. But most of them were forced to sink deeper and deeper on the social scale. Always confronted by the stigma of being Canadian Cree, these early pioneers of Montana — these Azures, LaPierres, Collins, LaFrambois, Poitras and all the rest — sought work where they could find it. Many of them congregated on a hill near the fast-growing city of Great Falls — later to be called Hill 57 — while others went to the areas they knew and loved the best — Choteau, Augusta, Dupuyer, and the Milk River towns of Havre, Chinook, Malta and Glasgow.

And here their descendants live today, scorned by both the white and the enrolled-Indian populations. All the assistance their forebears gave to the fur traders and to the early stockmen is forgotten. All of their struggle to receive recognition as United States citizens after their exclusion from the rolls at the time of the McCumber treaty is unknown. All that is remembered is the erroneous impression that they are Canadian Crees and therefore displaced persons, landless and unwanted.

Until the 1960's, Joseph Dussome still sat in his cabin with his good wife and went over his papers. He remembered the things that had happened to him — the false hope so often engendered. He also remembered the first organization he had effected, "The Abandoned Band of Chippewa Indians," in 1927, which seven years later he had incorporated under the name of "The Landless Indians of Montana." Without rancor, he recalled seeing a group of younger and more aggressive men split from his organization to incorporate one of their own, "The Montana Landless Indians."

He particularly remembered the hope of the 1930 depression years, for then the government promised to buy 37,000 acres of land lying near Box Elder for the Landless Indians of Montana. The government fulfilled its contract, but the jurisdiction of the land was placed under Rocky Boy's agency, with the Cree inhabitants of that reservation making the decision as to who should be adopted. As he viewed the adoption, the Canadian Crees — those who came to Montana after the Riel Rebellion — were the adoptees, so another dream vanished. The American Métis still wandered.

Dussome recalled, too, the purchase by the government of a forty-acre tract of land near Great Falls in the 1930's. Here was to be a chance for the Indians of Hill 57, the landless ones from the Turtle Mountains, to live in less squalid condi-

Cree roasting a dog

tions and to have subsistence garden plots. Too vivid in Dussome's memory was the opposition from Great Falls' residents to the occupancy of the site by the Indians, so the opportunity passed.

And then there was the government Resettlement Plan that was almost accomplished, early in the 1940's. In Phillips County, where the Farm Security Administration did remarkable things for white farmers, the plan developed whereby all of the Ben Phillips pioneer land holdings was to be purchased by the government for the Landless Indians. On this land, experienced Indian farmers would have separate units; inexperienced ones would work cooperatively. But the war came, and the idea became a forgotten one.

But hope, even now, is not entirely dead. Joe Dussome believed until his death that the federal government would eventually provide a rehabilitation program for his people; that the Indian claim to the hunting rights of the Turtle Mountain area would some day be recognized as being as significant as those cultivated rights of the white man; that eventually right would triumph and some of the inequities of the past would be rectified. Perhaps that belief of his someday will be justified.

NOTES

[1] Joseph Kinsey Howard's remarkable book, *Strange Empire,* William Morrow & Co., N. Y. 1952.

[2] For much of this information, I am indebted to Mrs. Joseph Dussome, Zortman, Montana, per personal interviews.

[3] For an excellent description of the Métis see "The French Half Breeds of the Northwest," by V. Havard, M.D. *Annual Report of the Smithsonian Institution for the Year 1879.* (Washington: Government Printing Office, 1880). 309-327.

[4] Here are simple entries:

"1855. The 23 Oct. of, the undersigned travelling missionary of Oregon during a trip to Ft. Benton in Nebraska Territory baptized the following half breeds whose parents are chiefly Canadians attached to the trading post. Rev. James Croke, S. J.

Sueqnet Antoine, age 1 year, son of Charles Sueqnet and Mary of the Bloods. The sponsor was Antoine Burdon.

Moran Charles, 1 year old, born to Charles Moran and a Blood woman. The Godfather was Simon Copineau."

"April 25, 1860, I, Adrian Hoecken, S. J. baptized:

Champagne Teresa Marie, daughter of Baptiste Champagne, Metis, and Pauline Agkippian. Born in the month of September, 1859.

Lespera Margaret, daughter to Joseph L'espera, a metis de la Rivere Rouge, and Siwaka. Born 20 January, 1860. The sponsor was Cadotte."

"Die 25 Marii 1879, Ego C. Imoda, S. J., in missione St. Petri coram hibito consensum pervebade praesenti solemniter matrimonio conjunsci Franciscum Xaverium LaPierre filiam Antonii et Caterntie LaPierre – et Mariam Rosam Swan, filiam Jacobi sr. et Maria Swan. Tests fuerunt Frances LaPierre et Paulus Nomee."

"The 25 of March, 1879, I. C. Imoda, S. J. in the Mission of St. Peter, having been presented with their mutual consent, solemnized the marriage joining Francois Xavier LaPierre, and Mary Rose Swan, daughter of James, Sr., and Marie Swan. The witnesses were Frank LaPierre and Paul Nomee."

For this information I gratefully acknowledge the assistance given me by one of my students, Joseph D. Marion, Jr., whose acquaintanceship with the Métis and their problems is unequaled by any other person in Montana.

[5] Havard, *op, cit.* 325.

[6] Personal Interview, John Barrows, Zortman, Montana, 9-14-57.

[7] Alexander Ross, *The Red River Settlements,* (London: Smith, Edler and Co., 1856. Reprinted, Minneapolis: Ross and Haines, Inc., 1957).

[8] J. M. Hamilton, *From Wilderness to Statehood,* (Portland: Binfords & Mort, 1957) 83.

[9] Joseph Marino gave me these family names from his notes concerning the movements of the early-day Métis.

[10] Obituary of Clemence Gourneau Berger, Lewistown *Democrat-News* December 31, 1943.

[11] Personal Interview, Mrs. Elizabeth Swan, a granddaughter of Pierre Berger and a resident of Lewistown. 9-18-56.

[12] For the complete and beautifully written story of the Métis in Canada and of the Riel uprisings, see J. K. Howard's *Strange Empire, op. cit.*

[13] An account of the trouble the Crees had in securing Rocky Boy's reservation appears in "The Rocky Boy Indians," by Verne Dusenberry, *Montana Magazine of History,* Winter, 1954.

[14] *Collections of the State Historical Society of North Dakota.* (Bismarck: Tribune State Printers and Binders, 1906) I, 384-405.

[15] *Senate Documents 154,* 55th Congress, 2d Session. 11

[16] *Report of the Commissioner of Indian Affairs for 1884,* 34-35.

[17] *Report of the Commissioner of Indian Affairs for 1888,* 41

[18] *Senate Document 154, op. cit.* 20.

[19] *Report of the Commissioner of Indian Affairs for 1892,* 353.

[20] *Senate Document 444,* 56th Congress, 1st Session. 33-36.

[21] *Ibid.,* 41.

[22] *Ibid.,* 31-36.

[23] *Senate Document 154, op. cit.* 26.

[24] *Report of the Commissioner of Indian Affairs for 1903,* 228-229.

[25] *33 Stat. L.* 58th Congress, 2d Session, Chapter 1402, 1904. 194

[26] *Report of the Commissioner of Indian Affairs for 1906,* 281.

[27] *Ibid.,* 154-155.

[28] *Report of the Commissioner of Indian Affairs for 1907,* 60-63.

INTRUDERS FROM
THE EAST

Lewis and Clark in the Mandan Village (Charles M. Russell)

The Lewis and Clark Expedition

AS SEEN THROUGH THE EYES OF THE INDIANS

By ELLA E. CLARK

FLATHEAD, SHOSHONE and Nez Percé Indians have their own history of the coming of the Lewis and Clark Expedition into the northern Rockies in 1805-06. Indian oral history describes their reactions to the strange-looking pale-faced men, curiously dressed, who suddenly appeared near their summer camps; and who delighted them with gifts of trinkets and garments they had never seen before. Strangest of all was a black man with short, kinky hair, "York."

Though probably altered during the decades and generations before being written, and colored by the imaginations of storytellers, these Indian "traditions" nevertheless provide information which the explorers could not have known. "We could not talk with them [the Flatheads] as much as we wish," wrote Private Joseph Whitehouse on September 5, 1805, "for all that we say has to go through 6 languages before it gits to them, and it is hard to make them understand all what we Say."[1]

Sixty-two years ago on the Flathead Reservation of Western Montana, Pierre Pichette was convinced that he should make himself an authority on the traditions and customs of his people. He was then in his early twenties and was shut off from normal activities by blindness. From his elders of more than half a century ago came this first story of Lewis and Clark, as Mr. Pichette recalled it in the summer of 1953:

> Our people were camped in a kind of prairie along the Bitterroot River, upstream from the Medicine Tree. The place is called Ross's Hole now; the Indians then called it *Cutl-khk-pooh*. They kept close watch over their camps in those days and always had scouts out, because they feared an attack by an enemy tribe. One day two scouts came back to report that they had seen some human beings who were different from any they had known. Most of the strangers had pale skins, and their clothing was altogether different from anything the Indians wore.
>
> "There were seven of them," the scouts told Chief Three Eagles (*Tchliska-e-me*). "They have little packs on their backs, maybe food or clothing."

The chief immediately sent his warriors to meet the strange men and to bring them to camp safely.

"Do no harm to them," he warned his men. "Do no harm to them at all. Bring them to me safely."

So the strangers were brought into the camp. All the tepees were arranged in a circle in our camps, with an open space in the center. The people gathered there in the middle of the camping place, and so when the warriors brought the strange men in, they were seen by the whole tribe. The Indians could not understand who the seven men were, but they knew they were human beings.

Chief Three Eagles ordered buffalo robes to be brought and to be spread in the gathering place. By signs, he told the strangers to sit on the robes. The men were a puzzling sight to all the Indians around them.

After the white men had sat down, they took their little packs off their backs. The chief looked through their packs and then began to explain to his people.

"I think they have had a narrow escape from their enemies. All their belongings were taken away by the enemy. That's why there is so little in their packs. Maybe the rest of the tribe were killed. Maybe that is why there are only seven of them. These men must be very tired and hungry — perhaps starving. And see how poor and torn their clothes are."

The chief ordered food to be brought to them — dried buffalo meat and dried roots. He ordered clothing also to be brought to them — buckskins and light buffalo robes that were used for clothing.

One of the strange men was black. He had painted himself in charcoal, my people thought. In these days it was the custom for warriors, when returning from battle, to prepare themselves before reaching camp. Those who had been brave and fearless, the victorious ones in battle, painted themselves in charcoal. When the warriors returned to their camp, people knew at once which ones had been brave on the warpath. So the black man, they thought, had been the bravest of this party.

All the men had short hair. So our people thought that the seven were in mourning for the rest of the party who had been killed. It was the custom for mourners to cut their hair.

By signs, Chief Three Eagles and his counselors came to a little understanding with the white men. Then the chief said to his people, "This party is the first of this kind of people we have ever seen. They have been brought in safely. I want them taken out safely. I want you warriors to go with them part of the way, to make sure that they leave our country without harm."

So by the chief's orders, the warriors accompanied the white men to the edge of the Salish country. They went with the white men down the river from Ross's Hole and up to Lolo Pass. The strangers went on from there.

They did not take with them the robes and the clothing Chief Three Eagles had given them. Perhaps the white men did not know that they were gifts.

Pichette's explanation of the "death" color of Captain Clark's huge Negro servant, York, is different from that in a Flathead tradition recorded by the photographer, Edward S. Curtis, in 1909, or slightly earlier:

The two captains advanced and shook hands with the chief, who commanded his people to refrain from any evil-doing toward them. The white men removed their pack-saddles from their horses and sat down on the ground. The chief said: "They have no robes to sit on. Some Indians have stolen them. Bring them robes."

Buffalo skins were brought, but instead of sitting on them, the white men threw them about their shoulders. One of them had a black face, and the Indians said among themselves, "See, his face is painted black! They are going to have a scalp-dance!"[2]

The Medicine Tree of Mr. Pichette's version (he had previously related a legend about it) is a large yellow pine on the east fork of the Bitterroot River, twelve miles south of Darby, Montana. Ross's Hole is a wide valley near the head of the Bitterroot, where the main stream is joined by two creeks, one coming down from the northeast and one from the southwest. Lolo Pass is in the Bitterroot Range, the part of the Rocky Mountains that now forms the boundary between Montana and northern Idaho.

Some details in the Flathead traditions are corroborated by the explorer's journals. The white men had twenty-nine horses, obtained by barter ten days earlier from a band of Shoshones living along the Lemhi River, a branch of the Salmon River of present-day Idaho. Both Captain Clark and Private Whitehouse tell about descending from the "dividing ridge" (between the waters of the Salmon and Bitterroot rivers) on September 4 and finding a wide valley, where a creek met the main stream, a large encampment of "Tuskepaws" or "Ootlashoots" or "the Flathead Nation" — thirty-three lodges, says Clark; "about 40 lodges," says Whitehouse. Both explorers mention the robes placed over the men's shoulders and also the friendly welcome: "They received us as friends and appeared to be glad to See us."[3]

But apparently no Flatheads accompanied the white men to Lolo Pass. On September 6 Clark wrote: "We set out at 2 o'clock. At the same time all the Indians set out on their way to meet the Snake Indians on the three forks of the Missouri."[4]

The number seven in Pierre Pichette's account is a puzzle. The mystic number, which is found in many Flathead traditions and tales, is five. Clark's journal (in the Thwaites edition) makes no reference to a division of the exploring party at that time and place. Whitehouse mentions, not seven, but two men ahead of the main party: "Two of our men who were a hunting came to their lodges first. The natives spread a white robe over them and put their arms around their necks as a great token of friendship, then smoked with them. When Capt. Lewis and Capt. Clark arrived, they spread their white robes over their shoulders and smoked with them. . . ."[5]

In a Flathead tradition, written in 1899 by Father D'Aste of the St. Ignatius Mission in the Bitterroot valley, the exploring party is described as consisting of "about 20 men, each man leading two pack horses, except the two leaders, who were riding ahead." The missionary had obtained the story from a reliable old Indian, François Saxa, who had heard it from the widow of Chief Victor, famous chief of the Flathead Indians, with whom Governor Stevens negotiated the reservation treaty of 1855. Chief Victor was the son of Chief Three Eagles. Father

D'Aste's account is given in full in O. D. Wheeler's *The Trail of Lewis and Clark*.[6] In brief, it is as follows:

> One day when the Flatheads were camping at Ross's Hole, at the head of the Bitterroot valley, Chief Three Eagles left the camp to scout for horse-stealing Indians. He saw at a distance a party of men with pack horses — men strange in appearance because they wore no blankets. Reporting to his people, the chief commanded that all horses be driven in and watched. Then he went back toward the approaching party, hid himself among the trees and watched them.
>
> They were traveling slowly, the two leaders appearing to survey the country and then to consult with their men. A black man was especially puzzling. Chief Three Eagles decided that he must have painted his face black for a war dance (which the Flatheads often held to encourage one another to fight bravely), that the party had had a fight with their enemies and had escaped, losing only their blankets. From the easy and unconcerned way in which the strangers were traveling, the chief felt sure that their intentions were peaceful.
>
> Returning to his camp, Three Eagles told his people to keep quiet and to wait for the party to come near. The white leaders, when they arrived, showed such friendliness that there was a general shaking of hands. The best buffalo robes were brought out for the visitors' use. The strangers filled their own pipes with Indian tobacco, but did not like it. Their tobacco, to the great amusement of the party, made the Indians cough. Asking for some kinnikinnick, Lewis and Clark mixed it with some of their tobacco. The Indians liked this mixture, as well as the good humor of the visitors.
>
> Seeing the friendly disposition of the Indians, the white men decided to camp there, and so began to unpack their horses. By signs they explained that they did not need the buffalo robes, because in their packs were blankets, which were only used for sleeping. The Indians "were soon out of their wits" at the power of the strangers, who carried on their shoulders large logs for their campfires.
>
> "All went on friendly," the story from Chief Three Eagles' daughter-in-law ends, "and after three days they started off, directed to Lolo fork's trail by the Indians, as the best way to get to the Nez Perce's country." [The Nez Perce country referred to is on the west side of the Bitterroot Range, along the valley of the Clearwater River and the lower Snake, in what is now northern Idaho].

What is said to be the story of the Flatheads' meeting with Lewis and Clark was recorded in 1831, in the journal of Warren Angus Ferris, a young employee of the American Fur Company. Because it was related only twenty-six years after the event, by an Indian described as an intelligent Flathead, a member of a group in the village who had been present at the first meeting of his people with white men, this narrative might at first glance be considered fairly accurate. But Ferris wrote that the Indians had seen the explorers along the *Salmon* River,[7] that they had moved there from the valley of the Jefferson River[8] in the narrator's childhood.

The journal of Captain Lewis contains many pages of information about the band of Shoshone or Snake Indians he had found encamped along the Lemhi River, a few miles above its confluence with the Salmon, on the west slope of the Rocky Mountains. The enemies of this band were called Minnetaree by Lewis and Clark whenever they mentioned the capture of their Shoshone interpreter,

Captain William Clark

Captain Meriwether Lewis

Sacajawea. Sacajawea's brother used the name *Pawkees* for the "Minnetaree of Fort de Prairie," in his conversations with Lewis. *Pahkee*, according to a recent report, was a Shoshone name for the Blackfeet.[9] The narrative which Ferris preserved is of interest and of value, however, whether it is about the Flatheads and the Blackfeet or about the Shoshones and the Minnetarees:

"A great many snows past, when I was a child," Ferris begins the Indian's story, "our people were in continual fear of the Blackfeet. They had firearms, but we had none. Whenever we went into the plains for buffalo, they attacked us. They never came in reach of our arrows."

At last, foreseeing the destruction of the band if they remained near the plains of their enemies, their chief decided that they should leave the valley of the Jefferson. For a whole month they traveled southwestward, up and across mountains and down canyons, until they came to the Salmon River. There they felt protected by the surrounding mountains. They found that the river was alive with salmon, that there was an abundance of berries, roots and game in the area. Once again peace and happiness filled their hearts.

But after a lapse of time, they were alarmed by the unexpected arrival of two strangers, unlike any men they had ever seen. The two had come over the mountains by way of the Beaverhead River. "They gave us things like solid water, which were sometimes brilliant as the sun, and which sometimes showed us our own faces." But the Indians were terrified when they learned that these strange men also had firearms and that a party of beings like themselves was but a day's march behind them. The white men wanted the Indians to go back with them to meet their party. At first the Indians refused to go, sure that the strangers were in league with the Blackfeet. But their chief persuaded them that they should try to conciliate men so terribly armed, especially now that their mountain retreat had been discovered. The women wailed in anguish when their men departed with the two strangers.

To the surprise of the Indians, they found only a few men in the strangers' camp and they were treated with great kindness. The white men gave them many things that they did not know existed. When the chief discovered from the carelessness of the strangers that they were not accustomed to theft, he warned his men not to steal anything from them. The Indians took the white men over the mountains to their village, where the strangers remained for several days. Ever since then, that band of Indians ("the Flatheads," says Ferris) have been friends of the white men.[10]

The Flatheads have always had friendly relationships with the whites, but the explorers' journals contain no reference to a meeting with any of them in the Salmon River country. The comments of Clark and Whitehouse about the strangely guttural language of the Flatheads at Ross's Hole ("we take these Savages to be the Welch Indians, if there be any Such, from the Language")[11] indicate that the friendly encounter of September 4-6, 1805, was the first with that tribe. In the area of Beaver's Head Rock, which the explorers reached on August 8 and which Sacajawea recognized as a landmark not far from her people's summer retreat in the mountains, Lewis and Clark were determinedly searching for Shoshone or "Snake Indians."[12] In quest of them, Captain Lewis and three companions scouted ahead of the main party, who would come up the Beaverhead fork of the Jefferson River as far as boats could go.

Preparations for the greatly desired meeting with the Shoshones had really begun months before, at Fort Mandan, when the captains arranged with their French-Canadian interpreter to take with them one of his three "squaws," young Sacajawea. She had been captured by the Minnetarees five years before and carried eastward from the upper Missouri. With her as interpreter, Lewis and Clark hoped to negotiate with the Shoshones of the Rocky Mountain region. They foresaw that the success of the enterprise would depend upon their securing horses to transport their cargo over the Continental Divide, from the headwaters of the Missouri to some navigable tributary of the Columbia, and upon their finding a guide acquainted with the trails between the two great streams.[13]

So the explorers wooed the Shoshones from August 11, when Captain Lewis and three companions saw one of them on horseback and tried to lure him with mirrors and trinkets,[14] until August 30, when the white men and their guides started north for the Flathead country and the recommended pass over the Columbia (the Clearwater River).[15] It was in a group of Shoshones who were following Captain Lewis from the Lemhi River camp, on August 17, that Sacajawea recognized her brother, Chief Cameahwait, and her childhood companion who also had been captured by the Minnetarees but had escaped.[16] Unimportant though women were in Indian culture, it seems strange that any storyteller could omit from his tale these dramatic reunions of Sacajawea with her people.

The explorers saw other camps along the Lemhi and the Salmon rivers; groups of unidentified Indians passed them on their way to the buffalo plains east of the Rockies. But the only references to Flatheads in the journal records on that area are similar to this one: the Shoshones' "chief intercourse seems to consist in their association with other Snake Indians, and with the Flatheads when they go eastward to hunt buffalo, or during the occasional visits made by Flatheads to the waters of the Columbia for the purpose of fishing."[17] The guide of Clark's reconnaissance along the Salmon River, when the party learned the impossibility of descending that turbulent stream, either by boat or by horse — that kindly old guide was acquainted with the Flatheads and knew their route over the mountains to the salmon streams west of the Divide.[18] (Pierre Pichette tells a Flathead

Lewis and Clark Expedition (Harold Von Schmidt)

myth which explains why there are no salmon east of the crest of the Bitterroot Range.)

Some of the details in Ferris's story are strikingly similar to facts about the Shoshones that Captain Lewis learned from Chief Cameahwait and his people. Within their own memories, they said, they had lived on the plains east of the mountains, but they had been driven into the Salmon River country by the Minnetarees. Those enemies had firearms and ammunition; the Spaniards along the Yellowstone River would not allow the Shoshones to have any. Consequently, they were left "defenseless and an easy prey to their blood-thirsty neighbors to the east of them, who being in possession of firearms hunt them up and murder them without respect to age or sex and plunder them of their horses on all occasions." To avoid their enemies they had to remain in those mountains at least two-thirds of the year.[19]

As might be surmised, the Shoshones suspected that the white men with guns were in league with their enemies; and when Chief Cameahwait and eight warriors departed with Lewis to meet the main party of explorers, the women wailed and prayed for the protection of "their warriors as if they were going to certain destruction."[20] The major difference between Ferris's story and Captain Lewis's account is that the latter reported the wretched condition of the Salmon River Indians; with little opportunity to hunt buffalo, they were forced to pass "whole weeks without meat and with nothing to eat but a few fish and roots."[21]

It seems likely, therefore, either that Ferris's informant confused a story he had heard from Shoshones with one heard from Flatheads; or that Ferris, who had been in the West slightly over a year when he recorded the narrative, confused Shoshones and Minnetarees with Flatheads and Blackfeet. He does not say what language he used when conversing with the Indians.

An amusing and fanciful tale of a Shoshone's meeting with the exploring party was related to Thomas Farnham in 1839. Farnham became acquainted with the Shoshone, who was then an old man, at Brown's Hole, in the northwestern corner of present-day Colorado and adjacent Utah. The Indian said that he was the first of his tribe to see the Lewis and Clark party, that he had discovered them on the headwaters of the Missouri while scouting for his people. Suddenly seeing two strange men, "with faces pale as ashes," he was first fixed to the spot in astonishment. Then he galloped his horse toward his camp, but the strangers pursued him, caught him, and took him to their camp. There they loaded him with presents and showed him that they could make thunder and lightning. When he returned to his people and told his experiences, he was accused of lying to the chief and was sentenced to death. But when he showed some of the gifts he had received, he was granted the privilege of leading his judges to the place where he had seen the palefaces. They were found and the scout's story was corroborated. "Ever since he has been much honored and loved by his tribe, and every white man in the mountains."[22]

The tale is amusing and fanciful because the men were not pale, but bronzed from months in the sun; they did not fire their guns when trying to make friends with the Indian; Lewis and his companions were on foot, the Shoshone scout on horseback. Permitting Lewis to advance within 100 paces of him, the Indian must have seen the looking glass and trinkets held out to him before he gave his horse the whip and leaped across the creek. Perhaps he returned and found the articles the men tied to a pole and left on an elevation as a lure.[23] Two days later, after the four white men had crossed the Continental Divide, trinkets which Lewis gave three terrified women calmed their fears and a few minutes later won for him and his companions the cordial welcome and "fraternal embrace" ("of which the motive was much more agreeable than the manner") of Chief Cameahwait and his sixty warriors. The men were riding excellent horses. Perhaps the Shoshone camp had been alerted by the man on horseback; more likely, by three others who had fled in terror shortly before the three women saw Lewis.[24]

Among the Nez Percé Indians, when Kate McBeth came as a missionary in 1879, the story of the explorers' first visit and of Watkuese's rescuing the bearded strangers from probable death was such a familiar fireside tale that all the local children knew it.[25] In 1952, a Nez Percé woman about ninety-three years of age, knowing only her native language, related the picturesque version of that tradition of the white men saved by a dying woman of her tribe.[26] On the Wind River Reservation, Wyoming, in the 1930's, Shoshone school children recorded their elders' recollections of the story of Sacajawea, who had lived her last years among them and was buried there in 1884. A half century after her death from old age, her great-grandchildren and their contemporaries still remember some of Sacajawea's experiences on the long journey she had taken with the white men, her baby strapped to her youthful back.[27]

For 160 years, many listeners and many readers have been stirred by the purposeful adventures of those resolute, wise and kindly young explorers, who treated the Indians with such understanding and courtesy, who overcame almost unbelievable obstacles in order to accomplish their numerous objectives and to complete their mission. We can only wonder what the history of the United States would have been without them.

Crucial in the great historical enterprise carefully planned by President Jefferson and his secretary, Captain Meriwether Lewis, was the almost impossible journey over the Rocky Mountain, from the waters of the mighty Missouri to those of the westward-flowing great Columbia. For that journey, the cooperation of the natives was imperative. Their natural fears allayed by friendliness and sincerity, their own natures responding to courtesy and generosity, the Shoshone, Flathead and Nez Percé Indians played brief but important roles in this heroic drama of the Far West. For most of the tribesmen these were the first of the "New Breed" — men from the Land of The Rising Sun — strange men, white and black, the first they had ever seen. It was an amazing experience for the red men.

NOTES

1 R. G. Thwaites, ed., *Original Journals of the Lewis and Clark Expedition* (New York, 1904-05) VII, 150.

2 *The North American Indian* (Cambridge, Mass., 1907-1930), VII (1911), 44. (Curtis gives *Chehleskaiyimi* as the native name of Chief Three Eagles.)

3 Thwaites, III, 52-53 and VII, 149.

4 *Ibid.*, III, 54.

5 *Ibid.*, VII, 149.

6 (New York, 1904), II, 65-68.

7 The Salmon River flows northward in eastern Idaho, through a deep gorge, crosses central Idaho through mountains and joins the Snake River, one of the chief tributaries of the Columbia.

8 The Jefferson, Madison and Gallatin rivers join at Three Forks, Montana, to form the Missouri River. They were named by Lewis and Clark, who camped near Three Forks the last week of July, 1805 — on almost the identical spot where Sacajawea and other Shoshone girls and women had been captured by Minnetaree. From there Lewis and three men went ahead on foot, to search for Shoshones.

9 Citing Lewis and Clark in his description, J. R. Swanson gives "Minitari" as one name for the Hidatsa of the Siouan linguistic stock. The name Minitari was probably given them by the Mandan, with whom they were allied. The explorers found them on Knife River, a tributary of the Missouri in present western North Dakota. (*The Indian Tribes of North America*, Bureau of Ethnology, Bulletin 145 (1952), 275-76). Pah-kee is a Shoshone name for the Siksika or Blackfeet (*Ibid.*, 395-6). Several Lemhi bands of Northern Shoshoni lived along the Salmon River at the base of the Rockies (403-4).

10 Warren A. Ferris, *Life in the Rocky Mountains, 1830-35,* H. S. Auerbach and J. C. Alter, eds. (Salt Lake City, 1940), 75-8.

11 Thwaites, VII, 150, and III, 53.

12 *Ibid.*, II, 321-2.

13 *Ibid.*, I, 287.

14 *Ibid.*, II, 329.

15 *Ibid.*, III, 47-48.

16 Elliot Coues, *History of the Expedition under the Command of Lewis and Clark.* (New York, (1893) II, 509-510). For the geography-minded: The party crossed over the Continental Divide southwest of present Dillon, Montana, at what is now called Lemhi Pass. Lewis crossed there three times: (1) westward with three companions, searching for Shoshones; (2) eastward with Chief Cameahwait and about 60 of his people to meet Captain Clark and the main party, with the canoes, at the upper forks of the Jefferson River (that section of it is also called the Beaverhead); (3) westward with the main party, the Indians, and their horses carrying the baggage to the Shoshoni camp on the Lemhi River in present eastern Idaho. Clark went ahead of Lewis on this last crossing, in order to then explore the navigability of the Salmon River.

17 Coues, II, 569.

18 *Ibid.*, 535.

19 *Ibid.*, 493-4, 554-4, 559.

20 *Ibid.*, 500.

21 *Ibid.*, 555.

22 *Travels in the Great Western Prairies in Early Western Travels*, R. G. Thwaites, ed. (Cleveland, 1904-7, XXVIII, 272-4).

23 Coues, II, 477-81.

24 *Ibid.*, 488-490.

25 *The Nez Perces Since Lewis and Clark* (New York, 1908), 24-26.

26 For both of these traditions of the Nez Perce Indians, see the author's "Watkuese and Lewis and Clark," in *Western Folklore*, XII, (1953), 175-8.

27 For many Shoshone traditions about Sacajawea, see Grace R. Hebard, *Sacajawea: A Guide and Interpreter of the Lewis and Clark Expedition* (Glendale, Calif. 1933).

Sacajawea –
Inspirational Maid

By BERNARD DE VOTO

In a book which I published in 1952, *The Course of Empire,* I tried hard to do exact justice to Sacajawea.

It is an astonishing and delightful fact that Sacajawea, not a word of whom we know at first hand, has impressed herself on the minds of Americans as no other Indian woman has ever done. Part of this is due, no doubt, to the staunchness and loyalty which show in the journals of Lewis and Clark. But I have always been at a loss to explain the rest of it. Somehow she seizes hold of the imaginations of people who write about her. Men seem to fall in love with her and women identify themselves with her, with the result that their imagination takes over and creates an Indian woman who never existed. The most conspicuous examples were Donald Culross Peattie and Grace Hebard, whose treatment of her cannot be called history at all but must be classified as romantic fiction. Further evidence is the fact — or what the "Dictionary of American Biography" says is a fact, for I have never tried to verify it — that more statues have been erected to her than to any other American woman. I have seen half a dozen of these, the best being the one at Bismarck, N.D.

Doubtless Sacajawea was a more useful member of the expedition than her worthless husband, Charbonneau. She was always cheerful, ingenious and willing to work. She was able to direct the expedition to edible roots which they didn't know about; she sewed deer-skin shirts and made moccasins, etc. When the expedition drew near the Three Forks she was able to tell them how far they were from various places, and that they were getting near the Shoshone country. Once she even did a bit of what may properly be called guiding.

But though a useful member of the expedition, she was an important one in only a single respect. Charbonneau was hired for the winter at the Mandan village, as an interpreter for dealings with the Minnetarees, whose language he could speak. There was then no thought of taking him along when the expedition got started again in the spring. But during the winter Lewis and Clark learned that they would have to do a lot of overland travel for which they would need horses, and that they could get horses in plenty from the Shoshones. Saca-jawea thereupon became valuable to them, since Shoshone was her native language and she could interpret for them — also, no doubt, because they foresaw that the presence of a Shoshone woman would be a manifest token of peace. That is the reason why Charbonneau and Sacajawea were taken along in the spring.

Of course she did practically no guiding. How could she? She knew the Shoshone country: Lemhi pass and the immediate environs both east and west of it, and she knew the country between there and the Three Forks — for as a child she had gone with her family on the tribes' annual excursion to the buffalo country. Captured by the Minnetarees at the age of 12, she had traveled from the Three Forks to the Mandan villages, we do not know by

119

what route. That was the extent of it. Since then her movements were confined to those of her husband — going out some distance west of the Missouri for buffalo, and going to and from the British posts on the Assiniboin River, maybe twice a year. She knew no other country for she had seen none. She could not have guided the expedition up the Missouri or beyond the mountains — it was all a blank page to her. But as they approached the Three Forks and from there to Lemhi pass she knew where she was and told them where they were. That, in brief, was the contribution of Sacajawea, the most publicized Indian woman of the West.

— Bernard De Voto

Lewis and Clark and Sacajawea (bronze by Henry Lion)

A Savage Christmas...1813

By ARTHUR L. STONE

For nearly eighty miles after it emerges from Hell Gate canyon, the Missoula River skirts the base of Montana's Bitter Root mountains, gaining in volume and in picturesqueness as it receives accessions from the hundred tributaries which emerge from the rocky rifts in the magnificent chain of peaks which tower above it, until its current blends with the sparkling flow of the St. Regis de Borgia. The beautiful stream here becomes more beautiful and changes its course from the general westerly direction which it has followed, turns almost at right angles and, with accelerated speed, dashes through a narrow box canyon for twenty miles. In this canyon the river pours over tempestuous precipices, plunges between rocky walls — foaming, seething, swirling — for nearly the entire distance. Then its bed broadens, it flows between fertile fields, it becomes a placid almost mirrorlike river. It debouches into the beauty of Paradise Valley — rightly named if ever a spot upon earth were rightly named.

Here, in the midst of the beauty of Paradise Valley, the Missoula mingles its waters with those of the Pend d'Oreille or Lower Flathead, whose flow here is mighty mild, whose color is either blue or green, according to the point of view, but always brilliant. The union of these splendid streams forms the Clark's Fork of the Columbia, through which the drainage of the western slope of Montana finds its way into the Pacific Ocean. This, to my mind, is one of the beauty spots of Montana. It is a glorious place. The mountain background is rugged and substantial. Great shoulders of naked rock jut out from the somber green cloak of pine which covers the slopes and silver streams form shining threads all through the fabric. Broad benches slope away from the abrupt sides of the hills and, in turn, pitch — often suddenly — down to the level of the meadows which skirt the streams. There are groups of deciduous trees upon the benches; there are tall grass and brilliant flowers in the summertime. In the winter the snow banks high upon the mountain slopes; there is considerable depth upon the bench lands. But the valley is not often snowbound. It is like spring there, always.

It appears . . . that [some of] the first buildings erected by white men in the territory included in the present boundaries of Montana were constructed in the spring of 1813 at the point of land between these two rivers.[1] The builder was

Factor McMillan of the Astor fur traders, who had been sent inland from Astoria to establish trade relations with the Flatheads, after the arrival of the good ship *Beaver* at the mouth of the old trading post built here,[2] but we have an accurate and detailed account of the life at the post and there can be no reasonable doubt of its authenticity. The records of the fur company establish the fact that the post was constructed there; it was known as McMillan's trading post. A book, published in England in 1817, *Cox's Adventures on the Columbia River*, furnishes a really graphic description of the happenings at McMillan's post during the sojourn of the writer at that place. Also, the Flatheads tell of the coming of McMillan. For years, before he came, the Flatheads had been getting the worst of it in their annual engagements with the Blackfeet, the latter having been able to obtain rifles and ammunition from the Missouri River nomadic traders, while the Flatheads were yet primitively armed. The advent of McMillan brought a supply of arms and power which restored the prestige of the west-slope Indians and enabled them to wreak vengeance upon their foes, for — on equal footing — they were better fighters and braver men than their eastside enemies. So their tribal records show the turn of the tide in their warfare when McMillan came.

We may, then, assume the correctness of the statement that the first buildings erected in Montana by white men were those which McMillan constructed at the mouth of the Missoula River. Their site was, later, the western boundary of the Flathead Indian reservation. It had for years been one of the meeting places for council among the Pend d'Oreilles. The Upper Pend d'Oreilles spent most of their time in the Moiese Valley; they were "horse" Indians and possessed great herds. The Lower Pend d'Oreilles had their headquarters in the Plains Valley; they were "canoe" Indians and subsisted mainly upon fish. They seldom joined in the expeditions to the buffalo country. They obtained their skins by trading; they were not good riders. But they were great trappers and their store of beaver and mink and other desired pelts was great. They were wealthy and, of all the Salish tribes, they had suffered less in warfare than the others, on account of their comparative remoteness from the Blackfeet country.

Cox, the young Englishman who wrote the book which has been mentioned, was a cabin passenger on the Astor ship *Beaver*. Upon his arrival at Astoria,[3] he was placed in command of an expedition which was ordered to proceed to McMillan's post with a general stock of trading supplies, to replenish the post and to bring back the furs taken in trade from the Indians. The journey to the mouth of the Missoula was made without incident, except that the party was hard put for meat and was forced to kill some of the horses. There was a brief pause in the Spokane country, but no other stop was made on the march. Cox had received instructions from the head of the fur company at Astoria which ordered him, in case he was forced to kill any of his horses, to select the poor ones for slaughter. In his reminiscences, Cox admits that he disregarded this order and, when a horse was butchered, it was one of the best-conditioned in the bunch. He didn't think emaciated steeds would make good eating. Aside from the horse-meat diet, there was nothing on the journey to cause any discomfort.

Indian Hunter's Return, oil by Charlie Russell

It was the day before Christmas, 1813, when Cox and his party arrived at the mouth of the Missoula River and presented their credentials to the factor at McMillan's post.[4] The buildings of the post consisted of a good trading store and a comfortable house for the trader, his clerks and assistants. Here Cox and his companions established themselves for the winter.

A night's rest under roof was agreeable to the travelers and they rose on Christmas morning, refreshed and ready for the celebration of the day. They had not lost track of the date and their English habits called for a proper observance of the holiday, even though they were in a wilderness and in a land where Christmas was then unknown and unrecognized. It was a queer setting for a Christmas celebration — strange, indeed to the men from England and the Atlantic states. But they had a Christmas spirit and they had brought with them, also, some of the Christmas spirits which were in those days considered an indispensable feature to the celebration of the great holiday. They were cheerful over their successful completion of the long march through the forests and the snug cabin furnished a delightful contrast to the tent shelter which had been their protection during the weeks of their slow journey. The glow of the McMillan fire was enough to compensate for the absence of some of the features of the Christmas celebration to which they had been accustomed all their lives and they proceeded to make the most of the material at hand and to crowd all the cheer possible into the day.

Beaver Head and family (Flatheads)

Not long ago, I looked over the valley at the confluence of the rivers and thought of that Christmas celebration of so many years ago. It seemed to me then that the first Christmas celebration in Montana must have been a jolly affair. Certainly there could be no finer setting for such an event. The valley with its background of pine-clad hills, with its rivers and its broad meadows, with all its natural beauty and with the pleasant associations furnished by the permanent shelter and the warm fire — the valley on that Christmas morning almost a hundred years ago must have been a place indeed in which to observe the Christmas holiday. I could imagine the complete satisfaction which Cox must have felt in sleeping under a roof, even if that roof were in an entirely new place and amid surroundings which were strange to him.

Montana is so new that we don't often have an opportunity to write or talk of events more than fifty years removed. So this Christmas within two years of a century ago is a novel theme.[5] This was almost forty years before the Jesuit missionaries came to Montana with the true message of Christmas. Possibly there was a Bible in the McMillan camp, but it isn't likely that it entered to any great extent into that first Christmas celebration. There is, I take it, a distinction between an observance and a celebration, and the affair at McMillan's camp was probably a celebration. We know that rum played an important part in the program, though it was not, evidently, conspicuous enough to cause the celebration to become anything like an orgy as far as the white men were concerned. Cox, in his book, tells us enough about that celebration to warrant the belief that the day was orderly.

When Cox and his companions reached the fort, they found a great camp of Indians there. These were warriors of the Flathead tribe who had just come back from the buffalo country where they got a lot of hides and won a decided victory over the Blackfeet, thus avenging a disastrous defeat of the year before. They had brought back a lot of Blackfeet captives, men and women. The Flatheads had been in camp there for a few days when Cox came with supplies to replenish the depleted stock of McMillan. It was a welcome arrival on that account, as the tobacco had been entirely exhausted and the Indians had learned to like the weed. It was a coincidence that shaped matters so that the Flatheads had planned the torture of their prisoners — for Christmas Day. That they were dissuaded from carrying out in full their program of torture is what makes me believe that the whites did not dip too deeply into the rum.

The hunters had brought in some mountain sheep for the feast of the day and there had been a general distribution of tobacco. From his private store Cox supplied a sack of flour, a sack of rice, a generous supply of tea and coffee, some arrowroot and fifteen gallons of prime rum. Here was the material for the Christmas celebration as Cox had planned it. But he had arrived only the night before and he did not realize, as he made his program that Christmas morning, the influence the Indians would have in upsetting the arrangements. Their enthusiasm came from their joy over their victory and their elation over the prospect of a sufficient supply of rifles and bullets to repeat the defeat of the Blackfeet upon the occasion of the next journey across the range. They had many defeats and indignities to avenge, and it was their nature and their practice to make the torture of their captives atone for many of the humiliations which had been forced upon them. Indeed, the captives expected nothing else, for they had tortured Flatheads and they knew that torture was the inevitable sequel to capture.

In his book, Cox describes the remarkable experiences of that first Montana Christmas. He tells how his expected pleasure was spoiled by the Indians. It is best to quote his words. They are graphic. He says: "We spent a comfortable, comparatively happy Christmas, and by the side of a blazing fire in a warm room, forgot the sufferings we had endured in our dreary progress through the woods. There was, however, in the midst of our festivities a great drawback from the pleasure we should have otherwise enjoyed. I allude to the unfortunate Blackfeet who had been captured by the Flatheads. Having been informed that they were about putting one of the prisoners to death, I went to their camp to witness the spectacle. The man was tied to a tree, after which they heated an old barrel of a gun until it became red hot, with which they burned him on the legs, thighs, neck, cheeks and stomach. Then they commenced cutting the flesh from about the nails, which they pulled out, and next separated the fingers from the hand, joint by joint. During the performance of these cruelties, the wretched captive never winced, and, instead of suing for mercy, he added fresh stimulant to their barbarous ingenuity by the most irritating reproaches, part of which our interpreter translated as follows: 'My heart is strong; you do not hurt me; you cannot hurt me; you are fools; you do not know how to torture; try it again; I do not feel any pain yet. We torture your relatives much better, because we make them cry out loud like little children. You are not brave; you have small hearts; you are afraid to fight.'

"Then, addressing one Flathead in particular, the captive said: 'It was by my arrow that you lost your eye.' Upon which the Flathead darted at him and in a moment with a sharp knife scooped out one of his eyes, at the same time cutting the bridge of his nose almost in two. This did not stop him; with his remaining eye he looked sternly at another and said: 'I killed your brother and I scalped your fool of a father.' The warrior to whom this was addressed instantly sprang at him and separated the scalp from his head. He was then about to plunge a knife into his heart when he was told by the chief to desist. The raw skull, the bloody eyesocket and the mutilated nose presented a horrible appearance, but by no means changed his note of defiance.

" 'It was I,' he said, addressing the chief, 'that made your wife a prisoner last fall — we put out her eyes, we tore out her tongue, we treated her like a dog.' The chief became incensed the moment his wife's name was mentioned; he seized his gun, and, before the last sentence was ended, a ball from it passed through the brave fellow's heart and terminated his sufferings. Shocking, however, as this dreadful exhibition was, it was far exceeded by the atrocious cruelties practiced upon the female prisoners. We remonstrated against such horrible cruelties. They responded by saying the Blackfeet treated their prisoners in the same manner; that it was the course adopted by all red warriors and they could not think of giving up the gratification of their revenge to the foolish and womanish feelings of the white men.

"Shortly after this, we observed a young female led forth, apparently not more than fourteen or fifteen years of age, surrounded by some old women, who were conducting her to one end of the village, whither they were followed by a number of young men. Learning of their intentions to torture this young girl, we renewed our remonstrances but received nearly the same answer as before. Finding them still inflexible and wishing to adopt every means in our power consistent with safety, in the cause of humanity, we ordered our interpreter to acquaint them that, highly as we valued their friendship and much as we esteemed their furs, we would quit their country forever unless they discontinued their unmanly and disgraceful cruelties to their prisoners. This had the desired effect and the miserable captive was led back to her sorrowing group of friends. Our interference was nearly rendered ineffectual by the furious old priestesses who had been conducting her to the sacrifice. They told the young warriors they were cowards, fools and had not the hearts of fleas, and called on them in the names of their sisters, mothers and wives to follow the steps of their forefathers and have their revenge on the dogs of Blackfeet. They began to waver, but we affected not to understand what the old women had been saying. We told them that this act of self-denial on their part was particularly gratifying to the white men and by it they would secure our permanent residence among them, and, in return for their furs, they would be furnished with guns and ammunition sufficient to repel the attacks of their old enemies and preserve their relatives from being made prisoners. This decided the doubtful and the chief promised faithfully that no more tortures would be inflicted upon the prisoners, which I believe was rigidly adhered to, at least during the winter of 1813."

Thus there was something of the real spirit of Christmas in the first Montana

celebration, after all. Cox appears to have acquired some influence over the Flatheads by his square dealing with them. Later in that winter, he persuaded the war chief to return a party of Blackfeet men and women to their own country. The captives were furnished with horses and dried meat — for which Cox paid — and were told to go home. The Blackfeet did not understand it, but they went. The Flatheads were not enthusiastic over the decision of their chief, but they wanted to be sure of their supply of arms and ammunition and they did not dare antagonize the men who furnished them. The first lesson in forbearance was thus taught to the Flatheads on this Christmas Day, 1813 — ninety-eight years ago.[6]

This is a strange story — this tale of the first white Christmas in Montana — but it is vouched for by records which are unimpeachable. The site of the old McMillan post is all that remains. The last vestige of the ruins of those old log cabins has disappeared. The Flatheads have lost even their tribal relations now. But the two great rivers yet mingle their waters in Paradise Valley. And the lesson of peace and good will is better understood than it was on that far-back Christmas day when a young Englishman sought to teach it to the Indians of the wilderness and succeeded to a degree which is surprising when we consider the conditions which attended the effort. I have no doubt that, though he had been shocked, he enjoyed his Montana Christmas dinner all the more for having exercised the Christmas spirit. Thinking it over, I am inclined to recall what I said about this incident and to speak of Cox's Christmas as an observance, after all, and not as a celebration.[7]

A letter from the late Dr. Paul C. Phillips, Montana State University historian and an authority on the fur-trade period, dated Nov. 8, 1955, clarified some understandable errors which the venerable Dean Stone had made in this article: ". . . it must be realized that Dean Stone wrote this at a time [1911] when most early Montana history was preserved only in legends. David Thompson and his Salish House had been lost to memory and the Dean could only learn of them some years later. There was no post at the mouth of the Missoula River. But this article refers to Salish House, built by Thompson in 1809, located on the Clark Fork River a few miles east of Thompson Falls. McMillan was an associate of Thompson, but never 'factor McMillan of the Astor fur traders.' He was credited with building Spokane House, but he built no posts in Montana. While in command of Salish House in 1813 he was working for the North West Company. In December, 1813, Ross Cox was in the employ of the North West Company, although he was in the service of the Astorians until only a month previously."

NOTES

[1] In late November, 1807, at the confluence of the Big Horn River with the Yellowstone, Manuel Lisa built the first fur post in Montana — undoubtedly the first buildings erected. Lisa was an experienced fur trader. His partners were William Morrison and Pierre Menard, both prosperous traders of Kaskaskia, Illinois. And in his party were such competent frontiersmen as George Drouillard and John Colter of the Lewis and Clark expedition. The prospects of Manuel's Fort or Lisa's Fort, as it was variously known, were so encouraging that two years later Lisa organized the St. Louis Missouri Fur Company, including such notables as William Clark, Reuben Lewis (brother of Meriwether), Andrew Henry, and Pierre Choteau, in the firm. In June 1809, they dispatched a party of about 300 men to this first Montana fur-trading post. The following spring they erected a second post at the Three Forks of the Missouri to expand trading into the Blackfeet Country and as far west as the Beaverhead, but because of the hostility of the Blackfeet, this post soon had to be abandoned. Despite its promising beginning, Lisa's Fort, too, had to be abandoned in 1811.

[2] Between the time of the building of Lisa's first and second forts in southern Montana, the Canadians moved into extreme northwestern Montana. In the fall of 1808 David Thompson sent one of his clerks from the North West Company down the Kootenai River to build a rough warehouse and living quarters near the present site of Libby. This was the second trading post to be built in what is now Montana. A year later Thompson built Saleesh House post within a few miles of present Thompson Falls. In 1812, James McMillan, at Saleesh House, built yet another post at the junction of Thompson's River with the Flathead River. This was the post mentioned here as built in 1813.

[3] In the fall of 1811, the 480-ton vessel *Beaver* sailed from England for the mouth of the Columbia. Cox was with a party of North West Company people, including a partner, six clerks and a sizable number of artisans and voyageurs. They sighted land at the mouth of the Columbia River on May 5, 1812, after a hard journey which required six months and three weeks. In the year preceding the Christmas described here Cox with a party of 12 men and 14 loaded horses left "Spokan" on October 17 and reached the Flathead River three days later. Then they suffered two weeks of grueling hardship, traveling through almost incessant snowstorms and subsisting mostly on horsemeat plus one bighorn sheep, until reaching McMillan's post for the first time.

[4] Cox actually spent his first Christmas on American soil en route back from the trip described in note 2, in 1812. Before proceeding to McMillan's post he and his party built a log structure somewhere west of the Flathead country which he mentions here as "the house." His exact statement follows: "When the house was finished I got a good canoe built of cedar planks in which I embarked with six men, and taking leave of Farnham, on the 18th of December [1812] descended the Flathead river on my return to Spokan. Our progress was slow and full of danger . . . the banks in some places so precipitous that for three nights we could not find room enough to make our beds on shore. . . . On the 25th (Christmas Day) into . . . channels . . . and a lake five miles long . . . we were forced to land on a marshy island . . . In my slumbers I imagined I was sitting at my father's table surrounded by the smiling domestic group, all anxious to partake of a smoking sirloin, and a richly dotted plum-pudding, while the juvenile members recounted to each other with triumphant joy the amount of their Christmas boxes. . . ."

[5] This article appeared in the *Missoulian*, Dec. 23, 1911, two years before it was used in the book *Following Old Trails*, published just a century after the Christmas incident.

[6] Or 152 years ago if figured to the forthcoming Christmas, 1965.

[7] Prior to this, in both 1804 and 1805, the Lewis and Clark expedition made rather elaborate preparations and "celebrated" Christmas, first after a journey of more than 1600 miles, in the Mandan village in present North Dakota; and the following year at dreary Fort Clatsop facing the Pacific Ocean, where they moved that Christmas Day into seven crude huts to get out of the rain and "feasted" on "some poor elk, a few roots, and some spoiled pounded fish."

Iroquois in the Far West

By JOHN C. EWERS

I AM NOT aware that any student of the Iroquois, even in his most expansive mood, has claimed that the domain of the Six Nations extended westward from the St. Lawrence through the Great Lakes, across the Plains, over the Rocky Mountains, and down the Columbia River to the shores of the Pacific Ocean. Nevertheless, there is ample evidence that Iroquois Indians were on the Northwestern Plains before the explorations of Lewis and Clark, and that they were in the old Oregon Country nearly three decades before the covered wagons began to roll over the Oregon Trail.

Those were very early times in the northwestern interior, where the span of written history was two and a half centuries shorter than it was on the St. Lawrence. What roles did the Iroquois play in the history of the region? And what influences did they have on the cultures of the primitive western Indians? These are questions which ought to intrigue and challenge the ethnohistorian.

During the quarter-century following the organization of the North West Company in 1784, the Montreal fur trade expanded rapidly westward in lively competition with the Hudson's Bay Company. It was the stimulus of this fur trade that lured Iroquois canoemen and trappers more than 2000 miles toward the setting sun. Probably the first Iroquois to reach the shadow of the Rockies were strong-backed Mohawk canoemen in the service of the North West Company. However, the first sizable movement of woodland Indians to the Upper Saskatchewan appears to have occurred about the year 1789, when some 250 Iroquois, Algonkins and Nipissings, as free trappers, accompanied the canoes of the North West Company traders as far west as Fort Augustus, near present Edmonton, Alberta.

Traders at that post, among them the famed explorer David Thompson, warned these red-skinned greenhorns of the dangers of life on the plains. But the Iroquois would not listen to them. Two of their numbers nearly lost their lives while hunting buffalo. A third was badly mangled by an enraged grizzly bear. Thompson attributed these misfortunes to the fact that the Iroquois had been "accustomed to hunt only timid animals, and keeping about one hundred yards from one another, to cover more ground, did very well for deer; but to hunt . . . bison and bear . . . which are fierce and dangerous, requires the hunters to be close to each other, the one reserving his fire in case of the wounded animal being able to attack them; they were faulty in their hunting until experience taught them better."

White traders also warned the eastern Indians not to winter on the plains south of the Saskatchewan, which were peopled by the strong and warlike Black-feet and their Gros Ventre allies. But a party of seventy-five haughty Iroquois traveled south, entered a Gros Ventre camp, and by signs invited the plainsmen to take part in a gambling match. A quarrel ensued. The Gros Ventres killed some twenty Iroquois, and the rest ran for their lives back to Fort Augustus. With considerable difficulty, friendly Cree Indians dissuaded the irate Iroquois from organizing a revenge raid against the much more numerous and more mobile Gros Ventres.

Next day the Iroquois and Crees joined in a great feast, following which the Iroquois proudly demonstrated their favorite dance of the grand Calumet to the unsophisticated Crees. They were elated when the Crees told them that they had no smoking dance. Then the Iroquois danced their war dance and challenged the Crees to show them theirs, if indeed those simple folk possessed one. After some urging an old Cree warrior stepped forward and danced so expressively that he left the Iroquois speechless with admiration. Later they admitted rather sheepishly that "our dances please ourselves and also the white people and Indians wherever we go, but your dance is war itself to victory and to death."

Thompson reported that this dance contest had a very humbling effect upon the Iroquois. "It seemed to bring them to their senses, and showed them that the Indians of the interior countries were fully as good Warriors, Hunters, and Dancers as themselves. They lost their self conceit and arrogance and became plain well behaved men, left off talking of war, and turned to hunting."

Thereafter these Iroquois avoided the country of the aggressive Blackfeet and Gros Ventres. They took their steel beaver traps westward and northward among the forests at the eastern base of the Rockies. Yet Thompson observed, "None of the natives formed a favorable opinion of the Iroquois; for their whole number they had only about six women with them, each had a husband; and they could not conceive how men could live without women."[1]

Some of these Iroquois eventually married Cree women, and remained in Alberta. Their descendants, known as Michel's Band after their leader Michel Calihoo, did not mix with the Plains Indians south of the Saskatchewan. They were allotted a reserve of 26,600 acres in the vicinity of St. Albert, northwest of Edmonton, by the Canadian government in 1878. Eighty years later (on March 31, 1958) the members of Michel's Band renounced their Indian status and became enfranchised Canadians.[2]

The first Iroquois west of the continental divide may have been free trappers rather than company men. At his new post, Salish House, on Clark's Fork of the

Big Snake, Blood Indian —
painted by Paul Kane, 1848

Broken Arm, Cree warrior — by
George Catlin

Columbia (near present Thompson Falls, Montana), in the month of February, 1810, David Thompson obtained the assistance of six Iroquois Indians "who had come this far to trap Beaver" in searching for birchbark suitable for making canoes.[3] In May of the following year Thompson met three Iroquois "on their way to the Canoe River to trap Beaver, and hunt Moose Deer." He hired one of them, "Charles, a fine steady Iroquois, to accompany us as Bowsman being an excellent Canoe Man." A few days later in a camp of Kutenai Indians he found "Ignace, an Iroquois," and engaged him as steersman. With these two Iroquois occupying strategic positions in his white cedar canoe, Thompson descended the Columbia and reached its mouth on July 15, 1811, only five years and eight months after the men of the Lewis and Clark party had gained their first sight of the Pacific Ocean.[4]

During the next few years the North West Company engaged a number of "Iroquois, Nipissings, and others of the native tribes of Canada" as canoemen and hunters in its western fur trade. Ross Cox, writing in 1817, explained that these Indians were willing to work for lower wages than were the French Canadians. They were strong, ablebodied men, skilled in managing canoes in river rapids and on dangerous inland waterways.[5] This was no mean accomplishment. In 1811 the Superintendent of the Northern Department of the Hudson's Bay Company had bemoaned the fact that he had only one man, a veteran of twenty-seven years' service, who could steer a canoe in rough water.[6] Officials of the North West Company thought so highly of the birchbark canoe that they shipped birch rind from Montreal to London, and thence around Cape Horn to the mouth of the Columbia to supply their far western field men with the basic materials for making these vessels.[7]

The Iroquois were also expert hunters and beaver trappers, and the company officials reasoned that they "might by their example teach others."[8] Thompson regarded the use of castorum as a bait for taking beaver in steel traps as a northeastern Indian invention.[9] If so, the Iroquois may have introduced and certainly must have helped to diffuse the use of this most effective trapping technique into the rich beaver country of the Northern Rockies and upper Columbia Valley. It became the standard beaver-trapping method of the American mountain men.

However, the Iroquois canoemen and trappers were not exactly model hirelings of a big company. At times they could be as independent as hogs on ice. Ross Cox observed that they "are moderately attached to the use of ardent spirits, are rather quarrelsome, revengeful and sometimes insubordinate; and during their periods of intoxication the utmost prudence and firmness are necessary to check their ferocious propensities, and confine them within proper bounds."[10]

In 1816 the North West Company decided to pursue the fur trade of the Oregon country by sending out brigades of trappers and traders on extended expeditions into the best beaver country rather than by trading with the western tribes at fixed posts. The availability of numbers of skilled Iroquois trappers must have been a factor in the making of this decision. In succeeding years numerous Iroquois, as well as men of other eastern tribes, whites of different national origins, as well as a few Hawaiian Islanders, composed the motley crews of these mobile fur brigades. And when the Hudson's Bay Company absorbed the North West Company in 1821, it continued to employ the brigade system in working the Columbia Valley field. Shortly after that event Ross estimated that the Iroquois comprised "nearly a third of the men employed by the Company on the Columbia."[11]

Contemporary accounts of the fur brigades operating in the rich beaver country of the Snake River and its tributaries in present Idaho made frequent mention of the Iroquois. They were men who paid little attention to company policies and felt no strong loyalty for their leaders. The company frowned upon its employees engaging in private trade with the local Indians. But the Iroquois traded guns, ammunition, traps and other items to the Nez Percés, Shoshones or Blackfeet whenever it pleased them to do so. One of them gave ammunition to a Piegan in exchange for a feather headdress. He may have been the first Iroquois to acquire a Plains Indian war bonnet. Some of the Iroquois deserted their brigades to live with Shoshone women in the Indian camps. Others took French leave to accompany the Flatheads on extended and exciting buffalo-hunting excursions over the Rockies and onto the Great Plains.[12]

But the height of Iroquois perfidy, in the eyes of the Hudson's Bay men, occurred in 1825 when a group of Iroquois engagées deserted to the service of rival American trappers of the Rocky Mountain Fur Company, taking their furs with them.[13] Thereafter, a number of Iroquois were found among the mountain men in Wyoming. Alfred Jacob Miller painted a full-length portrait of an Iroquois, clad in western Indian garb, in 1837, probably at the trappers' rendezvous on Green River.[14]

Most Iroquois trappers were referred to in the literature of the west only by their Christian names. Repeated mentions of such common names as Charles,

Pierre, or Ignace make consistent identifications of most individuals virtually impossible. Nevertheless, there was one well known leader among them whose career in the West can be traced with some degree of assurance. Pierre Tivanitagon (more frequently called Grand Pierre or Old Pierre) served for many years in the Snake River brigades. He was killed by Blackfeet in the valley west of the Grand Tetons in 1828, and that valley has since been known as "Pierre's Hole." In 1832 it was the scene of the best known battle between trappers and Indians in the history of the Rocky Mountain fur trade. Yet rough old Jim Bridger flatly declared that Pierre's Hole, with its myriads of wild flowers, its sparkling stream, and its gorgeous mountain background was "the finest valley in the world."[15]

In the prolonged guerrilla warfare between the mountain men and the persistently hostile Blackfeet, at least one Iroquois distinguished himself. Early in June, 1838, Jim Bridger's trappers encountered a Blackfeet war party in the Gallatin Valley just east of the Rockies in Montana. Upon hearing the taunts of the Blackfeet, an old Iroquois trapper (who must remain nameless) turned to his white comrades, made a brief speech in broken English, "stripped himself entirely naked, throwing his powder horn and bullet pouch over his right shoulder and taking his rifle in his hand began to dance and utter the shrill war cry of his Nation." Then he led the trappers' charge which routed the Blackfeet. Next day this same Indian led a second trappers' attack which put the dread Blackfeet to flight.[16]

Writers who knew the Iroquois in the fur trade of the Columbia Valley observed that those Indians had been converted to the Roman Catholic faith before they came west. Alexander Ross, the leader of many a fur brigade, noted that the Iroquois members sang "hymns oftener than paddling songs," but that when they sang sacred music in camp, it was a sure sign that they were plotting some mischief.[17]

It was among the Flathead Indians in the Bitterroot Valley just west of the Rockies in present Montana that Iroquois Catholicism had its strongest impact upon a western tribe. Sometime between 1812 and 1828 a group of some twenty-four Iroquois, under the leadership of Ignace Lamoose, settled among the Flatheads. They are said to have comprised a separate migration, and to have wandered westward until they reached the land of the Flatheads where they were hospitably received and decided to stay. This explanation sounds reasonable only if we may assume that these men were encouraged, and perhaps even guided, by one or more Iroquois who had been among the Flatheads, and had returned east with flattering descriptions of the country and its people.

Ignace Lamoose (also known as Old Ignace or Big Ignace; to distinguish him from a younger Ignace of the same group) was an Iroquois neophyte. Married into the Flathead tribe, he taught the Flatheads to say the Lord's Prayer, make the sign of the cross, and to observe Sunday as a day of rest. They did not hunt, fish, trade or move camp on Sunday. Each Sunday they assembled to listen to the moral teachings of their leader. The service was interspersed with singing and dancing in a great circle after the fashion of the older, native prophet dance. The remainder of the day was a secular holiday in which the Indians indulged their love of horse racing, the hand game, ring game and other gambling delights.

"Water Hole," by Olaf Seltzer

In the summer of 1835 Old Ignace and his two sons journeyed more than 2000 miles southeastward to St. Louis. There the two boys were instructed by Jesuits and were baptized Charles and Francis. Assured by church officials that a priest would be sent to the Flatheads if circumstances permitted, Old Ignace and his sons returned home the following spring. A year passed and no priest came to the Flathead country. So Old Ignace, accompanied by three Flatheads and a Nez Percé Indian, set out again on the long trek to St. Louis. At Ash Hollow on the North Platte the Sioux attacked and killed all five of these Indians.

Two more years passed. Then in the summer of 1839 two Iroquois, Pierre Gaucher and Young Ignace, left the Flathead camp and journeyed the long, hard, dangerous route down the great Yellowstone and Missouri Rivers to St. Louis. After receiving assurances that a priest definitely would be sent to their people the following spring, Pierre set out for home alone to carry the news to the Flatheads. Next spring Young Ignace accompanied the famed missionary Father Pierre Jean De Smet to explore the mission possibilities. In 1841 De Smet returned with helpers to found St. Mary's Mission among the Flathead, the first of a chain of Jesuit missions to the Indians of the northwest.

Pierre and Ignace had told Bishop Rosati in St. Louis that only four of the Iroquois who had emigrated from Canada were still living among the Flatheads in 1839. Nevertheless, what some writers have interpreted as a Flathead quest for Christian missionaries must be recognized as primarily, if not entirely, an Iroquois enterprise. Only Iroquois participated in the two deputations to reach St. Louis to seek a priest, while the abortive second deputation was led by an Iroquois.

In the summer of 1854 Gustavus Sohon, a private on duty with the Railway Exploring Expedition, drew excellent pencil portraits of Young Ignace and Pierre. The former, known to the Flatheads as "Ignace Chapped Lips," was a restless wanderer. Yet his knowledge of the geography of the intermountain region of the northwest proved valuable to white explorers. Lieutenant John Mullan credited

Ignace with pointing out the gorgelike pass over the Coeur d'Alene Mountains over which he built the Mullan Road, the first wagon road over the Northern Rockies, which extended from Fort Benton on the Missouri to Fort Walla Walla on the Columbia. Sohon termed Ignace a "poor but honest and reliable man" who "has not the industry or forethought of his comrade Pierre."

Pierre was the most remarkable Iroquois among the Flatheads in 1854. Sohon captioned his portrait of him "Pierre Kar-so-wa-ta. An Iroquois who came to this country thirty years ago, and settled here. He is the most industrious Indian in the valley, cultivates a small farm raising wheat, oats, potatoes, etc., and owns a large band of cattle; he speaks the mountain French and English, besides several Indian languages." The missionaries hoped that Pierre's success in farming would encourage the Flatheads to give up hunting, fishing and collecting wild plant foods in favor of agriculture and stock raising. But it did not. When the commissioners at the first Flathead Treaty Council in 1855 called upon Iroquois Peter to give his opinion of the relative fertility of two sections of the Flathead domain, Pierre answered honestly that he did not know.[18]

The Crow Reservation also had its pioneer Iroquois farmer. He was Milo Seketer, an Oneida Indian born in New York State, who, in the year 1868 at the age of thirty-one, somehow had forged his way west to the far valley of the Yellowstone River, married a relative of a prominent Crow chief and had been adopted into that tribe. In 1874, Milo applied to the Crow Agent for seed to plant twenty-five acres in oats, wheat and barley. Agent Wright, trying desperately to get his charges to settle down close enough to the Agency to protect it from repeated Sioux raids, looked upon Milo's farming activities as an excellent example to the hunt-minded Crows. But the Crows themselves showed little disposition to forsake the joys of the hunt for the drudgery of grubbing in the earth until the buffalo disappeared a decade later.[19]

Descendants of these Iroquois pioneers in the American West are scattered widely. Gilbert Garraghan found that a group of Catholic Iroquois emigrated from the Rocky Mountains to the site of Kansas City, and that among the first baptisms in the history of that Missouri city, performed February 23, 1834, two were recorded as "Iroquois-Flatheads."[20] The official United States Census for 1910 listed only one Iroquois living in Montana. Yet there are descendants of the early Iroquois in all of the northwestern states. Absorbed in the populations of different western tribes, they have been lost sight of by historians and anthropologists as well as by the census takers.

My knowledge of the Iroquois in the West is based upon a review of the western literature and history, augmented by limited field work on the Flathead Reservation. Western sources generally identify these men simply as "Iroquois," although there are suggestions that some of them hailed from Caughnawaga or St. Regis on the St. Lawrence. I should like to see an Iroquois specialist help to round out this fascinating story by a careful check of archival and traditional sources available in the East. Might not church or local records help to identify some, if not many, of the Iroquois who left home to engage in the fur trade or to find homes among the Indian tribes on the other side of the continent? How much of a drain upon their home communities was the siphoning off of those adventurous, able-bodied canoe men and trappers? Did the stay-at-home Indians regard them as heroes or foolhardy adventurers? Recognizing the Indian's traditional love for his homeland, I should not be surprised to learn that a number of the Iroquois who went west eventually returned.

A fascinating facet of an American heritage, the role of the Iroquois in Far West history is worthy of much deeper probing and scholarship than it has yet received.

NOTES

[1] Thompson, David. *David Thompson's Narrative of his Exploration in Western America, 1784-1812.* Ed. by J. B. Tyrrell. Pp. 311-317. Champlain Society Publication No. 12, Toronto, 1916.

[2] Letter from M. M. Jones, Director, Indian Affairs Branch, Dominion of Canada, Ottawa, June 28, 1962.

[3] Thompson, *op. cit.*, pp. 418-419.

[4] *Ibid.*, pp. 475, 460, 501.

[5] Cox, Ross: *The Columbia River.* Ed. by Edgar I. Stewart and Jane R. Stewart. p. 364. Norman, 1957. Ross, Alexander. *The Fur Hunters of the Far West.* Ed. by Kenneth A. Spaulding. p. 194. Norman, 1956.

[6] Quoted in Phillips, Paul C. *The Fur Trade.* Vol. II, p. 327. Norman, 1961.

[7] Ross, *op. cit.*, p. 55.

[8] *Ibid.*, p. 56.

[9] Thompson, *op. cit.*, pp. 204-205.

[10] Cox, *op. cit.*, p. 364.

[11] Ross, *op. cit.*, p. 194.

[12] *Ibid.*, p. 215.

[13] Irving, Washington, *The Adventures of Captain Bonneville, U. S. A. in the Rocky Mountains and the Far West.* Ed. by Edgeley W. Todd. p. 383. Norman, 1961.

[14] Ross, Marvin C. *The West of Alfred Jacob Miller* (1837). p. 41. Norman, 1951.

[15] Raynolds, W. F. *Report on Exploration of the Yellowstone River.* p. 41. Washington, 1868.

[16] Russell, Osbourne, *Journal of a Trapper.* Aubrey L. Haines, pp. 87-88. Portland, 1955.

[17] Ross, Alexander, *op. cit.*, pp. 194, 211.

[18] All Flathead data are from Ewers, John C. *Gustavus Sohon's Portraits of Flathead and Pend d'Oreille Indians,* 1854. Smithsonian Miscellaneous Collections, Vol. 110, No. 7. 1948.

[19] The National Archives. Indian Office Records. Montana Superintendency. Microfilm Reel 500, 1874-1875.

[20] Garraghan, Gilbert J., S.J., *The Jesuits of the Middle United States.* Vol. II, p. 239. New York, 1938.

"Trading Post," by Olaf Seltzer

Literate Fur Trader

AMONG THE UPPER MISSOURI TRIBES

By JOHN C. EWERS

In North America the white man's application of knowledge of Indian cultures to the solution of practical problems long antedated the development of ethnology as a profession.

The first white men to seek knowledge of the Indian tribes of the Northern Great Plains were the fur traders. In order to gain a precarious foothold in that region, to establish and expand their business, it was imperative that they obtain not only a working knowledge of the Indian languages but also a fund of reliable, useful information on the locations and numbers of the several tribes and of their major subdivisions, their seasonal movements, their basic economies, forms of government, intertribal relations, methods of making war and social customs.

Some of the more intelligent traders (of whom few were educated) recognized that the information they had gathered on these subjects would be of interest to others, even to people far removed from the Indian country. Much of our present knowledge of the cultures of the Northern Plains Indians prior to 1850 has been derived from the writings of these men. The names of several trader-writers readily come to mind: Pierre La Verendrye, Jean-Baptiste Trudeau, Pierre-Antoine Tabeau, François Larocque, Alexander Mackenzie, David Thompson and the two Alexander Henrys. Each of these French or Canadian writers has made a substantial contribution to history and ethnology.

The United States has produced but a single trader whose contributions to the ethnology of the Indians tribes of the Northern Plains are deserving of rank with those of the individuals mentioned. He was Edwin Thompson Denig.

The son of Dr. George Denig, a physician, Edwin Thompson Denig was born in McConnellstown, Huntington County, Pennsylvania, March 10, 1812. The Denig family traced its descent from Herald Ericksen, a chieftain of the Danish island of Manoe in the North Sea. Although Denig's writings show clearly that he was a man of better-than-average education for his time, nothing is known of his activities prior to his entrance into the fur trade at the age of twenty-one. It is most probable that Alexander Culbertson, a native of nearby Chambersburg, encouraged Denig to seek a career in the fur trade. Culbertson, three years Denig's senior, had gained some experience in the trade on St. Peter's River prior to visiting his family in Pennsylvania in the summer of 1832. Denig joined Culbertson in the service of the American Fur Company the following year. Records of that company, in the Missouri Historical Society, St. Louis, dated April 10, 1833, credit Edwin T. Denig with $400 for "Services ending 1 year from date."

Denig first traveled up the Missouri River in the same year, and possibly on the same steamboat, as did the noted German scientist-explorer, Maximilian, Prince of Wied-Neuwied, and Karl Bodmer, author and illustrator respectively of *Travels in the Interior of North America,* a work which for more than a century has been regarded as a basic source on the Indians of the Upper Missouri. For the German prince and his talented artist companion the trip offered an opportunity for a year's adventure and observation in a strange and exciting environment. For Denig it marked the beginning of twenty-three years' residence among the Indians of the Upper Missouri as a fur trader. He became one of many subordinates in the employ of the American Fur Company (which became Pratte, Chouteau & Company in 1834, and continued under the firm name of Pierre Chouteau, Jr., & Company after 1838). This was the principal firm engaged in the fur trade of the Upper Missouri. Its network of posts ranged upriver to the country of the Blackfeet near the Rockies and that of the Crows on the Yellowstone.

Denig's early years in the fur trade were spent in the country of the powerful Teton Dakota. On June 3, 1833, he wrote from Fort Pierre, the principal trading post in Teton country, "I will remain here this year."[3] Four letters from William Laidlaw, bourgeois of Fort Pierre, to Denig indicate that Denig was in charge of a small winter trading house subordinate to Fort Pierre during the winter of 1834-35. This house seems to have been located on Cherry River, a tributary of the Cheyenne, some sixty or more miles northwest of Fort Pierre.

In the spring of 1837, Denig held the position of post bookkeeper at Fort Union on the Missouri near the mouth of the Yellowstone.[4] In a letter to Jacob Halsey at Fort Pierre, dated March 25, 1837, Denig stated that he was well satisfied with his position and much preferred Union to Pierre. This letter also revealed that he had followed the custom of many white traders in that region in taking an Indian wife, and that he was the father of a boy. When smallpox reached Fort Union that summer, Denig became infected but recovered "favorably."[5] Years later he wrote two accounts of the terrible ravages of that plague among the Assiniboins, based upon his first-hand knowledge of the circumstances.[6]

When John James Audubon, the noted artist-naturalist, visited Fort Union in the summer of 1843, Denig cheerfully assisted him in collecting bird and mammal specimens and helped him to obtain the head of an Indian chief from a tree burial near the fort. Denig enlivened Audubon's stay with stories of Indians and animals of the region. At the naturalist's request he wrote a description of Fort Union which has been published in *Audubon and His Journals.* Dated July 30, 1843, this is the earliest known example of Denig's descriptive writing. It is also the most detailed description of the construction and use of that most important In-

Deer Little Woman
(Mrs. Edwin T. Denig)

Charles Larpenteur

Edwin T. Denig

dian trading post on the Upper Missouri. Denig stated that he was then in charge of the office of the fur company at the fort, a position comparable to that of chief clerk. His old friend, Alexander Culbertson, was Fort Union's bourgeois at that time.

Charles Larpenteur, a fellow subordinate in the service of the company, criticized Denig severely for his love of liquor, mentioning an occasion in January, 1844, when Denig was unable to make a trip to Woody Mountain to trade for robes with the Crees and Chippewas because he had imbibed too freely.[7] Drinking was common among field employees of the company, forced to spend long, monotonous winters at isolated posts in the cold north country. Denig was no teetotaler. In a letter to Alexander Culbertson, dated December 1, 1849, he wrote, "I would also request as a great favor if you will bring me up a keg say 5 galls of good old Rye, to have the pleasure of drinking your health occasionally. I can hardly look upon myself as the infernal drunkard represented and presume as no accident happened to the 2 g.' keg of last spring, the 5 g.' keg will be equally safe." In the same letter Denig reported, "Next year after the post has been thoroughly purged of all superfluities In a trade of 400 packs, I shall clear 6000$ if 500 packs are traded 9000$ will be the profit . . . you can assure yourself of my showing a neat Balance to our credit."[8] This was the kind of report on Denig's activities that the company preferred to take seriously.

In the spring of 1847, Larpenteur[9] had referred to Denig as "the clerk at Fort Union." Denig's letter to Culbertson, quoted above, indicates that he was promoted to the position of bourgeois before the winter of 1849-50. Fort Union not only was "the principal and handsomest trading post on the Missouri River," as Denig himself termed it, it was also the company's key point in its control of the Indian trade of the Upper Missouri. There the Assiniboin, Plains Cree and some Crow and Chippewa Indians traded. From Fort Union, employees, trade goods and supplies were dispatched to the upriver Blackfeet and Crow posts, and to it came their returns of furs and skins in the spring for reshipment downriver to St. Louis. No field employee of the company then held a more responsible position than did Denig, except for his friend Alexander Culbertson, who had been promoted to general supervisor of the company's posts on the Upper Missouri.

Denig again rendered valuable services to naturalists during the winter of 1849-50. At the request of Alexander Culbertson and with the assistance of Ferdinand Culbertson, Denig prepared skins and skulls of birds and mammals of the Upper Missouri for use in scientific study. On December 1, 1849, he wrote Culbertson: "I am progressing with my specimens of animals for you as I have said I would & have already prepared the White Wolf, the Beavers, the War Eagle, the Caputi Argali or Antelope's head, and sundry other small matters which will be in order to put into every museum you think propper."[10]

The following June, Thaddeus Culbertson, Alexander's brother, visited Fort Union. His Journal, under date of June 17, comments: "We were received very kindly by the gentlemen of the post, Mr. E. T. Denig and Ferdinand Culbertson. They showed me quite a good collection of stuffed skins made by them for Professor Baird, at the request of my brother. This must have cost a great deal of labor and considerable expense, and they deserve many thanks from the students of natural history for whose benefit this collection was made."[11] Thaddeus Culbertson brought back many, if not all, of these specimens for the collections of the Smithsonian Institution, which was then only in the fourth year of its existence. The earliest accession book of the division of mammals of the United States National Museum records specimens from "E. T. Denig and A. Culbertson." A few of them are specifically indicated as "Prepared by Denig." Several other specimens include skins of the wolverine, plains wolf, lynx, beaver, mountain sheep, antelope, whitetailed jack rabbit and grizzly bear, the head of a bison, and skulls of elk, mule deer and bison. Thus in 1850 the Smithsonian acquired an extensive representation of the mammals of the Upper Missouri as a direct result of the interest and labors of Denig and the Culbertsons.

Father Pierre Jean de Smet, noted missionary to the Indians of the Northwest, spent more than two weeks at Fort Union in the summer of 1851. He found in Denig a man who knew the Upper Missouri tribes well and who was sympathetic toward them. Between the famous Catholic priest and Denig, who was Swedenborgian in his beliefs, a firm friendship developed that endured for the remainder of Denig's life. It is likely that during this visit to Fort Union, De Smet encouraged Denig to write for him a number of sketches of the manners and customs of the Assiniboin and neighboring tribes. Apparently Denig lost little time in initiating the project, for in September of the same year Kurz observed that Denig was recording "stories" of "Indian legends and usages" for "Pere De Smet."[12]

We may never know the full extent of Denig's writings for Father De Smet. However, it is possible to trace some of them with precision through the published correspondence of the priest. Father De Smet expressed his "gratitude for the manuscript you have had the kindness to prepare for me, and which I shall be most glad to receive and peruse," in a letter to Denig written in May, 1852. By the next fall the priest had received the manuscript. On September 30 he wrote, thanking Denig profusely for "your very interesting series of narratives. . . . I have read the present series with absorbing attention and growing interest. My imagination has often carried me back to scenes long familiar to my experience and to others of a general and kindred nature which your pen has so well portrayed, in your valuable descriptions of their religious opinion, of their great buffalo hunt, their war expeditions, and in the histories of old Gauche and of the family of Gros Francois."[13]

Father De Smet incorporated much of Denig's information in a series of letters to Father Terwecoren, editor of the *Precis Historiques*, Brussels, Belgium. These letters were reprinted in English in the book *Western Missions and Missionaries: A Series of Letters by Rev. P. J. De Smet*, published in New York City in 1863. Letters X through XIII, comprising pages 134-205 of that volume, deal in turn with "Religious Opinions of the Assiniboins," "Indian Hunts," "Indian Warfare," and "Tchatka" (a biographical sketch of old Gauche). In the thirteenth letter Father De Smet acknowledged his debt to Denig. "I cite the authority of Mr. Denig, an intimate friend, and a man of high probity, from whom I have received all the information that I have offered you concerning the Assiniboins, and who resided among them during twenty-two years." Denig's account of the family of LeGros Francois was not published in De Smet's lifetime. Father De Smet recorded the story in longhand in the Linton Album, from which source it was obtained for publication in Chittenden and Richardson's *Life, Letters and Travels of Father Pierre Jean De Smet* 1905.

Rudolph Kurz, a young Swiss artist, possessed of a burning desire to sketch and paint wild Indians in their home environment, spent seven months at Fort Union, from September 4, 1851, to April 11, 1852. *The Journal of Rudolph Friederich Kurz*, published by the Bureau of American Ethnology in 1937,[14] contains a vivid account of life at the fort during that period. Frequent references to Denig in this journal provide an insight into his character that cannot be found in Denig's own, very impersonal writings.

Before his arrival at Fort Union, Denig had been represented to Kurz by a former, dissatisfied employee as a "hard man, liked by nobody ... keeps two Indians wives ... squanders all he has on them; begrudges anything paid the employees, oppresses the engagees with too much work, is never satisfied, etc."

On first meeting Denig, Kurz described him as, "a small, hard featured man wearing a straw hat, the brim of which was turned back . . . He impressed me as a very prosy fellow. He stopped Bellange [Kurtz' traveling companion from Fort Berthold to Union] short, just as the latter was beginning a long story he wished to tell on the other hand, he ordered supper delayed on our account, that we might have a more plentiful and better meal. A bell summoned me to the first table with Mr. Denig and the clerks. My eyes almost ran over with tears. There was chocolate, milk, butter, omelet, fresh meat, hot bread — what a magnificent spread! I changed my opinion at once concerning this new chief; a hard, niggardly person could not have reconciled himself to such a hospitable reception in behalf of a subordinate who was a total stranger to him."[15]

It is apparent, however, from Kurz' later observations, that Denig exercised an authority over his men that would have been the admiration of his seafaring Danish ancestors. Denig's fur-trading crew of some fifty men included workmen of a score of nationalities, many of whom were neither skilled nor ambitious. He kept them "strictly under his thumb." When they worked satisfactorily he offered some diversion for all of them. If they shirked, he limited their victuals. He expected his clerks, as good petty officers, to give him moral and, if need be, physical support in handling his men. He insisted on economy and efficiency on the part of his clerks to keep the trading-post overhead at a minimum.

Kurz observed that Denig had risen to his position of command as a result of "his commercial knowledge, his shrewdness, and his courage at the posts where he

The One Horn, Minniconjou chief (painted by Catlin; probably seen by artist when he visited Ft. Union 1832)

was earlier employed."[16] As a successful trader he also had to gain and hold the friendship of the Indians. Kurz learned that Denig had "made a thorough study of Indian life — a distinct advantage to him in trade."[17] But it was not enough for him to know the Indian languages, their manners and customs. He must conduct himself in such a way as to win their respect. Denig believed that most Indians esteemed white men for those talents they did not possess themselves; that though he had a keen eye and was a sure shot, the Indians would never admire him for his hunting ability. He thought white men who adopted Indian dress and tried to follow Indian customs only succeeded in degrading themselves in the eyes of the Indians. Although Denig had two Indian wives, he encouraged them to live as much like white women as was possible in the Indian country. Records of Denig's purchases from the company[18] tell of his importation of fine clothes for his wives and children, fancy foods for his table, candy and toys for his children. He kept up with the news and thoughts of the day by reading newspapers and books on philosophy and religion brought upriver from St. Louis. Edwin T. Denig was far removed from the crude hunter-trapper-trader stereotype of fiction. His way of life undoubtedly helped him to maintain the high degree of objectivity toward Indian cultures (and historic fact) evidenced in his writings.

In his long conversations with Kurz, recorded in the latter's journal, Denig revealed a very limited appreciation of art, but a lively interest in religion and morals, about which he expressed very definite opinions. One evening Denig came around to the subject of love. "Love — damn the word! — is a madness in the brain; a contagious disease, like smallpox or measles. I would rather have a dose of epsom salts than to recall the folly of first love-pure love. If it is not stopped, that lunacy makes one ridiculous, childish, ashamed of himself." Kurz, a confirmed romanticist, probably swallowed hard before adding: "There is always something true and worthwhile in what he says, only he expresses himself in strong language."[19]

Much of their conversation concerned the Indians, in whom both men were interested. Denig enjoyed telling the young artist stories of his experiences among the Indians, of tribal customs and personalities. He also read to Kurz from the manuscript he was preparing for Father De Smet and told him of his concern for the future of the natives. He went out of his way to give Kurz opportunities to meet chiefs and outstanding warriors who visited the fort, to attend councils he held with these Indian leaders, to obtain Indian artifacts and animal specimens for his collections, and to study the wildlife of the plains in the field. Denig seemed to have been as eager to help this unknown Swiss artist as he had been to aid the famous Audubon and Father De Smet.

In the middle of the nineteenth century, Henry R. Schoolcraft, of the Office of Indian Affairs in Washington, was busy collecting information on the Indians of the United States. To students of the Indians and to individuals who had traveled extensively or lived in the Indian country he sent copies of a printed circular of *Inquiries Respecting the History, Present Condition, and Future Prospects of the Indian Tribes of the United States.* One of these circulars reached Denig at

Fort Union. Cooperative, as he had always been in furnishing information about Indians to earnest inquirers, Denig systematically set about assembling data for Schoolcraft. He submitted an Assiniboin vocabulary of more than 400 words which Schoolcraft published (1854) in the fourth volume (pp. 416-422) of his imposing six-volume compilation, *Historical and Statistical Information Respecting the History, Condition and Prospects of the Indian Tribes of the United States.* Eight years later F. V. Hayden referred to this as "the most important vocabulary of the language" of the Assiniboin "prepared by Mr. E. T. Denig, an intelligent trader."[20]

Denig also painstakingly prepared answers to the 348 questions regarding Indian cultures asked in Schoolcraft's circular. His reply was made in the form of a *Report to Hon. Isaac I. Stevens, Governor of Washington Territory, on the Indian Tribes of the Upper Missouri,* a manuscript of 451 pages. Internal evidence in the manuscript itself and a statement in Denig's letter of transmittal to Governor Stevens referring to the author's "constant residence of 21 years among the prairie tribes" attest that the manuscript was completed in 1854. After remaining in manuscript form for seventy-six years, it was published in the Forty-Sixth Annual Report of the Bureau of American Ethnology in 1930. Although, as its published title *Indian Tribes of the Upper Missouri* implies, the work was intended to cover all of the tribes of the region from the Dakota to the Crow and Blackfeet, the wealth of detailed information presented refers primarily to the Assiniboin. Much of the material on the other tribes takes the form of brief comparative statements. As it stands, Denig's *Indian Tribes of the Upper Missouri* certainly is the most detailed and important description of Assiniboin Indian culture in mid-nineteenth-century buffalo days known to ethnology and history.

By 1854 Denig had resided continuously in the Indian country for twenty-one years, except for one brief visit to his relatives in the States in the summer of 1845. His diligence and ability had brought him success as a fur trader. He held partnership in the company, receiving one-twenty-fourth of its profits from the trade. Yet in a letter to Bishop Miege, September 1, 1854, he revealed his intention "to leave this country in a year or two."[21] This decision was based primarily on his consideration for the welfare of his children. There were no schools in the Upper Missouri country. Denig had sent his eldest son, Robert, to Chicago to be educated.[22] Now he had three other children to be considered — Sarah (born August 10, 1844), Alexander (born May 17, 1852) and Ida, (born August 22, 1854).

In the summer of 1855 Denig took his Assiniboin wife, Deer Little Woman, and his mixed-blood children to visit his brother, August, in Columbus, Ohio. In St. Louis, en route, Edwin Thompson Denig and Deer Little Woman were formally married by Father Daemen and their children were baptized. Denig's daughter, Sarah, recalled that the family found the climate in Columbus too warm for them. Otherwise they might have settled there. Instead they returned to Fort Union by a roundabout route, traveling from St. Louis to St. Paul and the Red River Settlement of present Manitoba by horse and wagon. Throughout this journey Denig was searching for a suitable future home for his family. The party reached Fort Union on November 28, 1855, after a wagon trip of nearly three months' duration. Much of the route passed through unsettled Indian country.[23]

The Denigs spent the winter at Fort Union. In the middle of the following year the family moved to the Red River Settlement in Canada. Denig received a payment from P. Chouteau, Jr., and Company at Fort Union July 13, 1856.[24] His will, dated September 12, 1856, at Red River Settlement, Red River of the North, must have been drawn up shortly after the family's arrival there. Very little is known of Denig's life in Canada during the next two years. He placed Sarah and Alexander in Catholic schools. He is said to have "established himself as a private trader on the White Horse Plains west of the present city of Winnipeg."[25] His friend De Smet wrote him January 13, 1858, "I rejoice greatly at your success and in the welfare of your children."[26]

Later in the summer of 1858 Edwin T. Denig was stricken with an inflammation that his daughter, Sarah, believed was appendicitis. He died on the White Horse Plains, September 4, 1858, and was buried in the Angelican cemetery near the present village of Headingly, Manitoba, Canada.[27] He was only forty-six at the time of his death.

The Denig manuscript comprises a portion of the text for a book of extensive proportions. The manuscript is in two parts. Although the pages of one part are numbered 1 to 153 in pencil, pages 61 to 92 are missing. Present are chapter 1, comprising the author's introduction; chapters 2 and 3, entitled "Of the Sioux;" chapter 4, entitled "Of the Arickaras;" the latter and undoubtedly the greater part of chapter 6, comprising a description of the Assiniboin; and chapters 7 and 8, entitled "Of the Crees or Knisteneau." It is probable that the missing chapter 5 described the Mandan and/or Hidatsa. The second part, entitled "Of the Crow Nation," is separately paged (pp. 1-75). However, there can be little doubt that this was intended as a later chapter in the same book.

In his opening chapter Denig clearly states the purpose of his book:

> It would be well for the public if everyone who undertook to write a book was thoroughly acquainted with the subject of which he treats, but unfortunately this is not the case — authors spring up everywhere, and the community is saddled with an immense effusion of literature, the greater part of which when divested of the writer's own fancies and feelings, and submitted to the test of truth and experience, amounts to nothing. This is particularly the case in most of the works purporting to describe the actual life and intellectual capacity of the Indians of North America; much evil has been the consequence of error thus introduced, bad feelings engendered, and unwise legislation enforced, which will continue until our rulers are enlightened as to the real state of their Government, character, organization, manners and customs, and social position. Most information extant on these heads has been published by transient visitors amongst the tribes, travelers through a portion of their country, or collected from rude and half-civilized interpreters whose knowledge is but a degree in advance of their savage parents, and also impose upon their credulous hearers tales of fiction mingled with some ceremonies; which with a hastily collected and ill-digested mass of information form the

basis of works by which the public are deceived as to the real state of the Indians. Even foreigners who have possibly passed a winter at some of the trading posts in the country, seen an Indian dance or two or a buffalo chase, return home, enlighten Europe if not America with regard to Indian character; which is only the product of their own brains and takes its color from the peculiar nature of that organ. Hence we find two sets of writers both equally wrong, one setting forth the Indians as a noble, generous, and chivalrous race far above the standard of Europeans, the other representing them below the level of brute creation. People cannot form an opinion in this way — a correct knowledge of any nation, and more particularly of a savage one, must be and only is attained by being as it were raised in their camps, entering into their feelings and occupations, understanding their language, studying their minds and motives, and being thoroughly acquainted with their government, customs and capacities.

Of the few traders who reside in the Upper Missouri territory, but a small portion have had the advantage of education, and these are so variously and constantly occupied as not to be disposed to apply their talents to writing histories, indeed it has been their policy to keep people in ignorance as to the trade and real disposition of the Indians, thereby preventing competition and discouraging visitors, both of which greatly militate against their interests. Neither do the gentlemen at the head of the Indian trade desire on all occasions to advance their opinions to persons who cannot, or will not, appreciate them. Truth, though mighty, will not at all times prevail, although stranger than fiction, cannot be realized. The strange sights and occurrences incident to the country, be they ever so truthfully described, are rejected by previously formed opinion, and the narrator stigmatized, even in the mildest language he could expect, as a teller of strange stories. The author of these pages feels this in the commencement but cares little about it, having set out with the determination to present facts in as true a light as his powers admit, and with the experience of 22 years amongst the Indians, speaking their language, and having been placed in every possible position that men can be amongst them, presumes his opinions are entitled to respect.

Denig's first concern seems to have been with setting the record straight regarding the ethnology of the Upper Missouri tribes. He does not name those individuals who were the objects of his caustic jibes in the first paragraph quoted above. There can be little doubt, however, that they are aimed primarily at George Catlin and Prince Maximilian, whose books, published a decade earlier, had gained wide circulation. Doubtless Denig was familiar with them. Indian-loving Catlin had spent eighty-six days on the Upper Missouri from Fort Pierre northward in the summer of 1832. Maximilian passed the greater part of a year on the Upper Missouri in 1833-34, wintering among the Mandans. In his criticism of those writers, Denig revealed the common disdain of the old hand for the greenhorn. In the case of Maximilian, certainly this strong criticism does not appear to be justified.

In the letter of transmittal accompanying his *Indian Tribes of the Upper Missouri*, Denig had expressed his dissatisfaction with his organization of that report, due to the limitations imposed upon it by the nature of the questions asked by Schoolcraft and which he attempted to answer. In his book he sought to remedy that defect by adopting a new, carefully planned organization of his data. He explained this plan in his introductory chapter as follows:

The plan intended to be pursued in these pages, that the reader may understand the different traits of Indian character without difficulty or confusion, is,
first, to give a short history of each tribe, its geographical position and other peculiarities; after which an inquiry will be instituted into their government, condition, manners and customs as a body. Most customs and opinions are common to
all tribes, but wherever any great difference is observable, or marked traits be
noticed, they will be found in the compendiums of their separate history. This is
necessary to avoid a constant repetition that would follow if detailed accounts of
each tribe were presented.

The Indians of the Upper Missouri territory may be divided into two classes,
the roving and the stationary tribes — the former comprising the Sioux, Crows,
Assiniboines, Crees and Blackfeet; the latter, the Grosventres, Mandans and Arikaras. My object is to show the state of these Indians in former times, what their
present conditions and what circumstances have tended toward their general advancement or decline; and after a general and minute research into all their motives, acts, religion, government and ceremonies, conclude with a history of the
American fur trader embodying many statements of various matters incident to the
lives of trappers and traders.

This was an ambitious program of research and writing. Doubtless Denig
was unable to complete it before his death. Certainly the manuscript in the Missouri Historical Society contains no descriptions of the Blackfeet, Grosventres
(Hidatsa), or Mandans; no general description of the common factors in the cultures of the Upper Missouri tribes; and no history of the fur trade such as he
promised in his introductory chapter. If Denig wrote chapters dealing with all or
any of these topics those portions of his manuscript either have been destroyed
or their present locations are not known.

Charles van Ravenswaay, director of the Missouri Historical Society, has
kindly permitted this editor to make a typed copy of the entire manuscript in the
collections of that Society. Selected chapters were edited for publication by the
Missouri Historical Society. Mr. van Ravenswaay granted permission to the Smithsonian Institution to publish Denig's description of the Crow Indians.

Of The Crow Nation, from internal evidence, was written in the winter of
1856. It is the last known writing by Denig in the field of ethnology. In accordance
with the plan for his volume, Denig did not intend this as a detailed description
of Crow culture. Rather it stresses those aspects of the history and culture of that
tribe that were unique or more highly specialized among the Crows than among
neighboring tribes. The sources of Denig's information on the Crows are not revealed in his writings. We do not know the extent to which Denig traveled in
Crow country. It is certain, however, that he met parts of that tribe repeatedly
over a period of two decades when they came to trade at Fort Union. Undoubtedly
he also received considerable information on the Crows from Robert Meldrum
and other employees of the Chouteau Company who had lived many years with
the Crows as traders.

Denig's frequent errors in dating events suggest that he wrote from memory
rather than from a journal or diary maintained over the years, and that he had a
poor memory for dates. Some of the events he described may have become some-

what distorted through years of verbal retelling prior to the time he first recorded them in writing. Denig was not an infallible authority. However, he was an objective observer of the Indian tribes of his acquaintance. His long experience enabled him to distinguish significant differences as well as basic similarities among neighboring tribes of the same culture area. He knew Indians well enough to view them as human beings, rather than noble redskins or inhuman brutes. In *Of The Crow Nation*, Denig has written one of the most valuable descriptions of Crow Indian culture in nineteenth-century buffalo days known to ethnology. In many respects this account substantiates and elaborates previously published descriptions of that tribe. It also contains significant data on Crow history, biography and culture that cannot be found in any other source.

NOTES

[1] Edwin T. Denig's close friend and long-time colleague in the fur trade of the Upper Missouri, Alexander Culbertson, survived Denig by 21 years. Prior to 1936, the Missouri Historical Society of St. Louis purchased from A. C. Roberts, of Spokane, Washington, a collection of manuscript materials dealing with several Indian tribes of the Upper Missouri. Mr. Roberts stated that this collection had been in the possession of his recently deceased mother, Julia Culbertson Roberts, who in turn received it from her father, Alexander Culbertson. The writings bore internal evidence of composition in 1855 and 1856, but their authorship was not known. In the archives of the Missouri Historical Society this material became known as the Culbertson manuscript.

[2] Early in February 1949, Mr. Ewers read parts of the Culbertson manuscript in the Missouri Historical Society. He was impressed with its historical and ethnological significance. It appeared to him that the author's style, as well as some of the specific information in the manuscript resembled closely that of Edwin T. Denig's published work, *Indian Tribes of the Upper Missouri*. Upon request, the Bureau of American Ethnology kindly furnished Mr. Ewers an example of Denig's known handwriting in the form of photographs of his handwritten will, executed September 12, 1856, which he was able to compare with the writing in the Missouri Historical Society manuscript early in March of the same year. Similarities between the handwriting of the two documents appeared so marked as to justify obtaining the opinion of handwriting experts. Accordingly photostats of pages of the manuscript together with photographs of the will were submitted to the Federal Bureau of Investigation. On April 15, 1949, handwriting experts of the FBI Laboratory, Washington, D. C., confirmed Ewer's conclusion that the handwriting of the two documents was by the same individual. Thus nearly a century after it was written an important Denig manuscript was discovered.

[3] Denig-Sarpy letter, Missouri Historical Society.

[4] Larpenteur, 1898, *Forty Years a Fur Trader on the Upper Missouri*, Vol. I, p. 122.

[5] *Ibid.*, p. 132.

[6] Denig, 1930, pp. 399-400; Denig Mss., Missouri Hist. Soc., pp. 99-100.

[7] Larpenteur, 1898, Vol. I, pp. 162, 184-186.

[8] Letter in Missouri Historical Society.

[9] Larpenteur, 1898, Vol. I, p. 250.

[10] Letter in Missouri Historical Society.

[11] Culbertson papers, 1851, p. 121.

[12] Kurz, 1937, p. 133.

[13] Chittenden and Richardson, 1905, Vol. IV, pp. 1215-16, 1482.

[14] Kurz, 1937, p. 101.

[15] *Ibid.*, p. 120.

[16] *Ibid.*, p. 123.

[17] *Ibid.*, p. 126.

[18] Missouri Hist. Soc.

[19] Kurz, 1937, p. 180.

[20] Hayden, 1862, p. 381.

[21] Letter in archives of Missouri Province Educational Institute, St. Louis, Mo.

[22] Kurz, 1937, p. 136.

[23] Historical Society of Montana *Contributions*, Vol. X, p. 151. 1940.

[24] Company records, Missouri Hist. Soc.

[25] Vickers, 1948, p. 136.

[26] Chittenden & Richardson, 1905, Vol. 4, p. 1499.

[27] Vickers, 1948, p. 136.

The Spirit of the Past

Watching for the Signal

The Chief and His Staff

The Wood Gatherer

Wolf

Shot in the Hand

Crow camp on the Little Big Horn

Crow war group

Left to right:

Crow war chief

Two Leggings

Medicine Crow

Crow medicine tipi

Crows dressed for winter campaign

Upshaw, educated Crow who
assisted Curtis in field work

The Bull Chief

RED GODS AND WHITE

Famed Indian medicine tree on U.S. 93, East Fork of Bitter Root River

The Ram's Horn Tree

AND OTHER SACRED MEDICINE TREES OF THE FLATHEADS

By GEORGE F. WEISEL, JR.

ON THE EAST BANK of the East Fork of the Bitter Root River in Montana, between the towns of Darby and Sula, is a large yellow pine called the Ram's Horn Tree. The United States Forest Service years ago marked it as such with a placard where Highway 93 runs within a few feet of its trunk. Some controversy exists as to whether or not it is the original tree described in ancient Indian legend and in the earliest journals of fur traders. If so, it is one of the earliest curiosities to be noted in the region, and a stark reminder of Indian religion. The first written account of a ram's horn tree in this vicinity was made by the fur trader, Alexander Ross. He camped near one on March 11, 1824.[1]

> In no place of our trip, Hell's Gates itself scarcely excepted, did we meet such a gloomy and suspicious place. At every bend of the river, wild and romantic scenes opened to view; the river alone preventing the hill and cliffs from embracing each other. We had to cross and recross twelve times in half as many miles, until we reached a rocky and slippery path on its margin, where grew a few pine-trees, through which the narrow and intricate path led.
>
> Out of one of the pines I have just mentioned, and about five feet from the ground, is growing up with the tree a ram's head, with the horns still attached to it; and so fixed and embedded is it in the tree, that it must have grown up with it; almost the whole of one of the horns, and more than half of the head is buried in the tree; but most of the other horn, and part of the head protrudes out at least a foot. We examined both, and found the tree scarcely two feet in diameter. Here we put up at an early hour, and called the place Ram's Horn encampment.
>
> Our Flathead Indians related to us a rather strange story about the ram's head. Indian legend relates that one of the first Flathead Indians who passed this way attacked a mountain ram as large and stout as a common horse; that on being wounded, the fierce animal turned round upon his pursuer, who taking shelter behind the tree, the ram came against it with all his force, so that he drove his head through it; but before he could get it extracted again, the Indian killed him, and took off the body, leaving the head as a memento of the adventure. All Indians reverence the celebrated tree, which they say, by the circumstances related, conferred on them the power of mastering and killing all animals; hundreds, therefore, in passing this way sacrifice something as a tribute to the ram's head; and one of the Iroquois, not to incur the displeasure of the god of hunters, hung a bit of tobacco on the horn, to make his hunting propitious.[2]

157

Another participant in the fur trade, Warren A. Ferris, passing through the same locale in 1833, noted a ram's horn tree and was impressed enough to write in his journal:

> On the east side of the Bitter Root river, there is a singular curiosity, that I had not before observed, because it was situated under some rocky bluffs, almost impassable to horsemen, the proper road being on the west side of the river; it is the horn of an animal, called by hunters, "Bighorn," but denominated by naturalists "Rocky Mountain Sheep"; of a very large size, of which two-thirds of its length from the upper end, is entombed in the body of a pine tree, so perfectly solid and firmly, that a heavy blow of an axe did not start it from its place. The tree is unusually large and flourishing, and the horn in it some seven feet above the ground. It appears to be very ancient and is gradually decomposing on the outside, which has assumed a reddish cast. The date of its existence has been lost in the lapse of ages and even tradition is silent as to the origin of its remarkable situation. The oldest Indians can give no other account of it, than it was there precisely as at present, before their father's great grandfathers were born. They seldom pass it without leaving some trifling offering, as beads, shells, or other ornaments — tokens of their superstitious veneration of it. As high as they can reach, the bark of the tree is decorated with their trifles.[3]

Indians invariably conceived legends about any oddity, however slight, and the Ram's Horn Tree certainly did not escape their attention. As compared to the legend narrated in Alexander Ross' account, the more recent tales are much embellished. One published years later, in 1901, has the inevitable "Coyote" as hero of the incident, and suggests that more than a single tree was involved.

> Coyote took to the trail again, and went up to Medicine Tree between Ross's Hole and Darby. Coyote was going down the mountainside, and a big Mountain Sheep ran after him. There were big trees standing at the bottom of the mountain.
> Coyote ran and the Mountain Sheep ran after him. Then all at once Coyote ran out to one side. The Mountain Sheep ran on down the mountain and right into the big trees at the bottom. One of his horns stuck in the side of the big tree. It is up high now and can be seen quite plainly.
> Every time the Indians go there, they give earrings or beaded moccasins or anything they happened to have to that horn, because it is big medicine. That is why the trees are called Medicine Trees.[4]

The Indians' story kept growing with the years; undoubtedly their imaginations were encouraged by the interest evoked by the whites, until in about 1929 it went like this:

> One day while the Coyote was traveling, he accidentally stepped on something which cried out painfully, "Oh, you have broken my leg! I was just about warning you of some danger of which you are almost within reach. But as you have injured me, I will not."
> As the Coyote looked down, he saw a poor little lark with a broken leg. "I did not mean it," said the Coyote pitifully, "do not worry, I will heal it for you,"

Alexander Ross

so he did so magically. "Well now, listen," said the lark, "a little ways farther you will hear someone calling you. It is the Mountain Sheep Buck, who kills everyone who goes by, as he is very quick and powerful, and when you meet him you must be very watchful, for he may kill you."

"Thank you," said the Coyote, "I will see if I don't put an end to that wicked beast." And so Coyote went on and a little ways farther he heard someone calling, "Coyote, come this way." He went on until he saw the Mountain Sheep Buck coming down to meet him. They both walked up to each other until they were very close together, then they stood watching each other closely. The Buck said in a warning voice, "What right have you to tread over my private land without my consent? Whoever does so, it costs him his life." "Is that so," said the Coyote, "and have you killed many already?" "Certainly," said the Mountain Sheep Buck, "countless numbers of them." "Is that so," said the Coyote, "you must be very powerful." "Certainly I am," said the Mountain Sheep Buck. "Well," said the Coyote, "let me see how powerful you are with those horns. Strike this pine and let me see how deep they will go into it."

During all this time, the Coyote had his eyes pretty close. "All right," said the Mountain Sheep Buck, and suddenly jumped up and struck for it, and struck it way high above the trunk with one of his horns deep into the tree, and before he could get himself off, the Coyote was right there, holding fast to the tree.

The next moment Coyote drew his great flint knife and cut off the head of the Mountain Sheep Buck, and the body dropped to the ground. Then he cut off the head from the horns which were stuck in the tree, then the head dropped to the ground, and then he cleaned out the horn and jumped to the ground. He took the head and body and threw them up on the hillside. They splashed the rocks, and they only left a print carved on the rocks — a human face, looking toward the horn stuck in the tree.

After all this was done, the Coyote stood by the tree and said, "In the future generation this tree will be a Medicine Tree to all tribes."[5]

The present-day Flatheads are not able to augment this one, although they have been given the chance to do so. Their legends are essentially the same.

Another bit of early Indian lore demonstrates the powerful medicine of the pine. It seems that a Nez Percé, on his way to hunt buffalo with a party of the Flatheads, boastingly demonstrated his scorn of the tree by firing a rifle ball into its trunk. Directly afterward, while running some buffalo on the plains east of the mountains, his horse fell and he was killed. The Flatheads said it was because the Nez Percé had spoiled his luck by mistreating the Ram's Horn Tree.

Under the sponsorship of Sid Ward, annual celebrations were held around the tree by Indians and whites during September or October of the early 1920's. The whole affair was purely a white man's innovation. "Thousands of valley people listened to the legend of the Medicine Tree and to the story of Lewis' and Clark's reception by the Flathead-Salish residents of the Bitter Root. Folks from Missoula to Sula had a fine time."[7] The celebrations ceased after Mr. Ward was compelled to discontinue the expense of feeding so large a group of Indians.

Conflicting opinions were held by the white pioneers still living in the region in 1951 as to whether or not the true Ram's Horn Tree is the one so marked. Will Cave, a remarkably reliable informant on the early days in the Bitter Root, insisted that it is not. He claimed that the original was chopped down years ago and the section with the horn sawed out was given to someone in Victor, Montana. Another report had it that the horns were cut from the tree and sent to the Chicago World's Fair. On the other hand, W. H. "Bert" Lord of Darby, a resident of the valley since 1882, insisted that the original tree is the one still standing by the highway, and that some vandal had cut off the exposed portion of the horn. Sid Ward, who came to the Bitter Root in '84 or '85, stated frankly that he did not know whether it is the original. He had heard that early loggers in the valley cut it down, and fearing retaliation by the Indians, had instituted another one. An old sawyer named Billy Rombeaux declared that he and his partner were the ones that felled it.

The Indians, who should know more about it than the whites, say that it is the same medicine tree their ancestors revered. Ellen Big Sam, an aged full-blood, recalled first passing it when she was about eight. Her mother told her to pull out some of her hair and hang it on the trunk, for then she would live to an old age. Other squaws in the same party led their children there to make wishes. Ellen traveled past the tree nearly every year of her life. She was taken there in the spring of 1951 to voice a particular wish she was anxious to have granted.

There is no doubt that the pine contains the horn of some large mammal. The only external evidence that it might contain the horn, or horns, of a mountain sheep are two scars on the trunk. A few flakes of material chipped from within these scars give a weak protein test when treated chemically, and have a typical odor of burning hair or horn when treated. Microscopically, they have the same appearance as pieces of sheep horn whittled from a skull in the museum of the Montana State University.

The horn was unquestionably placed there years ago by man, and has been completely overgrown. It is still not an uncommon practice for people to hang deer and elk antlers in the crotches or cavities of trees. The opinion that a charging ram drove his horns so firmly into the wood that he could not extricate himself is hardly tenable. The scars are exactly seven feet from the ground, and must have been at this height from the time they were formed, as the main trunk of a tree does not grow up, it grows only in circumference. Large male sheep may attain six feet in length, and stand forty inches at the shoulder. They do rise on their hind legs when jousting during the breeding season, sometimes meeting head-on in such a position.[8] But even while rearing, they would barely reach seven feet, and in such a position would hardly have forced enough to drive the horns into wood.

Other means by which the ram could have caught his horn at such a height are also ruled out. He could not have leaped off a bank into the tree because the scars are on the north side, almost at right angles to the rising slope to the east, and the rocky bluffs are too far off. The possibility that the ground eroded down several feet since the implantation of the horn is hardly possible, since the soil consists mostly of decomposed granite, which does not wash out easily, and the base of the tree itself gives no such indication. The ram may have stood on several feet of hard-packed snow, but that is unlikely because the surrounding country lacks browse plants suitable for a wintering ground, where the snow becomes packed by numerous animals in a relatively small area.

The age of this pine makes it possible for it to be the true tree. It is between 300 and 340 years old. The trunk has some internal rot which makes it impossible to get an accurate determination with increment bore. But, besides a bore from the tree itself, the age was checked on yellow pine of similar diameter growing on the same slope, and by counting annual rings on neighboring stumps. To clamp an average sized sheep's horn about the trunk of a tree would require a trunk with a diameter of close to eight inches. Counting back on the annual rings of the bore, the tree would have been fifty years old at this diameter.

Quite probably, the pine presently called the Ram's Horn Tree is the same as that described by Ferris in 1833. The height of the scars coincide with his description, and as he mentioned, it is situated under some rocky bluffs directly across the river from a small flat where the original trail probably went. The horn would have been in the tree for approximately 150 years when he saw it 132 years ago. He stated that it had been there for a long time.

From Ross's statement, it is not possible to fix so exactly the location of the tree he saw. However, it was along the East Fork of the Bitter Root where the valley was very narrow, so must have been within a mile or so of the tree in question. It is unlikely that his horn-tree was the same as that described by Ferris, although it was in the same locality. Ross' comments on the curiosity do not jibe with those of Ferris, although both these men were accurate observers, trained by the school of necessity. The Ross tree had a skull with horns embedded rather than a single horn, and it was only five feet above the ground.[9]

Supporting the contention that Ross' and Ferris' trees were not identical is the fact that ram's horn trees were not uncommon. In the Hell Gate Trading Post, Missoula, there are two sections of trees, each of which contains the horn of a mountain sheep. One is a portion of a large fir that came from the Jocko. A horn is completely entombed in its trunk. The Walter Custer family, which operated the unusual trading establishment, remembered that it was venerated by the Indians, and that even at the time it was cut down about forty years ago, there were beads and trinkets at its base. The other is a section of a tamarack which has only partly grown around a horn. The Custers did not recall where this one came from.

Ernest Thompson Seton recorded two more horn-trees, and added further information to the subject:

It seems that at one time, it was the custom of the Indians to hang sheep horns on trees — to mark the spot — to make a kind of monument. I remember hearing a tradition that the hunting grounds of the Blackfeet were demarked from those of the Shoshones by a "horn-tree."

Two such trees have been cut down, and the embedded horns added to collections of the curious. A picture of one appears in *Forest and Stream* for April 11, 1896, with this notice:

"I send you photos of a Big-horn head embedded in a large, green, quaking-asp tree, found on Porcupine Creek — tributary of upper West Gallatin River — Gallatin County, Mont. The tree was near a rocky ledge or wall. As you will notice in the photo, the skull is completely embedded." (Aug. Gottschalck, Bozeman, Mont.)

On Jan. 28, 1914, I saw in the store of J. P. Evans of Livingston, Mont., a horn-tree with two pairs of ram's horns embedded in the wood.[10]

Ellen Big Sam asserted in 1951 that there is a ram's horn tree not far north of Arlee, Montana, which is used in the Indian Bluejay rites. The Bluejay dancers first hold their ceremonies around a small fir decorated with various trinkets. After the dance, the fir is tied to the horn-tree, where it is left to wilt and the ornaments fall to the ground.

There were other medicine trees in the Flathead country that were apparently not ram's horn trees. One was about five miles south of Ravalli. The Salish have this legend connected with it:

Well, this side of the road [west] cross the river there is an old road that is just to a pasture, a big pine there which the Indians used as a place for making their wish — like a wishing well or something like that. Whenever the Indians come through there on their way to the hunting grounds back east or anywhere — that is where they make their wish — shoot arrows over there on up the tree. Long ago you could see hundreds of arrows sticking on the tree. Later the arrows dropped off, dropped until no arrows left.

Some years ago I found out after the reservation thrown open, that there was a fellow who lived around that district, kind of an old fellow — a white fellow cut the tree down — cut it up into blocks. Year or two after that, that old fellow passed away. He [I] think he passed away because he cut the tree down — brings the fellow bad luck.

They always do — whenever Indians going down the river make their wish — throw some arrows on the tree whenever they pass by coming back just as they do with the medicine tree.[11]

Another sacred tree stood on Medicine Tree Hill near the old McCarty bridge on Hell Gate River. It formed the southwest corner for the survey in 1883 which marked the boundaries between what then constituted Deer Lodge and Missoula counties.[12] This one also had its own legend:

Many years ago a young Indian, while slowly ascending a hill, discovered that he was being pursued by his enemies. Requiring rest, he sought a secluded spot where he hung his medicine talisman on the limb of a tree, under the sooth- ing shade of which he soon fell asleep and from which he was suddenly awakened by the yells of his enemies who, discovering his position, began making him the target of their arrows. To the young Indian's surprise not an arrow touched his body, all seemed to fly off and veer into space before reaching him. This occa- sioned great surprise on his part, as he was entirely surrounded, and being encour- aged by the belief that he was being protected by his "medicine" he quickly replied to the enemies' arrows by those from his own bow and was gratified to see that every arrow found its mark, resulting in the killing of many foes. His quiver soon became exhausted of its stock of arrows when behold! as by magic, more came to his hand enabling him to continue his battle against great odds in numbers.

One Indian, observing the great slaughter going on among his friends, and believing that the young Indian's medicine was strong and its power saving him from harm, became desperate and seeing the medicine talisman hanging on the tree over the young Indian's head made a dash for the tree and snatching the medicine from the limb threw it away. The very next arrow aimed at the single- handed warrior reached a vital spot and he sank to earth to rise no more.

This legend is still current among the Indians of the Western slope who never pass the tree without hanging some article from their personal effects upon one of the limbs as a token of awe from their superstitious natures and to keep green the memory of the medicine-wrought tragedy enacted beneath its shade and to the present day the eminence is known as "Medicine Tree Hill."[13]

Until some irresponsible boys cut it down in 1949, Sentinel Pine, which grew on the west slope of Mount Jumbo, was a familiar sight to the residents of Mis- soula. It was not considered a true medicine tree by the Salish, but it was supposed to bring good luck. When the Indians held horse races and stick games in Hell Gate Ronde, losers would climb the hillside to Sentinel Pine and pray for luck. The tree told them how to win. Sometimes a gambler would have to remain on the slope of Jumbo for a week before he received a sign from the tree.[14]

These last three medicine trees mentioned have been cut down or their iden- tity lost. The only remaining monument of this sort in the land of the Flatheads is the Ram's Horn Tree. Whites have maintained a mildly superstitious veneration of the tree by driving pennies into its bark. Unfortunately, others have carved their initials into its trunk. May the spirit of the tree visit them with misfortune! As the curiosity dates back at least 130 years in historical record and more than that in Indian legend, it should continue to be carefully preserved as a memento of the days when the Indian's religion all related to Nature.

NOTES

[1] Alexander Ross was a chief trader with the North West Company and later with the Hudson's Bay Company. He was instructed by the latter company to lead a trapping and trading expedition to the Snake country. His outfit — consisting of 54 whites and Indians, 206 traps, 62 guns, 231 horses, and 20 lodges — left the Flathead House in February, 1824. It followed the Clark Fork and Flathead rivers to the Jocko, crossed the Coriacan Defile into Hell Gate, (Missoula), and proceeded south up the Bitter Root River. See "Journal of Alexander Ross — Snake Country Expedition, 1824," edited by T. C. Elliott, *Oregon Historical Society Quarterly*, Vol. XIV, 1913; 366-388.

[2] Alexander Ross, *The Fur Hunters of the Far West*, 2 Vols., (London, 1855), II, 18-19.

[3] W. A. Ferris, *Life in the Rocky Mountains*, ed. by Paul C. Phillips, (Denver, 1940). 232-233. Warren Angus Ferris was employed by the Western Department of the American Fur Company. In 1833 he was with a party trading on Green River, but in July was sent with Robert Newell to resume trade with the Flatheads, whom he had visited earlier. On his way down the Bitter Root Valley he saw the Ram's Horn Tree. He remained in western Montana throughout the winter and made his camp in the mountains between Flathead Lake and Plains. *Ibid.*, 212-261.

[4] Louisa McDermott, "Folk-Lore of the Flathead Indians of Idaho: Adventures of Coyote," *Junior American Folk-Lore*, Vol. XIV, 1901; 245. Although the Ram's Horn Tree was merely a curiosity about which the Flatheads had some superstitious veneration, there was a hypothetical tree that evidently played a major role in their religion. One belief held that there was a great tree with roots sunk deep in the earth and branches which reached to the sky. The Good Chief sat on top of the tree, while the Bad Chief sat at the roots within the earth. The Good Chief was the deity who sent the culture hero, Coyote, into the world to make life easier for the people. See J. A. Teit, "The Salishan Tribes of the Western Plateaus," ed. by Franz Boas, *Forty-Fifth Annual Report Bureau of American Ethnology*, 1927-28; 383.

[5] From material collected about 1920 by Mrs. A. J. Gibson, late of Missoula. See also *Folk-Tales of Salishan and Sahaptan Tribes*, ed. by Franz Boas, (New York, 1917), 117, for another variant of this legend.

[6] Story from Mr. Sid Ward, Missoula, 1951.

[7] *The Western News*, Hamilton, Mont. Oct. 6, 1949; 3.

[8] See H. E. Anthony, *Field Book of North American Mammals*, (New York, 1938), 543; and C. C. Spencer, "Notes of the Life History of Rocky Mountain Bighorn Sheep in the Tarryall Mountains of Colorado." *J. Mammalogy*, (Vol. XXIV, 1943), 3-4.

[9] There must be a misprint in T. C. Elliott's footnote, *op. cit.*, 374, which places the Ram's Horn Tree in "Sec. 22, Tp. 30 N.,R. 20 E., B.M." This would be a good many miles from the route traveled by Ross. The present tree is in Sec. 22, Tp. 2., N.,R. 20 E.

[10] E. T. Seton, *Lives of Game Animals, Hoofed Animals*, 4 Vols. (New York, 1927), III, 529. See p. 543 of this volume for sketches of the two horn-trees mentioned above.

[11] Story by Baptiste Finley, a full-blood Indian. *Full Blood Flathead Indian Montana Study Group*, printed in mimeograph form by the Montana Study, Univ. Mont., Missoula, Mont., April 30, 1947.

[12] M. A. Leeson, *History of Montana*, 1739-1885, (Chicago, 1885), 552.

[13] Caleb E. Irvine, "Medicine Tree Hill," from notes edited by William F. Wheeler, *Contributions to the Historical Society of Montana*, (Vol. VI, 1907), 482-483.

[14] Story by Ellen Big Sam, Arlee, Mont., interpreted by Joe Big Sam Woodcock.

The Medicine Rock of the Marias

By JOHN C. EWERS*

IN AN ACCOUNT of Blackfeet Indian religion, published more than seventy years ago, George Bird Grinnell mentioned:

"Another sacred object is the medicine rock of the Marias. It is a huge boulder of reddish sandstone, two-thirds of the way up a steep hill on the north bank of the Marias River, about five miles from Fort Conrad. Formerly this rock rested on the top of the bluff, but, as the soil about it was worn away by the wind and rain, it is slowly moving down the hill. The Indians believe it to be alive, and make presents to it. When I first visited it, the ground about it was strewn with decaying remnants of offerings that had been made to it in the past. Among these I noticed, besides fragments of clothing, eagle feathers, a steel finger ring, brass ear-rings and a little bottle made of two copper cartridge cases."[1]

This "Medicine Rock" was a landmark on the old Whoop-Up Trail leading northward from Fort Benton to the American posts established in southern Alberta in the late 1860's. The sketch map of that trail in the Montana Historical Society collections, prepared by Harry Stanford, a Montana pioneer, shows it ascending "Medicine Rock Coulee" on the north side of the Marias. On the west side of the trail leading up the coulee the mapmaker placed a red dot and labeled it "Medicine Rock."

In the fall of 1943, Short Face, an elderly, full-blood Piegan living on the Blackfeet Reservation, told me the story of this "Medicine Rock" as it had been recited to him nearly a half-century earlier by an aged Indian, Spotted Calf, who claimed to have had personal knowledge of the origin of this shrine.

One time a war party of North Blackfeet went to fight the enemy. All but two of its members were killed by the Sioux. These two were returning northward over the Narrow Ridge Trail. One of them was armed with a muzzle-loader. The other carried only a bow and arrows. They were poorly clothed. By the time they reached the Marias the man with the muzzle-loader had run out of ammunition. They hadn't eaten in a long time. Both of them were very hungry.

Near the Marias they saw a large rattlesnake. One of the men said to his partner, "Let's kill him and eat him." The other replied, "No, we don't eat that

165

sort of thing." Nevertheless, the first speaker killed the rattlesnake, skinned it and cooked it. Then he said, "Now partner, take half of it." Again his friend replied, "No, I am not hungry. The smell has taken my appetite away." The other man began to eat and said, "Partner, you better eat some of this. It tastes good — like fish." Once more his friend declined, saying, "No, I am not hungry."

They spent the night there. Next morning the warrior who had eaten the snake was so bloated he couldn't move. His partner tried to help him, but the snake-eater said it was useless. "You can do nothing for me. Make a place where I can lie down and cover it with sage." This his partner did. Then the snake-eater continued, "Take off my necklace. When you get back to camp give it to my father, who gave it to me. Tell him what happened to his son. Tell him that in the spring of the year you two must come for me."

His partner followed his advice and went home, the only member of the war party to return. He gave the necklace to his friend's father, told him how his partner had eaten the rattlesnake and become so bloated he could not move, and how he had asked them to return in the spring. The old man said, "I want to see my boy right away. I'll give you horses and other articles if you will take me to him." But the young man replied, "No, my friend said for us to come for him in the spring. That is his wish."

When spring arrived the old father called upon the young man. "My boy, I can't go now. The coyotes must have taken my son's bones. But if you will join a war party of Blood Indians now forming, you can go by the place where you left my son, gather his bones and bury them."

Spotted Calf, a Blood Indian, was a member of this war party. When they arrived at a side hill overlooking the Marias River, the North Blackfeet warrior explained, "Here is where I dug my partner in." But there was nothing there except a large rock. Seeing this, another North Blackfeet member of the party said, "This man is lying. If his partner had been here surely we would find some trace of him — some of his hair or his bones." The critic then rolled the rock away. But the other members of the party prayed to the rock.

That night the party camped on the south side of the Marias. The skeptic continued to make fun of the snake-eater's partner and his unlikely story, saying that he had been lying, until he succeeded in getting the other members of the party to agree with him. They all made fun of the snake-eater's partner that night.

When the partner of the deceased snake-eater arose next morning he looked across the river and saw a man standing on the hill where the rock had been. He woke Spotted Calf and Spotted Calf also saw the man. They woke the others. All saw the man and believed him to be an enemy. The North Blackfeet and Spotted Calf crossed the river to get a closer view of the stranger. When they reached the other side they saw no one. But they rolled the rock back up the hill and placed it where they had first seen it. Spotted Calf left a blanket, tobacco and other small gifts at the rock.

Spotted Calf and the North Blackfeet agreed that the man they saw must

Piegan medicine man   Piegan medicine pipe

have been the snake-eater's spirit. The North Blackfeet addressed the rock, "If you, rock, are my partner, help this man [Spotted Calf] to be lucky. Give him power to get horses from the enemy." The two then painted the rock with earth paint and returned to their party on the other side of the river.

The war party, which numbered fourteen men, started to the enemy. But the Gros Ventres and Assiniboins sighted them coming and lay in wait for them. They surprised the party and killed every man except the North Blackfeet and Spotted Calf. They escaped, and on their way back found a large herd of horses. The two survivors separated near the site of an old fort, the North Blackfeet going north to his people.

Spotted Calf continued on up the Marias with his horses. He passed the rock on his way and decided to stop. He killed a buffalo, took out the liver and fat and left it by the rock. Then he spoke to the rock, "If you are the man, take this to eat."

That night the spirit of the departed snake-eater appeared to Spotted Calf in his dream, saying, "I thank you and my partner for giving me a blanket, tobacco and food. My partner was not lying to you. I thank you, and shall give you power to become a renowned warrior and to live to old age."

When Spotted Calf returned to his camp he told the people of his experience. Later it became known to all the Piegan, North Blackfeet and Blood Indians. From that time on members of these three tribes stopped by the rock and left presents of beads, paint, tobacco and other articles, when they traveled the Narrow Ridge Trail.

Geologists will take a dim view of Spotted Calf's explanation of the supernatural origin of this small but interesting Indian landmark. However, Spotted Calf's story may be helpful to historians and enthnologists in dating Blackfeet recognition of this rock as a sacred shrine. According to the Blackfeet Agency Census of 1901, Spotted Calf (also known as Old Running Rabbit) was seventy-four years of age. Thus he was born about the year 1827. If the Blackfeet tribes began to endow this rock with supernatural powers when Spotted Calf was a young warrior, as his testimony has indicated, the Medicine Rock of the Marias must not have become a Blackfeet shrine until the decade of the 1840's. This was roughly a quarter century before the Narrow Ridge Trail of Blackfeet war parties became the Whoop-Up Trail of white men's commerce, the first road into the country of the reluctant Blackfeet.

NOTES

° Published by permission of the Secretary of the Smithsonian Institution, of which the author is a prominent staff member.

[1] George Bird Grinnell, *Blackfoot Lodge Tales,* (New York, 1892). 262-263. Fort Conrad, built in 1875 by Sol Abbott and Henry Powell, was located near the present Naismith Bridge over the Marias River, near Glacier National Park in Montana.

Left to right: Medicine Man, Secrets of the Night, Sign Talk, Medicine Whip, bronzes by Charlie Russell

Flathead war dance

Flathead youngster

Flathead camp

Flathead chief

Flathead profile

The Flathead Apostasy

By RICHARD FORBIS

THE FLATHEAD INDIANS first discovered the mysteries of Christianity through Iroquois trappers and canoemen who accompanied the earliest fur traders into what is now Montana. Some Iroquois, in particular those who resided in the vicinity of Caughnawaga Mission near Montreal, had long been subject to Jesuit preaching. Even so, their indoctrination in Catholicism was not complete; in fact, the evidence indicates that they had taken Christianity primarily as "good medicine." The Indians around Montreal were desired by the North West Company for their dual abilities as trappers and canoemen, and also because they were readily available. However, they were fickle and indolent, and they frequently deserted the Company's expeditions in order to remain among the Indians of the Rocky Mountains, where they were well treated and highly respected.[1] It was in this manner that four Iroquois and one itinerant white came to live with the Flathead tribe sometime in the second or third decade of the nineteenth century.[2] One of these Iroquois, Big Ignace, was the most influential in converting the Flatheads to Catholicism, according to Father Gregory Mengarini.

> Big Ignace especially may be considered to be the first whom God made use of to dissipate the thick darkness which up to that time had enveloped the minds of our Indians. His words, reinforced by very virtuous behavior (this latter being a thing quite difficult, I should almost say impossible, to find among whites who live with the Indians), made a breach in the hearts of several, especially among the older ones, who spent not only days but sometimes entire nights in the tent of this precursor, as I may call him, in order to hear him talk of God, religion and especially baptism. Then it was that the Flatheads heard of certain white men clothed in black whose practice it was to instruct people, bring them to know God and all good things and enable them to live after death. Every time he spoke to the Indians (so old Gerve told me recently) he would finish by saying, "what I tell you is nothing compared with what the black robes (robe nere) know." Ignace would not teach the Indians any prayers, as he was asked to do, for fear, as he said, "of changing the word of God."[3]

Ignace offered only an appetizer, but he inspired the Flatheads with a zeal to learn more of Christianity. Since the Iroquois did not understand Christianity well enough to give them a comprehensive picture, the only recourse of the Flatheads was to seek the priests themselves. In 1831 the Indians sent their first delegation to St. Louis. Of the four Indians who began this journey, only one returned, and he reported the failure of the mission. The second party, which left in 1835, consisted of Old Ignace (Big Ignace) and his sons, Charles and François (Saxa). Unlike the first group, the second was able to communicate the desires of the Flatheads. However, the priests did not come, so the Flatheads tried again in 1837. The third expedition, of which Big Ignace again was a member, never reached St. Louis. All were killed by Sioux. The fourth delegation consisted of Peter Gaucher and Young Ignace. They reached St. Louis in 1839 and extracted a promise from Bishop Rosati to have a priest live among them.[4]

Bishop Rosati selected Father Pierre-Jean de Smet, a capable and energetic young Jesuit priest, to answer the call of the Indians. Less than one year after the last Flathead delegation arrived in St. Louis, Father de Smet met a Flathead committee on the Green River, in the present State of Wyoming. This was June 30, 1840. The Flathead party led him into the main camp at Pierre's Hole, where De Smet found also the Pend d'Oreille tribe and a sizeable portion of the Nez Percé tribe.

Father de Smet was astonished to find that Christianity had already taken a strong grip on the Flatheads. He noted that "The Flatheads had already for some years a custom of never breaking camp on Sunday, but of passing that day in devotional exercises."[5] That the Flatheads were firmly convinced of the efficacy of prayer is sufficiently demonstrated by Ferris's observation in the early 1830's that they never ate, drank or slept without giving thanks to God.[6] While these are the only specific examples of what the Flatheads accepted from Christian practice in those early days, the Indians are also more generally thought to have "conformed, as nearly as they could, to our creed and manners, and even to our religious practices."[7]

Two facets of Christianity particularly appealed to the Flatheads. First, they were inordinately attracted to the sign of the Cross. De Smet explained that they regarded this as a pledge of victory.[8] Second was their powerful regard for baptism. Apparently they did not see its symbolic significance, or if they did they held it to be of secondary importance. Instead, they felt that "when [they received] baptism, they . . . [could] conquer any enemy whatsoever."[9] The Flatheads did not emphasize these two aspects of Christianity in order to facilitate their entry into the Kingdom of God; they were more interested in using the force of Christianity to defeat their enemies and to preserve themselves. Their interests in the priests were of the same order. De Smet himself admits that the Indians wanted the black robes: "Because they think that all other imaginable blessings will come with them; not only courage to fight, but also every species of remedy to enable them to enjoy corporeal health."[10]

De Smet's friendly reception by the Flatheads, and their docile acceptance of his dictums, encouraged him to believe that their conversion to Catholicism would be quick and sure. With the idea of obtaining more help, he returned to St. Louis in the fall of 1840. In 1841, Fathers Gregory Mengarini and Nicholas Point accompanied De Smet to the Bitter Root valley, where they, with the assistance of two lay brothers, built St. Mary's Mission. During the next five years, the priests were well pleased with the success of their labors and sacrifices. They made steady progress in converting the Indians to Catholicism. There were a few changes in personnel. Father Anthony Ravalli joined the mission in 1845. Aside from some minor interruptions, the work proceeded smoothly. Then, in 1846, relations between the Jesuits and the Flatheads disintegrated.

The Indians left that year for their customary summer hunt, apparently on the best of terms with the missionaries. However, when the Indians returned in the fall, they revealed a complete change of attitude. In a pathetic letter to Roothan, Father Ravalli described the condition in these words:

. . . we were not a little astonished when on their approaching this reduction last fall, their camp, which was broken up in various bands, took different courses. Part of the Indians were unwilling or afraid to come up to their village, while the others on entering the village took up again their old-time barbarous yells, which had not been heard since we came among them. They gave a chilly salute to the missionaries and then drew off with their lodges far from the latter nor did they show themselves to the priest except rarely and then only to smoke in his cabin. They sold us grudgingly a little dry meat and that of the worst quality. We heard a little later that on Father de Smet's departure from their hunting-camp to descend the Missouri they had given themselves up to their old war-dances, to savage obscenity and to shameless excesses of the flesh. . . . We know that we were not to blame for such a change and we bewailed it all the more when we saw that they went on constantly getting worse.[12]

Father Anthony Ravalli

This passage reveals that De Smet's departure from St. Mary's to the east had something to do with the Indian's dissatisfaction. For one thing, the mission would now be under the supervision of Mengarini, whose zeal outweighed his common sense. Mengarini was not popular with the Indians, partly because of his lack of tact, partly because in previous times he had sheltered and protected some predatory Blackfeet.[13] Another thing disturbed the Indians. It seems probable that they were deeply hurt by the removal of the man who first brought orthodox Christianity to them. De Smet held the Flatheads in the highest esteem, and they very likely reciprocated this sentiment.

The fact that De Smet was to leave and Mengarini to replace him, however, could hardly account for the hostility of the Indians toward the other missionaries. There was a far more important incident, connected with De Smet's departure, which aroused the anger and resentment of the Flathead. Before he left them, De Smet discussed in the presence of both Blackfeet and Flatheads, the possibility of christianizing the Blackfeet. This, in Flathead eyes, was treason. Although De Smet had lived with the Flatheads for five years, he apparently did not appreciate the fact that the Indians were not particularly interested in the moral and non-material aspects of Christianity; they were primarily concerned with its protective powers. Consequently, when the Flatheads discovered that De Smet was as willing to baptize their mortal enemies, the Blackfeet, as he had been to clothe the Flat-heads in the armor of Christianity, they revolted. For when they alone had Chris-tianity, they were almost uniformly successful in repelling the attacks of the Blackfeet tribes. "Indeed," wrote De Smet, "their unbounded confidence in the god of battle is well rewarded; a truth which the enemies of the Flatheads in-variably acknowledge. The medicine of the Black Robes . . . is strongest of all."[14] But when the two tribes were on equal terms, there seemed little doubt but that the Flatheads would be exterminated. This was one of the goals of the Blackfeet and their superior numbers, plus the power of baptism, made their achievement of this goal seem likely.

However fallacious this reasoning may appear to a white man, when he un-derstands that the Flatheads accepted Christianity as a religion which was invested with superior power, he can see why the Indians were anxious to maintain their monopoly of it. In the case of the Flatheads, to control Christianity was to control their means of survival. In the light of De Smet's promiscuous proselytizing, Flat-head resentment and hostility toward the priests and toward Christianity then becomes logical.

There is no way to tell exactly how long the antagonism of the Indians toward the priests lasted. Probably the Indians discarded their haughty and overbearing manner shortly after they assumed it. At any rate, in 1848 they were once more on good terms with the missionaries, although they again broke with the priests in the winter of 1848-1849. Again the wound healed rapidly, at least superficially, and in 1849 Father Ravalli was able to write: "At present the Indians are well-affected toward our holy religion and toward us."[15]

In 1850, however, the situation had reversed itself again, and Ravalli wrote:

> The majority gave up "private prayer" and vented insult and injury every day upon the missionary. Though we were making sacrifices for their sick even so far as to deprive ourselves of a morsel of bread, they refused to sell us necessary pro-visions while under our very eyes they sold to an agent of the Hudson Bay Company.[16]

Why the Flatheads again revolted against the ways of the Jesuits is a problem which cannot be solved until further evidence comes to light. Very likely, they had never completely recovered from the blow they suffered in 1846 and, once having made a break, found it easier to revolt again. Then, too, they probably grew more disillusioned with Christianity as time passed. Father Accolti, Superior of Missions at the time, told of several erroneous ideas which had poisoned the minds of the Flatheads against the Jesuits. First, when Ravalli failed to heal a sick Indian, no matter in what condition the patient arrived, Ravalli was blamed for his death. This led to the belief that the Jesuits were scheming to kill all the Indians so that the Jesuits could assume ownership of the land. In other quarters some Indians felt that the priests had not been able to make a living elsewhere, so they came west to sponge off the Indians. Father Accolti traced these poisonous thoughts directly to Angus McDonald, a Hudson's Bay Company trader.[17] Mengarini, appointed to head St. Mary's Mission after De Smet left, assigned two more reasons for the shift in the Indian's attitude. First, he said, Little Faro, an Indian of some influence, damaged the reputation of Mengarini and other Catholic priests when Mengarini failed to support him in his attempt to become head chief. Second, Mengarini felt that all the good Indians were dying off.[18] It is true that many of those who greeted De Smet in 1840 had passed on. From Mengarini's remark, it is apparent that the younger generation was not so quick to follow the dictates of the priests.

The apostasy of 1850 was far more serious than the schism between the priests and their pupils in 1846. Instead of sulking in their tents, as they had done earlier, the Indians in 1850 reverted to their ancient mode of entertainment, the night "orgy," and practiced customs which the fathers expressly forbade.[19] Also, they remained around the mission so little that the priests felt their continued efforts were useless. Consequently, Father Joset, under orders from Father Accolti, leased St. Mary's Mission to John Owen. In the hope that the mission could soon be reopened, the fathers left St. Mary's shortly after the lease was signed, in the fall of 1850. The priests closed St. Mary's in retaliation for inconsiderate treatment by the Indians. Their intention was "to punish [the Flatheads] and bring them to a sense of duty."[20] When St. Mary's closed, the first chapter of Northern Rocky Mountain missionary history ended. The Jesuits had lost the first round.

NOTES

[1] Alexander Ross, *Fur Hunters of the Far West,* (London 1855) I, 295.

[2] Gregory Mengarini, *Memoria Delle Missioni delle Teste Piatte, 1848,* in Gilbert J. Garraghan, *The Jesuits of the Middle United States* (New York, 1938) II, 238-239.

[3] *Ibid,* II, 241. Old Gerve, J. B. Gervais, was the white man who joined the Flatheads with Big Ignace and his three Iroquois companions.

[4] Lawrence B. Palladino, *Indian and White in the Northwest,* (Lancaster, 1922), 25-28.

[5] Hiram M. Chittenden and A. T. Richardson, *Life, Letters and Travels of Father Pierre-Jean de Smet, S.J., 1801-1873.* (New York, 1905) I, 230-231.

[6] Paul C. Phillips, (ed.) *Life in the Rocky Mountains* by Warren Angus Ferris. (Denver, 1940), p. 89.

[7] Chittenden and Richardson, *op. cit.,* I. 289-290.

[8] *Ibid.,* II, 593.

[9] *Ibid.,* III, 952-953.

[10] *Ibid.,* III, 953.

[11] Mengarini, quoted in *De Smet a Nobili,* May 25, 1850, in Garraghan, *op. cit.,* II, 376.

[12] Ravalli, in *Ravalli a Roothan,* June 29, 1847; in *Ibid.,* 376-377.

[13] Albert J. Partoll, (ed), "Mengarini's Narrative of the Rockies," *Sources of North-West History No. 25.* Reprinted from *Frontier and Midland,* 1938, XVIII: 8 and 17.

[14] Chittenden and Richardson, *op. cit.,* II, 573.

[15] Ravalli, in *Ravalli a Roothan,* April 5, 1849, in Garraghan, *op. cit.,* II, 378.

[16] Ravalli, in *Ravalli a Roothan,* April 5, 1851, in *Ibid.,* II, 380.

[17] Accolti, in *Accolti a de Smet,* May 5, 1851, in *Ibid.,* II, pp. 382-383.

[18] Mengarini, *Woodstock Letters,* 18:148 et seq. in *Ibid.,* II, p. 378.

[19] Accolti, in *Accolti a de Smet,* May 5, 1851, in *Ibid.,* II, pp. 382-383.

[20] Mengarini, *Woodstock Letters,* 18:149, 152 in *Ibid.,* II, pp. 379-380.

Issiwun–Sacred Buffalo Hat of the Old Cheyennes

By FATHER PETER JOHN POWELL

IN ALL THE NORTHLAND there was the dull despair of hunger. It seemed that Maiyun — the sacred Powers — had forgotten the People, for the animals starved, the land shriveled under the icy winds. The Suhtaio were grateful when there was dried vegetation or one of the shaggy travois dogs to fill the gnawing of the empty stomach. One evening they camped by a beautiful stream. The head men went to one side and sat in a semi-circle, as the rest of the tribe moved toward the water. One of the chiefs ordered the men to pair up and to beg food from the women they respected. Of the men who did so, one was a young man who possessed sacred power; and he stepped in front of the wife of the head chief of the Suhtaio. The woman answered his request, standing patiently as he finished the scanty meal. When he was done, he informed her that he had chosen her to go with him to the far north. The woman was to take dogs, a travois and camping equipment, for they would be gone ten times the days of the sacred number four.[1]

After days of travel, they saw a forest stretching before them, and rising above it a great mountain. This was Black Mountain and the older Cheyennes today describe it as the site from which the Suhtaio came.[2] A large rock stood before the mountain. When it was rolled away, a passage was revealed. At the end of the passage they found themselves in the great lodge of the mountain. What they beheld there is mirrored even today in the beauty of the Sun Dance lodge and its altar. There, Maiyun instructed them for four days. Roaring Thunder also spoke to them of sacred things, his words coming from the top of the mountain peak. The older Cheyenne drawings of this scene show the blackness of the sky surrounding the mountain, and the vividness of the lightning flashes that pierced the darkness as Roaring Thunder spoke to them. Maiyun taught them that by following the sacred teachings they and their children would be abundantly blessed. As they moved back to the Suhtaio camp, the heavenly bodies would follow them. Roaring Thunder would awaken the moon, the stars, and the rain. The animals would gather round the sacred mount and would follow them. "Take this Horned Hat to wear when you perform the ceremony I have given you, and you will control the buffalo and all other animals. Put the cap on you as you go from here and the earth will bless you." Made from the skin of a buffalo cow's head, the horns attached, Issiwun — the Sacred Hat — thus came to the Suhtaio.

The whole world seemed to become new as the medicine man and the woman came from the mountain. The buffalo followed them, as did the other animals. Grass was everywhere. Fruit was plentiful. At the end of each day the animals rested around them.[3] When they reached the Suhtaio camp, the medicine man, wearing the sacred hat, informed the people that they no longer need fear hunger. He at once ordered the Medicine Lodge ceremony (or Sun Dance) to be performed exactly as the Powers had taught him in the mountain. When the dance was completed, the land was black with buffalo. Grass was abundant, so they had plenty. When the Suhtaio people saw the holy man with his horned hat, they named him Erect Horns.[4]

Firewolf, one of the oldest and most respected of the Northern Cheyenne priests, states that the Cheyennes and Suhtaio first met near the pipestone quarries in a land of many lakes. The Cheyennes proper (Tsistsistas) used to travel north in a season when the birds shed their feathers. During one of these trips Cheyennes and Suhtaio met, and fought. In the midst of the battle, a Cheyenne warrior named Wise Buffalo recognized the Suhtaio language as similar to his own. "After talking together, crying out from a distance, four of the Desert People (as the Cheyennes anciently called themselves) and four of the Suhtaio came out. They motioned each other to come on, and met in the middle. The Cheyennes said, "We are Desert People." The Suhtaio said, "We are Suhtaio." After that — nobody remembers how — they came together. A long time after, they roamed together, south and west. They crossed the Missouri, long before the White Man came West."[5]

With the Suhtaio came the Buffalo Hat and the Sun Dance, the gift of Erect Horns. The Cheyennes possessed Mahuts — the Sacred Arrows — as well as the Chief's Bundle. The Watchers Below the Ground (supernatural powers) had given these sacred objects to Sweet Root Standing, the Cheyenne cultural hero. In the years after, the Suhtaio would continue to retain traces of their former independence. They became a separate band in the great Cheyenne nation. As late as 1830, they still camped by themselves and still retained much of their ancient language.[6] Indeed, George Bird Grinnell states that the Cheyennes used to say the Suhtaio were Cree Indians. As late as 1902 some Cheyennes said the Crees were their close relations. The Cree name for Cheyenne is said to mean, "They talk a little Cree"; and here, perhaps, is the clue to the earlier origins of the Suhtaio themselves.[7]

The older differences were laid aside, however, when all the Cheyenne bands gathered each spring for the Medicine Lodge ceremonies. The Sacred Hat tipi stood at the west end of the inner camp circle, in front of the lodges of the Suhtaio band. The other Tribal sacred object — the Arrows — hung in their tipi at the east end of the inner circle, before the lodges of the Arrow men.[8] As the Suhtaio and the Cheyenne proper were now one tribe, so Issiwun — the Sacred Buffalo Hat — and Mahuts — the Medicine Arrows — were the "Great Mysteries" around which the nation was united. They were the spiritual rallying points of the Cheyenne tribe. Indeed, when the great central pole of the Medicine Lodge was raised, the two forks of that pole mystically represented Erect Horns and Sweet Root Standing.[9]

In the old days, when the construction of the tipis for these two sacred objects was to take place, a chosen warrior would walk to the pile of buffalo hides and count coup on them before the actual sewing began. Formerly, the Hat and Arrow lodges were painted black below and red above. It is not clear whether this was to harmonize with the colors of the shafts of the Medicine Arrows or to symbolize night and day. Today, however, the tipis of both are made of white canvas.[10]

The Sacred Hat lodge has always been a center of spiritual activity. Oaths are taken by the Hat, and it is believed that misfortune will befall him who breaks such an oath. The Hat tipi has long been a place of sanctuary, and enemies who might find their way there were safe from harm. During the Medicine Lodge (or Sun Dance) ceremonies, any chief who wanted to announce anything went to the Sacred Hat tipi, purified himself with smoke and prayed before Issiwun.[11] When warriors returned from a successful war expedition, a scalp or a cloth "blanket" might be offered to the Sacred Hat. The victorious fighters would come down the hill to the sacred tipi singing, "I put the blanket on God," offering pieces of fine cloth to cover the resting place of the sacred object. Thus, in a multitude of ways, the Buffalo Hat was the spiritual focal point of Cheyenne life. After these centuries since Erect Horns' appearance, many a Northern Cheyenne still enters Issiwun's tipi, there to sit in the presence of the sacred object, to pray for the People and to receive in turn the blessings of the Sacred Hat.

In the good times long ago, the Buffalo Hat and the Sacred Arrows rode to war together. Before the reservations were established, the two Great Mysteries were never separated. On those six occasions in recorded Cheyenne history when the Hat and Arrows went against the foe, the entire tribe marched with them.

The men rode first, with the women and children following. Before battle, certain sacred ceremonies were performed. An attack on the enemy before these ceremonies were completed neutralized the power of Issiwun and the Mahuts. The eagerness of individual warriors to count coup led to the power of the sacred objects being neutralized in three of these cases. One move was fruitless. Only two were successful.[12] Worse still, in 1830 the Sacred Arrows fell into the hands of the Pawnees — the worst spiritual misfortune ever to befall the tribe before the violation of the Sacred Hat in 1873. However, even prior to that sad affair, the Sacred Hat was to have its troubles.

In 1853 the Cheyennes moved the Sacred Mysteries against the Pawnees. Upon arriving within four or five miles of the enemy camp, they paused to perform the sacred ceremonies. Issiwun rested on the ground on a bed of sage. One of the Sacred Arrows was taken from the bundle and pointed toward the enemy camp. Wooden Leg, a noted warrior, pointed the Arrow at the Pawnee lodges and sang the Arrow song, dancing and thrusting the sacred objects at the enemy. The warriors ranged behind him, dancing in time to the song and making motions with their shields and weapons toward the foe. As the fourth song was sung, all shouted the war cry. The Arrow was restored to the three other Arrows as Stone Fore-head, the great Arrow Keeper, held the bundle.[13]

Meanwhile, another fighting man, Long Chin, had asked for the privilege of wearing Issiwun into battle. The Hat Keeper complied. As Long Chin tied the chin string in place, it snapped. Here was misfortune indeed! The trouble did follow, for Big Head and seven others had already slipped away in order to count the first coups — thus neutralizing the power of the Great Mysteries. In doing so, they had also warned the Pawnee camp of danger. To add to the discomfiture of the Cheyennes, a band of Potawatomies, armed with good rifles, came to the rescue of the enemy. With the power of the Hat and the Arrows broken, seven-teen Cheyennes lay dead in the buffalo grass. [14] It was not until 1854 that the Cheyennes would find solace in a victory that overwhelmed and killed — to a man — 113 Pawnees.[15] Truly, without proper respect for the Sacred Mysteries, all-out war was futile. . . .

(It should be noted in passing that one of the Cheyenne scouts who found the Pawnee camp that fateful day was Tall Bull. It was his son who, 106 years later, was to preside over the opening of the Sacred Buffalo Hat.)

The gradual division of the Cheyennes into Northern and Southern tribes seems to have been hastened by the establishment of Bent's Fort, whose building was completed in 1832. The Southern bands gravitated to the Fort, and Bent strengthened his relationship by marrying the daughter of White Thunder, the Arrow Keeper at that time. The Northern bands roamed the beloved North Country — west of the Black Hills, through southeastern Montana, Nebraska and Wyoming. At Sun Dance time, nevertheless, the bands still came together to offer the sacred ceremony that had been brought them with the Sacred Hat. With the pursuit by the white soldiers, however, it became increasingly difficult to keep the Buffalo Hat and the Medicine Arrows together.

Wooden Leg, the Northern Cheyenne warrior, says that the Sacred Hat tipi stood in their camp on the Rosebud in May of 1876. Coal Bear, the Keeper of Issiwun, set up the Hat lodge in the midst of the camp circle. "It put good thoughts and good feelings into the hearts of all Cheyennes."[16] After the battle with Crook on the Rosebud, the Buffalo Hat was hung up, and in the camp on the Little Big Horn, the Cheyennes tied a scalp to it.[17] As the darkness fell on the evening of June 24th, before the greatest of all Cheyenne victories, a social dance was beginning in the camps. Again Coal Bear "brought the buffalo skin that reg-ularly hung from the top of the sacred tipi. He tied it to the top end of a long pole before he raised it."[18] This probably refers to Nimhoyah, the buffalo hide "Turner" upon which the Sacred Hat rested. Again, after the victory over Custer, the "Turner" hung on the pole and the victorious coups were counted in the presence of this sacred object which was part of the Hat bundle.[19] As the Chey-enne camp moved from the Little Big Horn, Coal Bear kept Issiwun's tipi set up at every place of camping. The days stretched into autumn and the Cheyennes were camped along the Powder River. It was there, on November 26, 1876, that General R. S. Mackenzie attacked Dull Knife's camp.[20] By this time, Black Hairy Dog, the Keeper of the Sacred Arrows, had brought that other holy bundle to the Cheyenne camp, and the Great Mysteries were once more united.[21]

The Cheyennes were aware of the proximity of Mackenzie's troops. Scouts had infiltrated the Army lines and had reported the enemy's presence to the chiefs. Black Hairy Dog, aware of his responsibility to the people, urged that the camp be moved to the foot of the nearby Big Horn mountains, nearer Crazy Horse's large Lakota camp. However, Last Bull, chief of the Kit Fox society, arbitrarily ordered his warriors to keep everyone in camp, adding, "We will stay all night and dance." It was such high-handedness that resulted in the destruction of Dull Knife's camp. The Arrow Keeper, Black Hairy Dog, first spotted the troops at dawn, raising the alarm.[22] After the battle, the surviving Cheyennes fled to Crazy Horse's camp. There the Sioux received them hospitably.[23] Some days later, at Hanging Woman Creek, the tribes decided to separate. Most of the Lakotas went eastward up Hanging Woman Creek; the Cheyennes, with some of the Lakotas, started up the Tongue River valley. Just as the tribes began this separation, scouts brought news that soldiers were coming. Lakota and Cheyenne again faced the enemy together. It was in this skirmish with Colonel Nelson Miles on January 1, 1877, that Medicine Bear carried Nimhoyah — the "Turner" that was part of the Sacred Hat bundle — against the white soldiers. The bullets failed to touch him because Nimhoyah's power turned them aside.[24] After this fight, the Dull Knife band traveled to a winter camp on the upper Little Big Horn. Coal Bear was still with them, having survived the Mackenzie battle. He had "kept posses-

Wooden Leg, Northern Cheyenne, 1913

Chief Wooden Leg, in mufti

White Bull, or Ice, Northern Cheyenne   Two Moon, 1877

sion of the sacred buffalo head through all our distress. We now had as good a lodge for it as we ordinarily had," says Wooden Leg.[25]

When Miles attacked, he captured a small band of women and children.[26] One of these was an elderly female named Sweet Taste Woman. One winter day she suddenly reappeared in the Cheyenne camp, bringing John Bruguier ("Big Leggings") with her. She had warned Bruguier to seek sanctuary in the Sacred Hat tipi if the Cheyennes showed signs of hostility. This he did with great alacrity.[27] Sweet Taste Woman and Big Leggings told the tribesmen that they had been well treated by Miles, and that he offered the rest the same treatment. A lengthy council followed, with the opinions sharply divided. Two Moon, Ice and others surrendered to Miles at Fort Keough, becoming the nucleus of the famed Cheyenne scouts — so effective in the Nez Percé and Ghost Dance troubles. Little Wolf and Dull Knife chose to go to Fort Robinson, Nebraska Territory. Coal Bear said that the Sacred Hat and its tipi should follow them. "Their choice influenced the course of most of the Tribe."[28] After surrendering to Crook at Fort Robinson, the terrible news was given them: they must go to the hated south-land, with its death-bringing winds. On that sad journey to Oklahoma, Issiwun traveled on the back of Coal Bear's wife, as befitted the sacred object. When Little Wolf and Dull Knife made their heroic flight to the north, Coal Bear chose to remain with Plenty Bears, one of the minor chiefs.[29] Charles Sitting Man, the oldest man among the present-day Northern Cheyennes, states that Coal Bear brought Issiwun back from Oklahoma, in company with Black Wolf's band, in 1881. After a year's stay at Pine Ridge, that band journeyed to Fort Keough and the Montana country.[30] There, at the forks of the Lame Deer, the sacred tipi was pitched, back home in the beloved North Country once more. Coal Bear was to guard it faithfully there.[31]

The strength and holiness that emanated from the Sacred Hat bundle must also be mirrored in the lives of the Keepers of Issiwun. The Keeper must be of the Suhtaio band, and a man of peace. Cheyenne history, be it oral or written, does not recall a Hat Keeper as noted as Stone Forehead — the great Keeper of the Sacred Arrows. True, he had forsaken the war trail for the peaceful ways of the Arrow priesthood, when they had become his responsibility. However, his name as a fighting man lived on.

Today, when older Cheyennes recall the former Keepers of Issiwun, such as Coal Bear, they mention as their chief qualifications: "He was a man who was kind to everybody. He was very peaceful. He was qualified to keep the Sacred Hat because the law that concerns the Keepers says a man who is Keeper must be honest, peaceful and kindly to everyone."[32] For the majority of the Hat Keepers, this has been the rule in actuality as well as theory. However, there were exceptions. For instance, take the celebrated case of Broken Dish.

When Half Bear, the Keeper, was dying in 1865, Issiwun was supposed to pass to his son Coal Bear. However, at that time, Coal Bear was absent. Thus, Half Bear entrusted the Hat to his friend Broken Dish. The explicit understanding was that the Sacred Hat would go to his son at his return.[33] When Coal Bear did arrive back at the camp, he took four fine horses to the tipi of Broken Dish, thus paying him for his temporary care of Issiwun. Broken Dish accepted the horses, but refused to relinquish the sacred object.

The Kit Fox soldiers were called together, for further complications had developed. Under cover of night, Broken Dish and his wife had fled to a neighboring band of Lakotas, seeking refuge among these long-time allies of the Cheyenne. Bodies painted yellow, their lower arms and legs black, two eagle feathers upright in each warrior's hair, the Kit Foxes advanced in a line on the Sioux camp. The two sacred bow-spears were borne on high by their chosen keepers. The Foxes were joined by the Red Shields and the other warrior orders. The theft of the Sacred Hat brought peril to the entire nation! Luckily, before a pitched battle could begin, Broken Dish surrendered Issiwun. Coal Bear placed the Hat on his back, in the good sacred way, and rode off in triumph.

This was not the end, however. The Hat seemed uneasy as it rode on the back of Coal Bear's wife, or hung on its tripod in the black and red tipi. "The Cheyennes and Suhtaio had kept on suffering, with much sickness. Game became scarce. So they searched the Hat bundle and found one horn missing. Then they knew! They found out why they had such a hard time and suffering."[34]

Ho'ko, wife of Broken Dish, was the villain. Here was disaster indeed — as bad as the trouble that had followed the tribe when the Pawnees captured the Sacred Arrows! However, the deep spirituality of the Cheyennes is not lacking in practicality. The Buffalo priests prepared a substitute horn for Issiwun, and new sweet grass was placed in the bundle. Once more the Hat seemed to rest quietly.

However, what was done could not be entirely altered. The Sacred Hat had been defiled. Maiyun would not take such profanity lightly. It was predicted that ill fortune would follow both the tribe and the family of Broken Dish. Sure enough, Broken Dish soon died, and Ho'ko saw her children quickly follow their father. For years she lived as an exile among the Lakotas, spending her last years among the Southern Cheyennes, far from her Northern relatives. The tribe would suffer also. This was 1873, and the great victory on the Little Big Horn still lay ahead. However, the Cheyennes would still know the horror of their slaughter at the Sappa River by Lieutenant Heneley and the buffalo-hide hunters. There would be the destruction of Dull Knife's camp and the removal to Oklahoma. Unceasing sorrow would be the lot of those who saw their loved ones frozen in the snow during Little Wolf's march to the north. There would be the dull pain that never quite left the hearts of those who survived the destruction of Dull Knife's band at Fort Robinson. "Almost all the Cheyenne troubles are believed to have followed close on the loss of their medicine arrows and the desecration of the sacred hat."[35]

There was an epilogue. Ho'ko, the source of the trouble, outlived her family. The Cheyennes believe that her special punishment was the death of her children. Even Coal Bear, the true Keeper who was blameless in the entire affair, felt the effects of her sacrilege. When he died in 1896 he was no more than sixty years old. This was in marked contrast to the earlier Keepers, who traditionally were never killed, wounded in war or seriously ill. Tradition says they lived to a full age; some said of nearly 100 years. Coal Bear's death at such an early age was said to have been brought about by the increasing lack of reverence for Issiwun since that day in 1873.[36]

Ho'ko lived on to about 1906. When she was being prepared for burial, there — worn like a pendant — was the missing horn. It passed to Three Fingers, a Southern Cheyenne chief. He, in turn, sent word to Montana, where Wounded Eye now sat in the Sacred Hat tipi. Wounded Eye traveled south and the horn was returned to the bundle. However, there was still doubt. Should it replace the substitute horn that was prepared long before? The Spirit Ceremony — a Cheyenne sacred seance — was performed, and the question was placed before Maiyun. Maiyun were those mysterious powers which controlled men's fortunes, bringing blessing if they were reverenced or misfortune if they were neglected. Maiyun spoke and declared that Ho'ko's horn was a mere husk, that it should be buried, as the sacred power had long since departed from it.[37] (This, incidentally, was the same answer given the Cheyennes when General Hugh Scott offered to be their intermediary in recovering the two original Mahuts captured by the Pawnees in 1830. Maiyun said the Pawnee-owned Arrows were without power, that the two substitutes now in the Sacred Arrow bundle were true Mahuts.[38])

For Issiwun and its Keepers the reservation days were quiet days. Coal Bear died in 1896, and was buried as befitted one who had lived for the good of the People. His body was placed on a hill and was covered with stones. Above the stones, at each of the four sacred directions, a buffalo skull was placed. In older days if such a tribute were not paid the Keeper of the Sacred Hat, the buffalo would go away to the north — from whence they first came — and the range would be deserted. Even then, there was still the hope that the buffalo, the namesakes of the Sacred Hat, would again return, once more to blacken the plains of the Cheyenne country.[39]

When Wounded Eye succeeded Coal Bear, he was already elderly. He was "an honest man who believed in the old ways" and a Crazy Dog society member as well. Another warrior had become a man of peace.[40] Before he became Keeper, he enjoyed moving about, building a new cabin in each stopping place. When Issiwun was placed under his care, he moved into the tipi — for the Sacred Hat could not be kept in a white man's shelter. True, some excitement followed him. In the summer of 1906 he left the Sacred Hat for a time. Maiyun showed him the error of that move, for a great wind arose and blew over the Hat tipi. No one knew what to do. Issiwun lay on the ground; for no one had authority to move it. At last an unidentified Cheyenne, with many prayers asking forgiveness if he was in error, picked up the Hat and hung it properly. When Wounded Eye returned, the man was purified, his body rubbed with the sacred white sage, while the prayers were offered. Wounded Eye told the people that a storm would follow; and it did. Within two weeks, the most severe storm in years had uprooted trees and upturned tipis, all except the tipi of Issiwun.[41]

Black Bird followed Wounded Eye: a good, quiet man in the old-time Cheyenne way. He was a generous and gracious person, and the Cheyennes still talk of the joy in the summer camps when he pitched the sacred tipi among them, and the prayers and ceremonies were again observed with devotion by all.

Rock Roads, a member of the Kit Fox society, was next in succession. Some older Cheyennes today mention that he was criticized because he occasionally left the Sacred Hat tipi alone and unattended. However, he was one of the three sponsors of the great Medicine Lodge (Sun Dance) of 1911, indicating that he held fast to the sacred ceremony linked to the Buffalo Hat.

Sand Crane, "a quiet and good man," who had been a warrior in the end of the old days followed. Head Swift, his brother, succeeded him. An intelligent man who knew his duties well, he was strict in seeing that the utmost respect was paid Issiwun. Nobody could trespass in the tipi.[42]

At Head Swift's death in 1953, a new period of history began for Issiwun. The Keepers who had known the old buffalo days were gone, and eligible Suhtai men were becoming harder to find. The Suhtai have always been a small band, and this added to the difficulty. Many of the younger Suhtai males felt themselves unworthy, or unwilling, to bear the responsibility of the sacred office. Not only must the Keeper stay close to the tipi, but the prayers must be offered morning and evening. In the Medicine Lodge and the Buffalo Ceremony the Hat Keeper played an honored role, one he must know and live. Thus, up until 1958, Josephine Headswift, daughter of the former Keeper, watched over the sacred tipi at Birney. She was, by her own reckoning, the thirteenth Keeper of the Sacred Hat in her family. True, as a woman she could not open the Sacred Bundle. However, her father had carefully instructed her in the woman's role in the Hat cere-

Two Moon's tipi, Lame Deer, 1896   Two Moon in white-man clothes

monies; and she offered the prayers to Issiwun with great devotion. She knew how to wrap the sacred "blankets" on the Hat bundle; and when there were too many, she knew how to remove them. Thus, Issiwun was to receive at least some of the honor due the Great Mystery of the Northern Cheyennes.[43] So the years passed; but the problem of finding a male Keeper continued.

Finally, in 1958, a young Suhtai — Ernest American Horse — sent word to the military bands that he wished to be Keeper. Josephine Headswift, with her usual graciousness, allowed the Sacred Hat to pass to the younger man. Days were different now. In older times, when such a transfer was made, the Hat would have been borne on horseback to its new resting place. Now automobiles waited to carry the new Keeper and the warrior societies from Birney to Busby. However, the ancient prayers were recited, and the Keeper carried the Hat on his back — as Erect Horns had first taught the Suhtaio in the long-ago days. For over a year, the white tipi of Issiwun stood behind American Horse's cabin, near the Two Moon's monument at Busby.

However, the restless times had come again — just as they had come in Coal Bear's early years as Keeper. Last April, American Horse left for Sheridan, Wyoming, and with him went Issiwun. Here was trouble! True, American Horse stated that he had been told never to leave the Hat alone; so he took it with him. However, there were rumors and fears that the Cheyennes were in danger of losing this holy thing which was the supreme link that bound the past, the now and the tomorrow — making them all one.[44]

The Sacred Hat was intercepted and returned to the Tribal Office. There it rested uneasily — just as it had when the horn was removed. The military bands met and the chiefs delegated Elmer Brady and Davis Wounded Eye to carry Issiwun to its new Keeper. David Wounded Eye, the son of the earlier Keeper who had brought the horn back from Oklahoma, placed the Hat bundle on his back. Then, while he sat in a station wagon with it on his back, Issiwun was driven to Albert Tall Bull's home. There a tipi stood. There the Hat rested until the chiefs appointed Henry Little Coyote the new Keeper.[45]

The Cheyennes believe in the harmony of time. All that has been, all that is, all that will be, are one harmonious whole. Therefore, it is not strange that the new Keeper be the nephew of another great Cheyenne holy man — Sauts the Bat, or, as the White Men know him better, Roman Nose.

Thus, the Sacred Hat tipi now rests below the cabin of the eighty-three-year-old Little Coyote. Issiwun's Keeper must be a gentle man, a gracious quiet man, a man who is faithful in his prayers. Little Coyote possesses these attributes. Weasel Woman, his wife, is equally fitted to fill the woman's role in the sacred tipi. In her younger days, she was a noted beauty among the Northern Cheyennes. Once the widow of the great Ghost Dance priest, Porcupine, she became Little Coyote's wife after Porcupine's death. She is a credit to the Cheyenne nation, whose women have long been pre-eminent for their virtue. . . .

Now, on only one other occasion in the last thirty-odd years has the Sacred Hat been exposed for public veneration. During Black Bird's term as Keeper, General Hugh Scott and Congressman Scott Leavitt were interested in the contents of the sacred bundle. The military societies agreed that it could be opened. Both Scott and Leavitt made an offering to the Keeper. Wolf Chief assisted Blackbird in opening the bundle. Afterward, it is said that Blackbird gave a ceremony in which he purified himself.[46] Then the bundle was closed, the strings of the buffalo-hide container pulled tight, as it rested against Nimhoyah the "Turner" on the tripod in the sacred tipi. The offering cloths were still brought by the faithful. Nimhoyah still was carried forth to hang outside the lodge on its long pole. It turned away disaster from the Cheyenne warriors of two World Wars, and it protected them during the Korean campaign.[47] But Issiwun remained unopened . . . until July of 1959.

Even prior to the Hat's brief journey to Sheridan, there were those Cheyennes who believed the bundle should be opened. Many years had passed. Keepers had come and gone. Was Issiwun with its sacred contents still secure? Was not this the time to inspect it and again to bring its sacred power to the Tribe?

Affairs came to a head during the Sun Dance ceremonies last July. The Hat hung in its honored place above the tipi door on the Sun Dance site near Lame Deer battlefield. However, when Abraham Spotted Elk and Frank Redcherries, the Sponsors, and Albert Tallbull, the head Sun Dance priest, went to the Hat tipi to obtain the scalps which are included in the bundle, they could not be found. Here was more trouble! And the scalps should be carried in the sacred Medicine Lodge, just as Maiyun had instructed Erect Horns centuries before! The chiefs and the military bands agreed to gather when the Sun Dance was over. If the Hat should be opened, what priest was qualified to perform such a sacred task? they asked. Surely this was a serious problem.

While the Cheyenne leaders pondered this, I was fortunate enough to obtain the sacred "blower" (used to keep the ceremonial fire burning) and the pipe which had also disappeared from the Hat bundle at an earlier date. These holy objects had found their way to Frank Cady's trading post at Lame Deer. Mr. Cady graciously allowed me to purchase them, with the understanding that they were being returned to the Sacred Hat Bundle. Mrs. Forrest Liberty, of Birney, shared the costs of so doing.

In company with John Stands-in-Timber, the noted Northern Cheyenne historian, we sought Firewolf, one of the most respected of the older Cheyenne priests. Instructed by Firewolf, we arranged to return the sacred objects to Issiwun's bundle. The cloth "blankets" which are offered to the Hat were procured and, with the pipe and "blower," carried to the home of Little Coyote. The Sacred Hat Keeper sat in his place to the left of the outside of the tipi door, and we approached with Firewolf and John Stands. As we neared the tipi, Firewolf broke out into the ancient song belonging to the Sacred Hat lodge. In the good days, the victorious warriors sang it as a scalp was carried to Issiwun:

"The Spirit cries out all over.
He took pity on me.
He gave me charcoal.
Therefore I rejoice.
I dance the victory dance."

The song was repeated the sacred four times. I placed the "blankets" on the ground before Little Coyote, and the pipe and "blower" were laid at his feet. The Keeper received them with thanks, saying to Mrs. Liberty and me: "I am the Keeper of the Sacred Hat. By right I can ask the Spirit to bless people. He himself [i.e., the Hat] received the blankets and the pipes. You two will receive a blessing from him. Also, I declare that both of you shall find better life and better things in the future." Then Little Coyote carried the pipes into the tipi, and Issiwun was covered with the cloth "blankets." Turning to the Hat, the Keeper addressed it as a living person. He asked Issiwun to bless us — who were now his relatives — giving us long lives.

However, though two of the missing objects had been restored, the Hat bundle itself had not been examined. A meeting of the military bands was called for the next day, July 12. Finally, after hours of discussion, it was decided that that hot Sunday afternoon would see the opening of Issiwun.

Fourteen persons were present in the sacred tipi on that occasion: Little Coyote, his son Eugene Little Coyote, Elmer Brady, Alex Spotted Elk, John Stands-in-Timber, Frank Lonebear (a Southerner), Charles Sitting Man, Charles Whitedirt, Francis Yellowhair and August Spotted Elk. John Woodenleg represented the Northern Cheyenne Tribal Council, of which he is president. Fred Last Bull, whose father had been present when Issiwun's chin string snapped and when Mackenzie destroyed Dull Knife's camp, was the priest presiding over the opening. As such, he was the chief instructor in the ceremonies. Mrs. Hanks, of Kirby, Montana, Mrs. Forrest Liberty and I were the only non-Cheyennes present.

It was a paradox that the ceremony began with my reading from Grinnell's account of the Cheyenne Sacred Mysteries — written fifty years before, while Wounded Eye was still living. John Stands-in-Timber and John Woodenleg interpreted, so that all could be certain that they recalled and carried out the old-time rules regarding the Sacred Hat.

Then the Hat Keeper and his son removed Issiwun from its tripod. It was handed to Fred Last Bull. John Woodenleg knelt by to assist. The ancient ritual of the Keeper blowing on the palms of the priest's hands followed. Little Coyote knelt in front of the bundle and smoothed the earth in circular motions. The piece of sweet root (representing Sweet Root Standing, the other ancient cultural hero) was untied from Nimhoyah, the Turner. It was touched by Little Coyote, who then touched his tongue, blowing the medicine on Last Bull's hands the sacred four times. Then the Keeper, followed by all present, moved his hands in the ceremonial motions, covering the body with the blessing. This touching of the earth and touching the limbs and body are said, by the older men, to represent the Creator making the human body and blowing life into it from the earth. Last Bull then raised his hand to the east, calling on the name of Sweet Root Standing. He asked a blessing for all the Cheyenne people, their families and "our relatives that are here with us" (that is, the non-Cheyennes).

The cloth blankets had been removed from the bundle, which now rested on the ground on Nimhoyah, the buffalo-calf-hide Turner. Slightly tugging on the string that closed the Hat container four times, Last Bull untied it. One by one the sacred contents were removed. There was braided sweet grass, the incense of the Plains tribes. Next came the scalps. They were not gone after all! Five in number, they were graduated in size and were mounted on willow hoops, in the old-time way. Next came a large buffalo-hide bag containing Issiwun itself. The holy object was finally revealed! A quiet "ah-h-h" went up from the watchers. As the Cheyennes have always maintained, even after all these centuries it showed no sign of deterioration. An unwrapped otter (or mink) skin followed. Next was a package of "old-time" tobacco. Finally, a bundle of fluffy substance, identified as animal hair, emerged. With the exception of the Sacred Hat and the otter skin, the other objects were wrapped in cloth.

All these holy things were viewed with infinite respect, as was fitting for the Sacred Buffalo Hat of Erect Horns. Those present were called upon to witness that the bundle was now intact.

Last Bull then prayed to Issiwun in Cheyenne and English, the tears streaming down his face in the old sacred manner. The families of the witnesses then reverently entered. Adults and little children alike stood in silence and awe before the sacred object that had so long been at the heart of the Cheyenne Way.

The Sacred Hat itself is formed from the skin of a buffalo cow's head, with the horns attached. The horns are shaved, so that they are about one-half the ordinary thickness of a buffalo horn. There is carving on the horns, and this has been rubbed with red paint. Across the brow, there is a broad beaded band of pony beads — the large beads the earliest traders brought to the northern Plains tribes. The beads are blue and white; and the base of the browband is rawhide. The beaded design is the "tipi design," with three inverted triangles projecting above it. Some older Cheyennes claim that this is the source of the similar design frequently seen on the headbands of the older warbonnets.

The upper hair of the Buffalo Hat is clearly exposed. At the front, along the top of the browband, the hair is red and bristly. At the rear of the Hat, it appears that another skin, probably mink, has been sewed to the buffalo-skin base. The beads are clearly sewed on — not glued, as Grinnell states.[48]

When all had viewed the Hat, Last Bull and John Woodenleg began to re-place the contents of the bundle, repacking the objects in the same order in which they had been previously placed. When this was completed, Last Bull again prayed, giving thanks for the safe return of the pipe and the "blower." The offer-ing cloths were replaced, and Issiwun was again hung on its tripod.

It was with a feeling of relief and joy that all moved up the hill to the feast that awaited us beneath Little Coyote's sun shade. Issiwun was safe. The Sacred Thing that had always been so much a part of the life of the people was in good hands. Maiyun was pleased. We should celebrate this good thing together; and we did.

Shortly after the opening of the Sacred Hat, John Stands and I journeyed to Oklahoma to visit the Southern Cheyennes. There, the news of Issiwun's safety was also received with joy. Some weeks later, just prior to my return to Chicago, I again visited Little Coyote to bid him and Weasel Woman good-by. In com-pany with John Stands-in-Timber we drove down to the sacred tipi. Issiwun was hanging over the door, covered with its "blankets." As sunset was near, the Keeper and his wife carried it carefully into the lodge. There the pipe was lighted and offered to the four directions, just as the Keepers had done for centuries. Again Little Coyote prayed to the Buffalo Hat, which he addressed as "My God." Interceding for the Cheyennes, he also prayed for the white priest who was now "a relative of the Cheyenne people." He continued on: "Wherever you guide him, protect him to follow the roads, so that nothing will happen to him. And I am always grateful to you, Issiwun."

John Stands and I quietly left the tipi after these prayers, and climbed the hill together. The Keeper and his wife still sat before the Sacred Bundle, their heads bowed in reverence.

In their devotion, they mirrored the proud, strong, natural spirituality always so characteristic of the Cheyenne nation. Issiwun, the Sacred Buffalo Hat, has seen the life and culture of the Northern Cheyennes rise, fall and begin to rise again. It is the sacred symbol of the changing, yet enduring, greatness of the Cheyenne People and the Cheyenne Way.

NOTES

1 There are at least three versions of the origin of the Sacred Hat. Some present-day Cheyennes speak of God visiting four villages. At the last village, He found the people in need of everything — health, strong hearts, strong minds, etc. To this last village He gave the Sacred Hat. A second version tells of two young men, dressed, painted and speaking alike, mysteriously appearing in camp. The young men together dove into a spring of water, and there they found an elderly woman. She gave them the gifts of corn and meat. To Erect Horns (also called Standing on the Ground) she gave the Buffalo Hat. Grinnell identifies the other youth as Sweet Medicine (or Sweet Root Standing). See *Journal of American Folklore*, Vol. 20, No. 78, July-September, 1907; also *By Cheyenne Campfires*, George Bird Grinnell, Yale University Press, New Haven, 1926, page 257ff. The account given here is based upon field interviews with Northern and Southern Cheyennes, and George Dorsey's account in *The Cheyenne Indians*, Vol. 1, Field-Columbian Museum Anthropological Series, Vol. IX, No. 1, 1905, p. 46ff.

2 Interviews with Firewolf, Northern Cheyenne Buffalo and Sun Dance priest.

3 Interviews with Rufus Wallowing, Northern Cheyenne.

4 *Ibid.*

5 Firewolf.

6 *Social Organization of the Cheyennes*, George Bird Grinnell, Vol. XIII, New York, 1902, p. 135.

7 *Ibid;* p. 141f.

8 *The Cheyenne Indians*, Vol. II, George Dorsey, Chicago, 1905, p. 62, plate XIX.

9 Dorsey, Vol. I; p. 49.

10 *The Cheyenne Indians*, George Bird Grinnell; Vol. I, Yale University Press, 1923, p. 230. Also, personal observation.

11 John Stands-in-Timber.

12 *The Fighting Cheyennes*, George Bird Grinnell, University of Oklahoma Press, 1956, p. 72ff.

13 *Ibid.;* p. 92f.

14 *Ibid.;* pp. 84-96.

15 *Calendar History of the Kiowa Indians;* James Mooney; Annual Report, Bureau of American Ethnology, XVII, part 1, Washington, 1896, p. 175.

16 *A Warrior Who Fought Custer*, T. B. Marquis, Minneapolis, 1931, p. 187.

17 *Fighting Cheyennes*, p. 344.

18 *Warrior Who Fought Custer*, p. 215.

19 *Ibid.*, p. 274. The "Turner" is so-called because it turns sickness and misfortune from the Cheyenne camps.

20 *Ibid.*, p. 281f.

21 *Fighting Cheyennes*, p. 396f.

22 *Ibid.*, p. 375.

23 *Warrior Who Fought Custer*, p. 287.

24 John Stands-in-Timber.

25 *Warrior Who Fought Custer*, p. 294.

26 Field interviews; also, *Ibid.*, p. 293.

27 John Stands-in-Timber.

28 Marquis, p. 299.

29 *Cheyenne Autumn*, Mari Sandoz, McGraw-Hill, New York, 1953, p. 25.

30 Field interviews with Sitting Man.

31 John Stands-in-Timber.

32 Frank Waters, Northern Cheyenne Old Man Chief, describing Coal Bear, 1958-59.

33 *Great Mysteries of the Cheyennes*, George Bird Grinnell, American Anthropologist, New Series, Vol. XII, 1910, pp. 542ff.

34 Charles Sitting Man. (*The Cheyenne Way*, K. N. Llewellyn and E. A. Hoebel, University of Oklahoma Press, 1941, adds additional details.)

35 *Great Mysteries of the Cheyennes*, p. 567.

36 *Ibid.*, p. 562.

37 Llewellyn and Hoebel, p. 156.

38 Southern Cheyenne informants to author.

39 *Great Mysteries*, p. 567.

40 Frank Waters, interviews with the author.

41 *Great Mysteries*, p. 568.

42 Frank Waters, Rufus Wallowing, John Stands-in-Timber, interviews with the author.

43 Josie Headswift, to the author.

44 This is a story in itself. I have only outlined it here, for the sake of the more important section concerning the granting of the Hat to Little Coyote and the opening of Issiwun.

45 Henry Tall Bull, Vice President of the Northern Cheyenne Tribal Council, interviews with the author.

46 Rufus Wallowing.

47 John Stands-in-Timber and others.

48 Personal observation. It should be noted that Grinnell's description in *Great Mysteries of the Cheyennes* is largely incorrect concerning the physical appearance of the Hat, with the exception of the horn and its carving. Apparently, Grinnell recorded this description from someone who had not seen the Sacred Hat, or else hesitated to describe such a sacred object to a non-Cheyenne — even one as much respected as Grinnell.

CHARACTERS,
WHITE AND RED

Intruders, water color by Charlie Russell

Watching the Settlers, oil by Charlie Russell

Chief Black Robe

FATHER PIERRE JEAN De SMET

By ALBERT ANTREI

A BANNER FLAPPING from a pole was stuck in the hollow center of a circle of squatting humans, composed of a council of hostile chiefs, a Jesuit priest and an interpreter. A silent multitude of Unkpapa, Oglalla, Minneconjou and other white-hating Indians strained to catch the council's words and to look curiously at the banner (which bore a picture of the Blessed Virgin surrounded by a halo of stars on one side and the words *Holy Name of Jesus* on the other). It was June 20, 1868. The light rains of early summer were past, the sun blazed on the high plains of the middle Yellowstone, and waves of heat rose from the grass bottoms of the Powder River. It may have occurred to Father Pierre Jean de Smet, S.J., seated on the warm ground, that it was uncomfortably hot for an old man.

He may have wished he were back in St. Louis, but this is doubtful, for the great Jesuit's last significant act in behalf of the Western Indians was about to be performed. Thirty years of tireless devotion were climaxed under the strain of Bright's disease, old age and fatigue in the midst of Indians unapproachable by the United States Army. But Father de Smet was no stranger to the Sioux, to the Powder River plains, or to the processes of peacemaking.

He spoke slowly, pausing occasionally to allow his English (affected by a Continental accent) to be translated into Sioux by his good friend, squawman-trader Charles E. Galpin. De Smet blessed the council and offered a prayer. Invoking the "Great Spirit," he spoke solemnly of the dangers to the whole Indian race of opposing a powerful government. Some Army and political minds of the times were thinking of the Indian in terms of genocide, which horrified the priest. Couching his references to God in general terms, he reminded them that peace among men was God's will and hence pleasing to Him. They should go to Fort Rice and let their headmen sign the treaty which many of their kinsmen had already signed at Forts Larned and Laramie. He described the benefits of government aid in agriculture and the education their children would receive to make their medicine as strong as the white man's.

The unsophisticated Sioux were flattered that a hostile government with so much firepower would trouble itself to send such an eminent peacemaker across more than 200 miles of grassland, just to council. About learning to farm, they

193

were not so sure: their favorite meat was still bison. Sitting Bull muttered something vague about protecting the oak trees, but he was not so vague about no more forts and no more reservations.

Black Moon said his feelings were good toward the Chief-Blackrobe-of-the-Frenchmen, but admitted they had not been so good of late toward other white men. He reviewed his grievances in detail. He thought Father de Smet's suggestion to go to Fort Rice was a good one, and he agreed that peace was desirable. All the important chiefs and medicine men then spoke. With few exceptions they supported the Fort Laramie Treaty of 1868 and urged the headmen to sign it at Fort Rice.

How much faith Father de Smet actually had in the Treaty of 1868 cannot be ascertained. He suspected the presence of gold in the Black Hills, and he must have comprehended that its discovery would make the treaty obsolete. It may also have been his hope that by the time gold was discovered the Indians might have become more sedentary in their habits. At any rate, in view of his illness, age and the bloodiness of events, it was a test of faith in his own works that he undertook to comb the plains for the most elusive and recalcitrant of the hostiles. For their part, the Sioux demonstrated sufficient faith in De Smet to stop their war drums and to listen to what he had to say.

De Smet had chosen his companions well. Charles Galpin had traded among the Sioux for many years and spoke their language fluently. Married to a Sioux woman, he had a daughter attending convent school in St. Louis. Two Bears, a Brulé chief, who had once been second to few in his hostility to white men, told the search party on June 14: "I hope they [the hostiles] will hear this time, for something seems to tell that this is the last opportunity they will have." These were prophetic words. Speaking of De Smet, he added: "May the Great Spirit, through the wisdom and goodness of this good man, now toiling with us, open our ears that we may listen to his words and our people and country be saved."

Aside from the testimony of Two Bears and the presence of eighty Sioux ready to defend him against their own people, if necessary, the priest experienced one more token of his labors. On the return to Fort Rice an older warrior, who had been with the Powder River bands, showed Father de Smet a weathered copper cross. "You gave me this twenty years ago," he said. The Sioux were willing to give peace another big try in 1868.

He was not a trailblazer in the sense of Lewis and Clark, but in an age of mare and shank's mare, Pierre Jean de Smet had long been associated with the vast Missouri-Platte, upper Great Basin and Columbia-Snake geographic complexes. Between 1840 and 1870 one might find him in almost any Indian village, blessing or baptizing children, instructing adults or simply talking. The unexpected knock on the lonely cabin door of a *coureur du bois* deep in the forest was apt to be made by the civilized knuckles of Father de Smet, come to make holy the natural wedlock of a trapper and his Indian woman.

Father de Smet was born "Pieter Jan de Smet," one of twins, on January 30, 1801, in Dendermonde, East Flanders. There was no Belgium at that time of history and hence the observation that he was "Belgian" is technically incorrect. In 1801, all of the southern Netherlands designated as Flemish was a political division of the Dutch Kingdom. Partly, it was the historical religious antipathy between the Catholic Flemish and the Protestant Dutch that made it customary among the Flemish to use the French or Latin equivalents of their names. Thus, "Pieter Jan" became "Pierre Jean," despite the solid Flemishness of the family.

Peter's school days were spent in Dendermonde and Mechelen. By the time he was twenty years old, he had heard of the Jesuit labors among the wild Indians of the wilderness of Kentucky from Father Charles Nerinckx, who habitually returned to Flanders in the interests of recruiting both young men and Flemish money for his missions. In 1821, Father Nerinckx tapped De Smet.

With the stars of faraway places in his eyes, Peter left with five others for America, departing from Flanders by stealth to avoid both parental and Dutch Protestant interference. Avoiding the Dutch was an adventure, but he did not lightly leave home. By letter he implored parental forgiveness, revealing his goal to be the Jesuit novitiate at Whitemarsh, Prince George's County, Maryland. He reached this destination on October 6, 1821. Docking at Philadelphia, he had found that city disappointingly civilized, with no Indians apparent.

On April 11, 1823, De Smet was one of six Flemish novices of the Society of Jesus who set out for Missouri to tame the wilderness with bell, book and candle. With them went six Irish, German and French novices and lay brothers to open a school for Indians near St. Louis (then an energetic little river port of five or six thousand half-tamed frontiersmen). Here, De Smet worked among both Indians and whites for more than ten years and helped build the Jesuit novitiate at Florissant, Missouri.

With the greater influx of white children in the area, the Indian school at St. Louis was made into a white college, the embryo of St. Louis University. De Smet served for a while both as faculty member of the college and as a roving missionary with Father Felix Verreydt among the Indians in the Council Bluffs area. De Smet, with tongue in cheek, wrote in a letter that "when I climbed the ladder to put (the cross) in place, Father Felix beheld the devil clap his tail between his legs and take flight over the big hills."

In 1840, the Jesuits responded to the heroic efforts of the Flathead Indians to acquire a mission in the Bitterroot Valley deep in the Rocky Mountains (then in "Oregon Territory") some 1500 miles west and north of St. Louis. During the preceding decade, four Flathead and Flathead-Nez Percé delegations had made the much publicized trek to St. Louis to seek religious light. Methodists had responded to the first delegation by sending out Reverend Jason Lee. Presbyterians and Congregationalists had followed with the Reverends Eels, Cushing, Parker and Spalding, and the famed medico-missionary, Marcus Whitman.

The fourth delegation met De Smet and Verreydt at Council Bluffs. Their story excited De Smet, who was always ready to see the hand of God in what more secular-minded men would have considered "chance." Catholic Iroquois in the employ of the North West Company and the Hudson's Bay Company, already settled among the Flatheads, had taught their new relatives something of the Catholic faith.

With the blessing of Joseph Rosati, Bishop of St. Louis, De Smet departed from Westport (Kansas City) with the last of Andrew Drips' rendezvous parties of the American Fur Company, in May, 1840. De Smet was a wide-eyed traveler. He speedily surrounded the wide western plains and mountains with a great spiritual embrace. He described the peculiar islands of the Platte River as ". . . thousands of islands . . . which might be taken for flotillas, mingling their full sails with verdant garlands or festoons of flowers."

On July 5, 1840, he celebrated the first Catholic Mass in Wyoming history on the open bluff overlooking the Green River flats and the fur rendezvous near Fort Bonneville (present Daniel, Wyoming).

At Fort Bonneville, De Smet met an ex-grenadier of Napoleon's army, a fellow native of East Flanders named De Velder. With this companion and an escort of Flathead Indians to their country, they proceeded by way of Pierre's Hole, the Teton River, the Henry Fork of the Snake to Henry's Lake and across a nearby pass through the mountains to Red Rock Lakes, in what is now Montana. (Meanwhile, Jason Lee had not gotten on well with the Flatheads, and he had moved out to the Willamette Valley, much further West.)

Finding the Flatheads receptive, De Smet and De Velder in late summer set out on horseback for the east, going by way of the Three Forks of the Missouri and Bozeman Pass to the Yellowstone River, which they followed to its juncture with the Missouri at Fort Union. This was dangerous country. Not only was the rambunctious grizzly still abundant, but De Smet and his companion experienced the chilly fears of all who chanced upon fresh and old aftermaths of bloody intertribal battles.

Using their wits all the way, priest and soldier-of-fortune made it through a maze of Blackfeet, Minnetaree, Gros Ventre and Assiniboin war parties by ruse and stealth, fear never leaving them until they reached Fort Union. Here the travelers were informed that with all the Indian brawls normal to the Yellowstone bottoms and the bluffs above them, they must have been in the care of the Lord's angels.

From Fort Union, De Smet and De Velder made part of their way to St. Louis accompanied by several fur trappers. Point-blank meetings with Sioux above Fort Pierre proved a bit edgy at first, but ended on a note of mutual respect. One of the trappers introduced the priest as *Chief-Blackrobe-of-the-Frenchmen* to the Sioux, who took the man's word for the appellation but expressed a desire to know more about De Smet's black robe and crucifix. They were not brushed off. The Indians listened attentively as he explained Christ and His Cross, as well as the Jesuit costume. When finished, everybody shook hands. From then on the

Indians and Scouts Talking, water color by Charlie Russell

Brave, by Charlie Russell

Sioux generally knew who Chief-Blackrobe-of-the-Frenchmen was — and that he demanded neither land, women, horses nor pelts. It was understood that he sold neither whisky nor guns but was a man of peace — a great rarity among white men!

By June of 1841, De Smet was traveling west again, this time with the ill-fated company of John Bidwell's Western Emigration Society, which he accompanied as far as Soda Springs, Idaho. There were eleven in the missionary group. Father Nicholas Point, a Frenchman, served subsequently for many years in missions to the Flatheads, Coeur d'Alenes and Blackfeet. Father Gregory Mengarini, Italian, was a linguist, a medical expert and a musician. An extremely versatile man, he was to take care of the mission's many needs — from Indian languages, pill dispension and bone setting to choir singing. More mundane needs were in the hands of a blacksmith, a carpenter and a tinsmith in the persons of the lay brothers William Claessens (Flemish), Charles Huet (Walloon) and Joseph Specht (German). De Smet had also engaged a hunter and three French-Canadians to handle baggage, wagons and animals. His guide was the able frontier trapper and mountain man, Thomas Fitzpatrick, better known as "Broken Hand." The mission group scratched their names on the south side of Independence Rock, later dubbed "The Register of the Desert."

De Smet's party reached the Bitterroot River in September, 1841. There the mission of St. Mary's was established (near present-day Stevensville, Montana). Their route of travel significantly avoided the more logical route by way of Lemhi Valley and Lost Trail Pass in favor of the somewhat longer, but lower and easier, trail across Monida Pass to the Beaverhead drainage.

St. Mary's would remain as De Smet's first and greatest joy among the missions he founded in the Northwest. Even when temporarily abandoned in the

1850's because of Indian troubles, St. Mary's was closest to being De Smet's heartbeat.

The winter of 1841-1842 was spent "in quarters" at St. Mary's. A stockade was erected and the beginnings of a chapel and living rooms were planned. The Indians' practice of plural marriage engaged most of De Smet's initial attentions, and for some time he struggled with it. It took some doing, because polygamy was part of the age-old Flathead culture and they were shocked to learn that it was a sin. Nor could the Flatheads easily grasp the significance of the Catholic priests' celibacy. They decided this was a hard religion and, being hard, it must have great virtues and truths.

Unlike Jason Lee, De Smet was happy among the Flatheads. Many of his lengthy, well written letters praise that tribe's staunch standards of character, occasionally to the point of the incredible. From De Smet's letters the Flatheads are described as almost untouched by the traders' whisky and capable of holding their own against the dreaded Blackfeet.

De Smet was not open-minded about religion. Most certainly he was a man committed to Catholic purpose. Nevertheless, he rarely preached fire-and-brimstone. When later he did so to the Crows, further east along the Yellowstone, they replied that they knew of only two of their whole tribe who were Heaven-bent, and the facts were not all in on them. Despite this pessimism about morals, the Crow Indians were curious about the whole concept of "prayer." De Smet always seemed to find Indians emotionally suited to religious ceremony and curious about prayer. He learned early that the Indian liked a little pomp, ceremony and theater with his religious learning. So he enlisted three American flags to fly in the breeze, and with the aid of ten neophyte Flatheads to intone two canticles, he recited all the prayers and explained the Apostle's Creed and the Ten Commandments to a gathering of 3000 attentive and solemn Crows. He was very careful to disclaim any magical powers or ability to heal the sick and infirm by mysticism, however. Only God, he told them, could remove evils; but he taught them to come to God with their troubles with pure hearts and in repentance. No one knows who enjoyed it the most, Father de Smet or the Crows, but his "great mass" in Absaroka Country was memorable.

For all of his emphasis on "correct" instruction in the ways of the Church, De Smet recognized the immensity of the gulf in time and space between the prehistoric world of the Indian and that of civilized Europe. "There are cases," he sighed one day, "when all the requisite dispositions may entirely consist in an act of faith, and in the sincere desire to enter Heaven by the right path."

The many place-name references in the land of the Flatheads to "Hell" and the "Devil" amused De Smet. Most of them were of French-Canadian origin. He wrote to a superior that he hoped His Reverence would not be alarmed to read that his humble servant had, on several occasions, "examined the Devil's Pass, went through the Devil's Gate, rowed on (his) stream, and jumped from (his) horns." He changed "Devil's Gate" of the Sweetwater River to "Heaven's Avenue" — because of the natural beauty of the river gap near Independence Rock, but the name did not stick. De Smet's humor was the equal of his courage.

The humble log cabins which De Smet erected or caused to be erected, and tried to join together in all this immense area, never equaled the elaborate chain of missions of Junipero Serra in old California, Eusebio Kino's "White Dove of the Desert" in Arizona or the battle-wracked Franciscan chains in the Rio Grande environs. Yet De Smet's successes appear in Lewis Henry Morgan's *Indian Journals of 1859-1862*, which are not generally kind to mission efforts among American Indians, whether Protestant or Catholic. When Morgan met De Smet on the Missouri River steamer, *Spread Eagle*, in May of 1862, he called him "a noble looking man" and "a most delightful gentleman." From De Smet, he obtained considerable information on edible and pharmaceutical herbs of the Northwest.

The attractiveness of De Smet's character and personality suggests that his greatest appeal were not photogenic edifices, as in the Southwest, but warm abstractions he constructed in the hearts of people, including many he could not convert. The basic ingredients of his labors were compounded of phenomenal good humor, a pristine and impressive faith and an unselfconscious sincerity which transcended the cynicism of all religions, politics and atheisms. De Smet's immunity to frontier dangers borders on benevolent protection. In violent times and places he achieved no enemies and suffered no harm. He traveled for thirty years among savage Indians, few of whom had any reason to love white men; yet he was never struck or threatened. He saw little bloodshed. But he prevented it between others on several occasions. His relations with the wilderness and its denizens were intimate, personal and generally serene.

De Smet was capable of the unjaded joy of an intelligent child. His description of Indians he met and passed in the Bear River Valley of northern Utah, where he paused to soak in the sight for as long as they took to come into view and to disappear over the last ridge, is typical: *"Represent to yourself a band of horses . . . loaded with bags and boxes to a height equal to their own, and these surmounted by . . . young and old, male and female . . . to which the pencil of a Hogarth or a Breughel could scarcely do justice. One of these animals, scarcely four feet high, had four large sacks of dried meat, two on each side, above which were tied several other objects, terminating in a kind of platform. On the summit . . . was seated crosslegged on a bearskin, a very old person smoking his calumet. At his side, on another Rosinante, was mounted . . . his wife, seated . . . on the tops of sacks and bags that contained all sorts of roots, dried beans and fruits, grains, and berries. . . ."*

Only a cultured, broad mind, at perfect peace and harmony with itself and in love with its whole world, could see Breughel and Cervantes in a savage Indian family. With perfect composure, Father de Smet traveled late that day. Well toward midnight, he and his guide, the Indian he called "Francis Xavier," reached the divide between the Bear River Valley and the watershed of the Portneuf

River. About them was a wilderness exceeded for savagery by few in the world. "Wrapped up in a blanket," he wrote later, "and with a saddle for a pillow, I stretched myself upon a rock and immediately fell into a sound sleep."

After establishing St. Mary's in 1841, De Smet ambitiously dreamed of a gigantic chain of Jesuit missions from the Rockies to the Pacific, and from the north rim of the Great Basin northward beyond what are now the great Canadian provinces of Alberta and British Columbia.

By 1842, French-Canadian Jesuits had established the mission of St. Paul in the Willamette Valley, near Fort Vancouver, in the midst of the fur trade. In the spring of 1842, De Smet visited Fathers Demers and Blanchet at that place, and the three Jesuits discussed plans for a consolidation of their missions and for recruiting the kind of help that was needed. A plan was drawn which must have been close to De Smet's heart, traveler that he was. Although an enthusiastic missionary, he bore Mother Flanders on his sleeve. Accordingly, he was delighted to be assigned the task of seeking funds and religious workers in Europe. De Smet departed from the Willamette Valley to follow the wild shores of the Columbia eastward and northward to its confluence with Clark's Fork, and up this stream to the Bitterroot and St. Mary's. This little jaunt took approximately forty days. He covered 500 miles, but went uphill all the way, using horses and mules to carry supplies from Vancouver to St. Mary's. He hardly greeted Fathers Mengarini and Point and Brother Huet at St. Mary's before he instructed the Reverend Mengarini to have Point and Huet open a mission for the Coeur d'Alene Indians, to be called "Sacred Heart."

In this jamboree spirit, De Smet then was off on a several-thousand-mile jaunt to the "Old Country." He first stayed two weeks in the Three Forks-of-the-Missouri area with some Flathead Indians, whose language he was learning fast. Following that, he took the dangerous Yellowstone trail again, accompanied this time by the Iroquois, Ignatius, and a half-breed Crow named Gabriel. At Fort Alexander, the trading post founded on the north bank of the Yellowstone by Alexander Culbertson, opposite the mouth of Rosebud Creek, De Smet's party was joined by two American hunters. From Fort Union on the Missouri, the Jesuit and his two Indians rode by boat into St. Louis, confronted only by low water, snags, sandbars and a tornado which blew the wheelhouse off the boat.

Over a period of several months De Smet recruited three sturdy recruits in the persons of Fathers Peter de Vos and Adrian Hoecken and an Irish Brother named J. B. McGean. He saw them on the American Fur Company's Missouri riverboat, the *John Auld*, at Westport, gave them instructions, prayed with them, and bade them Godspeed almost impatiently as he turned his restless feet in the direction of Europe.

By Christmas, 1843, De Smet left Europe again. (In the course of his life he was to make at least ten such round trips). He shipped himself, four other priests, six nuns and one brother from Antwerp on the *Indefatigable* to the Willamette in Oregon Territory, by way of Cape Horn. The little sailing vessel was well named, being nearly as durable as De Smet. Besides being nearly blown into the Horn by gales, the ravages of *mal-de-mer* beset the company and crew. Although they had said good-by to the homy sight of *Sint Mariaskerk* in Antwerp on December 12, 1843, they did not arrive at the mouth of the Columbia until the feast day of St. Ignatius Loyola, on July 31, 1844. Even in this, De Smet saw an omen of good cheer, for the *Indefatigable* made several passes at the Columbia's currents and only by trial and error and stubborn seamanship was a channel finally found.

Father de Smet then acquired a canoe somewhere, which he paddled to Fort Vancouver. But Father Blanchet, Grand Vicar of all the missions west of the Rockies, was not there when he arrived. De Smet arranged for the *Indefatigable's* passengers to go to St. Paul's mission in the Willamette, and by October 3 he set off up the Columbia again. It was a happy day for him to find Father Hoecken not only well, but happily surrounded by Kalispell Indians on the east shore of the Pend d'Oreille River (near present Cusick, Washington), about fifty miles above the Pend d'Oreille's mouth. Father Hoecken had christened his plot "St. Ignatius" (not to be confused with the St. Ignatius Mission on Montana's Flathead Reservation, established by Fr. Hoecken in 1854). De Smet arrived here sometime in late autumn.

After resting briefly on the "Bay of the Kalispel," he left to visit the new Sacred Heart Mission established by Father Point on the St. Joe River. According to Chittenden and Richardson, De Smet left for St. Mary's in February, and he returned to St. Ignatius before snow melt. He helped start buildings for St. Ignatius, returning to Fort Vancouver for supplies in March, 1845. He did not return until the last of July, with eleven horses loaded with implements and provisions. On his return, De Smet established new stations to serve the northwestern missions, one at Kettle Falls and the other at Lake De Boey.

Having learned while at St. Mary's that the mission there had been threatened by the Blackfeet from time to time, De Smet decided the time was ripe to challenge Satan on the state of the Blackfeet soul. He horrified his immediate colleagues with the simple statement of his intention of approaching the Blackfeet from an unexpected direction, as though in the belief that surprise would either awe or amuse them. The usual way to the Blackfeet country from the Bitterroot was through the Hellgate, over the Bozeman Pass to the Three Forks, and down the Missouri from there. From that point there seems not to have been any problem finding Blackfeet; the problem was to avoid them.

With a Flathead companion or two, Father de Smet left St. Ignatius on the Bay of the Kalispel on August 9, 1845, going up the Pend d'Oreille River to the lake of that name. From the shores of this beautiful lake he and his little party followed a dim trail through the dark forest swamps approaching the Bonner's Ferry country of northern Idaho. His purpose was to find and follow up the valley of the Kootenay River, called in his day the Arcs-a-Plat (and the McGillivray).

One suspects a sounder purpose in De Smet's decision to plunge into dank northern Rocky Mountain forests than to amuse three great tribes of the awesome

Blackfeet Nation. In a letter dated August 7, 1845 at "Kalispel Bay" he concludes: "I purpose to visit these two tribes (the *Flatbows* and the *Kootenays*), who have never yet had the consolation of beholding a 'black gown' among them." Furthermore, in his constant seeking across horizons, Father de Smet was as incurable a geographer as David Thompson. He showed more than a casual interest in compiling information on that whole vast mountain complex north and east of Lake Pend d'Oreille. On August 9, 1845, he began one of the boldest treks in Western frontier history.

There are times when De Smet seems to have been a man in a hurry. Father Hoecken had confided his knowledge of the presence of copper ore, and De Smet, always interested in matters scientific, had detected signs of gold and silver. He may have felt that religious efforts had to be consolidated before the influx of white miners could complicate missionary work. In any event, Father de Smet proceeded up the Kootenay River to its headwaters. The Blackfeet then were pressing hard against the Crows in the upper Yellowstone Valley, and De Smet could have found bands of them anywhere from Bozeman Pass to Edmonton. Antedating this period, men of the North West Fur Company and the Hudson's Bay people had found them fiercely at home in the drainages of the North and South Saskatchewan rivers. Acknowledged and feared as the most enthusiastic warriors and hunters of the Northwest, they now held the buffalo plains and beaver streams from the east face of the Rockies to the mouth of Milk River, and were known to contest ground with Sioux and Shoshones south of the Yellowstone and east of Fort Union. Unless De Smet had better reasons for his northern trek than contacting Blackfeet, his motives for crossing the Canadian mountain backbone in the autumn of 1845 are dubious indeed.

Indian woman, over 100 years old, who helped build Cataldo mission

A Kootenai family, western Montana

He did not pause long among the Kootenays, nor long enjoy the company of a band of Assiniboins for a portion of the trail. In early October he was knocking at the gates of Rocky Mountain House, an outpost of the Hudson's Bay Company at the juncture of the Clearwater and North Saskatchewan rivers. He made the acquaintance of some Catholic Crees, and eventually established contact with some small Blackfeet bands. But in trying to widen his acquaintance with them, he was led astray by a half-breed guide and left wandering dangerously lost on the plains south of Rocky Mountain House in November. Wisely, he postponed his efforts and returned to the comparative comforts of Rocky Mountain House and Mr. Harriott's fireplaces, well chilled and snowed-upon as he was. After a short rest he departed for Fort Augustus (Edmonton), where he decided to spend the winter.

The truth is, Father de Smet's trek nearly overwhelmed him. Blackfeet country was altogether too vast to take by storm. In March, 1846, he arrived at Fort Assiniboine on the Athabasca River with a dogteam obtained from Rocky Mountain House. His enthusiasm was not exactly dimmed, for his letters sparkle with the adventure of the trail, sometimes humorous and sometimes gasping. But northwestern geography awed him. He faced two problems of life or death, other than sheer distance: these were his tendency to corpulence, and the deep snows and mushy muskegs of the Canadian forests. Before Father de Smet "mushed" his dogs on the long, long trail back to St. Mary's he trained off twenty pounds of excess fat in thirty days. To avoid deep snow, dense forests and soft ground it was found necessary to travel on the ice of the Athabasca. De Smet and his few Indian companions mushed up the Athabasca to old Fort Jasper. Somewhere along the trail, probably at this Hudson's Bay post, Father de Smet disposed of his dog team, after accompanying Mr. Fraser, of the fort, to the "Lake of Islands." Some forty-four people went along on this little outing. In taking their leave of the good father, the men of the fort insisted on naming a nearby mountain for him and christening it in volleys of gunfire. Several of them insisted on accompanying his little party a distance of ten miles along their way to set their feet aright and point out the way. It was not exactly a Brussels boulevard, but neither was the trail untraveled, for along the way De Smet eventually met a party of Hudson's Bay Company employees near the pass. These men were on their way back to York Factory on the Hudson's Bay from the Columbia River posts. One of the men was well-known to Father de Smet — Francis Ermatinger, factor of the Hudson's Bay post, Fort Hall (Idaho).

Crossing the Canadian Rockies in March is hardly a social breeze, however, and in 1846 early spring thaws had made roaring water monsters out of what should have been freshets. Fearful of avalanches, combating high water, freezing nights and numerous sleetstorms, De Smet's party fought its way to Boat Encampment, at the westward bend of the upper Columbia. De Smet slid off hills into snowbanks, barked his shins and head against unresisting trees and rocks, ripped his clothing and froze the toenails off his bloody feet. His snowshoes tripped him and deceived him and he blacked and blued his skin from head to foot. He waded icy streams up to his armpits and crossed one such stream forty times along a meandering trail. Yet, at Boat Encampment he wrote in a letter about the joys of sleeping "under the beautiful canopy of the starry heavens ... and sweet murmuring rills. . . ." It was May when De Smet strode into Fort Colville. His round trip, by foot and dogteam, represented nine months' time and nearly 2000 of some of the hardest miles on the continent. His dismay — if any — was forgotten by the time he reached Fort Colville. Anticipating the needs of St. Mary's, he headed down the Columbia by skiff for Fort Vancouver to obtain supplies for its growing offshoots among the Spokane, Nez Percé, Pend d'Oreille, Kalispel, Kootenai, Couer d'Alene and other tribes. He did not return to St. Mary's until August 10, 1846.

It was then that De Smet learned that the Flatheads and Blackfeet were planning a peace smoke and a little buffalo hunt soon. He re-met the Blackfeet through the good offices of the Flatheads, and Nicholas Point was assigned to a dubious Blackfeet mission on the Sun River (to be called St. Peter's). De Smet returned to St. Louis by boat from Fort Benton.

For three years Father de Smet had been laying the foundation for what he hoped would be a vast empire of "Christian Indians." What he meant by "Christian Indians," of course, was "Catholic Indians." He was aware, all along, that Protestant clergymen and one medical missionary had beaten him to the pagan "vineyard" by a decade. Yet De Smet continued on good personal terms with most of the Protestants he met in the field and among the wagon trains. His letters describing occasional visits are pleasant. He counted Dr. Whitman and the Reverends Cushing, Eels and Spalding as men of great faith and solemn purpose, but he seemed not to be much taken with Mr. Lee. It was a Protestant friend who provided him with the gem of thought which he quoted in his letters from time to time, giving him as it did a fairly profound insight into his own work: "It is in a journey through the desert that we see how attentive providence is to the wants of men."

In his efforts to become acquainted with the Indian and his country, De Smet immersed himself in a manner undreamed of by most missionaries. Through letters to friends, relatives and superiors the whole immense frontier territory became more clearly understood to the outside world. Of the three-year period, 1844-1846, De Smet noted: "I was ... three years without a letter. I was two years in the mountains without tasting bread, salt, coffee, tea, sugar. I was ... without a roof, without a bed. I have been six months without a shirt on my back, and often ... whole days and nights without [anything] to eat."

Enthusiastic as he was, sometimes to the point of bubbling, De Smet was never anybody but himself among the Indians. Although he often seemed to be able to lose himself among them, there is no record that he was invited to be some chief's "blood brother." It was always abundantly clear to the Indians that all De Smet asked was a brotherhood in God's name to transcend their cultural dif-

St. Ignatius mission, established 1857 by the Jesuits

ferences. The cultural differences were real and great, and he never glossed over
them. It has been said by some historians that "De Smet never completely understood the Indian." They point out that, despite his fluency in Flemish, French,
English and Latin, and eventually in the Salishan tongue, Flathead, he was not
a working linguist. But he understood Indians well enough to anticipate when to
leave them alone, and he was able to communicate. He confessed, in awe, that the
Indian stomach baffled him in its ability to adjust to alternate feasts and famines.
Often he referred to the redmen as "savages," and he certainly demonstrated an
understandable caution in the proximity of war parties. When he discovered a
Blackfeet hiding in the brush while on an excursion with a group of Flatheads, he
did not report the discovery, but as calmly as possible recommended to his companions that they double the watch on their horses that evening. This demonstrated considerable practical understanding. The redman's exaggerated solemnity
amused De Smet privately. He was no believer in Jean Jacques Rousseau's concept of "the noble savage," and he possessed the nineteenth-century frontiersman's
sharp sense of omnipresent danger. He considered it a prime responsibility of the
missionary in the wilderness to be alert and alive, as well as holy in conduct.

Shortly after De Smet's return to St. Louis in 1846, the Diocese of St. Louis
began to place more official restraint on him. His letters, begun at Council Bluffs
in the 1830's, describing his experiences and impressions, had circulated well and

they gave him considerable popular acclaim. Some of the hierarchy considered this bad for a priest's humility; and his literary enthusiasm also led to official fears of impulsiveness. His efforts to obtain money abroad for his missions were misinterpreted by some as a violation of vows of holy poverty. Politely, with the obnoxious courtesy a sympathetic authority can sometimes exercise, he was made "procurator." This kept him traveling, but only over well established trails and through well worked channels closer to St. Louis. In this position he traveled from New Orleans to Fort Berthold, Dakota Territory. He chafed, but being trained in obedience, he functioned.

De Smet became increasingly worried by the speed with which the West was changing during the 1850's. He foresaw military clashes to come, especially with the Sioux. He suggested in the 1860's that if the Sioux were not treated more fairly they might be tempted to join hands militarily with the Confederacy. What he feared most was the more subtle effects of sudden large-scale contacts between the explosive, expanding, highly organized white man's culture on the weaker, more placid, less organized Indian societies.

Father de Smet was too well established to be hogtied completely by any such title as "Procurator." In 1851, in an effort to head off a series of bloody guerrilla wars threatening along the entire Oregon Trail, the United States Superintendent of Indian Affairs at St. Louis, D. D. Mitchell, requested De Smet's attendance at the intertribal council at Fort Laramie. Although historically unrealistic, the powwow accomplished a valuable truce.

De Smet was approached again by the government in 1858 to help settle the Yakima War, which had flared up in Oregon Territory. Among others, the Flatheads were involved (the only large-scale hostilities in which this tribe ever engaged white men). St. Mary's mission had to be abandoned.

De Smet's diplomatic efforts were most sorely tested in matters involving the Sioux. Although he had passed through their country many times, De Smet had never become as intimately acquainted with this sprawling nation as with other tribes. Effective missions among them were always high on his list of things to do after 1839, when he mediated a squabble between a band of Sioux and Potawotamis. The whisky-soaked Potawotamis, uprooted not long before from their ancestral lands in Wisconsin and Illinois, were at that time debauching the Omaha-Council Bluffs area, and De Smet's mediation kept them from getting their swollen heads bashed.

But when the Santee Sioux raided the Minnesota settlements in 1862, killed a thousand citizens and destroyed over two million dollars' worth of property, military retaliation was prompt, decisive and ruthless, despite the federal government's preoccupation with the Civil War. Hatred between the Sioux and the whites by then defeated all hope for the development of missions. Yet De Smet avoided neither the Sioux nor their country. He plied his way from agency to agency, village to village, up and down the Missouri and Platte rivers and their larger tributaries, visiting not only the Sioux, but weaker tribes in their midst as well.

Despite his later preoccupations with the Sioux, De Smet's thoughts never entirely left his old friends, the Flatheads. Visiting Montana Territory in the 1860's, he was delighted to find Father Ravalli renovating St. Mary's and building a pharmacy shop to adjoin it, the first one in Montana. On this trip, Father de Smet returned to the East by way of San Francisco and the Isthmus of Panama, a route he employed between the East and the West a time or two in his last years. This was partly because he was aware of the Sioux and Cheyenne moods. But another reason, he confided, was not so much wild Indians as the wilder whites, who were now killing for gold dust in western Montana Territory.

June, 1864, found Father de Smet at Fort Berthold in behalf of the United States government. With General Sully, he was to arrange peace negotiations with the Sioux. But when the Santees moved their village directly opposite the fort, across the Missouri, a bad state of jitters arrived with them. Only De Smet dared to cross the river to powwow. He and Sully could not agree closely on an approach to the Sioux problem although a sort of *modus vivendi* was finally worked out.

By August, De Smet had returned to St. Louis and another journey to Europe followed his efforts at Fort Berthold. On this significant voyage he received a decoration from the Belgian government, "Chevalier of the Order of Leopold." His health being bad, he remained in Europe for a full year. Flanders had never lost its appeal for him as the place of home and family, and like no other place on earth it represented a haven of rest.

De Smet's energy for years had been a product of his will, not of his health. His hearing had gradually become sub-normal. Between 1849 and 1867 he was afflicted with weakening eyesight more than is usually expected with increasing age. He suffered a series of throat infections, dyspepsia, erisepalas and gradually worsening nephritis. A tendency toward obesity further complicated his health. By 1869, he had experienced most of the symptoms of renal disorders except irrationality. He had suffered such attacks of blindness and near-paralytic strokes that for many months he was prevented from conducting Mass.

It was an ill and very tired peacemaker who plodded the monotonous plains west from Fort Rice in 1868.

Little Fort Rice, on the Missouri River ten miles above the mouth of the Cannonball, was well over 200 miles from the camp of the hostiles whom the government sought. When De Smet set out to look for them he was old at sixty-seven, and his weight had wasted away to 160 pounds. Yet, with an escort of eighty friendly Sioux, including some women, he pushed resolutely westward into spring rains and mud. Time was no longer on the side of either the Sioux or Father de Smet.

Awaiting the result at Fort Rice were Peace Commissioners John B. Sanborn and Generals William S. Harney and Alfred H. Terry, interpreter Nicholas Janis and the able Protestant missionary, the Reverend Samuel Hinman, B.D.

Current events did not provide even the dimmest hope for peace. Colonel Henry B. Carrington was besieged by Red Cloud at Forts C. F. Smith and Phil

Kearney, and in that locality Captain Fetterman and a detachment of men had been lured into a dress rehearsal for the later bloody melodrama on the Little Big Horn. The Peace Commission, organized by the government under pressure from Eastern humanitarians and abolitionists like Henry Ward Beecher and Peter Cooper, was unrealistic. (Neither Beecher nor Cooper had ever looked an armed Indian in the eye.)

Despite the advice of friends, red and white alike, De Smet's peace party left Fort Rice on Wednesday, June 3, 1868. On hand for the long trail were wagons and teams and some saddle stock. The hostiles, discovered by De Smet's scouts, who carried tobacco handouts with them, were met on June 19. "If the tobacco is returned," his Sioux escort had advised him, "you had better go back to Fort Rice." But the tobacco was accepted, and De Smet's scouts returned with wild-riding young men from the hostile camp, evidently curious about this blackrobe and wanting to see him for themselves.

The meeting of De Smet and the hostiles on the Powder River was an historic, if little known, event. Of several thousand Indians gathered there, 500 horsemen thundered out of the camp to greet the Chief-Blackrobe-of-the-French-men: "We moved slowly to within a half-mile of the main column, when they stopped and went through some of their war maneuvers," wrote Charles E. Galpin in his journal, "scattering in all directions, then circling around the main body. . . . All at once four dashing fellows with their bows and arrows and other arms came toward us. We halted to wait for them. Suddenly they rushed forward as if charging; three went straight to Father De Smet and took him by the hand; and a fourth merely waved his hand, and then dashed past us at full speed."

The "war maneuvers" mentioned by Galpin were probably the customary greeting recorded by other observers of a full charge accompanied by shooting in the air. Nobody was alarmed. Bullets fired into the air were intended to indicate empty guns.

At Fort Rice good feelings rode the plains on a high horse and General Alfred H. Terry was a grateful man. On June 28, 1868, he dispatched a message to the Reverend P. J. de Smet, S.J.:

> Dear Sir:
>
> Messengers bringing your letter of the 25th instant arrived this morning. We are delighted to learn that your expedition has been so successful, and we feel that not only ourselves but the nation owes you a debt of gratitude for the extremely valuable service which you have rendered to it. General Harney and Sanborn arrived here on the 21st and they will remain until a treaty can be consummated. I very much regret to learn from a letter to LaFramboise from Major Galpin that you are quite unwell. I sincerely trust that you are suffering from only a temporary illness and that the rest and quiet which will follow your return will speedily restore you to health.
>
> With sentiments of the highest respect, I am, dear Sir, your most obedient servant.
>
> Alfred H. Terry
> Bvt. Major-General

On July 3, the three members of the Peace Commission at Fort Rice collaborated on a second letter to Father de Smet:

> We are satisfied that but for your long and painful journey into the heart of the hostile country, and but for the influence over even the most hostile of the tribes which your years of labor among them have given you, the results which we have reached here could not have been accomplished. We are well aware that our thanks can be of little worth to you, and that you will find true reward for your labors and for the dangers and privations which you have encountered in the consciousness that you have done much to promote peace on earth and good will to men; but we should do injustice to our own feelings were we not to render to you our thanks and express our deep sense of the obligations under which you have laid us.
>
> > Gen. Harney
> > Sanborn
> > Gen. Terry

The Fort Rice treaty signed by the Indians was attested to by P. J. de Smet, S.J., the Rev. Samuel D. Hinman, Nicholas Janis, Frank La Framboise, and James C. O'Conner. On July 4, De Smet returned to St. Louis.

The vital service he had rendered was not even mentioned in the Peace Commission's official report, when it later appeared.

The Powder River Council climaxed the frontier career of Pierre Jean de Smet. His journeys from St. Louis after that were few. Whatever his pains, he could now turn to reverie to assuage them: councils with pagans and lectures at the Sorbonne; an emissary of peace from the Potawatami to the Sioux and bearer of tidings from President Pierce to European crowned heads; the embraces of Indian chiefs and Gregory XVI; the pressed hands in friendship of Sitting Bull and Abraham Lincoln; the virgin wilderness of the Kootenai forests and the soft blossoms of April in Paris. Sought out by the United States government in times of Indian troubles, in peace De Smet was largely ignored by officialdom in the matter closest to his heart — the Indian missions. But bitterness was too foreign to De Smet's nature to endure longer than the moment.

On May 13, 1873, Captain La Barge asked his good friend, Peter de Smet, to employ his offices to bless his new Missouri riverboat. He did so, standing on the deck of the *DeSmet*. It was poetic justice. Father de Smet had occasionally referred to the Missouri as "my river."

Like most other things in De Smet's life, it proved a happy event. The last sacraments were administered to him on May 20, and three days later he was dead.

Natawista: The Major's Lady

By MILDRED WALKER SCHEMM

BACK IN THE good days before the Civil War the people of Peoria, Illinois, were astonished to see a Blackfeet Indian tepee pitched on the lawn of one of the show places of that fair city. The fine property belonged to Major Alexander Culbertson, a former fur trader, and Major Culbertson's wife was the daughter of a Blood chief.

For most of the year Mrs. Culbertson came and went as a civilized gentlewoman. Her clothes were of the finest materials and in the latest style, and anyone seeing her with one of her daughters from the Moravian Seminary in Pennsylvania would have thought her completely civilized. But when Indian summer came, the Major's lady, born *Natawista Iksana*, Sacred Snake Woman, shed the many ruffled skirts and corset and tucked chemise, the heeled leather boots with fancy stitching, the gloves and bonnet and calash she wore with such grace, and clothed herself once more in a single garment of fine buckskin, ornamented with dyed porcupine quills. She walked out of the mansion Major Culbertson had built with the fortune he had made in the fur trade, away from the heavy carpets and lace curtains and carved walnut furniture, and returned to the simple freedom of a tepee on her own spacious front lawn. She paid no attention to the carriages driving ever so slowly beyond the shrubbery and the fancy picket fence, nor to the inquisitive faces peering out of the carriages. It was cool in the tepee on those breathless Illinois days and she could remember the mountains and the prairie and the streams running down from the glaciers of her ancestral home.

Natawista was no mere Indian squaw taken by a white man as a poor substitute for a woman of his own race, but, for once, a person of that great charm, dignity and beauty which the writers of romantic fiction and the makers of movies always ascribe to their fictitious Indian heroines.

There is a rare tintype picture of her, in which she looks about above her prim white collar, fastened with its brooch, with a stolid, enigmatic gaze that entirely conceals the wild flash of her eyes or curve of laughter on her straight-lined mouth.[1] Her black hair, parted in the middle and combed into two braids, lankly borders her face. It is difficult to conjure up any hint of beauty or estimate her charm from that picture, but both beauty and charm must have been there; for hardly a visitor to Fort Union or Fort Benton in those days refrained from writing in his journal about Major Culbertson's lady.

Alexander Culbertson

Isaac I. Stevens

One visitor, Rudolph Friederick Kurz, the young Swiss artist, wrote in 1851: "If Mr. Culbertson's Indian wife had not received news of her younger brother's having been shot by the Assiniboin, I should have had a chance to study one of the most beautiful Indian women. In token of her grief she had her long lustrous black hair cut short. She would be an excellent model for a Venus, ideal woman of the primitive race; a perfect 'little wife.' "[2]

Major Culbertson first saw *Natawista* in 1840 when she came down from Canada with her father, Chief *Men-Es-To-Kos*, to trade at Fort Union on the mouth of the Yellowstone River. The bright-eyed young Indian girl attracted him at once and he sent an *engagé* with nine horses to tie to her eldest brother's lodge and ask him for the girl. The next day the chief's daughter was sent to him with

Fort Union, 1866

nine horses in exchange for those he had given.[3] And after the proper speeches and smoking of pipes, *Natawista's* people went back to Canada, satisfied, and she became Major Culbertson's wife by proper Indian standards. She was about fifteen at the time of her marriage; he was thirty. He had had one Indian wife before and two children by her, whom he educated in the East. But *Natawista* was always accorded honor and respect by all of Culbertson's friends and associates. She and her husband were seldom separated for more than a few days for the next thirty years.

Culbertson had succeeded Kenneth McKenzie as head of Fort Union and was already widely known among the tribes for his fair dealing. Father de Smet described him as a "distinguished man endowed with a mild, benevolent and charitable temper, though if need be intrepid and courageous."[4] Perhaps more important in the eyes of his Indian wife, his skill as a horseman and buffalo hunter was greater than that of any other white man of his time and of most of the Indian braves.

Natawista seems to have taken her place as the first lady of Fort Union with grace and ease and assumed the ways of civilized living. When she journeyed with her husband back to St. Louis to the head office of the fur company or visited at the home of Mr. Pierre Chouteau, her bright black eyes were quick to take in the manners and styles. She had an instinctive taste in the matter of dress and ornament. (In jewelry she was fond of rubies and emeralds but found diamonds no more exciting than snowflakes or drops of water.) She never learned, or perhaps never chose, to speak English although she could understand it. Her husband spoke all the Indian dialects and the French *patois* of the fur trade so they had no need for another language. One passenger on a Missouri steamboat in 1859 wrote of meeting Mrs. Culbertson "dressed as a white lady and said to be a very fine woman." And he adds, as though disappointed, "I have been introduced to her but she cannot speak English so I can say nothing to her."[5]

So well did she take upon herself the ways of white women that even Governor Isaac I. Stevens was greatly impressed. He wrote in 1853, "Mrs. Culbertson, who had fully adopted the manner, costume and deportment of the whites, by her refinement presents the most striking illustration of the high civilization which these tribes of the interior are capable of attaining."[6]

The young minister, Reverend Elkanah Mackey, who was discouraged before he began his task of making good Presbyterians out of the Indians, wrote gravely in a letter to his Board in 1856: "I think she [Mrs. Culbertson] is a very remarkable woman . . . her influence on Mr. Culbertson seems to be of the most favorable kind."[7]

But it is in the excellent journal kept by John James Audubon, when he stayed at Fort Union in 1843, that we can see *Natawista* most vividly. At the same time, we catch a glimpse of the verve and gaiety as well as the primitive simplicity of life in a fur-trading post in the western wilderness. Audubon had come up the Missouri in search of animals to paint for his collection of American quadrupeds, and Fort Union was a natural vantage point.

When Audubon stepped off the boat in that vast empty country, Major Culbertson and some of the men from the fort came down on horseback to meet him. They dismounted and escorted him across the prairie to the most impressive of the Missouri trading posts. His host, and perhaps, his host's lady, brought out glasses of "first-rate port wine." Audubon had only a dark little room with one small window, and a bed of buffalo skins but it was the same room in which Prince Maximilian de Neuwied had spent two months some years before. Distinguished guests were not uncommon in this wilderness fort.

Audubon and his companions had retired early that first night in the fort when they heard music below and an invitation was sent up to them to come down to a ball in the dining-room, a room which boasted wallpaper and framed pictures! "There was no alternative; we all got up, and in a short time were amid the *beau monde* of these parts. Several squaws, attired in their best, were present, with all the guests, *engagés*, clerks, etc. Mr. Culbertson played the fiddle very fairly, Mr. Gueppe the clarinet, and Mr. Chouteau the drum, as if brought up in the army of the great Napoleon. Cotillions and reels were danced with much energy and apparent enjoyment, and the company dispersed about one o'clock."[8] *Natawista's* life in the fort did not lack for gaiety.

The Culbertsons were at pains to entertain their guest and give him a taste of the country, much in the manner of Westerners at the present time. One day, they put on a sham buffalo hunt; another day, everyone dressed in Indian garb and Mrs. Culbertson painted Audubon's young companion "in an awful manner," like a Blood brave. She, herself, put on her own "superb dress." Audubon's admiration shows through his words:

> The Ladies had their hair loose and flying in the breeze and then mounted on horses with Indian saddles and trappings. Mrs. Culbertson and her maid rode astride like men and all rode a furious race, under whip the whole way, for more than a mile on the prairie; how amazed would have been any European lady, or some of our modern belles who boast their equestrian skill, at seeing the magnificent riding of this Indian princess, for that is Mrs. Culbertson's rank. Mr. Culbertson rode with them, the horses running as if wild, with these extraordinary Indian riders, Mrs. Culbertson's magnificent black hair floating like a banner behind her.[9]

Audubon was interested in every new bird and animal on the prairie, "the little new lark," the lazuli finches, plovers, arctic bluebirds, the western deer and the antelope, but in none of these perhaps more than in his young hostess, who was a new species of woman to him.

And he was equally new to her. He went hunting, but he brought his prey home to paint! He looked at the claws of the beaver as though he had never seen anything like them before, and stroked the fur of a white wolf pelt as though it were more valuable than a blanket. He was an artist and she never tired of watching pictures grow beneath his brush. He was interested in woman-things; she made him a necklace of red berries and he fingered it like a squaw and admired the parfleche she decorated with dyed porcupine quills. He was French, but she had known French voyageurs and clerks and traders and he was different from all these. When she looked up she often found him studying her. What she thought of him there is no way of knowing except that one day she dove into the Missouri River and brought back six mallard ducks as a gift for him.[10]

Audubon was delighted. She, herself, must have been very like the lovely wild water fowl, swimming under water like a silent shadow, then cutting the surface with her dark head and raised brown arm and climbing up on the shore to dry.

He noted with pleasure all the little domestic things she did: "After a good dinner of Buffalo meat, green peas (from the Fort garden) and a pudding . . . we had an arrival of five squaws who came to see our fort and our ladies. The princess went out to meet them, covered them with a fine shawl, and the visitors followed her to her room. These ladies spoke both the French and Cree languages."[11]

But Audubon is repelled to discover savage traits in his hostess. He writes: "I lost the head of my first buffalo bull because I forgot to tell Mrs. Culbertson that I wished to save it, and the princess had its skull broken open to enjoy its brains. Handsome and really courteous and refined in many ways, I cannot reconcile myself to the fact that she partakes of raw animal food with such relish."[12]

Father Nicholas Point, a Jesuit priest who lived at the fort for some time, like Audubon was disappointed to find the Major's lady clinging to the primitive superstitions of her tribe after he had thought her completely Christianized and had baptized at least one of her children. When her child was sick with croup and the white man's remedies had done no good, she persuaded her husband to call in an old Blood woman. The crone heated rocks and poured water on them to give the child a steam bath, all the time chanting in a monotonous sing-song the lament that was part of the cure. When the heathen chant reached the priest's ears he tried to throw the old woman out of the fort but Culbertson intervened. *Natawista* was stubborn about certain things and, a miracle, the child was breathing quietly![13]

In 1845 Culbertson moved up the Missouri to build a fort above what had been old Fort McKenzie to tap that vast wilderness, rich in furs, farther west. In 1847, he moved the fort again to a point that was more advantageous for trading and built the walls of adobe. On Christmas night, 1850, a ball was given to celebrate the completion of the Culbertson house inside the stockade.

Music reached the banks of the Missouri that was never quite black, even at night, but it could carry only a little way across the wind-swept prairie before it was lost in space. Inside, the big room of the fort was warm with a fire on the hearth and the heat of a hundred or more living bodies swaying, jigging, stamping to the music. Perhaps the Major was not playing the fiddle that night, but dancing with his lithe little wife. Her hair may have been in braids, but her full red skirt had come from St. Louis and on her buttoned bodice hung a silver cross.

There was punch for all, for Natawista's relatives, for the young army officers, the clerks and the interpreter, the hunters who had brought in the game for the Christmas feast, and a dram apiece of liquor for the *engagés* and the

Ft. Benton, head of navigation on the Missouri, 1878

Indians. There was laughter and the start of a voyageur's song in French mixing with the music; then the fiddler tapped his bow and the Major raised his hand and the room hushed. The Indian women looked to their husbands to know what the white chief said and their husbands interpreted: The fort was henceforth to be called Fort Benton. Hands clapped, then the music began again and the major swung his lady and the long, lonesome range of the Highwoods looked coldly down on the prick of light on the banks of the Missouri.[14]

For the next ten years, Major Culbertson made Fort Benton his headquarters. It came to surpass Fort Union in importance in the fur trade. The Blackfeet and the Piegans and Bloods and Gros Ventres brought their bales of beaver skins in peace and trust. So heavy was the trading that by spring even the bedding and the cutlery from the fort kitchen went in barter and the boats sailed down the Missouri piled high with the winter's rich take. In St. Louis and even as far away as the capital in Washington, Culbertson was famed as the man who knew Indians and could smooth out any difficulty and bring back trade where it had fallen off. But who shall say how much of his success was due to *Natawista*?

When the Governor of Washington Territory, Isaac I. Stevens, set out to survey a route for the Pacific railroad that would go through the country of the treacherous Blackfeet, he had Major Culbertson appointed as a special agent to treat with the Indians, and he wrote in his report to the Secretary of the Interior: "I placed the more reliance upon the favorable influence which Mr. Culbertson might exert upon the Indians as he had married a full-blooded Blackfoot Woman."

Governor Stevens had not thought of actually taking Mrs. Culbertson with them on the expedition, but she insisted, saying to her husband: "My people are a good people, but they are jealous and vindictive. I am afraid that they and the whites will not understand each other; but my husband, if I go I may be able to explain things to them. I know there is danger, but, my husband, where you go I will go, and where you die, I will die."

When they camped for the night, the Culbertson tent was always pitched outside the line of sentinels so the Indians could come freely to talk with *Natawista*. Stevens writes: "I soon perceived the advantage to be derived from Mrs. Culbertson's presence. She was in constant intercourse with the Indians, and inspired them with perfect confidence. . . . She heard all that the Indians said and reported it through her husband to me." He was amazed to hear the squaws shrieking with laughter around *Natawista*'s tent and discovered that she was regaling them with tales and descriptions of the white ladies of St. Louis. He concluded that it was a mistake to think of the Indian as "silent and unsociable." "Mrs. Culbertson . . . rendered the highest service to the expedition, a service which demands this public acknowledgement," he puts down formally in the record. So *Natawista* helped to open the way for the railroad and the coming of the white settlers who would some day push her people onto reservations.[15]

Natawista had five children, these bearing the old-fashioned, all-American names of Jack, Nancy, Julia, Fanny and Joe. When the second child was drowned in the Missouri, the Major sent the others back east to be raised in convents and military schools or by his maiden sister in Illinois. But each year he and Mrs. Culbertson went back to see them.

The Major's lady was always with her husband, traveling thousands of miles between forts and Indian camps. Some expeditions to the Indian camps she made alone. There are notes in the diary of the Fort Benton clerk of outfitting a wagon "for Mrs. C" or of "Mrs. C's return." Whenever the Culbertsons arrived back at the fort after an absence, it was a signal for rejoicing. The clerk's diary reads: "September 1854. About noon, much to the delight of all in the Fort, Mr. Culbertson, Lady, and three men arrived from Fort Union. Received him with a proper salute." And the next day, "Mrs. Culbertson gave the men a feast and in the evening a ball."[16]

There is an almost medieval flavor about this life they lived, and their cavalcades winding across the prairie toward the fort, sometimes in the shade of the cottonwood trees along the river, are not unlike those parties on gaily caparisoned horses that passed through the oak forests in England or France toward some moated gray castle.

The Major and his lady went up and down the river by mackinaw, or keelboat, or steamboat. For miles upon miles, sometimes weeks at a time, there was no sign of a habitation along the river, only buffalo, or a wolf, or a magpie flashing across the immense sky, flying its pirate flag of black and white. Yet in this land of unmeasured space they seem never to have been impressed by the isolation or danger or loneliness. Those were the good years of their lives.

By 1858, Major Culbertson had amassed a fortune of some $300,000. He retired from the active management of the trade in the Upper Missouri country and settled on his estate outside Peoria, Illinois. A new and hilarious chapter began for *Natawista*.

A splendid nine-room mansion with sharp gables, trimmed with a scalloped border, was built for the Culbertson family. No expense was spared in furnishing it: a magnificent pier glass hung in the hall and the walls of the drawing room were decorated with original paintings by Stanley. One of them, painted to order, used *Natawista* as a model. An English gardener was imported to lay out the 300 acres surrounding the house, and it is safe to say that he must have been daunted by the corral on the property, stocked with antelope, elk and even panting buffalo, brought down from the upper Missouri. There were stables with the finest carriage horses that took blue ribbons in the horse shows at Cincinnati, and the estate was staffed with servants and stablemen.

In his new role as an established country gentleman, Major Culbertson bethought himself of his Indian marriage, or, perhaps, gossip was rife among the citizens of Peoria. At any rate, the Peoria *Daily Transcript* for September 12, 1859, carried the account of a marriage

> . . . Performed in this county on Friday last (Sept. 9, 1859). The parties were Major Alexander Culbertson and Natawista, daughter of the Chief of the Blackfeet Indians. Major Culbertson is the well-known Indian trader and was married to his present wife according to the Indian ceremony some sixteen or seventeen years ago, but having lately severed his connection with the American Fur Company and settled down to an agricultural life near this city, he was anxious that the ceremony be performed according to civilized rites. The parties have three [5] very interesting children, the eldest of whom is about fifteen years of age. The marriage was performed after the ceremony of the Catholic Church by Father Scanlon of St. Joseph, Missouri.

By 1860 Peoria citizens were fond of driving their guests out past Locust Grove, which was the name of the Culbertson estate, telling them stories of the amazing family who lived there; of Jack taking a goat into the house to butt his reflection in the lovely pier glass, or of his riding his horse right up those front steps into the parlor; how the cook said there were barrels of gold coins in the cellar, although there were rumors that the Major didn't pay his bills promptly.

Such reckless extravagance had never before been seen or heard of in Peoria, and people told over and over how Mrs. Culbertson had the coachman hitch two half-broken colts to a brand-new carriage that cost not a penny less than $300 and when they ran away and smashed the carriage to smithereens, she just stood there laughing and slapping her hands as though it were the best joke in the world! Some folks said Mrs. Culbertson was fond of firewater — this bit always accompanied by significant raising of eyebrows and the word "Indian" shaped by the lips.

Then, as suddenly as it began, the hilarious, musical-comedy chapter was over. It turned into something not quite tragedy. Major Culbertson had invested his money unwisely in projects promoted by his good friend Senator Thomas Benton of Missouri, for whom he had named the fort. His family had spent recklessly and the fortune was gone. The barrels in the cellar stood upended.

In the fall of 1869 thirty-three creditors filed claims against the property, but the Major and his wife had already gone back up the Missouri. Major Culbertson must have been glad many times in his life that he had an Indian wife; when he saw the young missionary's white wife, overwhelmed with homesickness and horror at the loneliness of life at Fort Benton, take to her bed weeping until her husband promised to take her back to the States before winter; when *Natawista* traveled with him all day across the endless prairie with the cold wind blowing against them and, still unwearied at the day's end, was ready to make their bed and cook the wild meat she had often shot herself; or when *Natawista* rode as furiously as he in pursuit of a wolf for the sheer joy of the chase.

But perhaps he was never more thankful than now to have an Indian wife who would not reproach him for his bankruptcy, or cry for her vanished luxuries and ease, or feel abused or martyred. Sitting quietly in the boat going up the Missouri, her eyes watched for old landmarks and she could have had few regrets for the life in Peoria.

Yet things had changed on the upper Missouri in those ten years. Fort Benton was now the only post owned by the Chouteau firm and the business was no longer trade with the Indians but a transportation-and-merchandise business with the white settlers pushing into the gold-rich new country.

Still, a man like Major Culbertson, even though he had turned sixty (and sixty is old on the frontier), was always valuable in the Indian country. He could make some money trading with the Indians on his own and acting as interpreter at the various Indian agencies. A comedown for a man who had been a feudal lord in that country, but one who lived so long in the wilderness had few material needs and his dignity needed nothing to bolster it — it was inherent in him.

And *Natawista?* Our sense of the brave ending would be pleased if we could say that she was faithful to her husband all the years of his life, dying where he died as she had vowed to do on Governor Stevens' expedition. But that is not the way the human record reads. Her daughters were in the East; they were to live all their lives as educated white women, marrying white men. Her sons found work around the forts, content with a life that was half-Indian, half-white. She stayed at Fort Benton awhile, since her name is on the census for 1870. Then she left the Major and went her own way.

We can only speculate about the motivations of her actions. She kept no diaries. Within a year or two of her leaving Fort Benton she, who had lived so well in a white man's world, turned her back on it and went north to Canada. The simple fact is moving. She had been away a long time and she chose to go back to her own people.

Major Culbertson was roving the country, trading with the Indians, even up into Canada. They may have met again on the Blood reserve, the old fur trader and the still-beautiful Indian woman who was his wife. Just before his death, Culbertson went back to visit his daughter, and in 1879 died at Julia's home in Nebraska. *Natawista* lived on the Blood reserve in Canada until her death, but she could never step back completely into the old Indian ways, for she was always known by her married name of Madame Culbertson. She died in the 1890's and was buried in the Indian cemetery near the Catholic Mission, northeast of Fort Stand-Off on the road to Cardston, Alberta.[17]

The story of the Major's lady has the beauty and strength of a legend, the strange mystery of an Indian ceremony and the disappointment of the cheap Indian wares bought in a tourist shop, but it has its own unique place in the history of the West. Every school child in Montana knows the story of *Sacajawea* but hardly a one has ever heard of *Natawista*. Yet she, too, helped the white men in their trailmaking and she is a woman worthy of a legend.

NOTES

[1] Historical Society of Montana *Contributions*, Vol. X, p. 8.

[2] "Journal of Rudolph Friedrich Kurz," Bureau of American Ethnology, *Bulletin 115*, (Nov. 6, 1851) 224.

[3] Journal of Lewis H. Morgan, 1862, No. 2, p. 20. Ms. Historical Society of Montana.

[4] Historical Society of Montana *Contributions*, Vol. X. p. 242.

[5] "Journal of Elias J. Marsh," South Dakota Historical *Review*, Vol. 1 No. 2, Jan. 1936, p. 100.

[6] U. S. Cong. 33:2 S. D. 86,403. Report of Governor I. I. Stevens on Expedition of 1853.

[7] Letter Fort Union, July 22, 1856, from Rev. E. D. Mackey to Walter Lowrie. *Journal of Department History*, Dec.

1941, Presb. Hist. Society, p. 337.

[8] Maria R. Audubon, *Audubon and His Journals* (New York 1900), in two volumes, II, p. 35.

[9] *Ibid.*, Vol. II, pp. 88-89.

[10] *Ibid.*, Vol. II, p. 112.

[11] *Ibid.*, Vol. II, p. 123.

[12] *Ibid.*, Vol. II, p. 111.

[13] Historical Society of Montana *Contributions*, Vol. III, p. 249.

[14] *Ibid.*, p. 264.

[15] U. S. Cong. 33:2, S.D. 86,404. Report of Governor I. I. Stevens of Expedition of 1853.

[16] Historical Society of Montana *Contributions*, Vol. X, p. 243.

[17] Culbertson File. Manuscript collection. Historical Society of Montana.

Bear's Belly (Arickara)

The Rush Gatherer (Kootenai)

Spotted Bull (Mandan)

Arickara medicine ceremony

Sitting Bull's White Squaw

By DAVID HUMPHREYS MILLER

THE DECADE of the 1880's was a particularly harsh one for the American Plains Indians. In 1883 the last great herd of wild buffalo was slaughtered by white hide hunters and sportsmen, and the old free roving line of the tribes was curtailed by the white man's armies. Defeated in war, the Indians were forced into dreary poverty and degeneracy on reservations of near-worthless land. By 1889 the government even wanted to open up the best parts of these reservations to white settlement, a move justified by the authorities as a rampant holdover of the Manifest Destiny which had peopled a continent.

Paradoxically, further exploitation of the red man was vigorously opposed by a group of whites — mostly Eastern philanthropists — who called themselves the National Indian Defense Association. Prominent among the Association's members was Catherine Weldon, an attractive, somewhat overdressed widow from Brooklyn, New York. An artist, Mrs. Weldon traveled west in the spring of 1889 — ostensibly to paint a portrait of Sitting Bull, famed old chief of the Hunkpapa Sioux. Actually her purpose was to expedite Association aims by helping Sitting Bull and other tribal leaders fight the further cession of Indian lands to the whites.

Flamboyantly garbed in the latest styles, she was a strange apparition on the desolate Dakota prairies. Her arrival at dusty Standing Rock Agency, Dakota Territory, generated considerable excitement among agency employees and Indian bystanders alike.

She had been corresponding with Sitting Bull, but had never met him. Having written the chief to meet her at the agency, Mrs. Weldon now awaited him uncomfortably under the stares of a growing crowd. Handsome, white-thatched, mustachioed Agent James McLaughlin emerged from his office to greet her. After introducing himself somewhat formally, the agent began at once to talk of Sitting Bull, though no one had mentioned the chief's name.

"Sitting Bull's a coward," he said. "He's a selfish man and no one's friend. He's of no importance. He's a heavy burden on our younger Indians who are more progressive."

McLaughlin then indicated his awareness of the true purpose of Mrs. Weldon's visit by pointing out that the National Indian Defense Association had "no foothold or influence at Standing Rock." The widow was surprised to learn that the agent already knew so much about her. It was obvious to her that McLaughlin had intercepted her letters to Sitting Bull and she felt an instant dislike and growing mistrust of this agent who ruled his Indian charges like a little king.

Any misgivings she may have had about Sitting Bull, however, vanished almost immediately with the chief's arrival. Sitting Bull, recovering from an illness, was also mourning the death of a favorite daughter named Standing Holy. Nevertheless, he had driven his team and wagon forty painful, bumpy miles from his camp on Grand River to meet the lady from the East.

Although he was fifty-five and long past his fighting prime, Sitting Bull seemed to Catherine Weldon to be the quintessence of the noble red man. In him she saw the vitality and integrity that could at last bring purpose and stability to her somewhat incoherent passions and enthusiasms, for she was nearing an age when some women do the strange and unaccountable. From that moment on, she devoted all her erratic energies to Sitting Bull and his people.

Sitting Bull was stirred considerably by the manner as well as the appearance of this graying, fashionably clothed lady from the East with her showy rings and brooches. Compared to the drab servile pioneer women and the modestly attired army wives he usually encountered among the whites, Mrs. Weldon was indeed a striking personage. The old chief's fighting and foraging days were long since past. Nearly thirteen summers had elapsed since the great day of victory over Long Hair Custer and his Seventh Cavalry at Little Big Horn. But Sitting Bull was far from senile. Sioux men often had several wives at a time, and Sitting Bull now had two. Moreover, marriage to a white woman was not unthinkable to a Hunkpapa chieftain. So when Mrs. Weldon brashly insisted on accompanying Sitting Bull to his Grand River camp, he warmly welcomed her into his household.

Agent McLaughlin was also impressed by the flashy Brooklyn widow — though by no means so favorably. He viewed Catherine Weldon's intrusion with annoyance. This business of her painting Sitting Bull's portrait was a lame cover-up for her true aims at Standing Rock and a gross insult to the agent's intelligence. At the same time he could scarcely overlook her great physical attractiveness and there can be little doubt that he was disturbed by it far more than he cared to admit.

The agent was married to a mixed-blood Sioux woman with whom he shared a consuming and calculating ambition — and little else. Mary McLaughlin strove constantly to rise above "the accident" of her birth as a part Indian and to achieve what she regarded as her rightful social place among the exclusive coterie of officers' wives at nearby Fort Yates, an army post within a mile or so of Standing Rock Agency. As civilian appointees or Indian office careerists, agents generally were looked down upon by the military. McLaughlin was no exception, although in his efforts to keep pace with the Fort Yates clique, he took pains to have himself called "Major" — a holdover from the days when army majors were in charge of Indian reservations.

Mary McLaughlin's abiding passion, second only to her ambition, was her unrelenting hatred and contempt for Sitting Bull. The chief's fondness for Indian ways and natural conservatism made him loom like a huge stumbling block in the path of her social progress. In her mind, at least, he was a public reminder of all that she hated in herself. Above all other Indians, Sitting Bull epitomized the reluctance of most Standing Rock Sioux to follow McLaughlin's program and augment his rise to prominence as an upcoming government official. Friction between the McLaughlins and Sitting Bull was long-standing, dating from the chief's refusal in 1887 to join the agent's wife in touring Europe and appearing at Queen Victoria's Jubilee in Buffalo Bill's Wild West Show. Mary McLaughlin had occasionally acted as interpreter for the chief and had planned to go along and hobnob with royalty in that capacity. She felt that Sitting Bull's unwillingness to leave the reservation had seriously hindered her own social advancement.

Catherine Weldon and Agent McLaughlin clashed soon after the widow established herself in Sitting Bull's menage on Grand River. For days she had been singing the chief's praises, showering him with gifts, and writing letters for him. She also began work on a flattering full-length portrait of him in full regalia — a labor of love in which she lingered painstakingly over each minute brush stroke.

When she proposed that Sitting Bull accompany her to other Sioux agencies to forestall Indian concessions to the land commissioners, the chief readily agreed. Before he could legally leave the reservation, however, Sitting Bull, like any other Indian, would have to obtain a pass issued by the agent. Mrs. Weldon offered to go to Standing Rock Agency to expedite what she regarded as a purely routine matter. McLaughlin flatly refused to issue Sitting Bull a pass. Of all Standing Rock Indians, Sitting Bull could not be absent from the reservation, the agent told her, since his signature might be needed on important documents when the commissioners arrived. Moreover, the agent refused to grant Mrs. Weldon permission to travel through the Indian country to reach other agencies with the excuse that it might be unsafe for her person. The widow lost her temper.

"Are you afraid of a woman or of a woman's influence?" she asked scornfully, adding a threat to report McLaughlin to the Indian Office in Washington. As she later wrote, "high words passed between us, and I rose indignantly and left the office." She sent word to Grand River, advising Sitting Bull that the trip was off and that he should drop his preparations for the journey.

Incensed at McLaughlin, Sitting Bull went to Standing Rock Agency. The agent, who had already circulated rumors among the idlers that Sitting Bull had planned to carry off Mrs. Weldon and therefore might be headed for the penitentiary, refused to see him. As Catherine Weldon subsequently wrote, "the old chief was so much surprised and pained that his heart ached when he heard these vile insinuations." Primly ascribing purely platonic feelings to Sitting Bull, she added that "he looked upon me as his own daughter and would have shielded and protected me from all harm. I felt much disappointed and pained, and resolved to leave Standing Rock at once."

Sitting Bull, wife No. 9, their infant child and five-year-old twins. White woman and child in group not identified. *Right:* Sitting Bull

Sitting Bull drove her down to the river to catch a steamer for her return to the East. "Straightway a romantic story was printed in *The Sioux City Journal*," she later wrote. "A story full of the vilest falsehoods, stating that I purposely came from New York to marry Sitting Bull, that the agent had tried to prevent a meeting, but that Sitting Bull succeeded in seeing me. . . . All this is the agent's work. He fears Sitting Bull's influence among his people and therefore pretends to his face that politics were not his motive for refusing the pass, but my welfare, and he took this opportunity to humble the old chief and make his heart more than sad. . . . If a white person becomes the true friend of a Dakota [Sioux] must he battle with the whole world?"

Back in Brooklyn, Catherine Weldon found herself the target of the press in a rising surge of protest over her unconventional friendship for an Indian. The *Bismarck Daily Tribune* editorialized on July 2, 1889, that Mrs. Weldon "is a great admirer of Sitting Bull, and it is gossip among the people in the vicinity of the Agency that she is actually in love with the cunning old warrior. Agent McLaughlin's position in the matter is unquestionably right, especially at this time, as Sitting Bull would surely prove a disturbing element at the lower agencies during the conference of the Land Commission on the question of opening the Sioux reservations to settlement."

Another newspaper commented that "Sitting Bull has been growing gradually worse, which is partly to be accounted for by the presence of a lady from

Sitting Bull, mother, daughter and grandchild

Brooklyn, N. Y. named Mrs. C. Weldon. While here she bestowed numerous presents upon Sitting Bull, considerable being money, which has a demoralizing effect upon him, inflating him with his own importance."

Defensively, the widow heatedly charged that "the agent fears my presence, and did all he could to destroy me." Undoubtedly, McLaughlin and his wife were mainly responsible for the ugly press releases emanating from Standing Rock Agency and picked up by various newspapers throughout the country.

Carrying on her crusade from afar, Catherine Weldon continued to fight the further cession of Sioux lands by bestowing more of her largesse on Sitting Bull and "inflating" the chief with further presents. During the winter months of 1889-90, Mrs. Weldon kept up a lively correspondence with Sitting Bull. By the spring of 1890 she made a bold decision. On April 5 she wrote Agent McLaughlin as follows:

"You will doubtless be surprised to receive a letter from me after our not very amicable conversations. . . . And indeed it is with reluctance that I humble myself to address you, knowing that you cannot feel friendly disposed toward me. . . . Even enemies can act magnanimously towards each other, and I hope you will extend to me the courtesy of a gentleman to a lady. . . . It has been my intention to spend the rest of my life in Dakota among or near my Indian friends. . . . I can be happy no where else. . . ."

If McLaughlin was shaken by this announcement, no records indicate that he opposed Catherine Weldon's return to the Standing Rock country later that spring. Though still *persona non grata* at the agency, the widow was not content to remain outside the reservation. Accordingly, she by-passed any contact with McLaughlin and traveled in triumph to Sitting Bull's camp on Grand River, where she moved into his cabin with the rest of the family and briskly resumed work on the chief's portrait.

In her unabashed zeal, Mrs. Weldon also washed dishes — most of which had been her own gifts to the chief — swept floors, cooked meals, and performed other menial household tasks, earning the Indian name Woman-Walking-Ahead — a sobriquet she bore proudly among Sitting Bull's followers. She was now more determined than ever to spend the rest of her life at Standing Rock if necessary to promote harmony between the old chief and the white "enemies" who surrounded him.

Inevitably, Sitting Bull's wives, Seen-by-Her-Nation and Four Times, grew somewhat jealous of the interloper. While polygamy was common among the Sioux, multiple wives were often sisters or cousins who easily maintained a harmonious household. The presence of a strange and aggressive white woman, however, was anathema.

For a while it seemed that the jealousy of the Indian women was indeed well founded. Catherine Weldon's extreme devotion to Sitting Bull was apparent to all and sundry, and in no time at all the wildest rumors were afloat. Indians and whites alike around Standing Rock Agency and Fort Yates speculated that the lady from the East had become Sitting Bull's third wife and was already with child by the chief. Stories went the rounds that his Sioux wives, furiously jealous, had chased Mrs. Weldon around the camp with their butcher knives. White women on the reservation, affronted by the apparent brazenness of the situation, openly regarded her "infatuation as a bitter disgrace" to their sex. The McLaughlins may have added fresh fuel to the fires of ugly gossip.

The agent certainly looked with distaste upon Catherine Weldon's "inordinate praise" of Sitting Bull. In one of his more truthful allegations, he maintained that the widow aroused Sitting Bull's martial ardor by reading aloud to him tales of Alexander, Achilles and Napoleon. Mrs. Weldon had by this time learned enough of the Sioux language to carry on conversations with the chief in his own tongue. She kept copious records on foolscap of these discussions, fragments of which remain to this day, indicating that a wide array of subject matter was covered. Even as simply as she must have described them, her readings of the exploits of historical figures could scarcely have failed to stir the old warrior's dormant fighting instincts.

Mrs. Weldon also acted as Sitting Bull's secretary, writing to other Indians in his name and translating all sorts of documents for his benefit. Unwittingly, apparently, the lady found herself caught in a most uncomfortable situation.

Among the Sioux, a woman made known her availability to a man by performing acts of wifely service around his home. Since Indian mating involved few preliminaries, the straightforward Sitting Bull took Catherine Weldon at face value and offered to make her his bride — the objections of his Indian wives notwithstanding. But when this carnal arrangement was bluntly suggested by the chief, Mrs. Weldon recoiled in shocked amazement.

Counting the two still living, Sitting Bull had had a total of nine wives. Now this strange pale lady had come into his home willing, even eager, to do all for him that a wife should do — save lying in his bed with him! In his perplexity Sitting Bull could only back away from this oddly chaste female.

Not long after Sitting Bull's unsuccessful courtship, rumors drifted into the Standing Rock country from the more southern Sioux agencies that the Son of God was again walking the earth. This redeemer, it was said, had returned to save the Indians from the white men who had defeated the tribes and penned them upon reservations and killed off the buffalo. Long ago, it was said, this same Christ had appeared among the white race. But they had not liked Him and had rejected Him. Finally they had killed Him by nailing Him to a tree. Now He had come back again as a living person — this time as a Paiute Indian medicine-man in Nevada, hundreds of miles from the Sioux reservations. There He preached and taught His followers to perform a sacred dance, a new ceremony that would bring a new earth sliding over the old, burying the white men and their civilization, but giving Indian believers a new land, fresh and verdant and teeming with wild game. Indian ancestors would return from beyond the grave to join their tribal descendants in a great revival of native life and culture. Before them the dead would drive back the vanished herds of buffalo. But to bring about this miracle living Indians would have to perform this new ritual known as the Ghost Dance.

Many Indians traveled to Nevada to see Wovoka, the Indian Messiah. Among them was the Minneconjou Sioux medicine-man, Kicking Bear, who brought the Ghost Dance back to his people. At the southern agencies the Sioux were already dancing desperately in the feverish belief that all the new religion's promises would soon be fulfilled.

Sitting Bull remembered Kicking Bear well, for the medicine-man had been a foremost warrior at Little Big Horn and other great battles. Eager to find out more about the Ghost Dance, Sitting Bull was now anxious to visit Kicking Bear at Cheyenne Agency, headquarters of Cheyenne River Reservation which bordered Standing Rock Reservation on the south. The chief applied several times for permission to go, but each time Agent McLaughlin refused to grant him a pass. Sitting Bull then turned to Catherine Weldon to make a final appeal.

Late one midsummer morning Sitting Bull drove his wagon up in front of the agent's office. Sitting on the driver's seat beside the chief was the lady from the East, somewhat grimed after forty dust-eating miles from Grand River, but still very much the picture of fashion.

News of the chief's approach, flavored with the usual gossip, had already reached James McLaughlin. He sauntered out on the office steps in vest and shirtsleeves, his shock of white hair bristling.

"Major," Catherine Weldon announced coolly, "I am going to Cheyenne River, and Sitting Bull is going to drive me there."

"Sitting Bull, as you may know, Mrs. Weldon, has no pass to leave Standing

Rock," McLaughlin answered. "Furthermore, I do not think it advisable to grant him one."

The sharp exchange which followed has not been preserved, but Mrs. Weldon apparently was disposed to argue the point — with the upshot that she was escorted by a detachment of Indian police to the reservation's north boundary and told not to come back.

The Cannonball River bounded Standing Rock Reservation on the north. Just beyond it lay Parkin Ranch, home of Mrs. Parkin and her sister, Mrs. Van Solen. Although these two women had been among Mrs. Weldon's more vociferous critics, she now appealed to them for shelter and advice. They refused outright to take her into their home, but permitted her to occupy an empty sod-roofed log shack a mile or so below the ranch house on the north bank of the Cannonball near its junction with the Missouri. Since McLaughlin's jurisdiction did not extend outside the reservation, there was little he could do to prevent the widow from taking up residence in this dreary region of drab sand bars, muddy water and stunted oaks and box elders. It was hardly a fitting setting for Catherine Weldon's Eastern elegance. But here she determinedly settled down, even adding a semblance of permanence and respectability by sending east for her sickly thirteen-year-old son, Christie, who joined her after traveling alone upriver on one of the antiquated side-paddle steamers that still plied the wide Missouri.

Sitting Bull came to this dismal place once every two weeks after each "issue day" through the long summer. Driving a team of half-wild, loose-jointed cayuses hitched to the running gear of his wagon, the chief looked like an aloof old mummy sitting on planks laid across the bolsters, his hot-weather blanket and leggings of white sheeting soiled as old parchment after the seventy-odd-mile trip from Grand River. Always riding with him on these occasions was one of his wives, for Mrs. Weldon thought to keep the tongues of soldiers' wives and ranch hands from wagging by insisting that Sitting Bull never come alone.

During this 1890 summer idyll, word came through channels that the Sioux were planning an outbreak. McLaughlin and other agents in the Dakotas were requested by the Indian Office to file reports on the extent of the Ghost Dance and possible revolt among the tribes. From the first vague reports of the new religion, the press and public had regarded the "messiah craze" as a prelude for a full-scale Indian uprising. Agent McLaughlin, however, attached no great importance to the Ghost Dance at this time. According to his best information, not even the wild Hunkpapas on Grand River, (i.e. Sitting Bull's followers) were performing the ritual.

Nevertheless, McLaughlin took advantage of outbreak rumors to submit a list of "nonprogressive" leaders it might be well to remove — removal meaning imprisonment at some remote military prison. This he recommended in spite of the fact that the Indians in question had committed no crimes but simply "stood in the pathway of progress." The list was topped with the name of Sitting Bull. Branded by McLaughlin in official reports as "a polygamist, a libertine, an habitual liar, an active obstructionist, and a great obstacle in the civilization of his people" — and therefore by innuendo responsible for any uprising which might occur — the old chief was thereafter a marked man.

Early in October Kicking Bear brought the Ghost Dance to Sitting Bull's camp. Overnight the new religion spread like wildfire among the Hunkpapas, who were eager to join in a seance where, as Kicking Bear promised, they might see and talk with their dead. Starting October 9, that first Ghost Dance on Grand River lasted five days. Sitting Bull danced as eagerly as any of his followers. He wanted, perhaps more than any other Indian, to experience such miracles as communicating with the dead. Nothing would have pleased him more than to see his lost daughter again. But, while other Hunkpapas fell to the ground in rigid trances, then awakened to tell of seeing and talking with deceased relatives, no magic vision came to the chief. Tired and discouraged, Sitting Bull moved to the sidelines.

Agent McLaughlin got wind of the Ghost Dance at Sitting Bull's camp soon after it began. On October 13, he sent a detachment of Indian police to arrest Kicking Bear and break up the ceremony. The policemen failed to carry out the arrest, but the Minneconjou medicine-man felt he had accomplished his mission and left Standing Rock Reservation.

The proud Sitting Bull deeply resented the agent's sending police to tell him what he could or could not do. While he had stopped dancing, he announced that he would do nothing to prevent his people from worshiping as they saw fit.

Thus, overnight, Sitting Bull became the unwitting archvillain of the entire Ghost Dance movement, although he personally did not fully believe in it. Throughout the nation, the new religion was misunderstood and feared as a fanatic Indian conspiracy against the whites. The situation in the Dakotas was viewed with alarm, and a relatively innocent Sitting Bull was suddenly caught up in a new maelstrom of notoriety.

High officials loudly echoed McLaughlin's demand for the chief's early "removal," and the agent began to enjoy his national publicity. Many newspapers pictured him singlehandedly keeping the lid on a powder keg of Indian violence. McLaughlin, privately, had little fear of the Ghost Dance. In his October report he even assured the Indian office in Washington that the new religion was "basically harmless" and would die out once the Indians "discovered the futility of such nonsense." Nevertheless, with the press building the Ghost Dance scare into outsize proportions, the agent publicly committed himself to a ruthless course of action guaranteed to suppress it once and for all. At Standing Rock this was tantamount to the elimination of Sitting Bull.

No one foresaw the chief's growing danger more clearly than Catherine Weldon. From her retreat on the Cannonball she now bombarded McLaughlin with correspondence, pleading with him to "have pity on Sitting Bull and the Hunkpapas who have been under the evil influence of Kicking Bear." Anticipating a move against the chief, she wrote:

Kicking Bear

"... Do not send the police or soldiers, and I will induce Sitting Bull to come to you of his own accord. He will surely accompany me to the agency; but please do not detain him; his brain has suffered, but his heart is good. He will be all right now that Kicking Bear has gone. My heart is almost breaking when I see the work of years undone by that vile imposter. ..."

Kicking Bear had indeed created havoc at the southern agencies in South Dakota where thousands of Sioux now defied the authorities by following the medicine-man into the Bad Lands, a remote region in which they could practice the Ghost Dance religion without interference from the whites. Mrs. Weldon had not been in regular contact with Sitting Bull since late summer, and she was increasingly worried by rumors of his participation in what she called "this absurd new religion." Fearful that Sitting Bull and his followers might join Kicking Bear, she wrote voluminous letters to him, begging him not to have anything further to do with the Ghost Dance. Then, convinced that letters alone were inadequate, the widow sneaked back into Standing Rock Reservation, arriving at Sitting Bull's camp during the third week in October.

Catherine Weldon plunged at once into an impossible task. She prepared a lengthy sermon which she painstakingly translated into Sioux and delivered to the assembled ghost dancers. Her message was completely wasted; she might as well have recited gibberish.

Desperate now, she offered to debate the new religion point by point with Kicking Bear, provided the Hunkpapas could somehow locate the medicine-man in the Bad Lands and persuade him to return to Grand River. She shrieked out her defiance of Kicking Bear's power, insisting that he was deluding the Indians. She warned her listeners that the white men would surely use the Ghost Dance as an excuse to wage war against the Sioux. The ghost dancers listened politely to the widow's heated arguments — then went right on dancing.

Sitting Bull was in a quandary. It was unconventional among the Sioux for a woman to address a group which included men. Mrs. Weldon not only flouted the tribal customs, but spoke with such vehemence about the Ghost Dance that the old chief almost regarded her as an enemy. After hearing her ravings, several ghost dancers convinced him that her talk of a coming war was a cover-up for a plot to destroy him — a plot she shared with Agent McLaughlin! Yet Sitting Bull could scarcely believe that she meant to have him killed.

"Perhaps, since you are no longer my friend, you want me to be locked in prison," he suggested sadly.

Catherine Weldon's harsh laughter puzzled him all the more.

"Do you suppose," she retorted, "that I have spent all these years working for you and your people — ready to share your every danger and tribulation — and am *not* your friend? Are you foolish enough to believe that I am your *enemy?*"

That night the Hunkpapas sang and wailed louder than ever as they shuffled in the great circle of the Ghost Dance. The wild saturnalia kept Mrs. Weldon awake well into the small hours of early morning. Seeking out Sitting Bull, she upbraided him mercilessly in front of his followers.

"If you do not stop this dance at once," she challenged, "I will leave this camp at daylight — forever!"

That broke up the dance — at least for that night.

Next morning the widow begged Sitting Bull to permit no more dancing lest the troops come and many people be killed, both whites and Indians.

"If the soldiers kill me, I will be glad," Sitting Bull said solemnly. "Our old way of life is almost gone. Now I want to die."

Mrs. Weldon seemed unsympathetic. "If you want to die, kill yourself. Don't bring other people into your trouble."

The old chief said nothing, even in answer to the widow's persistent demands that he step in to put a stop to the Ghost Dance when it resumed around noon. Later that day he watched indifferently as the ghost dancers shuffled past him. But he made no move to interfere with the ritual in which so many of his followers now believed.

Catherine Weldon was crushed by her failure to stop the Ghost Dance at Grand River. Disillusioned, she confronted Sitting Bull with her plan to leave the camp — this time for good.

"Do as your heart dictates," he told her simply. "If you want to go, go. If it says 'stay,' then remain as long as you like."

Had he been more emphatic, perhaps, Mrs. Weldon might have stayed. With a last ounce of spirit, however, she insisted on leaving. Sitting Bull himself offered to take her north to the Cannonball and, resignedly, she permitted him to carry her back to the Parkin Ranch in his wagon. The chief was beginning to realize the danger that surrounded him. He walked far ahead of the vehicle lest any soldiers try to take him prisoner and harm the widow. The journey was uneventful — save that it was the last time Sitting Bull and his "white squaw" ever saw each other. The chief returned to Grand River by an alternate route, foiling an attempt by three agency Indians to ambush him at McLaughlin's instigation. After that Sitting Bull stayed near his camp, his faith shaken in all but his closest followers.

From the Parkin Ranch Mrs. Weldon sent a final letter to Agent McLaughlin.

". . . I have turned my former Hunkpapa friends into enemies," she wrote. "Even Sitting Bull imagines that I seek his destruction, in spite of all the proofs of friendship which I have given him. His brain is so confused that he does not know friend from foe. . . ."

Yet Sitting Bull was aware of the growing gulf between himself and the whites. His reluctance to leave Grand River irked McLaughlin, who made a rare excursion to Sitting Bull's camp and attempted to lure the chief to the agency so that the agent "might convince him of the absurdity of the doctrine" of the Ghost Dance. Fearing for their leader's life, Sitting Bull's followers refused to let him go.

While McLaughlin set about to plan the arrest of the old chief, Catherine Weldon grew increasingly discouraged in her lonely isolation at Parkin Ranch. Clinging desperately to her dream of a better world for her Sioux friends, she had only her young son Christie to give her a small boy's meager comfort.

One day as wintry chill settled over the Cannonball and the daylight hours grew shorter, Christie stepped on a nail which pierced his shoe and badly lacerated his right foot. The wound refused to heal. When the injured foot grew worse, Mrs. Weldon took Christie out of Cannonball Landing to catch a downriver steamer. Pierre, the capital of South Dakota, was the nearest city where she might get proper medical attention for the boy. Aboard the steamer, however, Christie went into spasms of lockjaw poisoning. When the craft ran aground on a sand bar opposite Pierre, the boy died.

Catherine Weldon's grief was obsessive. She wrote to Sitting Bull on black-bordered stationery:

"If he had died on the Cannonball, I should be more content; for then I would have buried him there and remained near my Indians. Now I am far from all my Dakota friends and from you, and my only child gone too. Nothing left to me. . . ."

No longer affluent (in fact her money was gone) the lonely widow suffered a final blow when her last worldly possessions were lost in a baggage mishap aboard the steamer. Confessing that she no longer wished to live, she wrote Sitting Bull a final letter, from Kansas City, on December 1, 1890:

"If your prayers to the Great Spirit are heard," she implored the chief, "pray to Him to give me a speedy death, that my heart may find peace. . . . Let your heart be true to those who deserve it, that when death comes to both of us we may not be eternally separated, but meet again in a better world. . . ."

Death was close at hand for Sitting Bull. On December 12 orders came by telegram from Army Headquarters in St. Paul to "secure the person" of the chief of the Hunkpapas. McLaughlin persuaded Colonel W. F. Dru, commanding officer at Fort Yates, to let the actual arrest be made by Indian policemen with troops in reserve, thus saving face for the agent. Plans called for the arrest to be made on December 20, when most of the Hunkpapas would be drawing rations at Standing Rock Agency and Sitting Bull would be alone and unprotected in his camp.

The schedule was abruptly revised when McLaughlin got wind of a message sent from Kicking Bear to Sitting Bull asking him to join the ghost dancers in the Bad Lands "as God was about to appear to them." Unfounded reports had Sitting Bull busy fitting out horses for a long ride. McLaughlin at once ordered his Indian police to proceed with the arrest that night, December 14, 1890.

Fortified with cheap whisky supplied by the agent, forty-three Indian policemen rode through the night toward Sitting Bull's camp on Grand River. From another direction over a hundred cavalry troopers came riding, bringing one Gatling and one Hotchkiss gun. At daybreak on December 15, the police broke into Sitting Bull's cabin and roused the old chief. While they hurried him into his clothes, nearly 150 of his followers gathered outside, excited and anxious about their leader.

Lieutenant Henry Bullhead and Sergeants Red Tomahawk and Shave Head brutally forced Sitting Bull out the door of his cabin. At first the old chief had not refused to go with the police. But now he began to struggle with his captors.

"I'm not going!" he shouted to his followers.

One of them fired a shot at Bullhead who turned instantly and shot Sitting Bull in the left side, inflicting a mortal wound. The chief was reeling from the impact when Sergeant Red Tomahawk shot him from behind. Sitting Bull fell dead. A moment later during furious hand-to-hand fighting Shave Head was killed and Bullhead fatally shot. Four more policemen were killed as they carried the dying Bullhead into Sitting Bull's cabin for a stand-off. Sitting Bull's followers had also suffered casualties. Eleven Hunkpapas lay dead or dying around their fallen leader.

Troops arrived soon after sunup. Sitting Bull's followers had taken cover in timber along the river, and for a brief time the Indian police in the cabin were caught in a deadly crossfire. Then the Hunkpapas fled across Grand River, some of them reaching Kicking Bear's stronghold in the Bad Lands, others joining a Minneconjou chief named Big Foot with whom they were slain by white cavalry at the Massacre of Wounded Knee two weeks later.

Once the fighting was over at Grand River, policemen and troopers joined in ransacking Sitting Bull's camp. Everything of value was taken by the looters.

Red Tomahawk

Sitting Bull's body was treated with contempt by the police who battered the head and face to a shapeless pulp. Soldiers finally stepped in and put a stop to further mutilation. The desecrated corpse was tossed in a wagon and the bodies of slain policemen carefully placed on top. When Sitting Bull's remains were taken to Standing Rock Agency, Agent McLaughlin had them buried in quick-lime as though the leader of the Hunkpapas had been a common criminal.

McLaughlin's smug satisfaction with the success of his murder plot was ill concealed. He proudly announced to visiting newsmen that "the shots that killed Sitting Bull have put a stop forever to the domination of the ancient regime among the Standing Rock Sioux." At the same time the agent made a great show of bewailing the loss of the dead policemen and blamed Sitting Bull for all the trouble which culminated in his own death and "also the killing of much better men than he was."

Sitting Bull's personal belongings eventually came into the agent's possession. Former Indian policemen found that they did not want to keep such bloody mementos. McLaughlin and his wife profited handsomely from them, however, when they were put on exhibition in "Sitting Bull's death cabin," a part of the State of North Dakota's display at the World's Columbian Exposition and Fair at Chicago in 1893.

Featured among the simple artifacts and items of costume that had belonged to the dead chief was a full-length oil portrait of Sitting Bull in full regalia. During the arrest an Indian policeman managed to smash the frame with his rifle and to jab his gun barrel through the canvas before a young Army officer, Lieutenant Matthew Steele, grabbed it away and kept it for a while as a souvenir. In the lower left corner of the painting was a brief signature, "C. S. Weldon" — all that was left of Sitting Bull's tragic, disillusioned "white squaw."

Ceremony of the Sun Horse, by W. H. D. Koerner

Stolen Ponies, by W. H. D. Koerner

A Return to My Beloved Blackfeet

By JAMES WILLARD SCHULTZ

One of the most talented writers the Old West ever knew was James Willard Schultz. His name and that of Glacier National Park and the Blackfeet Indians form an indissoluble trinity. As long as these majestic mountains endure the three names shall be inseparable. After his friend, Hugh Monroe, Schultz became one of the first white residents of the mountains and lakes. He married into the Blackfeet, understanding this picturesque tribe as few whites have ever done. For many years he memorialized his adopted people through tomes of able writing.

This son of well-to-do Boonville, N. Y., parents had prepared to enter West Point for a military career when he visited an uncle at St. Louis in 1877. The stories he heard of the frontier region to the north fascinated him. He wrote to his mother for $500 and permission to visit the northern Rocky Mountains, promising to return to school in the fall. He never returned.

After an interesting 2100-mile river-boat trip, he reached Fort Benton in July, 1877. The country was even more exciting than imagined. Soon Schultz was a partner of the veteran Joe Kipp, trading in buffalo robes with the Indians. In 1880 they took in more than 4000 tanned robes at about $3 each; speedily sold to Boston buyers at an average price of $7. But the buffalo were almost gone and within two years the trade had vanished. With his profits he settled in the Glacier region, married Musti Ahwaton Ahki, was accepted into the tribe with the name Apikuni or Far-off-White Robe, and lived fully the life of his red brothers. Here his son, Hart Merriam — for many years an artist sculptor in Arizona, known as Lone Wolf — was born.

When his Blackfeet wife died in early 1903, James Willard Schultz's life as an Indian was ended. He plunged into writing, but the sadness of the mountain and Indian associations weighed too heavily. In 1904 Schultz became literary critic for the Los Angeles Times. *He spent most of the next two decades in California and Arizona. But in the summer months he returned religiously to his old haunts in Glacier Park. During this time he produced countless articles, including many never-to-be-forgotten juveniles for* The American Boy *and* Youth's Companion. *Because of his long association with George Bird Grinnell, whom he introduced to Glacier, much of his mature writing appeared in Grinnell's* Forest *and* Stream. *Houghton Mifflin Company published many of his fine books. In 1931 he married Jessie Louise Donaldson, an English instructor at Montana State College. She was with him at the time of his death, June 11, 1947, at eighty-seven, at Lander, Wyoming. He was buried among his brothers on Blackfeet soil. The material which follows, from* Blackfeet Tales of Glacier National Park *(Houghton Mifflin Co.,*

Boston, 1916) is brought back into print through the generosity of his widow. The title is ours. We are deeply indebted to Jessie Donaldson Schultz for these memorable reminiscences from the masterful pen of James Willard Schultz.

— Michael Kennedy.

AFTER AN ABSENCE of many years, I have returned [July 12, 1915] to visit for a time my Blackfeet relatives and friends, and we are camping along the [Glacier National Park] mountain trails where, in the long ago, we hunted buffalo, and elk, and moose, and all the other game peculiar to this region.

Today we pitched our lodges under Rising Wolf Mountain, that massive, sky-piercing, snow-crested height of red-and-gray rock which slopes up so steeply from the north shore of Upper Two Medicine Lake. This afternoon we saw upon it, some two or three thousand feet up toward its rugged crest, a few bighorn and a Rocky Mountain goat. But we may not kill them!

Said Tail-Feathers-Coming-Over-the-Hill: "There they are! Our meat, but the whites have taken them from us, even as they have taken everything else that is ours!" And so we are eating beef where once we feasted upon the rich ribs and loins of game, which tasted all the better because we trailed and killed it, and with no little labor brought it to the womenfolk in camp.

Rising Wolf Mountain! What a fitting and splendid monument it is to the first white man to traverse the foothills of the Rockies between the Saskatchewan and the Missouri! Hugh Monroe was his English name. His father was Captain Hugh Monroe, of the English army; his mother was Amelie de la Roche, a daughter of a noble family of French *emigres*. Hugh Monroe, Junior, was born in Montreal in 1798. In 1814 he received permission to enter the employ of the Hudson's Bay Company, and one year later — in the summer of 1815 — he arrived at its new post, Mountain Fort, on the North Fork of the Saskatchewan and close to the foothills of the Rockies.

At that time the Company had but recently entered Blackfeet territory, and none of its *engagés* understood their language; an interpreter was needed, and the Factor appointed Monroe to fit himself for the position. The Blackfeet were leaving the Fort to hunt and trap along the tributaries of the Missouri during the winter, and he went with them, under the protection of the head chief, who had nineteen wives and two lodges and an immense band of horses. By easy stages they traveled along the foot of the Rockies to Sun River, where they wintered, and then in the spring, instead of returning to the Saskatchewan, they crossed the Missouri, hunted in the Yellowstone country that summer, wintered on the Missouri at the mouth of the Marias River, and returned to Mountain Fort the following spring with all the furs their horses could carry.

Instead of one winter, Monroe had passed two years with the tribe, and in that time he had acquired a wife, a daughter of the great chief, a good knowledge of the language, and an honorable name, Ma-kwi-i-po-wak-sin (Rising Wolf) which was given him because of his bravery in a battle with the Crows in the Yellowstone country.

During Monroe's two years' absence from the Fort, another *engagé* had learned the Blackfeet language from a Cree Indian, who spoke it well, so that this man became the interpreter, and Monroe was ordered to remain with the Piegan tribe of the Blackfeet, to travel with them, and see that they came annually to the Fort to trade in the winter catch of furs. And this exactly suited him; he much preferred roaming the plains with his chosen people; the stuffy rooms of the Fort had no attractions for a man of his nature.

How I envy Hugh Monroe, the first white man to traverse the plains lying between the Upper Saskatchewan and the Upper Missouri, and the first to see many portions of the great stretch of the mountain region between the Missouri and the Yellowstone. He has himself often told me that "every day of that life was a day of great joy!"

Monroe was a famous hunter and trapper, and a warrior as well. He was a member of the *Ai-in-i-kiks*, or Seizer band of the All Friends Society, and the duty of the Seizers was to keep order in the great camp, and see that the people obeyed the hunting laws — a most difficult task at times. On several occasions he went with his and other bands to war against other tribes, and once, near Great Salt Lake, when with a party of nearly 200 warriors, he saved the lives of the noted Jim Bridger and his party of trappers. Bridger had with him a dozen white men and as many Snake Indians, the latter bitter enemies of the Blackfeet. The Snakes were discovered and the Blackfeet party was preparing to charge them, when Monroe saw that there were white men behind them. "Stop! White men are with them. We must let them go their way in peace!" Monroe shouted to his party.

"But they are Snake white men, and therefore our enemy: we shall kill them all!" the Blackfeet chief answered. However, such was Monroe's power over his comrades that he finally persuaded them to remain where they were, and he went forward with a flag of truce, and found that his friend Jim Bridger was the leader of the other party. That evening white men and Snakes and Blackfeet ate and smoked together! It was a narrow escape for Bridger and his handful of men.

Monroe had three sons and three daughters by his Indian wife, all of whom grew into fine, stalwart men and women. Up and down the country he roamed with them, trapping and hunting, and often fighting hostile war parties. They finally all married, and in his old age he lived with one and another of them until his death, in 1896, in his ninety-eighth year. We buried him near the buffalo cliffs, down on the Two Medicine River, where he had seen many a herd of the huge animals decoyed to their death. And then we named this mountain for him. A fitting tribute, I think, to one of the bravest yet most kindly men of the old, old West!

At the upper east side and head of this beautiful lake [Upper Two Medicine] rises a pyramidal mountain of great height and grandeur. A frowse of pine timber on its lower front slope, and its ever-narrowing side slopes above, give it a certain resemblance to a buffalo bull. Upon looking at a recent map of the country I found that it had been named "Mount Rockwell." So, turning to Yellow Wolf, I said: "The whites have given that mountain yonder the name of a white man. It is so marked upon this paper."

The old man, half blind and quite feeble, roused up when he heard that, and cried out: "Is it so? Not satisfied with taking our mountains, the whites even take away the ancient names we have given them! They shall not do it! You tell them so! That mountain yonder is Rising Bull Mountain, and by that name it must ever be called! Rising Bull was one of our great chiefs: what more fitting than that the mountain should always bear his name?"

"Rising Bull was a chief in two tribes," Yellow Wolf went on. "In his youth he married a Flathead girl, at a time when we were at peace with that people, and after a winter or two she persuaded him to take her across the mountains for a visit with her relatives. Rising Bull came to like them and all the Flathead people so well that he remained with them a number of winters, and because of his bravery, and his kind and generous nature, the Flatheads soon appointed him one of their chiefs. When he was about forty winters of age, some young men of both tribes quarreled over a gambling game and several were killed on each side. That, of course, ended the peace pact; war was declared, and as Rising Bull could not fight his own people, he came back to us with his Flathead wife, and was a leader in the war, which lasted for several years. When that was ended, he continued to lead war parties against the Crows, the Sioux, the Assiniboins, and the far-off Snakes, and was always successful. Came the dreadful Measles winter [of 1859-60], and with hundreds of our people, he died. He left a son, White Quiver, a very brave young warrior, and two years after his father's death, he was killed in a raid against the Crows.

"Ai! Rising Bull was a brave man. And oh, so gentle-hearted! So good to the widows and orphans; to all in any kind of distress! We must in some way see that this mountain continues to bear his name," said Tail-Feathers-Coming-over-the-Hill.

And to that I most heartily agree.

We left Little River on the 5th [of August, 1915], crossed the big ridge dividing the Arctic and the Atlantic waters, and made camp here on the big prairie at the foot of the Upper St. Mary's Lake.

In the old days this great valley, hemmed in by gigantic mountains, was my favorite hunting ground after the buffalo were exterminated and there was no more sport to be had upon the plains.

Hugh Monroe, or Rising Wolf, was, of course, the first white man to see these most beautiful of all our Northern Rockies lakes; with the Piegan Blackfeet he camped at them in 1816, and long afterward, with his growing family of hardy sons and daughters, this became his favorite hunting and trapping ground. When, in the 1830's [sic] that valiant and much beloved missionary, Father De Smet, S.J., was visiting the various tribes of this Northwest country, Monroe was engaged to take him to a conference with the North Blackfeet, then camping on the Sas-

Little Plume and son, Yellow Kidney   Piegan tipis at water's edge

katchewan River. En route they camped at the foot of the lower of these lakes, and there erected a large wooden cross, and named the two sheets of water, St. Mary's Lakes. Later, the Stevens expedition named them Chief Mountain Lakes, but that name did not last. Monroe and his brother trappers were all Catholics, and they continued to use the name that the great priest had given them, and on the maps they are St. Mary's Lakes today.

During my long friendship with him, Monroe told me many stories of his adventures here in early days. This was his favorite mountain resort on account of the great numbers of moose that inhabited the heavily timbered valley and mountain slopes, and of the great variety and numbers of fur animals that were found here. The valley swarmed with elk and deer; there were countless flocks of bighorn and goats on the mountains, and herds of buffalo everywhere along the lower lake, and below it; but Monroe liked best of all the flesh of moose, and killed large numbers of them every season that he camped here.

His method of catching wolves was simple and unique. He would build an oblong, pyramidal log pen about eight by sixteen feet at the base, and eight feet in height, the last layer of logs being placed about eighteen inches apart. Easily climbing the slope of this, the wolves would jump down through the narrow aperture at the top to feed upon the quantities of meat that had been placed inside to decoy them, but they could not jump out. Often, of a morning, the trapper and his sons would find ten or more big wolves imprisoned in the trap, and, powder and ball being very costly, they would kill them with bow and arrows, skin them, and drag the carcasses to the river and cast them into it, then take the hides home and peg them on the ground to dry. In this manner they would often, in the spring, have several hundred wolf pelts to pack in to Fort Benton for sale, and prime pelts sold at five dollars each, in trade. Their catch of beaver, otter, mink, martin and fisher was also large.

Monroe always camped at the foot of the lower lake, near the outlet, and was there more than once attacked by roving war parties of Assiniboins, Crows and even the Yanktonais. The horses were kept at night in a strong corral just back of the lodge, and in the daytime were watched by some member of the family while they grazed on the rich prairie grasses. All the family — John and François, the sons, Millie and Lizzie, the daughters — and even the mother had guns, flintlocks, and a good supply of powder and ball. Early one morning a large war party was discovered approaching the camp, sneaking from bush to bush, some crawling on all fours through the high grass. Lizzie opened fire upon them and killed her man, and then the fire became general on both sides. But the Monroes, in their trenches surrounding the lodge, had the best of it from the start, and eventually made the enemy retreat with a loss of five of their number. Late the following night the Assiniboins crept in to make another attack, but the Monroes were expecting them, waiting for them, and in the bright moonlight could take fairly accurate aim. They again drove them off, with a loss of two more of their number, and that time they kept going. Nothing more was seen of them. But for some days the Monroes did not venture far from their camp.

I first saw the St. Mary's Lakes in October, 1882, in company with Charles Phemmister, James Rutherford, Charles Carter and Oliver Sanderville, all old plainsmen, good company, and best of hunters. We outfitted for the trip at the Old Agency, on Badger Creek, Blackfeet Reservation, and started northward. There was no trail after leaving the crossing of Little or Milk River, and we struck up country toward the big gap in the mountains, in which we knew the lakes must lie, and that evening camped on the shore of a large prairie lake that was black with ducks. I shot a dozen or more of them as they flew over a long point, and to my surprise and delight found that they were all canvasbacks and redheads, and very fat from feeding upon the wild cherry beds of the lake. I named the sheet of water Duck Lake.

The next day we made a trail down the long hill, and camped at the foot of the lower lake, close to the outlet. Then began two weeks of most glorious sport. We shot elk, deer and several grizzlies in the valley, and bighorn on a mountain that I named Flat Top, and combed that mountain from one end to another and on all sides for an animal known to us as the Rocky Mountain ibex. We had seen several skins of them, bought from the Stony Indians by Captain John Healy, of Fort Whoop-up and Fort Benton fame, but none of us nor any man of our acquaintance — and we knew every trapper and trader in the country — had ever seen one of the animals alive. Of course we found none, as this sub-Arctic animal, which we later learned is a true antelope, and not an ibex or goat, seldom leaves the high cliff mountains for the outer and lower ones of the range. When, later, we did find them, we in our ignorance named them Rocky Mountain goats, and that is the common name for them today, despite the fact that they are antelopes.

On this first visit to the St. Mary's Lakes country I was so impressed by the grandeur of its mountains, the beauty of its many lakes, and its plenitude of game, that thereafter for many years it was, more than anywhere else, my home. In 1883 I brought out to the lakes a good boat that I had had built for me at Fort Conrad, and with it learned that both lakes were alive with whitefish and Mackinaw, Dolly Varden and cutthroat trout. During the summer of this year I named Red Eagle Mountain and Red Eagle Lake, after my uncle-in-law, Red Eagle, owner of the Thunder medicine pipe, and one of the most high-minded, gentle-hearted Indians that I ever knew. In the autumn of this year Dr. George Bird Grinnell joined me, and we hunted around the lower lake, and went up Swift Current far enough to see what we thought would possibly prove to be a glacier. We had not then time to learn if our surmise was correct. During our hunt Dr. Grinnell killed a large ram at long range, offhand, with one shot from his old Sharps rifle, on the mountain next above Flat Top, and I therefore named it Single-Shot Mountain.

In the summer of this year I also named Divide Mountain, because it is the outermost mountain on the Atlantic-Arctic watershed. At the same time I named Kootenai Mountain, also for a very good reason. Some members of that tribe were encamped beside me at the foot of the upper lake. I noticed often that they would ride out of camp at daylight and return at noon or a little later with all the bighorn or goat meat that their horses could carry, and finally I asked them where they went to make their killings so quickly.

"Come with me tomorrow and I will show you something," one of them answered. And the next morning I rode with him up Red Eagle Valley and part way up a mountain, where we tied our horses and went on afoot for a couple of hundred yards. Then, looking down into a *coulee*, we saw a dozen or more bighorn in the bottom of it and killed four of them. They had been eating salty clay and drinking from a salt spring that oozes from the ground there, so I named the place Kootenai Lick, and also gave the mountain the name of Kootenai. Thereafter I knew where to go for bighorn when I wanted one.

In 1884 I named Almost-a-Dog Mountain, after one of the few survivors of the Baker massacre, which took place on the Marias River, January 1, 1870. At that time Colonel [Major] E. M. Baker, with a couple of companies of cavalry from Fort Shaw, Montana, was trying to find the camp of Owl Child, a Piegan Blackfeet, and murderer of a settler named Malcolm Clark, and arrest him. By mistake he struck the camp of Heavy Runner and his band of friendly Indians, and although the chief came running toward him waving his letters of recommendation and his Washington medals, Baker ordered his men to begin firing, and a terrible massacre ensued, the Indians firing not one shot in defense, as about all the able-bodied men were at the time on a buffalo hunt. When the firing was over, 217 old men and women and children lay dead and dying in their lodges and in the camp. The soldiers then shot the wounded, collected the lodges and property of the Indians in great piles, and set fire to them and departed. [As later attested by Joseph Kipp.]

In the autumn of 1885 Dr. Grinnell, J. B. Monroe, and I made a trip up Swift Current River, and discovered and roughly measured the big glacier at the head of its middle fork, Dr. Grinnell killing a big ram on the ice while we were traversing it and avoiding its deep crevasses. That evening Monroe and I named the glacier in honor of Dr. Grinnell, and also named the mountain to the north of it after him. On the following day we were joined by Lieutenant — now Major — J. H. Beacom, Third Infantry, and he gave my Indian name, *Apikuni*, to the high mountain between Swift Current and the South Fork of Kennedy Creek. Upon our return to Upper St. Mary's Lake, Dr. Grinnell named Little Chief Mountain, Monroe gave Citadel Mountain its name, and I named Yellow Fish, Goat, Going-to-the-Sun, and Four Bears Mountains. Yellow Fish (*O-to-ko-mi*) was an Indian who often hunted with us, and Four Bears (*Nis-su-kyai-yo*) was the Blackfeet camp crier and a most amusing man.

It was in 1886, I believe, that we three, and my old-time friend, William Jackson, one-time scout for General Custer and General Miles, cut a trail to the head of the St. Mary's Valley and discovered the great sheet of ice that we named the Blackfeet Glacier. We at the same time named Gun-Sight Pass, and named the peak just west of the glacier, Mount Jackson. It should be *Sik-si-kai-kwan* (Blackfeet Man), Jackson's Indian name. He was a grandson of Hugh Monroe, a real plainsman, and one of the bravest men I ever knew.

Going-to-the-Sun has been climbed this day, and a flag has been planted upon its summit, by Paul E. Walker, Esq., of Topeka, Kansas. Owing to a high cliff upon its upper shoulder, the mountain has always been considered unclimbable. But after long search, and with no little risk, Mr. Walker finally worked out a way up the wall, and out upon the extreme crest, and was undoubtedly the first man, white or red, ever to stand there. He reports that a magnificent view of the mountains and plains is to be had from the great height. [Any man who could live among the Blackfeet, under the Big Sky and the beautiful mountains of what is now Glacier could indeed count himself among the most privileged of all mortals.]

Sign Talker with a Straight Tongue

FRANK BIRD LINDERMAN

By HAROLD G. MERRIAM

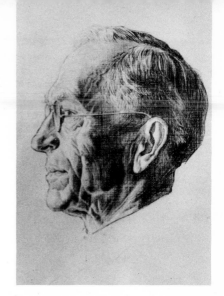

Frank Bird Linderman, drawn by Carl Link, 1937

This is a necessarily brief account of the life and writing of Frank Bird Linderman, with some tentative judgments and some words of encomium. Linderman's writings should be revived from the comparative neglect that has fallen upon them. A complete biography is overdue. His unpublished writings should be examined and the best of them published. Indeed, Montanans should take him to their hearts as they have taken his long-time friend, Charles M. Russell. Both men were authentic and able artists of days they were almost too young to experience. The works of Russell have come into their own; those of Linderman have not — yet. It is time they did. This account is intended to awaken interest in the man and his writing fully as much as to record his history.

The Plains Indians, both naturally and because of abusive experience, were suspicious of white men. They felt and knew, however, that Frank Linderman truly wished to know about their life — their customs and beliefs — and they trusted him. This trust made possible two fine books about them, "American" and "Red Mother," and many racial tales of real merit.

Linderman loved the free life of the open country, which he knew as a lad through his astounding intrepidity. He wrote of it interestingly in two novels, "Lige Mounts: Free Trapper" and "Beyond Law."

Frank Linderman was engaged in writing about early life in Montana and about Indians during all but a few of the last twenty years of his life. Previously, while living in Helena 1905 to 1917 he had promised himself, as he told me more than once, that as soon as he had made money enough selling insurance for his family to live on for a dozen years or so he would build a log house on Flathead Lake at Goose Bay and spend his full time writing. In 1917 he built that house and set to work. Two years earlier he had had published by Charles Scribner's Sons a collection of Indian tales entitled "Indian Why Stories." Eleven books followed, the last one five years before his death in 1938.

These writing years held both disappointment and elation for Linderman and his family, which was always devoted to his work. He was often disappointed and discouraged because, as author and critic Frederic Van de Water expressed it: "He did not give the public what it wanted. He offered them truth, a doorway into verity. He recreated authentic fragments of an already forgotten era."[1]

Linderman's books sold steadily but not in quantity. The sale of books about Indians has seldom been lively unless specifically written for children. Children loved Linderman's tales, though they were not written definitely for them; they were a record of Indian tales told, as nearly as possible (as he himself explained) in the Indians' style of story-telling.

When Frank had written and published six books and was "half done with the seventh," his friend Harry Cunningham wrote him on June 28, 1922, from Helena and offered him work once again selling insurance. In his reply, Linderman wrote that he was getting along fairly well, his books were being well received, he felt it "a duty to, in some way, preserve the Old West, especially in Montana, in printer's ink," that he wanted to do his work well and up to standard of the West itself as he knew it and that therefore he was "going to stick for a while, . . . and play the string out or until I see that I am in financial danger."2 In the autumn of the following year he felt that danger, realizing that more money must be brought into the family coffers. In December, 1923, he bought the Hotel Kalispell, in that city, ran it for two-and-a-half years, sold it, and returned to his home and writing at Goose Bay.

The elation during his writing years came, at its highest moment, after a long, highly successful and exciting visit to New York from October, 1929, to mid-April, 1930. He wrote me from there on December 14, 1929, that he had "contracts for 'Plenty Coups,' a republication of 'Lige Mounts,' 'Old Man Coyote and the Crows' and 'Beyond Law,' besides a contract to publish the first as a school book — all by the John Day Company except the last named. Lorimer, [editor of 'The Saturday Evening Post,'] sent for me to come down to Pa. and I've years of work to do now, old man, years of it. You'd be surprised as I am at the — well, I'll have to tell you, by word of mouth. . . ."3 All worked out as planned. "For New Yorkers," wrote Jean Pauline Smith, Mrs. Linderman's niece, "he was a refreshing breeze from his own mountains. He was feted and made a host of loyal friends who persuaded him to remain seven months."4 He was literally worn out by the round of luncheons, dinners and business.

The manuscript referred to as "Plenty Coups" came out under the title of "American" in 1930; "Lige Mounts: Free Trapper," was first published by Scribner's Sons in 1922, as "Morning Light," (a completely inept title) also in 1930; "Old Man Coyote and the Crows" came in 1931; "Beyond Law" in 1933. All bore the imprint of the John Day Company of New York. Linderman, meanwhile, under the impetus of his enthusiasm and profitable reception in New York City, was at work on the life of an old Crow woman in an effort to do for the Indian woman what "American" had done for the Indian man. As he consulted Plenty Coups through an interpreter and through the old man's use of sign language, which Linderman knew well, so Pretty Shield was telling of her life, using sign language. Her story was published in 1932 as "Red Mother."

"American" is one of two classics about Plains Indians. The other is James Willard Schultz' "My Life as an Indian."5 Two or three generations from ours, these classics will probably be read by more people than have read them in the last generation. Both of these volumes have appeared on school and college reading lists and will continue to appear there. Both men based their many writings on long and sympathetic life or association with Flatheads, Kootenais, Blackfeet, Chippewas (Ojibwas) and Crees. Both men had deep respect for Indian life and beliefs. Both recognized, as I have written elsewhere,6 in the Indian's life an atmosphere of communal interests, realistic courage and endurance, and an awareness of spiritual relationships with animals, earth and sky. Both men found him in partnership, so to speak, with the country, the man having adjusted himself to nature reverently and understandingly, not exploiting the land or its wild things

Harold Merriam before Thunder Lodge, painted for Frank Linderman by Mrs. Running Rabbit and Mrs. Buffalo Body

but using them as was necessary to his existence. Of course, both men found the Indian a human being much like ourselves. (Not all writers have — especially military men who turned to writing about the Plains Indian.)

Linderman, to the end of his life, believed that the white man could never fully understand the Indian who lived before white civilization reached him. But this is what he strove to do, and it took him thirty years of learning through contact and experience before he attempted to write his first book about Indians.

As A BOY Frank spent holidays and vacations "roaming the woods of Ohio, watching the wild animals and birds." His mother told Norma Linderman, her granddaughter, that she dressed him "in velvet suits with lace collars" and he would tramp off to hunt squirrels with his sawed-off musket over his shoulder. How he would flinch recollecting such a costume! "He liked to trap even then and once tried his hand at taxidermy and ruined his freshly papered bedroom wall with his stuffed birds." His mother also told the story of his filling the family cistern with toads, watersnakes and fish, of his pets dying and the cistern having to be drained and cleaned.[7]

In his teens he sprawled on his belly on the floor of his room in Chicago examining "for the hundredth time" a huge map of the United States in an effort to locate the least civilized part of it. "I remember that I felt glad when the Flathead Lake country in northwestern Montana Territory seemed yet to be the farthest removed from contaminating civilization. I'd go as straight as I could to Flathead lake."[8] A friend his own age agreed to go with him, taking along, through the chicanery of letter changing, a Negro coachman of his father's. They took off in March, 1885. Frank's father traveled with them a short way. "I had saved up seventy-five dollars and out of this sum I paid sixty-seven dollars and fifty cents for a ticket to Missoula, Montana Territory, for the Negro . . . My chum had much more money than I and I do not remember why I paid the fare for the Negro." This footing the bill (and not just in financial matters) was typical of Linderman to the day he died.

Arriving in Flathead country on March 20, 1885, the three set about falling logs and building a log cabin, windowless, floorless, without a fireplace or stove, and with the green skin of a whitetail deer for the door. "The uncovered pole roof leaked for hours after the rain outside had ceased to fall." They had no night covering except their light overcoats. Wolves howled about the makeshift cabin. The grubstake was light.

After four or five days of grumbling, Linderman's two companions proposed to leave. But Frank had cut his foot to the bone by stepping on the sharp blade of their ax, hidden under boughs of felled trees. The Negro bound it with Frank's only handkerchief: "the wound dampened my ardor so much that when my partners left me I felt mighty blue." And why not? A lad not yet seventeen years old, wounded, without sufficient food or clothing, with no money — it wouldn't have helped much anyway — alone in a vast wilderness which was uninhabited, so far as he could tell.

The stoicism of Frank Linderman's decision to remain reveals the kind of man he was. His total possessions were an old percussion-lock Kentucky rifle which had belonged to his father in Ohio, and the ax. By the time he could walk with a stick, the grub was gone. As yet he had seen no Indian, and no white man and he had no idea whether the Indians in that area were friendly or hostile to whites. One morning while cooking venison over the campfire, Frank heard a horse whinny. He picked up his bowie knife, slipped it into its scabbard at his belt, snatched up the rifle, power horn and bullet pouch, and hobbled over some knolls, where finally he hid and waited, watching some grazing horses. Within an hour or so an Indian "with a rifle across in front of him rode into the prairie on a pinto horse." The Indian nosed the wind and rode straight to the campfire by the cabin, which contained Frank's overcoat and ax. After an hour of waiting, Frank cautiously approached the cabin. There was the Indian sitting on a log filling his black stone pipe. "His blanket, a white Hudson's Bay, was tucked tight about his lean hips, his rifle leaning against the log beside him." With a stick from the fire he lit his pipe and then settled back "with such an air of peace and contentment that I fairly ached to shake hands with him."

The Indian's ear had caught the sound of crackling snow crust as Frank stepped on it: "Without the least startle or show of surprise his head turned until he saw me. Then he stood up with extended hand, 'How! How!' he said so pleasantly that I answered, 'Very well, sir, how are you?' giving his hand a good shake. He was a Flathead who instinctively knew that I was a rank pilgrim. His smile said as plainly as words that he thought me a babe in the woods."

The Indian's name was Red-horn, "a renowned Flathead warrior who had counted several coups and had taken more scalps than any other living member

of his tribe.... For many years after our meeting I knew my first Indian intimately."[9] "There in 1885," wrote Mrs. Waller, "began his interest in the history
of the Indians, their customs and their stories."[10]

Soon the lad entered into partnership with an old trapper, Alvin Lee, "who
had grown gray in the wilderness." Like other trappers "he felt pride in owning
a fast horse, a deadcenter rifle, the shortest camp equipment and the scantiest
bedroll in the Territory [of Montana]; and nothing stirred him as did the sight of
a fence. I shall never forget his displeasure and chagrin when he learned that
Montana had ceased to be a Territory and had become a State in the Union.
'Now she's gone to hell for keeps,' he sighed. And I believed him."[11]

The two of them built a new cabin in the autumn of 1885. Lee had built a
ferry over the Flathead River and because Frank had been around water much of
his early life and Lee knew nothing about boats, Frank was elected to run it.
This ferry was near what is known now as Holt Ferry but at that time was called
Lee's Landing.[12] In *My Camp-Kettle Career* Linderman states that they went
weeks without a single passenger.[13] About this time Frank's father sent him some
traps and camp gear. During his years as trapper he had two other partners,
both Indians, and, presumably, Flatheads: Dominick (Left Hand) and Koonsaw.
During these years also Lincoln Lee (Link) joined his brother in the Flathead.
From 1923 to about 1934 he lived in a cabin as caretaker of Goose Bay.

At times Linderman acted as a guide for hunting parties. After he had had
more than five years of the free life of the trapper he served as guide for Governor Sam Hauser, Judge Frank Woody, A. Sterne Blake and G. A. Wolf, "all
pioneers and prominent in the young state's affairs." One evening when the
Governor could not give a quotation from Shakespeare accurately, young Frank
did: "Boy," said Sam Hauser, "don't spend too much time running wild...
When you come out of the wilderness look us up, any of us. We'll help you get
your stride, someway." Characteristically, because he liked these men, he refused
pay for his services, "which had included horses, camp outfit, and even a sail-
boat and canoe."[14] Major Peter Ronan, Indian agent on the Flathead Reservation, had advised them to employ Frank.

About a year after meeting his first Indian, a Flathead, he met Crees and
Chippewas (Ojibwas). In 1892 as he left the Flathead on the steamboat *State of
Montana,* the boat passed a Cree village; he waved to Muskegon, who stood in
front of his lodge. Muskegon had told him many of the Cree legends.[15]

Then Linderman met the lady of his life, Mary Jane Johns, who had come
to the old town of Demersville to visit her brother, Sam. The course of Frank's
life changed. He promised her to leave the free life of the trapper and come back
into "civilization." But getting out of the much-loved wilderness proved almost
more than he could manage. From that time on, about 1892, the love of plains
and mountains and streams and freedom struggled with love for Mary Johns, although soon after meeting her he determined to marry her. They were not married until April 18, 1893.

In the meantime he tried tending store in Demersville, but his feet were uneasy and he soon gave up. He tried other means of livelihood, but the pull of the open life was too strong for him. Finally, he decided to take the Governor at his word. He happened upon Sam Hauser and a party on Flathead Lake, but he pushed on to Missoula. He had no money for getting to Helena. In Missoula, A. Sterne Blake proposed that he guide a party of Hauser, Dan Floweree and himself into the Clearwater country after elk. Linderman succumbed. The trip, however, because of weather, was not the success the party had hoped for. Frank took Tom, the Governor's son, over the mountain to get an elk. A week later he rode up with Blake to the Curlew mine near Victor, Montana, to become its watchman. Soon he found himself both bookkeeper and assayer, though he knew little or nothing about either. He sent off for books and from them taught himself some bookkeeping and also how to assay for silver and lead and later for other metals.

The time set for his marriage approached. He was without money. While repairing machinery at the mine he had chipped his knee and consulted Dr. Hanbridge, who told him he must rest for at least a week. Linderman refused to rest and the doctor accompanied him to Missoula, intending to put him in a hospital. But in the face of possible lameness for life, he still did not rest. He commissioned Dr. Hanbridge, however, who had lent him $100, to meet Mary Johns at the station, not wishing to appear lamed before her. When he did see her and told what the doctor said about possible lameness — and probably about his lack of money and the loan — Mary replied: "We shall get along well enough." Linderman, in his account, added "And we always have."[16]

Mrs. Linderman was a woman of perception and sympathy. Those qualities plus her courage sustained her husband over the many periods of hard times and discouragement. Once, in 1917, she wrote him, "... We ought to have lots of pleasure planning and building our new home. After all, that is what life consists of, improving one's surroundings and having a personality that brings the right kind of friends ... I shall get pleasure through seeing you daily again [he had been traveling the state for seven years] and listening to the people who will seek you for yourself in your new home."[17] The friends came and they were generally of "the right kind," and Mrs. Linderman was an excellent listener. She was devoted to his career.

After a short while at Victor he moved, in 1894, to Butte, as an assayer for the Butte and Boston smelter. There the first child, Wilda, was born. From Butte he moved the family in the spring of 1898 to Sheridan in Madison County. There he set up a furniture store with an assay office included and the weekly newspaper *The Sheridan Chinook*, which he bought with a down payment of five dollars — "all," wrote his daughter Norma, "he could afford at the time."

The family lived in Brandon, just above Sheridan, and in that area Frank prospected, without success. Andrew M. Balfour, a Scotch mining engineer, graduate of Edinburgh and Columbia Universities, met him there. In the papers of the Linderman Estate is a letter from him to Frank, written in 1917, which reveals the impression Frank made on people: "It is now 17 long years since you and I had our first medicine talk. There were lots of them. I shall never forget that little furniture store in Sheridan. To me, the memory of those days will always be a chapter, the reading and rereading of which fulfills adequately all that I require in the nature of a rite — a sacred rite. It was a new world to me entirely. Just to watch the play of your features as you read your own and the works of others, to me, was pure joy. I felt then that I had made a discovery — I had found a type — a new type of man." Mr. Balfour recalled a conversation he had with the senior Mr. Rossiter of Sheridan: "I said I believe Frank is the only man in the Legislature with courage enough to think for himself. Asked why I thought that I replied, he has the face. Mr. Rossiter replied, 'so you've noticed that too, have you?' "[18]

In his Sheridan years Linderman was elected representative in the Montana legislature in 1903 and again in 1905. This interest in politics earned him the nomination in 1918 as candidate on the Republican ticket for U. S. Representative in Congress. But he was defeated, as he was when he ran against Senator Tom Walsh in 1924. Herman Hagedorn, his friend, wrote: "these essays in Montana politics were gallant but futile."[19]

His family and friends were not ill-pleased by these defeats, for they meant additional years for writing about Indians and early life in Montana. Had he been elected to either office, his output would have been more limited than it is. Had he gone to Washington he would have given his all to either office, though his heart, it is pretty clear, would have remained in Montana with early days and Indians. In either office he would have been nobody's tool. But this gets ahead of the story.

In the late spring of 1905 the family moved to Helena. Linderman had become not only assayer, newspaperman and businessman, but a successful insurance agent as well. He rose to high position in Masonic ranks, becoming a Potentate of Algeria Temple.[20] He always had the courage of his beliefs on all issues and this frank expression of his honest convictions doubtless contributed to his political defeats.

During his Helena years, 1905-1917, Linderman was active (with his friends Senator Paris Gibson, William M. Boles and Charley Russell) in the establishment of the Rocky Boy Reservation around old Fort Assiniboine and in locating on it the wandering, displaced Crees and Chippewas. "He spent many days in our national capitol in December 1912, at his own expense, presenting his plea before Congressmen and Senators, staying on until he was assured the bill would be presented. The bill was first introduced in January, 1913, and became law in the spring of 1916. The Indians were allowed to move to Fort Assiniboine in the fall of 1914. It was from there that Chief Rocky Boy of the Chippewas wrote Frank Linderman asking his opinion on a tribal matter, and ending the letter with, 'You are Chief'."[21]

During the Helena years the old men and women of the Blackfeet, Chippewa,

Cree, Kootenai and Crow tribes often visited and told him their stories and customs, their beliefs and disappointments. They also showered him with gifts and prized possessions. The idea of giving full time to writing probably became strong when in January, 1911, he met in Helena his first author, Opie Reid, and gave the author a welcoming dinner at the Montana Club. It is a good guess that he told Reid of his desire to write and dead certain that he filled Reid's mind with Indian lore. In July, 1914, he was in Forsyth, Montana, when the Chautauqua was there, with Reid as one of the lecturers. Unexpectedly, the two men met and Reid declared, "Thank God, the town is now redeemed," less downgrading the town than expressing pleasure from meeting Linderman again. When they parted Reid said: "Go at it . . . be sure to print the Indian lore." Immediately he wrote his wife telling of Reid's encouragement and stating, "I wonder if I could make a good living with my pen — I know I could for you and me." . . .[22] However, there were three daughters to be raised and educated.

Soon after this he sent the manuscript of *Indian Why Stories* to the Curtis Publishing Company. The editors, feeling that they could not use the tales but liking them, sent the manuscript to the Century Publishing Company with a comment, "wonderfully interesting." To Linderman the Curtis editor wrote that he had "taken the liberty of sending the manuscript to the Century people who would be deeply interested in the stories and the writer." However, it was Charles Scribner's Sons, in the following year, who published the book. This was nearly two years before the move to Goose Bay and the devotion of his full time to writing. Three other books of Indian tales followed: *Indian Old-Man Stories* (1920), *Kootenai Why Stories* (1926), and *Old Man Coyote* (1931).

The commodious and handsome log house on Goose Bay had been completed in 1917. It sat so nicely among evergreens and other trees and bushes that from the highway above it only its roof could be seen. In front it looked out over the beach and the bay onto Flathead Lake, which Linderman had known and loved for more than thirty years. Beside it usually stood a tepee, a most comfortable dwelling-place, Frank assured me when I appeared skeptical, in summer and winter. The Linderman family moved in and made the log house a home, always a hospitable one, and when the daughters were there a gay one.

"A visit in Linderman's home on Goose Bay," wrote Jean P. Smith in the *Frontier* article already cited, ". . . is like stepping back into frontier days. Each bronze figure he has cast, each trophy, each picture breathes the beauty, the humor, the friendships, the hazards of an earlier life. For example, I asked the author as he stood beside his open fire in his red voyageur's cincture about the portrait of Aeneas. 'Oh, he slapped my mouth once. That's Big Knife. He wanted me to leave the country.' Frank Linderman chuckled reminiscently, 'And by George, I did.'"

Frank Linderman passionately wished to understand the Plains Indian, yet although he had "studied the Indian for more than forty years, not coldly, but with sympathy" he did not feel that he knew "much about him." "You have felt my heart," said Plenty Coups, "and I have felt yours." But still Linderman believed that because of the widely different views of life held by the two races, red and white, "any writing by a white man about the Indian must suffer." "I am convinced that no white man has ever thoroughly known the Indian."[23] The key to his concern is the word "thoroughly," for no writer could be more meticulous in search for truth. He tried persistently to get under the skin of the Indian, yet felt constantly baffled. In his search he trusted only the fullbloods and among those only the old ones. Younger Indians had experienced too fully the white man's ways, and the breed's knowledge of Indian myths, stories, dances, religious views, ways of responding to life he felt to be almost non-existent: "the real Indians are gone." This conviction appears again and again in his writing and his talk and his letters. It is "far too late to study the Indian now."[24]

An incident Linderman liked to tell ran this way: In Glacier Park he saw a young Blackfeet entertaining a group of tourists with hand talk, the common sign language of the old-time Plains Indian. He marveled to see a youngster so deft in what had become almost a lost art. He asked the lad where he learned hand talk; the lad replied, "From General Hugh L. Scott's book." Frederic Van De Water, who relates this incident, continues: "When a Blackfoot [sic] must turn to a white authority to recover an invention of his own people, it is easy to imagine how much of incredible worth that no one at the time troubled to fix in print is gone forever from the West."[25]

Linderman's collections of tales and his biographies of Plenty Coups and Pretty Shield clearly show that he was particularly concerned with the imaginative and the spiritual sides of the Indian. None of the materials in them is his invention. Except in short forewords they are accompanied by no explanation or gloss. The telling is simple, as the Indian told them. In his first two collections he has an old Indian, War Eagle, tell the tales to his grandchildren in his great painted lodge.

The emphasis which Linderman placed on getting his tales from the oldest Indians is extreme. For pristine lore, he felt, the time was too late for gathering: "With the passing of the blanket Indian . . . we have lost much of the aboriginal folklore, rich in its fairylike characters and its relation to the lives of a most warlike people." Though convinced that the white man could not fully know the red man, he himself penetrated into the Indian nature deeply enough to assert that the Indian is "a poet by nature." The tales show that he was. The Plains Indian he also found "intensely religious and profoundly superstitious."[26] The tales show these characteristics also. It is not clear how much the Indian associated religion and superstition. The medicine dreams were principal and guiding experiences in life and those from which the Indian derived his "medicine." To the white man today (especially one who has no mysticism in his nature) these dreams are superstition; yet they served the Indian well. To have them he had to be alone, to fast, to cleanse his body many times. Sometimes the dream did not come for several days when the lad — for always the dream must be sought when the Indian was

Pretty Shield   Plenty Coups

young — was exhausted. Of course today, under such conditions, we say that hallucination occurs. Any person who has experimented with fasting over a period of days knows that strange experiences come to the mind. When we do not understand a spiritual experience we are likely to label it superstition or hallucination.[27]

In any case, the Plains Indians believed that God (white people usually think of Him as Manitou) made all animals, all flora, man, the world and everything in it. God created heaven and earth. Some creations, however, He put into the hands of Napa and Napa made the mistakes. To each creation, to each creature God gave special characteristics and qualities; these the Indian respected, not thinking of himself as superior except in his own special characteristics. The coyote, for instance, had a keener sense of smell than man. The Indian acknowledged that superiority. The eagle had keener eyesight and could travel the skies as he could not. The Indian acknowledged the eagle's superiority to him in those respects. Linderman wrote: "If you ask an Indian whether the sun is God he will say yes, for he believes that you know that ALL is God."[28]

The ideas here roughly outlined indicate the sincerity of Linderman's writing.

In *Indian Why Stories*, which are Blackfeet, Chippewa and Cree tales, we learn reasons why the deer has no gall, why the mountain lion is long and lean, why Blackfeet never kill mice, how the ducks got their fine feathers, and other whys and hows. These are simple tales as most folklore tales are, but often they have depth, again like most folk tales. They are to be read with imagination, even, at times, with spiritual response, and they are seldom understood without the play of humor.

Linderman, like every other white man who knew the Plains Indian well, found in him a developed sense of humor. One sees this in Plenty Coups and in Pretty Shield as they tell their life stories. "Napa or Old-Man appears [in these stories] as a god and a creator, and again as a fool, a thief, or a clown." Somebody kept making mistakes in the world. They would never, by the Indian, be attributed to God, whom he would never tell idle tales about or mention irreverently.[29]

In *Indian Old-Man Stories* (1920) — Chippewa and Cree tales — the Indian tells why our sight fails with age, why children lose their teeth, and why dogs howl at night. In this book one learns of an old man's courting, of Old-Man's new weapons, about Quo-too-quat the cripple; about Ca-mee-ne-wa-sit, the most evil person in the world (who, significantly, had left the world before War Eagle, the teller, came to it); and about Strikes-and-Kills, a tale which mixes animals and men.

In *Old Man Coyote* (1931) the tales are Crow in origin. They are longer, have more body, the red man's mind is less obviously moral or ethical, and the tales deal with animal-man and man-animal, the two intermixed even more than in tales of the earlier books. One must believe that they have meanings which escape the white-man mind. This collection was published also as a Junior Literary Guild selection. To white children, the tales offer enchanted incident after enchanted incident until what was animal and what was man are indistinguishable. The last story in the book, "Morning Star, Son of the Sun," appeared in *The Frontier* in 1928. It carried an excellent foreword about the Crows (Absarokees), similar to the foreword in his volume. The book is the last of Linderman's significant collections of Indian tales.

The illustrators of the Linderman Indian tales were artists in sympathy with the materials, although some obviously knew the Indian better than others. The best, of course, was Charley Russell, who illustrated *Indian Why Stories, Indian Old-Man Stories* and a school edition published by Scribners Sons in 1918 entitled *Indian Lodge-Fire Stories*. The author and the artist were friends; both knew the West and both knew Indians well. Both were good workmen. They were doing much the same thing, interpreting the Indian, one in words, the other in paint. Russell delayed making drawings for another Linderman book, which resulted in a long delay in its publication, and a temporary estrangement between the two old friends. The affection which existed between them, however, is shown in an interesting excerpt from Linderman's "Recollections of Charley Russell" written of their last hunting trip together in the fall of 1925.[30]

Kootenai Why Stories carried pictures by C. L. Bull, who was an illustrator of the day specializing in drawing and painting animals. The publisher assigned the work to him.

The *How It Came About Stories* (1921) were the invention of Frank Linderman's mind. He is careful to warn the reader in the foreword that they are purely imaginary and are not to be taken as Indian folklore. Although he used Old Man, he was writing to interest young readers in nature. "I believe in the cultivation of appreciation for the work and beauties of nature as a firm foundation for better citizenship," he stated in the foreword. The book is divided into two parts, *At the Big Lake When the Moon Is Full* and *Near the Foot of the Mountain When the Moon Is Dark*. It is a pity that this book has not been recently illustrated and reprinted. The author, here relieved of responsibility for truth to the Indian's telling, had pure fun in the conceiving and writing of it. A Dutch artist, C. M. Boog, again assigned by the publisher, created the illustrations.

When *American* appeared in 1930 critics (myself among them) hailed the book as a classic. Nothing quite like it had been done before for the Plains Indian. It is the life story of a Crow chief, Plenty Coups, then eighty-three years of age. Since the chief had been born in 1847, the earliest years of his life were probably largely but not wholly free from white-man influence. Furthermore, one must remember that the white-man influence he did not escape was that of the trapper, a type of person who learned more from the Indian than he taught the Indian. The earliest years, therefore, must have been comparatively Old Indian in nature. His accounts of the games of boys, their swimming, their imitation of fighting, their play at counting coups, their longing to be men (and they were, at very early years), the ways of their parents with them (the parents never struck their children and before them were constantly speaking of the deeds of their elders in order to incite challenge), these all probably ran back to the fairly primitive Indian. The self-discipline of the boys, their endurance, physical and spiritual, obedience to their elders and to their "medicine" are remarkable. And all of these characteristics are universally human and universally delightful.

The young age at which they undertook tasks, especially in search for dreams, involving bodily suffering and spiritual anguish, appalls the reader.

The making of this book was a painstaking task. When Plenty Coups said he would tell his life story, Linderman went repeatedly from his home on Goose Bay almost across the state to the Crow Reservation. There, using an interpreter and asking the chief to use the sign language as he spoke, Plenty Coups and he sat day after day, the former recalling his life, the latter listening and carefully watching the sign talk. Being adept in that talk, time and again Linderman was able to correct the interpretation given him. There was no pushing of the chief and only occasionally were there leading questions. "I am glad you asked me that," Plenty Coups would say. The two men respected and trusted one another. "I know," the chief said as he signed the manuscript with his thumb, "you will tell only what I have said, that your writing will be straight like your tongue."[31] Linderman does insert paragraphs of interpretation of Indian words, symbols, customs, meanings for his reader, but does not attempt to analyze or expand upon the chief's words or experiences.

The method of getting the material and of writing it was both pleasant and laborious. No detail was too small for Linderman's patient research for exactness and verification. I recall that when Professor Lowie, a famous anthropologist at the University of California, in reviewing the book, noted one error in a detail about the sun dance, Linderman traveled once more across the state to the Reservation to learn whether he or the professor was right. As he returned he stopped at my home to say that "the damned professor was right."[32]

In spite of meticulous care "such a book as this must suffer," Linderman states in the foreword, "because of the widely different views of life held by the two races, red and white." True enough. However, other differences such as different stages of development in civilization at a given time make the understanding difficult, and the white man's feeling of superiority doesn't help one bit. *American*, however, I am convinced, comes as close to understanding and authenticity as any straightforward and honest account, not an analysis or labored interpretation, will ever come. This is autobiography as nearly as man can talk about himself without self-consciousness. It is a gay book as Plenty Coups tells of his early days; a book of courage when he tells of Crow raids and fights; a tragic one as the Indian's position in life comes clear. "In this brave story," wrote Linderman's niece, Jean Pauline Smith, ". . . we realize the deep significance of the philosophy of the Indian – 'I am standing in this world alone'."[33]

Red Mother (1933) was meticulously taken down from the talk of Pretty Shield, a Crow woman, eleven years younger than Plenty Coups, in the same manner. She, too, used sign language as she talked. The account may be slightly less interesting, partly because an Indian woman was shy in the presence of a white man and in part because the life of an Indian woman was more humdrum than that of the man. Yet the account is charming in portrayal of young-girl life: the girls romp, kick the ball, swim, are teased by the boys (it was ever thus no matter what the race), are curious about the places over the hill. Then they grow up, enter the lodges of their men, perform the many arduous duties of the Indian wife, become mothers and grandmothers. Like the boys, they have much fun when young.

These two biographies are Linderman's finest work. As a workman he reveals in them a sense of word values and a rhythm of expression that spring, no doubt, from love for his task. In these writings in particular he demonstrates his artistry.

H. M. Stoops of New York City illustrated *Old-Man Coyote, American* and *Red Mother*. Linderman had not known him, but immediately upon meeting they knew they would be great friends, and they were. From New York City Frank wrote me on March 29, 1930: "Wonder of wonders – my illustrator was employed to make 4 pictures for 500.00. He made *42* and then donated his 500.00 to advertise the book *American*. Can you believe such things?" The illustrations by

Stoops in the three books are the most artistic of any illustrations in the Linder-man books, but for me when compared with Russell's they have less "the smell of the Injin," as Linderman would say. And possibly it is my imagination which sees in them the eastern Indian more often than the western. Linderman, however, was quite happy about them.

With *Red Mother* the published writings about Indians cease, except for a brief and interesting history of the Blackfeet Indians written to accompany the paintings of them by Winold Reiss. The account he gives here applies pretty much to all Plains Indians: "Although they brought their social customs from the northern forests, they [the Blackfeet] did not differ greatly from those of the Plains Indians," he wrote in the foreword.[34] This succinct account is for the reader who desires a short statement of facts. An astounding fact in it is Linderman's finding one of the Blackfeet Indian hero tales in a translation from the Sanskrit.

Linderman's first love had not been the Indian but the free life of the outdoor man in contention or compliance with nature. It was to be expected, then, that sooner or later, once he had begun writing in earnest, a novel about early western life would come from his pen. *Lige Mounts: Free Trapper* (1922) tells of fur trading in Cree country. Like many first novels it drew heavily upon personal experiences and to that degree is autobiographical. But Lige, in spite of the young man's longing to go west becomes nostalgic: "A feeling of sure enough home-sickness settled down on me," says Lige, "and I wanted to go back. I *would* go back, and stay. I made up my mind to that." But he didn't. In spite of such mat-ters, Lige is not Frank Linderman. However, with his knowledge of the plains and mountains, of the trapper's life and of Indians, and with his extreme care for accuracy, the novel certainly is as authentic as any book about early days in Montana. Much the same can be said of *Beyond Law* (1933). Both novels have unmistakable feeling for the country and the wise ways of living in and with it and its people. This last characteristic many novels of the West utterly lack. Fred-eric Van De Water, author himself and critic, placed Linderman's in the first rank of novels of the West. He found them possessed of "a baffling sense of reality."[35]

Lige himself is a bit idealized and so does not assume that same reality, but the author was less interested in the man than in the country, the action and the way of life. There probably is a good deal of Al Lee in him. At this period of his life, Frank Linderman was close to the edge of ideality, in some of his thinking and writing. His Indian did not become the noble savage but he was clearly in the approach to that state. So, too, was his free trapper. A Montana artist, Joe de Yong of Choteau, protegé of C. M. Russell, illustrated the novels and illustrated them well.

In *On a Passing Frontier* (1920) Linderman gathered seven tales told mostly in the anecdotal manner. He was himself a master of anecdote. Some are tales that circulated orally over a large territory. For instance, I have heard "Jake Hoover's Pig" from more than one old-timer. All of the tales have the flavor of the early period hankered for by the writer. Significantly, the dedication is to "the good town of Malta and to the mining camps in the Little Rockies where the old west is making its last stand." Prefacing the collection is one of Linderman's best poems, with the characteristic die-hard surrender of the old-timer to contemporary ways.

The Indian tales and the two biographies of Crow man and woman have ethnological value as well as artistic, and should be studied by anthropologists. The novels and sketches are of particular value, as Van De Water has pointed out, because they were written by a man who "had been Doer before he became Teller."[36] This means that experience guides imagination as the writer works; thus inaccuracies, absurdities and misinformation are avoided. Western stories have become so standardized and routine that a writer need never even see the West in order to write them. What a writer who has first been a doer produces is likely to ring true, as Linderman's writing does. Tap it anywhere and you get a clear, true tone.

During many years Linderman wrote verse western in character and form. A few poems were published in *Scribner's Magazine*, in *The Frontier* and in *The Literary Digest*. What he really wished to preserve is in the volume *Bunch Grass and Blue Joint*, dedicated to his wife.[37] The poems are often nostalgic for the early days and often have a clever or humorous twist at the end. Several describe nature, which was always close in his affection. The packrat, the burro, the endlessly hopeful prospector, the packer, the cowpuncher and the coyote all have their say. At times a moral slips in. The three poems in Canuck dialect are among the best. I am reminded of a passage between Linderman and Lew Sarett, the poet, the former maintaining that a dialect poem should have every word exactly in the dialect and the latter inclining to the thought that enough dialect should enter a poem to put the reader "in the groove" but not so much as to make reading difficult. With Linderman the choice was always complete accuracy. The opinions arose over a poem Sarett entitled "Two Woodsmen Skin a Grizzly Bear" in which one of the two men was a "Canuck." The poem was published in *Frontier and Midland*.[38] The first poem in the book, "Git Down and Come In" is the traditional greeting of the plainsman in days that are gone.

In Linderman there was nothing of the city man, although he enjoyed its life and opportunities when in a city. The spread of space, the silent places, mountains, plains and streams untouched by man, animals in their natural habitats, life in *cooperation* with nature, freedom to be alone and to think and feel without distraction, generosity toward other men, minding one's own business, living with a reverence for life and for all created things, these were what he felt that life in the city lacked. He was not an enemy of progress but its commercial aspects he could hardly respect. He was not hostile to art, but he wished it to be honest and as inspiring as he found nature to be. His lungs needed the fresh air of mountains, his eyes the blue sky and the green tree and flowing water, his mind had to have honesty, his spirit integrity and bravery, and his heart, love. These qualities one finds in good measure in the writings of Frank Bird Linderman. Small wonder the Indians called him "Sign-Talker-With-Straight-Tongue."

NOTES

[1] "The Work of Frank Bird Linderman," *The Frontier and Midland,* Vol. 19:149.

[2] Ibid., p. 146.

[3] Letter in possession of H. G. Merriam.

[4] Frank B. Linderman: "Sign Talker," *The Frontier,* Vol. 11:59.

[5] Published in 1907, republished in 1914.

[6] In "Montana Writing," *A History of Montana,* edited by Burlingame and Toole, Lewis Historical Pub. Co., N. Y., 1957, Vol. 2, p. 271.

[7] Letter to H. G. Merriam from Mrs. Waller, Apr. 15, 1962.

[8] See "My Camp-Kettle Career," *Frontier and Midland,* Vol. 19, 153-167.

[9] Ibid., p. 156.

[10] Leaflet prepared by Mrs. Waller for distribution at the Linderman exhibit, June through September, 1962, Museum of the Plains Indian, Browning, Mont.

[11] Foreword to *Lige Mounts: Free Trapper,* Chas. Scribner's Sons, N. Y., 1922.

[12] Letter to H. G. Merriam from Mrs. Waller, Apr. 19, 1962.

[13] In a section of the manuscript among the Linderman Estate papers not published in *Frontier and Midland.* In a letter to H. G. Merriam, dated Nov. 20, 1930, Linderman wrote: "Wish I had you where I might pour my 'Camp-Kettle Career' into you, so that I'd at least have one good man's opinion of it. I don't like the thing at all, didn't want to do it."

[14] "Camp-Kettle Career," *op. cit.,* p. 159.

[15] Among the Linderman Estate papers.

[16] "Camp-Kettle Career," *op. cit.,* p. 167.

[17] Letter to the writer, Apr. 15, 1962.

[18] Ibid.

[19] *Frontier and Midland,* 19:144.

[20] H. G. Pickett, Past Potentate of Algeria Temple, Helena, sent H. G. Merriam on March 11, 1939, a letter and a typed appreciation of Linderman: "For some months in the early 90's I was bunkmate with Frank Linderman, among the mountains, at a mine. Of the many things he told me, the following incident is now first in my mind: It was night on the Flathead, darkness had dropped from the sky of night until it rested on the wide expanse of the quiet waters of the lake. On a bed of blanket, moss and sand, in front of a driftwood log, a slender youth was sleeping. A small campfire near his feet lifted a little of the darkness of the near waters of the lake. Some sub-conscious alarm wakened the sleeper to see an Indian standing tall and straight behind the log. The sudden call from perhaps a dream, with an instant's loss of memory, sent a sharp thrill of fear through him but his eyes did not waver and his voice was calm as he greeted with 'How' and asked his silent visitor what brought him to his campfire. The unbending Indian returned his 'How' and said 'you have trapped with our young men, you have been in our lodges, you have eaten with us and have entered our hearts. I have been sent by our chiefs, from where our Council Fire is burning, to bring you to them that they may adopt you into our tribe and make you a real brother to us all. Come with me my brother to where they wait.' It was from there the real Indian life of Frank Linderman began."

[21] Leaflet, *op. cit.*

[22] Letter among the Linderman Estate papers.

[23] Quotations from the brief Foreword to *American* and the words of Plenty Coups, vii.

[24] Foreword to *Indian Old-Man Stories.*

[25] *Frontier and Midland,* 19:149.

[26] Foreword to *Indian Old-Man Stories,* xix.

[27] For a detailed and fascinating account of the dream, see *American,* pp. 34-44.

[28] Foreword to *Indian Old-Man Stories,* ix.

[29] Quotations from Foreword to *Indian Why Stories.*

[30] *Frontier and Midland,* 19:167-171.

[31] *American,* vii. *American,* under the title *Plenty Coups,* is now on sale by the University of Nebraska Press. The World Book Co. published it as a school textbook, which the State of Texas adopted.

[32] Linderman's respect for professors was not large; all they know they learn from books, he once told me.

[33] *Frontier and Midland,* 11:59.

[34] *Blackfeet Indians,* published by Brown and Bigelow, St. Paul, 1935, for the Great Northern Railroad. That company later published the history separately.

[35] *Frontier and Midland,* 19:151.

[36] Ibid., p. 148.

[37] Charles Scribner's Sons, N. Y., 1921.

[38] Vol. 12, p. 1.

CONFLICT
AND ACCOMMODATION

Ft. Keogh, built in 1887 as base for troops engaged in final subjugation of the Indians

Lt. John J. Pershing, 6th Cavalry,
was stationed at Ft. Assiniboine

Cavalry inspection, Fort Assiniboine

War Paint Against Brass
THE ARMY AND THE PLAINS INDIANS

By ROBERT G. ATHEARN

THE SURRENDER at Appomattox was more than a death knell to the Confederate forces; it also marked the beginning of a period later called the Federal Army's "Dark Ages." While the gray-clad soldiers disconsolately stacked their arms, knowing that militarily their cause had ended, the day of triumph for the boys in blue was only momentary. Within weeks, demobilization seriously decimated their ranks and a year later a force that once numbered nearly a million men was a mere shadow of an army. Subsequent reductions cut it to a corporal's guard.

Yet, during the post-war years events — particularly related to Indians — in the American West demanded a larger frontier force than ever — a fact never quite fixed in the public mind. It was a period when capital avoided the shattered South in preference to an untouched frontier; when settlers by-passed arable lands in the East for arid plots in what was still called the "Great American Desert." And it was a period that witnessed successive economic assaults on the land by hunters, miners, cattlemen and bonanza wheat farmers.

Above all the Plains Indians made a frantic effort to stem the tide of emigration, only to be deluged by waves of wealth-seekers. The white advance was so enormous that despite some spectacular battles it generally appeared as if its cutting edge was not even dulled by resistance. The natives, whose efforts provided only temporary obstacles, never a permanent barrier, repeatedly struck at the invader, causing howls of pain but no real retreat. These ham-stringing attacks goaded the whites into a fury of retaliation and produced bitter denunciation against the Army for failing to destroy the enemy. Futilely troops chased the better mounted Indian raiders, and even if there was a battle civilians were generally unhappy about the way it was conducted. When the troops won, Eastern humanitarians complained of the slaughter; when the Indians won, charges of negligence leading to a "massacre" were heard.

Americans never discovered a solution to the Indian problem, but prior to the Civil War period the availability of land beyond the Mississippi at least gave their government an opportunity to temporize merely by pushing the tribes westward. During Jackson's administration, when the President told Congress that the

Indians could not live with the whites and prosper, extensive removals were effected. But now, with a restless population poised at the edges of the remaining unsettled regions, time was running out for the tribes. There was no great unsettled area to which they might be again removed. After the whites gained sufficient control they marked off unlikely sections of the West as reservations and assigned the Indians to their new homes.

During the post-war years the direction of Indian affairs continued under an unhappy partnership between two governmental departments. In 1849 the War Department had surrendered its control to the new Interior Department, but events showed that the military was never quite free of responsibility. Under normal conditions agents from any civilian branch could carry on day-to-day business with the tribes but with disturbing frequency the Indians resorted to warfare and excited calls for troops followed. As a rule there was a brief and violent struggle, after which the Indians sullenly returned to the reservation, driven there by troops or by hunger. The ebb and flow of resistance continued until the Indians were exhausted.

The Interior Department frequently objected to Army methods of pacifying the Indians. Hardly was the problem of the Plains Indians faced, after the Civil War, before Interior Secretary James Harlan complained that some "gentlemen of high position, intelligence and personal character" openly advocated a policy of extinction. This, he said, was an impossible notion. The liquidation of 300,000 Indians appeared to be impracticable, if for no other reason than the financial one. He estimated that each regiment of troops maintained on the high plains then cost two million dollars annually and the previous summer's campaign in the West had resulted in the destruction of not more than a few hundred natives.[1] The Indians must be fed, not fought.

For the remainder of the nineteenth century, and after, the American people were divided into two camps with regard to what was generally known as the "Indian Problem." The Interior Department, jealous of its powers, opposed force and advocated a policy of pacification by feeding. Easterners, in general, and a group of vocal humanitarians, in particular, applauded this stand and never lost an opportunity in the press or from lecture platforms to preach a crusade of gentleness and enlightenment toward the benighted savages. Many who fought in abolitionist ranks before the war now turned their attention to the American Indian and he became the object of their sympathy.

Army men were placed in the dilemma of having the responsibility of peace in the new West and yet treading carefully to avoid offending the sponsors of the *beau savage*. General W. T. Sherman, who commanded the Western Army, expressed the military view when he said, "My own opinion is that unless we have absolute control of Indian affairs, we cannot be responsible for harmony of action, and the safety of the Frontiers. . . ."[2] His belief was unnoticed in the crescendo of maudlin sympathy voiced for the oppressed race. Both he and his subordinates were placed in the false position of being called "exterminationists." Except for a few young and ambitious warriors like George Custer and Nelson Miles, army men wanted neither Indian war nor extermination. To thinking men the question was one of law and order. They believed that if the races were to be separated the operation should be done with strictness and equity. Those Indians assigned to reservations ought to be fed and cared for, just as the Interior Department advocated, but should they transgress and stray they must be returned, by force if necessary. In short, reservation Indians were to be regarded as good Indians and so treated; those who wandered and committed depredations were to be regarded as hostile and punished accordingly.

Simple as the reservation plan seemed to be, it was difficult to operate. The government constantly reduced the size of Indian holdings amidst loud complaint by the residents that they did not understand the latest treaty, while young braves periodically left the reservation in raiding parties, returning to safety after committing depredations. These hit-and-run tactics disturbed not only the surrounding countryside, but the army as well. The Interior Department had strong objections to soldiers chasing Indians across land assigned to its control and constantly complained that the military men went beyond their jurisdiction. They feared, quite correctly, that in the enthusiasm of the chase, troopers might fix their gun sights on peaceful and obedient inhabitants of the reservation. Soldiers were not noted for discriminating between enemy and friend when the skin was brown.

Army men, driven near to desperation by the hard-fighting, shifty Plains Indians, showed a surprising understanding of the enemy's dilemma. Those who knew the western country saw what was happening. From the East came settlers, cattlemen and miners, while from the Pacific Coast the mineral frontier edged through Oregon and Nevada into Idaho and Montana, closing the vise, cutting off further retreat. Treaty by treaty, the Indians gave up land, moved to reservations, and tried to understand their shrinking boundaries. Unfortunately the buffalo did not comprehend these demarcations and neglected to join the retreat. This resulted in hunting parties ranging far from home in search for food. General Sherman saw the matter clearly while out at Fort Laramie shortly after the war. He wrote sympathetically of the Sioux that "The Indian agents over on the Missouri tell him to come over here for hunting and from here he is turned to some other quarter and so the poor devil naturally wriggles against his doom."[3] It was a case of death by starvation or death by combat. That the Indian chose the latter was not surprising to old soldiers like Sherman.

The high plains region had remained surprisingly quiet during the Civil War but as that conflict drew to a close there were uneasy stirrings among the Indians. Colonel John M. Chivington's ill-considered attack upon the Southern Cheyennes at Sand Creek, Colorado, in 1864 touched off a flame of resentment and promises of retaliation among the tribes. Western residents, hopeful of receiving considerable help from the army now that its major tasks against the Confederacy had been completed, advocated sudden and forceful punishment for warlike Indians.

Soldiers like General Patrick E. Connor, who kept open the California Trail route during the latter part of the war, personified their wishes. His instructions to his men were crystal clear: "You will attack and kill every male Indian over twelve years of age."[4] His immediate superior, General John Pope, reacted with equal firmness: "If any such orders as General Connor's are carried out it will be disgraceful to the Government and will cost him [the officer] his commission if not worse."[5] The two points of view were, in the coming years, to characterize on one hand the attitude of Westerners, and on the other the Army. While one usually wanted to dispose of the Indian with local volunteer troops, the other was torn between the cries of eastern humanitarians and the realization that the government had to protect the native as well as fight him.

It was the high plains that witnessed the most violent struggle between the Indians and settlers, for over this region ranged the nation's fiercest red warriors. Mobile, well armed and able to live off the buffalo herds, they posed a threat that puzzled the best military minds. Sherman, studying the empire of grass lying between the Mississippi and Rocky Mountains, admitted that "It is plain to me that we cannot undertake to keep any part of our army massed according to the systems of Europe, but will be forced for years to come to adapt our conduct to the prevailing sentiment and necessities of the Frontier."[6] The adaptation proved to be difficult, for with each succeeding army appropriation fewer troops were available. To divide up and pursue the small Indian bands to the death was theoretically sound, but it required a superior force and the army did not have it.

Before the Sioux made their final bid at the Little Big Horn in 1876, the entire Army of the United States was reduced to about 20,000 men. While most of it saw service in the West, the effectiveness of the organization was seriously diminished by the fact that some men were needed to guard government property in the East and in the West distance diluted it to a point of near uselessness. For this financial malnutrition the Army could thank Congress, some of whose members were former Civil War Volunteer officers who had little love for West Point. Under the abrasion of Indian wars in the West and attacks by Congressional braves out to decorate their political coup sticks in Washington, military strength was constantly drained.

Concerned by increasingly complicated problems of command, General Sherman endeavored to lay out some comprehensive plan that would at once protect the settlers and then do justice to the tribes in the land-rush years that followed. As he wrote to his old friend, Admiral David Dixon Porter, the Plains resembled the high seas in their limitless extent and uncharted paths. It was a comparison that was widely employed, so striking was the parallel. Far out in the grassy waters were little islands of settlement and occasional military outposts. Sherman's primary task was to maintain communications with these widely scattered strongholds and prevent them from being engulfed by a red population that still controlled much of the land. Once the permanency of major routes was guaranteed, additional roads could be developed and protected. Ultimately the

Soldier shooting abandoned horse for food, Crook's 1876 expedition against Sitting Bull

West would be interlaced by travel routes and whites could safely go to any part of it, a situation that in itself would help to contain the tribes. Meanwhile, troops must stay close to the few main roads, even at the expense of the more isolated settlements, and work at the problem from the standpoint of military defense. In the spring of 1866, well aware that his move would be unpopular in the West, Sherman made his recommendations.

Let settlement be encouraged, "as far as the land will yield corn and grasses," he wrote. But beyond that point, travel would have to be funneled into two or possibly three principal routes. All other avenues should be closed until the Indian problem was better under control.[7] Accordingly, General John Pope, now commanding one of the departments in Sherman's military division, issued an order on February 28, 1866, defining the rules of travel across the Plains. Places like Forts Ridgley and Abercrombie in Minnesota, Fort Kearny in Nebraska, and Forts Riley and Larned in Kansas were designated as points of departure into hostile country. Emigrants moving west of these locations were required to organize in a semi-military fashion, electing a captain and other officers and providing no less than thirty armed men. Violators would be arrested by the army. By means of these precautions it was hoped that travelers would reach their destinations safely and, above all, contact between whites and Indians could be cut to a minimum. The plan envisaged the near-impossible: peaceful Indians hunting over their lands with peaceful whites quietly making their way through the country along narrow and sharply defined routes. Visionary as was the scheme, it was the only course, for the Army was not prepared to fight a major Indian war.

That there would be a sharp increase in plains travel was obvious. The mountain communities, made rich by their mineral wealth, were growing with great rapidity and men were using all available routes to the diggings. To control the rush, to guide it westward the safest way, was the Army's desire. Already there were several familiar and well traveled roads leading to important sections of the West; they were deemed sufficient to bear the traffic. The two oldest and best known were the Santa Fe Trail and the Overland Route along the Platte River. Since the gold rush to Colorado in 1859, the Smoky Hill route through Kansas had become heavily used. Also used more widely now was the line of the Missouri River, from which travelers branched off at different points and proceeded overland to mining regions.

As the post-war population movement increased, an alarming number of offshoots from these main lines were developed by travelers. Already the Bozeman Trail, branching north from the Overland Route at Fort Laramie and hooking around the Big Horns into Montana, was disturbing the Sioux. Other branches, like the Niobrara Road across Nebraska and present South Dakota, put pressure on the tribes. Sherman saw that a showdown was shaping up as a result of the white pressure and he warned President Grant's office that clashes between the two races lay directly ahead. The once independent Indians were increasingly in need of the white man's cattle for food, now that the buffalo herds were vanishing, and the white man's cattle became an overpowering attraction. Such hunting of the "pinto buffalo" infuriated the stock owners and their hostility further encouraged Indian raids on white settlements.[8] The situation would be tense enough without complicating it by cutting new roads across hostile country.

Even Westerners were alarmed at the recklessness with which newcomers crossed Indian country, ignoring all signs of danger, taking any short cuts available, bent only upon reaching the yellow metal. *The Montana Post* of Virginia City, M.T., agreed with Sherman's desire to control the traffic and warned that those who had "cut-off on the brain" risked not only their own scalps but invited a general Indian war.[9] Such warnings were lost in the din of preparation for the great treasure hunt beyond the Missouri and those who saw gain for themselves discounted warnings by gloomy army officers.

It was not only the prospective travelers who were unwilling to listen to talk of control. So were the merchants who lived in thriving cities along the Mississippi and up the Missouri. They saw no reason why their towns should not become great entrepots of trade and they openly promoted the establishment of any and all roads leading to the mines. It angered them to think that a few dirty savages could threaten what promised to be the biggest boom of all. During the spring of 1866 Sherman was beset by requests for military escorts along various projected routes. Iowans wanted their own road to Montana, as did Minnesotans, and the Governor of Dakota Territory cried out for protection of local travel routes. Sherman said "No," with his accustomed vigor. "We have not troops enough to guard and build a separate road of near sixteen hundred miles to accommodate every village and set of emigrants," he told his superiors when Senator Alexander Ramsey of Minnesota applied pressure on the War Department.[10]

To accede to such local clamor was impossible; there were not enough troops for the protection of routes already in use. The establishment of more roads would merely goad the Indians into further depredations.

Laws and restrictions meant little to the pioneer. It was soon clear that no force on earth could keep the Indians out of the white man's way. The great emigrant road along the Platte River was a continuous cloud of dust during the travel season as settlers and freighters churned along it in their heavy wagons. In a period of only six weeks during the summer of 1865, no less than 6000 wagons, each carrying from one to four tons of freight, passed Fort Kearny in Nebraska.[11] Sherman himself, fascinated by the westward rush, could not suppress the enthusiasm he shared with those who were bound for new lands. He told General W. S. Hancock that already more than fifty steamboats were trading regularly on the Upper Missouri, a part of the country he called the "best region of all our Territories."[12] At the same time he realized the effect of the movement upon his own problems and warned headquarters that with the growth in importance of the mountain regions military protection of the routes connecting them was an absolute necessity. The nomadic tribes, however friendly, were increasingly obliged to live, in part, by raids upon wagon trains and small settlements. The very presence of white men offered a temptation that meant trouble.[13]

The Indians were not the only ones tempted by the presence of another race; the whites themselves found it difficult to refrain from attacking the natives. In the new states and territories governors frequently regarded the solution of local Indian problems as falling within their province. They knew that such duty normally belonged to the Federal Army but in cases of emergency local volunteers had in the past been called upon. The governors were too often guilty of yielding

Thomas Francis Meagher   Indian Territory, oil by W. H. D. Koerner

to local clamor and declaring a state of emergency before the facts warranted such action. They were torn between a desire to wait for the army, or take to the field at the head of locally raised troops with an opportunity for personal glory in the offing.

The case of Montana furnishes the classic example of ready-made Indian war and its local management, as well as the desire of a federal appointee to capitalize upon his situation. In 1867, Acting Governor Thomas Francis Meagher, a former brigadier general, loudly called for federal troops at a time when Sherman had but a single regular cavalry regiment in the entire mountain region. When Meagher discovered that no troops were available, he seized upon rumors that Red Cloud and his Sioux warriers were about to wipe out communities along the Yellowstone. Hopeful of enhancing his own reputation, he called for volunteers. Despite Sherman's warning that no money was available for such activities, Meagher raised a small force of miners, anxious for a grubstake, and took to the warpath. While the campaign fortunately resulted in few casualties for either side, since the volunteers seemed to have difficulty in locating the aggressors who were about to conquer their territory, a bill of over a million dollars was assessed against the federal government. Horses and equipment brought fancy prices in a mining community and many a half-broken Indian pony was sold to the volunteer organization for a sum that opened even a miner's eyes. Meagher, who had hoped to gain sufficient fame to send him to the Senate when Montana became a state, did not live to realize his dreams. He fell from the deck of a river steamer at Fort Benton and was drowned, while on a trip to that river port to get more guns with which to fight. Sherman, who had correctly called Meagher a stampeder, realized that with the growth of the white population he would have the problem of restraining his own race, as well as the Indians.

Another of the army's great enemies in the West was distance. Tiny settlements, hundreds of miles apart, demanded protection that could not be given. No sooner did soldiers go to the aid of one of them than another cried out for help. The hit-and-run tactics of the Indians kept the soldiers constantly moving. Yet when the cavalrymen returned from a long chase, tired and hot, they usually had to resume the mundane task of repairing their quarters in anticipation of winter or haul firewood from miles away. "With almost everything to do you can understand they have not much chance to hunt down horsethieving Indians whose lodges are in the Black Hills of the Cheyenne 400 miles off," wrote Sherman from Fort Laramie in 1866. "It is these awful distances that make our problem out here so difficult."[14]

Fortunately a great shrinker of distances was poised at the Missouri River, ready to move across the forbidding stretches to the West. For decades the army had faced the problem of supplying its remote frontier outposts. Now with its area of operations swelled to new proportions, the coming of the railroad offered the only hope of combating apparently insoluble problems of logistics. The great plains, with their continually shifting buffalo herds and rapidly moving horse-Indians, presented quite a different picture than had the terrain east of the

Mississippi. But there were compensations. The prairie was sufficiently level to accommodate a roadbed with a minimum of cutting and filling. In some cases the ties were laid directly upon the sod. The builders of the great Pacific Road demonstrated that as many as ten miles of track could be laid in a single day.

Army men were delighted at the expansion of the railroad in the Trans-Mississippi West during the years immediately following the war. From the time Sherman took command of the Military Division of the Missouri, in the summer of 1865, to his retirement in 1883 he regarded it as the final solution to the Indian problem, and said so repeatedly. One of his first duties, in the new command, had been the inspection of the Union Pacific's first few miles west of Omaha. Always the conservative, he did not expect great results from the construction for a few years. But to his surprise his old friend General G. M. Dodge, the Union Pacific's chief engineer of construction, pushed the tracks westward with amazing speed. Meanwhile, in Kansas, the Union Pacific Eastern Division (soon to be known as the Kansas Pacific) sped toward Fort Riley and instead of arching northward to join the main road, continued on toward Denver. Within a few years the parallel lines marked off a wide corridor of country from which the Indians were driven. Now a wedge of white population projected westward to the mountains, shoving aside the tribes like a great snowplow. It was the beginning of the Indian's final stand.

The importance of the railroad to military planning was demonstrated in the spring of 1866 when a new department, named after the Platte River which it followed, was marked off from Omaha westward to Utah. Long and serpentine in appearance, the Department of the Platte covered the Union Pacific's main route and its commanding general was ordered to give full protection to working parties along the road. As Sherman explained, the railroad was eminently suited to military purposes and he proposed to support it to the limit.[15] Enthusiastically he told Grenville Dodge that "I regard this Road of yours as the solution of 'our Indian affairs.'"[16] When the Indians objected to the appearance of railroads in their country, Sherman bridled, and bluntly told them: "We will build iron roads, and you cannot stop the locomotive any more than you can stop the sun or the moon, and you must submit, and do the best you can."[17] This brought cheers from the young city of Cheyenne and a prediction that the advance of the road meant "the grave of the Lo family is dug."[18]

But the final resting place of the natives was not quite prepared. There were to be many examples that Lo, the poor Indian, was alive and kicking. However, the coming of the rails into western country had already begun to alter the military-Indian situation, proof of which was seen in their influence upon the much-contested Bozeman Trail. That cut-off, used by the whites at considerable risk, had necessitated the building of a string of protective forts north of Fort Laramie into Montana. The objections of the Sioux were sufficiently violent to keep them under a constant state of siege. It was with considerable relief to Sherman that General Grant approved their abandonment early in 1868. Army men argued that Montana could be as easily reached by way of Corinne, Utah, soon to be served by rail, and the intervening country was not controlled by particularly dangerous Indians. The Sioux regarded the Bozeman Trail's abandonment as a victory, and Sherman did not argue. He was glad to free the troops who had tried to guard it for other equally pressing duties.[19] In effect, the railroad had given him more men.

Upon the completion of the Pacific Railroad, Sherman, now commanding the Army of the United States, turned his attention to other sections of the West. He advised Phil Sheridan, who had succeeded him in the western command, to watch the construction of the new Northern Pacific with particular care for "it will help to bring the Indian problem for a final solution."[20] Even the Indian Bureau had to agree. In 1872 its commissioner admitted that the new line would "solve the great Sioux problem" and serve as part of a great corral for that war-like tribe. In places like Colorado, Utah, Arizona and New Mexico the coming of the railroad would accomplish a like result and "multiply fourfold the striking force of the Army in that section."[21]

Sherman had said these things for some time and as the rail network spread, he continud to preach its worth. There was no single enterprise in which the United States had a greater interest, he told the Secretary of War, than the extension of the Northern Pacific.[22] The Southern Pacific was likewise important and he personally thanked its Vice President, predicting that the line would be a "great civilizer" in the Southwest.[23] After touring the West with President Hayes in 1880 the general was willing to say that the railroad had completely revolutionized the country during the past few years. In his final report, written in 1883, he attributed the general condition of peace in the West to three principal factors: the presence of the army, the heavy influx of settlers and the railroads. Of these factors he called the railroads the most significant.[24]

Gradually the West was fenced off, and as the rails criss-crossed its great stretches of mountains and plains, the tribes were surrounded. Meanwhile, along the sprouting branches of steel, settlements clung like fungi, gradually spreading over the land. When danger from the Indians threatened, troops were quickly dispatched, traveling in a single day distances that formerly took them a month. At last the great enemy — distance — was controlled. But years of discomfort, sacrifice and frustration on the part of the army had preceded the arrival of this condition.

The defense of the last frontier had presented the United States Army with problems that were both unique and perplexing. If the great plains altered methods of farmers who had learned their trade in the tree area east of the Mississippi, the change was no less true for the soldiers. Some understanding of the new conditions by the American public would have made the transition easier for military men, but as the century progressed they came to expect little sympathy and patiently they made the necessary adjustments.

Gone now was the earlier notion of a fixed frontier, a chain of protective posts to fend off Indians from the West. The frontier's advance guard now plunged headlong into Indian country in a frontal attack and was momentarily

Maj. Gen. Philip H. Sheridan

swallowed up in a land of illimitable distances. So rapid was the ensuing change, so fluid the situation, that the military frontier was never quite fixed until the final battle had been fought. Like a traveling road show, the troopers periodically struck their tents and moved on. They were, in Sherman's words, the picket line of civilization.

Gone too were the solid, even comfortable, posts of old. In exchange the soldier found himself deep in hostile country, opposed not only by a dangerous human adversary but threatened by nature itself. His waking hours were usually occupied with the ever-present task of keeping alive. The search for fuel, water and building materials was constant. Easterners found it difficult to believe the distance these necessary items frequently were hauled.

Transportation of both men and supplies was arduous in the extreme and the navigable rivers of the Mississippi and Ohio valleys were sorely missed. Only an unsatisfactory facsimile, the shallow and snag-filled Missouri River, served the plains. Other western waterways, dignified with the name "river," were not only unsuited for transportation purposes, but were mean and treacherous just to cross.

Physical difficulties were not uncommon to the soldier and their presence was within his comprehension. Ideological barriers were harder to understand. From the establishment of the government there had been Indian wars, conducted, with some modifications, like other wars. If the technique of fighting was somewhat different, the general purpose was not. A tribe on the warpath was an avowed enemy, and a body of soldiers was sent out to give battle. The American people approved and supported the idea. But in the post-Civil War era the country was at peace and, in general, military collisions with the Indians were regarded as campaigns, not wars. The duty was in the nature of a police action. That it should be short-lived, and effective, was assumed by the public.

It was the enemy at his rear that the soldier did not understand. A rising body of humanitarians, bent upon saving the last of the natives, cried out in protest at every collision and filled Eastern papers with condemnation of the Army. The general public took the position that since this was a time of peace, the army should be reduced and there was an inclination to support the new sponsors of the Indians, rather than the military men. As a crowning blow an old soldier, now President, appeared to have cast his vote with the peace camp. Grant's Quaker Policy confused an already complex and controversial problem at a time when the army was beleaguered by enemies at both front and rear.

Historically, the peacetime army has been held in rather low esteem by the nation; for two decades or more after the Civil War, a period of revulsion to war after four years of bloody conflict, this was the situation. Unfortunately they were decades of unprecedented development, of extreme pressure upon the remaining Indian tribes, and a time when an adequate military force was required to separate the races in collision. Because it was not available the nation was confronted by what it chose to call its "Indian Problem," the solution of which brought glory neither to the Army, the Interior Department nor the American people.

NOTES

[1] Report of the Secretary of the Interior, 1865, *House Executive Document* 1, 39 Cong. 1 Sess. Serial 1248, p. viii.

[2] Sherman to General John Pope, March 5, 1866, Division of the Mississippi. Letters Sent, 1865-1866, Records of the War Department, U. S. Army Commands, National Archives.

[3] Sherman to Rawlins, August 31, 1866. Division of the Missouri, Letters Received, 1866-1868, Special File. Records of the War Department, U. S. Army Commands, National Archives.

[4] Fred B. Rogers, *Soldiers of the Overland*, 168.

[5] *Ibid.*, 183.

[6] Sherman to General W. R. Price, November 16, 1865, Division of the Mississippi, Letters Sent, 1865-1866, Records of the War Department, U. S. Army Commands, National Archives.

[7] Sherman to Colonel T. S. Bowers, January 13, 1866. *Ibid.*

[8] Sherman to Rawlins, February 17, 1866. Division of the Missouri, Letters Received, 1866-1868. *Op. cit.* Department, U. S. Army Commands, National Archives.

[9] *The Montana Post*, May 26, 1866.

[10] Sherman to Colonel George K. Leet, Asst. Adjt. Gen., Headquarters of the Army, April 17, 1866. Division of the Mississippi. Letters Sent, 1865-1866. *Op. cit.*

[11] Charles F. Lummis, "Pioneer Transportation in America," Part II, *McClure's Magazine*, XXVI (November 1905), 84.

[12] Sherman to Hancock, March 12, 1866. Division of the Miss., Letters Sent, 1865-1866. *Op. cit.*

[13] Sherman to John Rawlins, February 17, 1866. Division of the Missouri, Letters Received, 1866-1868, Special File. *Op. cit.*

[14] Sherman to Rawlins, August 31, 1866. *Ibid.*

[15] Sherman to General Philip St. George Cooke, March 28, 1866. *Ibid.*

[16] Sherman to Dodge, January 18, 1867. Grenville Dodge Papers, XIV, State Department of History and Archives, Des Moines, Iowa.

[17] Henry Morgan Stanley, *My Early Travels and Adventures in America and Asia.* (New York, 1895), I, 210 and 211.

[18] Cheyenne *Leader*, November 14, 1867. "Lo" was a term frequently used to denote Indians.

[19] Sherman to General C. C. Augur, February 28, 1868. Augur Papers, Illinois State Historical Library, Springfield, Illinois.

[20] Sherman to Sheridan, September 26, 1872. Sherman-Sheridan Correspondence, Volume I, Division of Manuscripts, Library of Congress.

[21] Report of the Commissioner of Indian Affairs, 1872.

[22] *Reports of Inspection Made in the Summer of 1877 by Generals P. H. Sheridan and W. T. Sherman of Country North of the Union Pacific Railroad*, (Washington 1878), 28.

[23] Sherman to David D. Colton, September 26, 1878. *Alta California* (San Francisco), October 2, 1878.

[24] Annual Report of W. T. Sherman, October 27, 1883. 48 Cong., 1 Sess. *House Exec. Doc. 1*, pt. 2 (Serial 2182), 45, 46.

Which Indian Killed Custer?

By EDGAR I. STEWART

THE BATTLE of the Little Big Horn River, fought nearly ninety years ago, still remains one of the great question marks of American frontier history. Almost everything about it has been made the subject of controversy, and since there is so much about the battle that never will be known, in fact which never can be known, that sanguinary engagement probably will remain a source of speculation and controversy for as long as the American people have a history, or at least for as long as there is anyone left to write it or to read it.

No guarantee is made as to the historical accuracy of any of the stories which follow. I have simply presented some of the accounts — both preposterous and plausible — which have come to my attention during many years' study of the Custer Fight.

Two of the subjects most productive of speculation have been as to whether or not there was a white survivor of the approximately 250 men who followed their Lieutenant Colonel down the long hog-back ridge which runs parallel to the Little Big Horn, and who died with him on a similar ridge a few miles farther north; and which one of the hostile tribesmen was responsible for Custer's death. For many years after the battle "lone survivors" were fairly numerous, so much so that it took a rather fanciful and extreme story to attract more than passing attention. So numerous were these claimants that it is doubtful if room could have been found for all of them on that dusty ridge where Custer and the members of his five companies made the supreme sacrifice.

Similarly an almost equally large number of Indians have claimed, or have had their friends claim for them the dubious distinction of having killed the white chief whom they knew by many names. While most of the tribes seem to have referred to Custer as the "Long Hair" or the "Yellow Hair" the Crows also knew him as "Son of the Morning Star" and the Sioux as the "Chief of the Thieves," this last being in reference to his leadership of the Black Hills expedition of 1874, which was made in violation of a solemn treaty, to the observance of which the faith of the United States had been pledged, and resulted in the opening of the Black Hills to white settlement. Appropriately the road which the expedition made was known as "The Thieves Road."

Steamer *Far West,* first boat up Yellowstone with Custer in 1876

The last claimant of the distinction of having killed this white chief was no other than White Bull, a Sans Arc nephew of the renowned Sitting Bull, and himself a warrior of no mean ability. His claims were put forth in a rather oblique way by no less a person than the late Walter Stanley Campbell, better known by his pen name of Stanley Vestal, probably the greatest authority on the tribes of the Great Plains, and whose death constituted a distinct loss to American historical scholarship. The Vestal story, as received from White Bull himself, was first published in an article in the February, 1957, issue of *American Heritage* (Volume VIII, Number 2) and then repeated in the revised edition of Mr. Vestal's biography, *Sitting Bull, Champion of the Sioux.*

White Bull's story is unique in that he did not come out point-blank and say that he killed Custer. Instead he related in considerable detail, and probably with a normal amount of exaggeration, the story of a terrific fight that he had had with one of the soldiers as the battle neared its end, and in which he at last succeeded in killing his adversary. The next day in passing over the battlefield, White Bull had his attention called to the naked body of his victim of the day before and was told that was the great chief of the soldiers, which if it were true meant that White Bull had been the slayer of Custer. While most of the Sioux did not know that they were fighting Custer's troops or indeed that he was even in the vicinity, there were some of them, including White Bull's informant, Bad Soup or Bad Juice, who had been around Fort Abraham Lincoln and knew the white leader at least by sight. Custer was also well known to many of the Cheyennes, whose large circle was almost directly across the river from Battle Ridge.

Mr. Vestal said that he had known of White Bull's story for several years but had kept it secret for fear that some pro-Custer fanatic might try to harm the old chief. This explanation is hardly convincing for although White Bull may not have been over-popular with his neighbors, it is doubtful if there has been anyone possessed of such intensity of feeling on the Custer battle since at least the turn of the century, or even before. If Mr. Vestal had said that it was his desire to protect White Bull against the publicity seekers and the writers who would have immediately tried to capitalize on the story, his explanation might have been sounder. It has also been suggested that another reason for keeping the story under cover until after White Bull's death was to keep students of the battle from doing some cross-examining and possibly revealing some flaws in the story. (Not that such flaws would necessarily invalidate the story since human memory is notoriously fallible and uncertain.) In relating the story, White Bull implies that while his adversary was the stronger, he had had more experience in rough-and-tumble fighting. Yet Custer was of medium height, weight, and build, if we may judge from his uniforms, while White Bull was six feet tall and weighed in the neighborhood of 200 pounds. Also White Bull says that this hand-to-hand encounter occurred near the end of the fight. There is other evidence to indicate that Custer was killed early in the battle and farther down the ridge, toward the position occupied by Captain Keogh and his men.

But although the story first came to general attention in the pages of *American Heritage*, it was by no means unknown to students of the Custer fight before that time. Nor did it come as any surprise to many persons with more than a passing knowledge of the literature of the battle. Nor was it the first time the story had appeared in print, for Reginald K. Laubin (Tatanka Wanjila), an adopted member of the Sioux tribe, in an article in *Adventure*, 1955, entitled "Who Killed Custer" told substantially the same story although with considerably less embroidery. He points out that White Bull said that Custer did not have long hair at the time of the battle and seems to feel that that gives his story a "ring of authenticity" although the chief could have learned that fact long after the battle.

For many years after the battle, the killing of General Custer was quite generally attributed, at least in the popular mind, to the celebrated Sioux warrior Rain-in-the-Face, an association that found expression in the poem "The Revenge of Rain-in-the-Face" by Henry Wadsworth Longfellow. But it is probable that his unusual name contributed as much as anything else to the notoriety that this Sioux warrior received. But the Sioux had a very poor reputation for veracity; in fact "to lie like a Sioux" was a common saying of the day, and it may very well be that in making this claim Rain-in-the-Face was merely living up to a well established tribal reputation. As a matter of fact he probably did not even par-

Two Moon looks over rows of headstones dotting contours of Little Big Horn. *Center:* Rain-in-the-Face. *Right:* Chief Gall, Oglala.

ticipate in the Battle of the Little Big Horn River, being miles away at the time. And the wound which lamed him permanently and was said to have been received at the battle was self-inflicted when he accidentally shot himself in the foot. But Rain-in-the-Face was not one to refuse to accept a distinction that people insisted in thrusting upon him. While he at first tacitly admitted that the story was true, he later denied it, and said that Custer had been killed by a young Cheyenne warrior named Hawk. He explained that the two of them had been painted and dressed similarly so that confusion of identity was only natural. But on his death-bed Rain-in-the-Face again changed his story and admitted that the original story was true and that he was so close to his victim when the fatal shot was fired that the discharge of the gun inflicted a powder burn on the body of the white commander. One witness of the scene expressed the belief that he was telling the truth.

Other Indian claimants for the distinction of having killed the Lieutenant-Colonel of the Seventh Cavalry include Flat Hip, who was a member of Sitting Bull's band of Uncpapa Sioux; Two Moon, a Cheyenne who is said to have had a personal grudge against Custer, and Red Horse, a Santee, who was a son of Inkpaduta, the leader of the Spirit Lake Massacre in June, 1857.

One of the most interesting stories is that of the Cheyennes who maintain that no one knows who killed the leader of the troops, but who give the cere-monial honor to Brave Bear, a Southern Cheyenne. Then there is, of course, the widely circulated but generally disbelieved story that Custer took his own life, committing suicide to escape capture and the certain torture that he knew awaited him.

All of these stories presuppose that Custer was killed near the northern end of that dusty and sun-baked ridge where the monument now stands. This is by no means certain, since as indicated earlier there is evidence to indicate that he was killed farther down the ridge and closer to Keogh's position.

There is also a story — which exists in several versions — to the effect that Custer was shot as he led his troops into the ford across the Little Big Horn River, at the foot of Medicine Tail Coulee, in an attempt to cross and attack the hostile Indian village. This claim was first advanced by Frank K. Linderman in his book *Red Mother*, which is the story of Pretty Shield, the wife of Goes Ahead, one of the Crow scouts with the Custer column. According to this story, which Pretty Shield had from her husband, Custer rode into the river to test its suitability as a crossing when a group of hostiles, concealed on the opposite bank, suddenly opened fire, killing him, his body falling into the water and being swept away downstream. Dr. Thomas B. Marquis, who as an agency physician lived among the Cheyennes for many years and who knew personally many of the warriors who had participated in this most famous of all Indian battles, expressed doubt as to the accuracy of the story, believing that somewhere a mistake had been made in translation. There is some corroborative testimony although its accuracy is by no means beyond question. Two other witnesses, apparently independent of each other, claim that they saw Custer's body in the stream. One account was that of a squaw man living in the Indian camp who claimed that because of his white skin and buckskin dress, it was feared that he might be mistaken for a scout serving with the soldiers by some of the Indians who did not know him, and that they might shoot first and ask question afterwards. Thus he was advised to hide in the bushes along the banks of the Little Big Horn and remain there until the battle was over. The advice was followed and shortly after the firing began he claimed to have seen Custer's body floating down the stream.

The other story is that of a Sioux warrior who was shooting at a group of soldiers in the area where the monument now is and where the Last Stand was made. As the battle neared its end and the number of the soldiers steadily diminished, a small group of them broke away and ran toward the river in an obvious effort to escape. Most of them never made it, but from his place of observation it seemed to this warrior that one or two of them might possibly have reached the temporary safety of the bushes that line the banks of the Little Big Horn. So he started out to investigate and made his way carefully in the underbrush, alert for anyone who might be in hiding. While he found no survivors he did see the body of Custer in the water and caught by a snag projecting from the bank. (Another account says that the body had stranded on a riffle or gravel bar, but the discrepancy is not serious.) In neither account is there any mention of how the identification of Custer was accomplished. It is interesting to speculate as to what the result would have been had this Sioux warrior searching for possible survivors hiding in the bushes encountered the squaw man, who according to his account was hiding in those same bushes and probably was not too far away.

But these stories receive at least a slight amount of confirmation from the fact that almost ever since the news of the battle reached the outside world there has been at least the shadow of a doubt as to just how positive the identification of Custer's body really was. While most students of the battle reject the theory entirely, it has been contended that Custer's body was one of those never found or at least never identified. (One possible explanation of this rumor might be that the body of George A. Custer was confused with that of his brother Tom. In the latter case the body had been horribly mutilated, which led to the story that Rain-in-the-Face had fulfilled a threat made earlier and had cut the Captain's heart out and eaten it, so that identification was difficult and was finally accomplished only by the fact that the captain's initials had been tattooed on his forearm.)

If George Custer's body had not been found the obvious explanation would have been that he had been captured alive by the Indians and had died under torture in the infliction of which the Sioux were known to be past masters. And with their hatred of Custer being what it was, it was a foregone conclusion that he would have been spared nothing and would have suffered everything in the way of calculated agony that the fiendish ingenuity of his savage captors was able to devise. And so, according to the story, when the search parties organized after the arrival of the Montana Column failed to find the body of the Lieutenant Colonel of the Seventh Cavalry among the group on Custer Ridge and realized the implications involved, they came to the obvious conclusion that he had been captured, and in order to spare the feelings of Mrs. Custer agreed upon a polite fabrication, not only concealing the fact that his body had not been found but adding the further adornment that it had not even been scalped or mutilated. Apparently no one thought of the possibility of his having been killed in the river. Although there is some corroborative evidence this story of Custer's body not being found is generally rejected as unworthy of credence. But it achieved enough credibility in the weeks after the battle so that Lieutenant James Bradley, Seventh Infantry, whose detachment found the bodies of the Custer command, issued a statement describing the position in which he found the body and the nature of Custer's wounds.

It is this story of Custer's body not having been found that led to the most fantastic story of all: that Custer was not killed at the Little Big Horn at all, but escaped from that stricken field and lived ever afterward in obscurity. There are two versions of what happened. One is that he was captured by the Cheyennes, who because of the great respect which they had for his bravery and the fact that they considered him a blood brother, although an erring one — he had a son in the Cheyenne camp — concealed and protected him from their Sioux allies and after his wounds were healed brought about his return to white civilization on his solemn promise that he would never fight against the Indians again. The other version is that Custer led a small group of soldiers that escaped from the battlefield and made their way eastward toward Rosebud Creek in the direction from which the regiment had come. He made good his escape and when he became aware of the magnitude of the tragedy on the banks of the Little Big Horn realized that he should have died with his men and that he would now be branded as a craven coward, and so never made known the fact of his survival. This yarn is further embroidered by the additional detail that a former acquaintance is supposed to have encountered Custer on the streets of New Orleans and that the latter readily admitted his identity and freely discussed the series of events leading up to the battle! As to just how Custer was providing himself with the basic essentials of living, deponent sayeth not.

And so the controversy over the Custer battle continues, not only in its broader aspects, but in regard to the more minute details as well. The entire subject of the Battle of the Little Big Horn River has become so overlaid with myth and legend, so encrusted as it were with historical barnacles, that it has become more a matter of folklore than of proper history.

But regardless of which Indian killed Custer — and the best conclusion still is no one knows or ever will know — that anonymous warrior conferred upon the Lieutenant-Colonel of the Seventh Cavalry an immortality and fame that the latter could have achieved in no other way. The greatest and most overwhelming of victories would not have given him the notoriety that came with defeat and death. And when that great Indian camp moved in savage and majestic splendor up the valley of the Little Big Horn, leaving Custer and every member of his five companies dead on Battle Ridge, they left behind all unwittingly the matrix of a great American legend — perhaps it might even be called an epic — and conferred upon the leading white actor in the tragedy a reputation, perhaps unmerited, which shows no signs of diminishing with the passing years.

Crazy Head, Cheyenne chief in Custer fight. *Center:* Curly, Crow scout with Custer. *Right:* Dewey Beard, last of the Sioux who fought Custer at the Little Big Horn (died 1955 at age 97). Painted by William R. Leigh, 1913

The Battle of Wolf Mountain

By DON RICKEY, JR.

THE CENTENNIAL SUMMER of 1876 witnessed the completely unforeesen and shocking defeat of the Seventh Cavalry in the Custer tragedy at the Little Big Horn on the 25th of June. Telegraph wires hummed the message of disaster to Washington and to army headquarters at Chicago and St. Paul, and by early July several regiments had been ordered to the theater of hostilities in southern Montana. General Nelson A. Miles' Fifth Infantry Regiment, which had served continuously on the frontier since 1856, was among those ordered north against the Sioux and Cheyennes from its station at Fort Leavenworth.

Companies of the Fifth Infantry began construction of a log cantonment on the Yellowstone River, at the mouth of the Tongue River, in late August, 1876. From September to late December, Miles' regiment and a few companies of the 22nd Infantry engaged in a series of small, arduous winter campaigns against the scattered bands of hostile Sioux and Cheyennes.

The winter of 1876-77 was extremely severe in Wyoming, Dakota and Montana. Deep snows and sub-zero weather came early to the high plains and mountains of eastern Montana. Buffalo and other large game were scarce, and the Tongue River camps of the Northern Cheyennes and Oglala Sioux contained little food for the winter.

Miles' soldiers had made many strikes against other bands, mainly those with Sitting Bull, north of the Yellowstone River. In every engagement the Indians had abandoned the field. Crazy Horse, the Oglala leader, and the head men of his Cheyenne allies were considering peace negotiations by mid-December, as the general's Indian scouts had spread the word that "Bearcoat" Miles would treat them favorably and justly if they came in to surrender.

The matter was much talked of around the camps, and it was decided that peace delegates should be sent to meet with Miles at his log cantonment at the mouth of the Tongue. The peace party arrived in the vicinity of the post just before noon, December 16. Captain Simon Snyder, an officer at the post, described what followed:

Crazy-in-the-Lodge, Sioux (erroneously identified as
Crazy Horse, of whom no known photograph exists)

Gen. Nelson A. Miles

... [at] 11:15 A.M., rapid firing was heard in the direction of the Crow
[scout] camp. The command was immediately turned out and deployed around
the garrison, when it was discovered that five Sioux . . . had attempted to come in
under a flag of truce, were discovered by the Crows after they had passed their
[scout] camp, and all killed before they could reach the garrison. Genl Miles was
angry . . . and ordered Capt. Dickey to at once disarm the Crows, which being
partly done, the Crows left in a body. . . . Of the Indians killed, Bull Eagle, Tall
Bull, Red Cloth and Red Horse have been recognized. All chiefs and head men.[1]

The fate of the peace negotiators was soon known in the Sioux and Cheyenne
camps located up the valley of Tongue River, and all thoughts of early and peaceful surrender were abandoned.

General Miles dispatched two of his Sioux scouts to find the hostile camp the
day after the peace envoys were killed. However, the scouts either couldn't or
wouldn't find Crazy Horse's camp, as they returned on December 21, with the
peace gifts Miles had sent, reporting they had been unable to locate the hostile
camp.[2]

On December 26, Sioux raiders ran off the post beef herd grazing near the
cantonment. Miles was now convinced that only an immediate and determined
campaign could compel the surrender of the Oglala Sioux and Northern Cheyennes.

Scouts informed Miles that the stolen cattle had been driven up the valley
of Tongue River, toward the supposed location of the hostile winter camps. Miles

at once ordered out Companies C and F, 22nd Infantry, and Company D, Fifth Infantry, all under Captain Dickey's command, to pursue the raiders. Lieutenant Carter and Company K, Fifth Infantry, followed Captain Dickey's command the next day, and Miles left the cantonment on December 29, with Companies A, C and E, Fifth Infantry, and two cannon, to assume personal command of the expedition.[3] Miles' command numbered 436 infantry officers and men, and included a twelve-pound bronze Napoleon cannon, one three-inch rifled Rodman gun, a few white scouts, one Bannack and two Crow scouts and several supply wagons. He intended to pursue the Sioux and Cheyennes through the ice and snow until they would be forced to fight or surrender, and he was prepared to remain out as long as need be, regardless of winter storms and sub-zero temperature.[4]

The infantry marched up Tongue River through drifted snow, and at times on a somewhat less strenuous route on the river ice. Mounted scouts ranged several miles ahead, and the artillery pieces and supply wagons brought up the rear. Miles' men skirmished with a few hostiles on January 1 and 3, and a soldier was killed while rounding up stray draft animals behind the column.

"A blinding snowstorm . . . [raged] early in the morning . . ." of January 6, and the troops passed through several recently abandoned Indian campsites that afternoon.[5] The Sioux and Cheyennes were withdrawing up the valley as Miles advanced. The late afternoon of January 7 witnessed a hard fight between Miles' advance scouts and a large number of hostiles. Miles led a detachment of troops to their rescue, and the Sioux and Cheyennes withdrew.

That same afternoon the scouts had captured a young Cheyenne warrior and seven women and children. Miles had the captives fed and given shelter, and learned that Crazy Horse and his Cheyenne allies were only a few miles farther up the river.

The troops camped for the night in a grove of trees, near Tongue River, with many high, rugged ridges and hills on the left and right, and a cone- or pyramid-shaped butte immediately in front of them in the river valley. Miles and his scouts felt certain that the Sioux and Cheyennes would offer battle the next day. Snow fell during the night, while the temperature hovered near zero. By morning fresh snow, added to what was already on the ground, resulted in an accumulation of from one to three feet. A cheerless, gray dawn, with heavy leaden storm clouds moving in from the west, greeted the numbed soldiers as they lumbered out onto the valley bottom to build cooking fires on the morning of January 8, 1877.

Patches of snow were scraped bare, and coffee was quickly boiling while the soldiers broiled their frozen salt pork and munched hardtack crackers. As the troops ate their meager breakfast, the hills and ridges in front, to the right and left, and partly across the river behind them were quickly covered with more than twice their own number of Sioux and Cheyenne warriors.[6] A warrior's voice rang out across the valley taunting the soldiers, advising them to eat well, as it would be their last meal.

Miles immediately ordered his artillery placed on the bench facing the Indians ". . . to resist attack; or be held in reserve. . . ."[7] His infantry companies were posted to battle formation, ready to repel an assault or begin an advance. Firing broke out at 7:00 A.M., with many warriors concentrating on the soldiers' right and others attempting a thrust to encircle the troops on the opposite side of the river.[8] E Company was moved to intercept the thrust to the right, and a detail of soldiers was sent to dig in on the commanding point across the river.

The warriors ". . . fought entirely dismounted."[9] Launching a loosely maneuvered charge on the right, the Sioux and Cheyennes were forced back by E Company, and a detail of soldiers seized the top of the dominant high knoll now designated Battle Butte, removing the threat to Miles' right.[10] Miles commanded from his position near the Napoleon gun, where he ". . . stood with a little switch in his hand directing operations."[11]

The "wagon gun" artillery crashed and reverberated through the valley, but did not seem to frighten the warriors, as they were now massing on ridges to the left of the troop positions.[12] Artillery had previously been greatly feared by the Indians, but the big guns apparently did not of themselves tip the scales of battle at Wolf Mountain, as Miles finally had to order his infantrymen to charge the Indian-held ridges to dislodge the warriors.

Two companies were ordered forward against the ridges where Indian riflemen lay ". . . hidden behind rocks shooting toward the soldiers."[13] Encumbered by heavy coats and footgear, Miles' infantrymen began their charge, at a labored walk through snow two to three feet deep.

Just below the crest of Crow Butte, Big Crow, a leading Cheyenne warrior, danced and sang war songs proclaiming his invulnerability to white bullets. His feathered warbonnet tail swinging wildly as he moved, Big Crow was a striking figure in his red-daubed war shirt and red blanket — shouting, gesturing and occasionally stopping to fire a shot from his Springfield carbine.[14]

Companies A and D moved steadily ahead until they had almost reached the Indian positions. Bullets plowed little furrows in the snow, but most flew high, over the soldiers. Stopping to concentrate their fire on the enemy, A and D companies fired away hundreds of cartridges. Fearing these men would run short of ammunition, Captain Frank Baldwin grasped a heavy box of rifle cartridges, held it in front of him on his saddle and raced to the skirmish line. Baldwin lost his grip on the ammunition box and many shells spilled out on the snow. Though most of the cartridges were lost, Baldwin's arrival was very timely, as he ". . . hat in hand, and with a ringing shout, . . . newly inspired the weary men. . . ."[15] Company C meanwhile had moved forward to support Companies A and D, and all three companies went up the glassy slopes toward the hostiles. A few men were wounded as the assault began, and one soldier was killed.

Deep snow and rugged terrain compelled the soldier line to break into uneven groups of struggling attackers. Two soldiers in advance of their comrades halted at a rock ledge, on the lower slopes of Crow Butte, and began firing at Big Crow. One of the soldiers was wounded by an Indian bullet, but between

Gen. Crook's supply train near Custer City, 1876

General Nelson Miles, center, and staff, Dec. 1876

them they concentrated a carefully aimed fire on the red-clad warrior, and Big Crow fell mortally wounded.[16]

Captain Frank Baldwin had only just joined the advance, swinging his hat to lead the men on. The ridge top ahead still spouted Indian bullets, but a few minutes later the hostiles abandoned their position and retreated, carrying the stricken Big Crow with them, as the troops approached within fifty yards. Stumbling, slipping, and occasionally falling down, the soldiers ". . . took the ridge in storming fashion."[17] The last shots were fired about noon, as the continuing snowfall increased to near-blizzard intensity.

During the engagement one soldier was killed and eight were wounded, one of whom died the next day.[18] All Indian casualties were carried away by their comrades. Wooden Leg stated that Big Crow was the only Cheyenne killed, and that two Sioux warriors were killed, which agrees with Red Sack's (Sioux) contemporary statement.[19] Red Sack further advised that three other warriors had been wounded, two of whom later died.[20] The engineer officer reported that many blood spots were seen on the snow in the abandoned Indian positions.[21]

Miles' men pursued the fleeing Sioux and Cheyennes for several miles up the valley of Tongue River, passing through the Indian camp where much of the hostiles' winter supplies and *materiel* was lost. The snowfall warmed to rain during the early evening of January 8, and Miles moved his campsite up onto the bench where his cannon had been during the action. Unable to pursue the hostiles, the tired soldiers retraced their route, down Tongue River, and arrived at the cantonment (Fort Keogh) January 18, after a total march of 242 miles.

Though casualties were light on both sides at Wolf Mountain, the hostile Oglala Sioux and Northern Cheyennes had suffered a severe blow in having their winter camp uprooted. "If a Crazy Horse camp could be struck, where would the people be safe?"[22] Some Cheyennes soon drifted into camp to surrender at Miles' post; others, remaining with Crazy Horse and his Oglalas, turned themselves in to the authorities in South Dakota.

Miles' victory at the Wolf Mountain Battle convinced Crazy Horse and his followers that further resistance was futile. Less than six months after the allied Sioux and Cheyennes had experienced their peak of triumph at the Little Big Horn, only a few scattered remnants remained dangerously at large. Sitting Bull and his followers fled to Canada, Crazy Horse and his cohorts were preparing to surrender, and with the capture of Lame Deer's Village of Minniconjou Sioux May 7, 1877, the powerful hostile bands of mid-1876 had been swept from eastern Montana, Wyoming and Dakota.

NOTES

[1] "Diary of Capt. Simon Snyder. 5th Infy, 1876," MS, Snyder-Ronayne Collection, Custer Battlefield National Monument, "Dec. 16."

[2] *Ibid.*, "Dec. 21."

[3] "Troop Operations, Tongue River Cantonment, Aug. 28, 1876-Oct. 1, 1877," in Letters Sent, Fort Keogh, 1877, MS, Record Group 98, National Archives, 55.

[4] Miles' infantry marched 11½ miles the day they departed, December 29, with the temperature at −30° below zero. *Report of the Chief of Engineers, 1877* (Washington: Government Printing Office, 1878), 1693-94.

[5] *Ibid.*, January 6, 1877.

[6] "Troop Operations, Tongue River Cantonment, Aug. 28, 1876-Oct. 1, 1877," MS, "January 8, '77."

[7] Luther S. Kelly (Milo M. Quaife, ed.) *Yellowstone Kelly* (New Haven: Yale University Press, 1926), 172.

[8] *Report of the Chief of Engineers, 1877,* 1694.

[9] Col. N. A. Miles to Assist. Adjt. Gen'l., Department of Dakota, telegram, January 20, 1877, in *Annual Report of the Secretary of War, 1877* (Washington: Government Printing Office, 1878), 494.

[10] Statement of battle participant H. C. Thompson, Sgt., Co. E, 5th Infy, 1877, in newspaper clipping by "Montana Lou" Grill, Montana State Historical Society, Helena, Montana. Thompson went over the battle site with Grill in 1926 and stated that the hostiles attempted to counter-attack at this point, and came within fifty yards of the infantry line before breaking and falling back.

[11] Kelly, *Yellowstone Kelly,* 173.

[12] Mari Sandoz, *Crazy Horse, The Strange Man of the Oglalas* (New York: Alfred A. Knopf, 1942), 352.

[13] Thomas B. Marquis, *A Warrior Who Fought Custer* (Midwest Publishing Co., 1931), 169.

[14] The hostile Sioux and Cheyennes captured about 250 .45-caliber model 1873 Springfield carbines from Custer's men at the Little Bighorn. Wooden Leg's drawing-text states that Big Crow used one of these carbines.

[15] Maj. G. W. Baird, "General Miles' Indian Campaigns," in *Century Magazine,* Vol. XX, No. 3, July, 1891, 357. Sgt. Thompson recounted the same incident in Grill, "Crazy Horse's Last Stand," 3rd installment, in Miles City *Daily Star,* June, 1926. Also *Kelly,* 174.

[16] Lou F. Grill, "Crazy Horse's Last Stand," 3rd installment, in Miles City *Daily Star,* June, 1926 (no other date). Marquis, *Warrior Who Fought Custer,* 170.

[17] *Kelly,* 173-74.

[18] Capt. O. M. Smith, "The Twenty-Second Regiment of Infantry," in T. F. Rodenbough and W. L. Haskins (eds.) *The Army of the United States.* (New York: Maynard, Merrill & Co., 1896), 687. Private Bernard McCann, Co. F, 22nd Infantry, was the man who died on January 9. He was posthumously awarded the Congressional Medal of Honor for bravery at Wolf Mountain. The three men that Miles reported killed included Pvt. McCann, one man killed during the assault, and the herder killed on January 3. *The Report of the Chief of Engineers, 1877,* reported only one man actually killed on January 8, 1695.

[19] Marquis, *Warrior Who Fought Custer,* 171.

[20] "Feb. 13, Cheyenne [Wyoming Territory] *Sun,*" in Missouri *Republican,* February 14, 1877.

[21] *Report of the Chief of Engineers, 1877,* 1695.

[22] Sandoz, *Crazy Horse,* 353.

The Northern Cheyennes
at Fort Fetterman

Edited by JOHN E. PARSONS

Colonel George A. Woodward, author of this sketch, was a Philadelphian and son of the Chief Justice of Pennsylvania. As organizer and captain of the "Penn Rifles (Company A of the 2nd Pennsylvania Reserves), Woodward saw service with the Army of the Potomac at the outset of the Civil War. Wounded in the foot at Charles City Cross Roads in the Peninsular Campaign of 1862, he was captured and confined in Libby Prison until exchanged. Lieutenant Colonel of his regiment in 1863, he commanded it at Gettysburg although still lame from his wound. The Pennsylvania Reserves defended Little Round Top on the second day of the battle.

After the war, though not a West Pointer, Woodward received an appointment as lieutenant colonel in the regular army. Transferred to the 14th Infantry in 1869, he was in command at Fort Fetterman, Wyoming, when the events here described took place. Later he commanded at Fort McPherson, Nebraska, and Fort Cameron, Utah, before becoming colonel of the 15th Infantry in 1876. Three years later he was retired for disability due to Civil War injuries.

Col. Woodward became an editor of The United Service, in whose columns the account that follows appeared in April, 1879. Significantly, perhaps, he wrote it on retirement, for evidently he did not subscribe to the usual Army view of "good" Indians. The need for diplomacy, fair dealing and compassion toward the native wards of the Government is a theme running through the story.

It sketches at first hand several Cheyenne chiefs conspicuous in the annals of the tribe: Old Bear, leader of a band of irreconcilables and a participant in the Battle of the Little Big Horn; Turkey Legs, wily entrepreneur, the exploits of whose band included the derailment of a U. P. freight train; and Little Wolf and Dull Knife, epic leaders of the homeward march of the Northern Cheyenne exiles to Indian Territory in 1878. Portrayed likewise are two Arapaho chiefs, Friday and Black Coal, the former a Jesuit pupil returned to savage life.

Colonel Woodward was mistaken in accepting the current report that Dull Knife lost his life in the midwinter breakout from Fort Robinson. This chief survived the escape to find eventual sanctuary at Fort Keogh, Montana, whence Little Wolf had already gone after surrender to Lieut. Clark. But Dull Knife did not live to see the creation of the Northern Cheyenne reservation in 1884 between the Tongue River and the Rosebud. Near it Little Wolf ended his days in self-exile and there descendants of their bands still live. Col. Woodward's account follows:

— JOHN E. PARSONS

Little Wolf   Two Moon   His Horse Bobtailed

THE LATEST BLOSSOMING of our Indian policy, as exemplified in the case of "Dull Knife's" band of the Northern Cheyennes, has attracted wide-spread attention, and not a little adverse comment. It exhibits, in epitome, the baneful consequences that must ever attend the working of a system of divided responsibility in the conduct of Indian affairs. Not being in possession of sufficient authentic and detailed information on which to base an intelligent judgment, I shall not attempt to impute blame to either the civil or military officials connected with this affair; indeed, had I such information, I should have neither the disposition nor the right to criticise or find fault, my purpose and only legitimate province in this paper being to jot down for the entertainment of the readers of *The United Service* some experiences of my own with the Northern Cheyennes in times gone by, when Dame Fortune was more benign to them than she has proven of late.

I cannot, in passing, however, restrain expression to the thought that has doubtless occurred to many of us, of how great the pity is that gallant soldiers, the peers of the best humanitarians in all the refinement and susceptibilities that belong to gentlemen, should be compelled by the stern requirements of duty to turn their arms, under such circumstances as attend this occurrence, against a people whose wild love of liberty and home could make them do, and dare, and die so bravely as have these Cheyennes.

In the spring of 1871 the Fourteenth Infantry, of which I was then the lieutenant-colonel, was ordered to Forts Laramie and Fetterman, in the Territory of Wyoming; the regimental headquarters, with six companies, going to the former post, and I, with the remaining four companies, to the latter. Fort Fetterman, named for the gallant but unfortunate officer who, with his entire command, was slaughtered by the Sioux Indians, near Fort Phil Kearny, in 1866, is situated at the junction of La Prele Creek and the North Platte River, and was, at the time of which I speak, the extreme outpost of the Platte River region.

Fort Laramie was eighty miles distant, in a southeasterly direction, but, for all that, was our nearest neighbor; and Medicine Bow Station, on the Union

Pacific Railroad, ninety miles to the southwest, was the nearest point to us touched by that great artery of travel and commerce. We had a mail once a week, which we got by sending a party to Horseshoe Creek, half-way between us and Fort Laramie, where it was met by a similar party from the latter post, between whom our outgoing and incoming mails were exchanged. We had, besides, telegraphic connection with Fort Laramie, and with department headquarters at Omaha.

At this time we were, nominally, at peace with all of the Northwestern tribes. This peace was not exactly of the kind that politicians habitually denominate "profound," but was rather a one-sided affair, in which we were to presume all Indians to be peacefully inclined until the contrary were shown; a principle that did not operate beneficently as to parties that might meet the copper-colored gentry at the moment their savagery — emotional, like the insanity of the modern murderer — got the better of their plighted faith.

The situation of Fort Fetterman made it a convenient house of call for roving bands of the Ogallalah Sioux, the Northern Arrapahoes, and the Northern Cheyennes; the two latter of which tribes, although claimed by Red Cloud to belong to his jurisdiction, and therefore appurtenant to his agency, repudiating such claim, had been allowed by the government to receive their supplies at Fetterman, and the post had therefore become practically their agency, and its commanding officer *ex officio* their agent.

I had been in command at Fetterman but a short time, when one day runners came in bringing intelligence that "Little Wolf," one of the three headmen of the Cheyennes — the other two being "Turkey Legs" and "Dull Knife" — would arrive the next day with the larger part of the tribe, who were returning from their great autumn hunt in the Powder River country. And the next day, about ten o'clock in the forenoon, the sentinel whose beat commanded a view up the valley of the Platte reported the approach of Indians. Although still some miles away, we could easily, by aid of field-glasses, separate what to the unaided eye seemed only a dark moving mass into its constituents of warriors, squaws, children, ponies, and dogs.

The column came on, moving slowly, but with such order and precision as gave token of skilled leadership and soldierly discipline. Arrived near the post, a halt was called, and immediate dispositions made for camping, the labor involved falling, as all labor does among savages, upon the women. The unloading of the ponies and their picketing out, the erection of the "tepees," the carrying in and stowing away of the bundles of robes, bags of pemmican, strings of dried meat, and the few utensils employed in culinary operations, that constitute the *impedimenta* of Indian marching, all devolve upon the squaw.

Leaving the women to their labors, Little Wolf, accompanied by a select few of his warriors, came up to the post for a talk with the commanding officer, stopping on his way at the log cabin just outside the fort, where lived our guide and interpreter, Joe Merival, "Old Joe," as he was popularly called, whose services were indispensable on all occasions of council or talk.

Joe was a grizzled Mexican, whose whole life had been spent among the

Indians, formerly as a trapper, but for many years in the capacity he held at Fetterman, of guide and interpreter. Joe was a character, and his dialect was something all his own. Indeed, until use made it familiar and to some degree intelligible, his speech needed interpreting nearly as much as that of the Indians themselves. One of Joe's dialect peculiarities was the excision or clipping off of the last syllables of words, as though he disapproved of redundancy, and boldly rejected what he regarded as surplusage in language. For example, "Bible" with Joe became "bibe," and "you ain't the Bibe" was Joe's mode of telling one with whom he differed in opinion that he was not infallible. Joe was also indifferent to gender, and habitually spoke of woman — "gooman" he called her — as "he." On one occasion he was telling a party of officers about a game of *monte* he once saw in Mexico, and was illustrating how deftly the dealer cheated the players. "But, Joe," said one of the officers, "I should have thought they would have knifed him." "Oh, no, no," said Joe; "he was a gooman."

Well, Little Wolf having secured Joe's services, came to my office, and filing in with his dusky aids, each as they entered shaking my hand and ejaculating "how," he took a proffered chair, while the others ranged themselves around the walls of the room, squatting or sitting on the floor. The Indian in council is the most deliberate of mortals, and beyond uttering his "how" on entering — and that is not invariable — not a word will he speak until the pipe has been produced, slowly filled with kinikinnik, passed to the end man at the right, by him lighted, devotionally tendered, first, by a downward gesture, to Mother Earth, and then, by an upward one, to the Great Spirit above, then a whiff or two taken, and the pipe handed to the next man towards the left, who, repeating the proceedings of the first, hands it to his left-side neighbor, and so on till its circuit of the assemblage is completed. At least once, often twice or three times, the pipe makes its rounds before the talking begins. Then the chief, or head-man, of the party rises, offers his hand to the person he is about to address, says "how," and begins his speech.

On this occasion, Little Wolf, after telling me that he was glad to see me, and "that his heart was good towards me," went on to say that they had had a prosperous hunt in the fall, and had procured a large supply of skins, which they had dressed, and were now anxious to trade for the various articles of use and ornament that suit the Indian taste. Besides our regular post trader, there had gathered near the post a number of others provided with Indian goods, in anticipation of this coming in of the Cheyennes, and Little Wolf wanted me to say what rules should be observed in dealing with them. He informed me that he had "made soldiers," — equivalent to posting sentinels, — and that none but those I saw with him would be permitted to leave their village, or camp, till he had my permission to open trade. Having listened to what I had to say in reply, and receiving permission to make the best bargains he could, and with whom he chose, he and his companions took their departure, and spent the rest of the day in stalking solemnly about from one trader's camp to another, getting from each of the competing dealers a "feast," consisting mainly of coffee and crackers, and receiving at the same time proposals for their robes and other peltry.

The next day Little Wolf gave his people loose rein, and they were soon everywhere about the post. Many of the women and children, more curious than avaricious, dropping out of the crowds that pressed around the counters of the post trader, would come up to the officers' quarters and hang for hours about the windows, peering in, and frequently flattening their noses against the panes to get a more satisfactory view of our interior life, which seemed to possess for them irresistible attraction. Most of our ladies were sufficiently familiar with Indians not to be seriously alarmed by their presence, but to the more timid and nervous among them the sudden apparition of an aged crone, whose hand, no doubt, had often brained or scalped the white victim of Indian savagery, would be far from exhilarating.

Others of the Indian women, however, were not a whit behind their sisters of the pale-face in their propensity for "shopping," and would stand hour after hour, ranged two and three deep, along the counters in the post trader's store-house, feasting their eyes on the bright beads and parti-colored calicoes and flannels with which his shelves were loaded, producing from time to time, for the purposes of barter, a buffalo tongue, dried and cured, or a dressed skin of some of the smaller objects of the chase, which, up to that moment, had been carefully hidden somewhere about their persons. Some of them on this occasion perpetrated a fraud on the post trader that for a time gave promise of largely increasing their personal estate at his expense. In the rush of business, which he was taking at its flood, he and his assistants had no time to make any orderly disposition of the wares he was receiving, and, as fast as gathered in, the buffalo tongues and peltry were tossed under the counters, discovering which, some of the Indian women managed quietly to detach one of the boards forming the front of the counter, and, reaching in, would abstract the wares already once paid for and unblushingly "swap" them again.

From this time forth, during nearly my whole stay at Fetterman, I had a good deal of experience with the Cheyennes. Every five days, when they were in the neighborhood, they came in to receive their rations, the issuing of which nearly always had to be prefaced by a council or talk, the object of which, however it might at first be masked by a pretence of other business, generally proved to be a demand for an increased supply of subsistence stores. I was not giving them credit for the number of people they had, and, to prove it, they would bring to the councils a bundle of small sticks of uniform size and length, which constituted their census, each stick counting for a person, and they thought it very hard that I would not accept this return as final and conclusive. I invariably told them that whenever they would submit to be counted I would increase the number of their rations if my enumeration proved their claim to be well founded; but, until such time, I would adhere to the existing practice of estimating their number from the number of "tepees" or lodges constituting their village.

In common, I believe, with Indians generally, they were averse to being counted, whether because of some superstition or because their actual number being once ascertained it would not be so easy to magnify it on occasion, I do not know. However, they finally yielded, and at an appointed time they formed a great circle in a grassy spot just across the Platte, and, accompanied by my adjutant and quartermaster and the interpreter, I rode over, and, passing slowly around inside the circle, made my count, while each of my companions made his, and when we were through we compared and verified our several enumerations. The result was that they were found to have a considerably greater number than I had been issuing to. On this occasion the whole Northern Cheyenne tribe were present, with the exception of one small band whose numbers were pretty accurately known, and as this was the first time that an actual enumeration of them had been successfully attempted, the information obtained was not without value.

Of the three head-men of the Cheyennes, Dull Knife was, I think, greatly the superior. Tall and lithe in form, he had the face of a statesman or church dignitary of the grave and ascetic type. His manner of speech was earnest and dignified, and his whole bearing was that of a leader weighted with the cares of state. Little Wolf had a less imposing presence, but looked more the soldier than the statesman. Turkey Legs looked his character, which was a very bad one. His appearance was mean and forbidding, and bespoke the very incarnation of treachery and cruelty. The ascetic-looking Dull Knife was, however, not superior to a fondness for sweets. Somebody about the post had given him once a can of preserved pine-apple, and this he had found so toothsome that he resolved if possible to have it included in the issue of rations made to him. Accordingly, the next issue day, he told Joe that he wanted him to ask the colonel for some pine-apple. Joe told him that it was useless to ask for it, as he would only be refused. "You do as I tell you," said Dull Knife. "You ask the colonel for it, and *accident* (Joe, for 'accidentally') he may be in good humor, and may give it to us."

Turkey Legs distinguished himself on one occasion at Fetterman by a wonderfully successful fishing exploit that he and his people accomplished with a seine belonging to one of the companies at the post, which had been loaned him on condition that all the pickerel he should take with it should go to the company, he retaining such other of the finny denizens of the Platte as might be captured. Taking the seine, the whole band — men, women, and children — proceeded to the river, and selecting a spot where the channel was much narrowed by a projection of the opposite shore, the men, wading in, stretched the seine across the upper end of the narrowed part, while the women and children, mounted on their ponies, formed a line across its lower end, and, closing in upon the party with the seine with a great noise of shouts and splashing of water, they drove the fish into the seine as it was slowly swept shoreward, the *net* result being a take of nine hundred fish, of which the pickerel, the part going to the company, filled a hand-cart to overflowing. Much elated at their success, they were about to repeat the experiment, when Joe, fearful that they would depopulate the stream, forbade further attempt in that direction.

The only hostile act of which any portion of the Cheyennes was guilty during the time the tribe was under my supervision — at least the only one committed anywhere in the region over which the protection afforded by Fort Fetterman could be regarded as extending — was an attack, made by a small party of them, on a quartermaster's wagon-train at La Bontee Creek, twenty-two miles from the post, on the Laramie road, in the Month of May, 1872; and the subsequent killing of Sergeant Mularkey of my command, who, being in charge of the mail party *en route* for Horseshoe Creek the same day that the wagon-train was attacked, had incautiously ridden ahead of his party, and, coming upon the Indians just after they had been repulsed in their attack upon the train, fell a victim to their rage and disappointment. In this affair the Indians succeeded in killing the sergeant, taking the mule he rode, and escaping into the hills before his party could come up, the first intimation the latter had of the presence of the hostiles being their coming upon the dead body of the sergeant lying in the road, watched over by a faithful dog that had accompanied him.

This was the work of Cheyennes, not, however, of those of them that had been receiving the bounty of the government at Fort Fetterman, but of a small band of irreconcilables under a leader appropriately named "Old Bear," who persisted in maintaining an attitude of hostility towards the whites despite the influence and example of their more tractable brethren. Indeed, the great body of the Cheyennes were on the very day of this occurrence encamped near the post

Dull Knife, seated, and Little Wolf

Turkey Legs, seated, and Little Chief

preparing to start for their hunting-grounds on the Powder River, and their presence there materially complicated the solution of the problem as to who were the perpetrators of the Mularkey murder, for Indians never, when it can be avoided, expose themselves with their women and children to the danger of reprisal and retaliation. Their own maxim of conduct being "a life for a life," their presence with their families near a military post is pretty good *prima facie* evidence of their innocence of any act of killing committed in that immediate neighborhood.

The Cheyenne village on this occasion was perfectly commanded by a gun that could at any moment have been trained upon it, hurling destruction and death upon all it contained; and I found it very difficult, therefore, to believe that with such means of retribution menacing them the Cheyennes were the perpetrators of this outrage.

Besides the Cheyennes, the Arrapahoes were also encamped near the post; so that the same presumption of innocence as to this particular act existed in their case also, thus leaving the Sioux, roving bands of whom were frequently in the neighborhood, obnoxious to the strong suspicion of being the slayers of Mularkey. Having no mounted force, any attempt to find and take up the trail of the hostiles in time to effect a successful pursuit would be futile. I, however, sent for the headmen of the Cheyennes and Arrapahoes, and giving them to understand that I was very angry with Indians generally, asked them if they had anything to say respecting this outrage. They of course denied all participation in or knowledge concerning it.

Then, addressing myself to the Cheyennes, I told them that I had reason to think that the party who killed the sergeant had gone up the Powder River road, the same that they were about to move on, and that I should expect them to find out the guilty ones and arrest and bring them back to me, and that they should recover and return to me the mule and equipments. This they finally promised to do if they could.

I did not rely very confidently, however, on anything coming of it all, and therefore my surprise was as great almost as was my gratification when, a few days after the Cheyennes had departed, runners from them returned to the post bringing me word from Little Wolf and Dull Knife that they had ascertained that "Old Bear's" band were the perpetrators of the Mularkey murder, and that they intended to catch and punish them, and this was supplemented a few days later by the arrival of Little Wolf himself, bringing back the mule the sergeant had ridden. Little Wolf informed me that they had come up with "Old Bear's" party at night, and that his young men had charged their camp and had captured it and the mule, but that "Old Bear" and his followers had escaped. Some of this I took *cum grano salis,* but the substantial fact of the rendition of the mule there was no disputing. Having properly acknowledged this evidence of good faith on their part, I made Little Wolf and his companions a present of some rations, and they set out to rejoin their people.

The most powerful influence operating within our Indian system is that of the traders. From top to bottom of the Indian service its *personnel* from time to time changes — all except the trader; he is perennial. Theoretically, he too has his time to fall, but practically he stays. His counting-room is the point of radiation of lines of influence as minute as the capillary ducts of the human body, and as powerful. If *his* Indians go to Washington to visit their Great Father, he goes with them; the interpreter, who is probably deep in his debt, varies the utterances of the chiefs to suit his purposes, and by his wily machinations he manages to defeat all efforts in behalf of Indians that do not coincide with his interests.

My relation to the Cheyennes at Fort Fetterman was detrimental, of course, to the trading interest at the Red Cloud agency, where it was claimed these Indians properly belonged, and unceasing were the efforts made to effect a rupture of that relation. The Cheyennes themselves, although connected with the Sioux by marriage, and generally allied with them in war, were extremely averse to being associated with them in their village life, for the reason that, being weaker in numbers, they were robbed and lorded over by the Sioux, and for the further reason that the principles and the practice of the Sioux in regard to female chastity differed widely, for the worse, from that of the Cheyennes.

What the Cheyennes most earnestly desired was the establishment of an agency for themselves, somewhere in the Northern country, or, if that could not be compassed, their continuance under military management at Fort Fetterman. The scheme of the government respecting them was to effect their transfer, peacefully if possible, to a southern reservation, and it was the partial consummation of this scheme that led to the recent tragic events in their history. In all of my councils with them I persistently endeavored to bring their minds to an acceptance of the government scheme of removal to the south, but without much success.

Meanwhile, I regarded it as of prime importance that, pending their final disposition, they be kept away from the Red Cloud agency, because I knew that the influences to which they would be subjected there would be opposed to the realization of the government scheme; and, moreover, anticipating the hostilities with the Sioux that have since occurred, I deemed it better military policy, while the Cheyennes should remain in the Northern country, to have them so in hand that we might utilize them as our allies against the Sioux, rather than add them as a reinforcement to the latter.

Finding my efforts to induce them to acquiesce in the policy of a removal to the south ineffectual, I tried to persuade them to ask for permission to visit Washington, hoping that, by an interchange of views with the authorities there, either the government might succeed in winning them over to acceptance of its scheme, or, if that failed, they might be permitted to have an agency of their own. After repeated refusals to accept this advice they finally adopted it, and coming to me asked that I would communicate to the Great Father their request to be allowed to visit Washington; this I immediately did, but the moment was inopportune, for, as it happened, Red Cloud was just then on one of his periodical visits to the Capital, accompanied by his retinue of traders and interpreters, and, the request of the Cheyennes being communicated to him, he was made to say that a delegation from them was unnecessary, that they belonged to him, and that he would represent them. In consequence of this opposition of Red Cloud to their suit the Cheyennes failed to obtain the personal hearing at Washington which they so ardently desired, and which, had it been accorded them, I cannot but think would have resulted happily, both for the government and for them.

Even after my *quasi* agentship had been terminated and both the Cheyennes and Arrapahoes had been remitted to the Red Cloud agency for their subsistence and government oversight, they were constantly touching at Fetterman in their journeys to and from the Powder River country and their forays against the Shoshonees, and it was seldom that the tepees of members of one or the other of these tribes were not visible near the post. The Cheyennes and Arrapahoes got along very peaceably together. The latter were only half as strong in number as the former, and although originally among the most fierce and warlike of the Indians of the plains, they were, much more rapidly than the former, taking on a milder type of manners and character. Their declining numbers had doubtless much to do with this decadence from their pristine eminence in savage traits, and they had among them, moreover, a man whose influence probably operated as an auxiliary towards the same result.

The man to whom I allude was "Friday," whose singular history, albeit not falling strictly within the purview of my subject, merits a passing notice. The tribe, many years ago, breaking up their village on the Cimmarron branch of the Arkansas River, divided into two bands, each taking its own direction. Friday was at that time a boy of about seven years of age. By some misadventure he found himself accompanying one band while his parents and family had gone with the other. Upon making this discovery he left the party he was with and started to find the one his parents had accompanied. He lost his way, and wandered about for days in a vain search for the right trail, till at last, overcome by hunger, fatigue, and cold, he lay down, as he supposed, to die.

A passing trader found him, however, before life was extinct, and carrying him to Missouri, turned him over to the Jesuit fathers at St. Louis. By them he was cared for and instructed, with a view to making him, in after-years, a missionary to his people. He proved intelligent and apt, and became a respectable scholar in Hebrew, Greek, and Latin. When he had attained the age of sixteen, his parents then for the first having learned his whereabouts, made requisition on the government for him, and with much reluctance, both on his part and on that of the worthy fathers who had so long nurtured him, he was delivered to his parents at a spot near one of the military posts, in what is now the State of Colorado. So little, however, did he enjoy the prospect of a return to the savage life, that as soon as the shades of night had fallen upon the Indian village he stole forth, and made a break for the camp of the party that had brought him out from the States.

His attempt at escape was speedily discovered, and promptly frustrated by pursuit and recapture, and he was compelled to take up again the nomadic life of the plains. Had he been of maturer age at the time of this rendition, or, perhaps, had his character been of tougher fibre, the store of languages, dead and living, and, let us hope, the precepts of religion and morality with which the good fathers had furnished him, might have proved a valuable equipment for effort on his part toward civilizing and Christianizing his people; but, being what he was, only a boy, and sharing with us all that human tendency towards vagabondage that makes descent in savagery much easier than rising out of it, he became what he was when I knew him, — as thoroughly an Indian, to all outward seeming, as any of his companions. Almost his only distinguishing characteristic, beyond his knowledge of English, was a fondness for "fire-water," that could only be regarded as distinctive by reason of the proportions it had attained.

And yet, despite all this, I believe, as I intimated before, that unconsciously to himself, and imperceptibly by his people, Friday had been an auxiliary of no mean effect in toning down the savagery of the tribe, and so rendering them somewhat more amenable to civilizing influences.

The Arrapahoes at the time of which I speak were without a recognized chief, their headship being divided between Friday and a splendid specimen of the young Indian brave named "Black Coal." The two called one day at my quarters on some business just as I had finished dinner, and as I was alone at the time, my family having gone to the States, I invited them to eat; an invitation which an Indian as invariably accepts as does that approximate congener of his, — civilization's latest human product, — the tramp.

Friday's reminiscences of civilized ways enabled him to possess his soul in patience until the board, duly set, was ready to receive him and his companion, when he still further indicated the training of his youth by displaying a perfect familiarity with the several table articles and their uses, while Black Coal was much hampered in the appeasing of his appetite by the necessity he was under of learning by observation of his more accomplished friend the mode of using the knives and forks and spoons with which civilization has supplemented aboriginal fingers.

My last council with the Cheyennes was a stormy one. It was after Fort Fetterman had ceased to be their appointed base of supplies that one day about 500 of them came in hungry and cross, asking for food. At the beginning of the council they were glum and moody, but not insolent. I received them kindly, but told them that I could not issue rations to so large a number of them without first obtaining the permission of the Great Father at Washington, as it was no longer intended that they should be subsisted at Fetterman, but at the Red Cloud agency, all of which they perfectly well understood. I further said to them, as they seemed to be really suffering for food, I would ask the Great Father, by telegraph, for permission to issue them bread and beef sufficient to subsist them *en route* to the agency; that I might receive a reply that afternoon, but that possibly it would be delayed till next morning; that I would see them again in the afternoon and tell them whether I had received an answer to my dispatch or not. At the time for the reassembling of the council in the afternoon no reply had been received, and upon my informing them of this fact they began to manifest a very ugly spirit.

Two of their young men had been killed by whites just previous to this, between Fort Laramie and the railroad, and one of their speakers commenced arraigning me and the whites generally for this offense, his harangue finding great acceptance with his companions, who, by their grunts of applause and angry looks, were evidently being worked up to a high pitch of excitement. When he had finished, I replied to him that the young men who were killed were stealing cattle, and had no business to be where they were under any circumstances; furthermore, that I had an unsettled account with them in the matter of my sergeant, whom their people had killed. To this they vouchsafed no immediate reply, but one of them, rising with great excitement of manner, ejaculated somewhat after this fashion: "What are you doing in this country, anyhow? You come here and kill our game; you cut our grass and chop down our trees; you break our rocks" (prospecting for mines), "and you kill our people. This country belongs to us, and we want you to get out of it."

Joe having got thus far in his interpreting, I stopped him, and directed him to tell the Indians that I had heard all that I proposed to listen to of that kind of talk, and that if they were not more civil I would turn them off the reservation, and if they ever set foot on it again I should treat them as enemies. The aspect of affairs at this juncture was threatening: the Indians were all armed, while the few of us who were present were unarmed; they were angry and excited, and, except for a diversion which most opportunely occurred, serious results might have ensued. But, fortunately, just at this moment the telegraph operator came in and handed me a reply to my dispatch, authorizing me to issue the bread and beef.

Transferring it to Joe, I told him to interpret it to the Indians. The effect was magical, and strongly controverted the traditional stoicism that they are credited with, for no sooner did they learn the contents of the dispatch than all their sullenness disappeared, smiles took the place of scowls, they crowded around me and the other officers present with a general shaking of hands and ejaculations of "how," and one enthusiastic brave, seizing my hand, intimated to me his opinion that the killing of my sergeant and of their two young men about balanced matters in that line, and that we ought now to drop the subject.

This, as I have said, was my last council with the Cheyennes. The Sioux were becoming restive, and the greed of traders, made potential by the unfortunate system, at the core of which it nestles like the "worm in the bud," had forced the Cheyennes to amalgamate with them, and undergo conversion from peaceful wards and possible allies of the government to active and relentless foes. Now, nearly eight years since the incidents I have narrated, old Dull Knife lies stark and stiff among the Nebraska bluffs, his warriors are either dead or in irons, the widows of his braves find refuge with their sisters of the Sioux, and Little Wolf plays the avenger among the ranchmen of the Niobrara.

GEO. A. WOODWARD,
Colonel U.S.A.

The Indian Reservation System of the North Central Plains

By EVERETT W. STERLING

IN CHOOSING TO COMMENT upon the role played by the Indian reservation system in the history of the north central plains, the writer opens himself to criticism that could be avoided by addressing himself instead to the details of one particular reservation. The reader might then agree that the article was carefully documented and undoubtedly true, but complain in somewhat the same way as the boy who ordered a book from a publisher and, after it had arrived, wrote back complaining: "This book tells me more about pelicans than I wanted to know." Instead, the writer opens himself to the criticism that what he writes, or a part of what he writes, is not even true. For the subject calls for a drawing of conclusions, an assessment and to some extent a passing of judgment; and in these matters few men are ready to accept without revision the conclusions of others.

The subject still calls for facts, but facts are often less important than the context within which they are seen. In 1867 a group of Irish nationalists shot a policeman of Manchester, England, while rescuing two fellow nationalists from a paddy wagon. The bald fact is that certain men shot and killed a policeman. To ardent Irish nationalists, however, the men doing the shooting were patriots striking a blow against tyranny. To many Englishmen, and particularly to policemen, an officer was murdered while acting in the line of duty. Wherever passions become involved, this same difficulty arises and it is needless to remark that passions have been involved and are still involved in relations between red men and white. For that reason it may be helpful to begin with an explicit statement as to the context within which the facts to follow are presented.

First, and most basically, it is assumed that the struggle between red men and white was one which had an inevitable result; namely, the subordination of a people living in the hunting-and-fishing stage by a people who made their living by agriculture and commerce. Whatever beauties or merit there may have been in the way of life of the Indians, it was doomed as soon as Columbus landed. There was no way in the world to have kept the great plains of the United States as a huge buffalo preserve, occupied by a relatively few inhabitants. There is tragedy involved, but tragedy in which there are, broadly speaking, neither heroes nor villains. Who is hero and who villain among the Indians, the stalwart brave who resists the inevitable or the Indian who takes up the white man's way of life and tries to make a living as an agriculturist? Who is hero and who villain among the whites, one who insists that a way of life based upon hunting and fishing cannot survive in the face of a more advanced culture, or one who tries to preserve the Indian way of life, together with Indian ownership of the vast areas of land necessary to that life? There are, of course, individuals on both sides who behave in such a fashion as to earn the name of villain in any society of which they may be a part, but their wanton disregard for the human dignity or even the right to life of other humans is a weakness to be found wherever the human species abounds and is a problem independent of the tragic and unyielding process by which one way of life takes precedence over another.

It follows from the above that the Indians would ultimately have to adjust to the disappearance of buffalo and other wild game and learn to support themselves by other means.

Lastly, it is assumed that the proper long-range goal of Indian policy is full-fledged membership as citizens of the United States, with all that citizenship implies in terms both of privileges and responsibilities. Secretary of the Interior Stewart L. Udall makes the same point when he speaks of "the ultimate goal of full and equal participation by Indians in all aspects of our national life."[1] Such a fate is not one we need to apologize for nor is flag-waving or cultural pride in any way involved. One wishes for his own children nothing better than equality with other citizens, which is not the same thing as saying that he desires to be *like* other citizens in matters of morals, religion, esthetic taste or a thousand and one other things.

Left: Knife (Indian police), Red Cloud, Jack Red Cloud, Baptiste Guarnier (interpreter)

Indian agent with chiefs of Yankton Sioux, at Greenwood Agency

The reservation system was first applied in this area in 1851 under the terms of the treaties of Mendota and Traverse des Sioux. The reservations provided for bordered the St. Peters or Minnesota River along its upper reaches. In Dakota, the first reservation was established in the southeastern corner of the Territory under the Yankton treaty of 1858.

To start with the most obvious point, the establishment of these reservations was a means for quieting Indian title to vast areas of land that were now demanded by the westward-tumbling settlers or by the land speculators who generally preceded them. With Iowa in the 1840's and eastern Nebraska in the 1850's filling up with settlers, the Indian Office was under pressure, primarily from the frontier sections affected, to enter into negotiations for the opening up of the next few hundred miles of agricultural land. The stage was reached, in both instances, after the Sioux tribes in the area coveted had already been softened up for the blow in a number of ways.

Areas so close to white settlement as to be destined for colonization in the near future were already losing their ability to support Indians dependent upon the chase. As an old man, Gabriel Renville, a chief of the Sisseton and Wahpeton of South Dakota, commented on the process:

> I remember the big council fire when we signed away our first land. At that time the country was full of buffalo and when I was 20 summers I killed a cow and calf with one arrow. Then came swarms of grasshoppers and ate up all the grass for four seasons. Then bones of the buffalo became white on the hillsides and they were poor and of little meat, so that the hunter got not much but the blanket in the hunt. Then the grasshoppers turned into white men and killed off all the buffalo that did not starve. This made great changes to the Indian. He could eat the buffalo and the grasshoppers, but he could not eat the white man. So we had to sell off more of our land to the great father at Washington for meat and blankets.[2]

Fur traders also were affected by the reduction in wild life. Charles Larpenteur, employed by the American Fur Company at a post on the Missouri below the James River, abandoned the fur trade in 1851, several years before the Yankton treaty. "The post, the country, all pleased me well enough," wrote Larpenteur, "but I found there was nothing more to be made in the Indian trade . . ."[3] In 1854, the Indian Agent for the Upper Missouri reported that the Yankton Indians "know they must resort to the cultivation of the soil for their subsistence."[4]

A further soft spot prior to the negotiation of treaties was the presence of a few Indians who were early converted to a Protestant brand of Christianity, and with it, an agricultural way of life.[5] In addition, half-breed families and Indian traders served as convenient instruments through which treaty makers operated.

The treaties which called for the establishment of these reservations were but a step in the relentless process by which a more advanced culture and a more numerous people moved to the enjoyment of a sparsely settled area rich in nat-

304 | Conflict and Accommodation

ural resources. Broken promises, bribery, intimidation were incidental; the disappearance of a stone-age culture was certain to be accomplished by one means or another. The political arm at Washington might for a time employ the machinery of treaty-making.

The bald fact was that the native inhabitants had, by the end of the 1820's, become wards of the state. It was in that decade that the Supreme Court was asked to rule on the position of the Indian nations. Were Indians citizens of the United States, covered by the usual constitutional legal systems, and hence subject to the laws of the states within which they resided, or were they, on the other hand, members of political entities which were on the same level as the central government and hence to be dealt with solely by the treaty-making process? In 1831 Chief Justice Marshall ruled in the case of *Cherokee Nation v. the State of Georgia* that the Cherokees were a "domestic dependent nation" rather than a "foreign state." The Court shortly also ruled, in *Worcester v. Georgia*, that Indians were not, because of the domestic aspect of their status, subject to the laws of the states within whose boundaries they resided.

The elements of compromise is at once apparent. One might almost say that the court temporized. The phrase "domestic dependent nation" tells the story. Indians will be handled through the treaty-making process but, as dependent nations, their treaties are not as other treaties. Indian tribes are separate nations, but are subject to the sovereign power of the Congress of the United States. It is a line of judicial reasoning similar to the "insular" cases at the end of the century made famous by Finley Peter Dunne in one of his syndicated columns. In commenting upon the Supreme Court decisions on the status of Puerto Rico and other recent territorial acquisitions, Mr. Dunne concluded: "Some say it laves th' flag up in th' air an' some say that's where it laves th' Constitution. Annyhow, something's in th' air. But there's wan thing I'm sure about . . . That is . . . no matter whether th' Constitution follows th' flag or not, th' supreme court follows th' iliction returns."

Both sets of decisions made sense at the time because they squared with the facts. Indians were without question not like other citizens of the United States and would have to be handled in some special fashion. At the same time, it was equally true that the sovereignty of the United States overshadowed the sovereignty of Indian tribes. This superiority of the authority of the federal government, and the dependence of Indian tribes, have been consistently applied by the Supreme Court. Most recently, in a case arising out of the condemnation of Indian lands in the State of New York for the construction of a reservoir, the Court has ruled that the Seneca Indians are as vulnerable to the power of eminent domain as other citizens of the United States, even though they have a treaty signed by George Washington himself, promising them permanent possession of the lands in question.[6]

The recognition of tribes as "domestic dependent nations" and the employment of treaty-making machinery were both adaptations to existing circumstances and, to some extent, expedients used in handling the Indians. Rules and pro-

Early-day Crow Indian farmers, Black Lodge District　　　Girls at boarding school, Crow agency, 1896

cedures existed to cover relations with truly sovereign foreign nations and to cover the rights and obligations of full fledged citizens. Because Indians fell somewhere between the two, existing machinery had to be adapted.

To some the terms "expedient" and "temporizing" may carry a connotation of duplicity or shady practice. This does not necessarily follow. The establishment of Indian tribes as, in fact, either full-fledged citizens, on the one hand, or full-fledged foreign powers, on the other, would have involved a miraculously sudden acculturation or a bloody, last-ditch struggle. The means employed were part of a compromise solution which avoided both extremes.

This temporizing policy is to be seen in the establishment of Indian reservations. Ideally, reservations were to be a transitional stage. The ascendant society, having separated the native population from the natural resources essential to their old way of life, so that they were no longer self-supporting, undertook to supply food and clothing until the natives might learn to make their living by other methods. The reservation system might serve to ease the conscience of re-

Crow tipis near Fort Custer, M.T.

sponsible citizens troubled by the process of expropriation. More importantly, however, the establishment of reservations was a means for avoiding a direct confrontation of the natives with the alternatives of adapting at once or resisting by force of arms.

A third alternative was provided. For the conservative Indian, the reservation could be held forth as a sanctuary where much of the old life might be retained. To the progressive, the reservation might be held forth as a schooling place where, with the help of government farmers and government teachers, they might learn to be self-supporting in a new fashion. In either case, the reservation was a way between the old and the new.

The role reservations played in preparing, or helping to prepare, individual Indians for self-support under the new conditions is the most difficult part of the story to trace. Groups or group activities are comparatively easy to follow. Adaption, however, has been an individual thing and, for a number of reasons, the successful individual has tended to leave the group. Any assessment of the part reservations have played in facilitating adaptation must give considerable credit to the several religious denominations, Protestant and Catholic, that have maintained manual-labor training schools on the reservations.

In a very real sense the reservation has served as a transition place for many Indians. During the first years of the Sioux reservation along the Minnesota River, members of several bands deliberately made the break with their old way of life, either because of a recognition that it was doomed or because of the attractiveness of the new. With assistance and guidance from agency personnel, they took up quarters in brick houses, tilled fields, adopted the clothing of the white man, became Presbyterians or Episcopalians and even organized as a separate band under the name of "The Hazlewood Republic," with elected officials replacing their former chiefs. This particular endeavor was short-lived, being destroyed by an attack from less progressive members of their own tribe.[7] When the Minnesota Sioux left the state, however, similar movements arose both at Santee in Nebraska and at Sisseton in Dakota. In both instances, when the reservation atmosphere appeared to be unsatisfactory for progressive change, a body of Indians left the reservation to take up the struggle on the outside as homesteaders, either at Flandreau, north of Sioux Falls, or at Brown Earth, west of Milbank.[8]

A second category can be identified on a number of the reservations, consisting of Indians who saw the necessity or even the advantage of readjusting their lives in part, but desired at the same time to hang on to many of their old ways. The families of Indian traders, so prominent in both Minnesota and the Dakotas, ordinarily fell into this group. Gabriel Renville, half-breed chief of the Sisseton, is a good example. The brand of Christianity which he adopted had to be one which would accept or at least wink at his retention of all three of his wives.

Something of the mood in which this group approached the new way of life is suggested by the 1868 report of the first of the agents assigned to the new Sisseton reservation. To show the eagerness of the Indians to take up a sedentary life on the reservation he announced with evident satisfaction that they had their wives out cutting hay with the only implements at hand — butcher knives.

There were features of both the old and the new that could be attractive. If the Great Father in Washington wanted to build a cabin for you, send an agency farmer to do the plowing for you, an agency blacksmith to repair your equipment and other employees to issue such staples as could not be grown, why not accept gracefully the fact that buffalo were no longer to be found?

To the Indian who was unwilling or unable to learn new skills or to adapt old ones to new situations, the reservation has been a sort of poor house. Uncle Sam has taken the place of the buffalo as the source of food, implements, clothing and housing. Logically, the buffalo as a totem should have been replaced by the Great Father in Washington and children should have been named not "White Buffalo," but "White Uncle" and not "Sitting Bull" but "Sitting Sam." That such has not been done is perhaps attributable to the fact that the pursuit of Uncle Sam is less ennobling and less productive of satisfaction than pursuit of the buffalo. It may be, on the other hand, that it is a matter of cultural lag and that, given enough generations to whom pursuit of the Government has been a way of life, a new symbolism will emerge.

The place of Indian Reservations in the rather well developed political spoils system of the post--Civil War period is a subject that invites extended treatment. Only a few observations are possible. That Indian agencies were in some way connected with political spoils is a matter of common knowledge. There is a famous story of a Republican job-seeker by the name of Walter Burleigh who claimed to have been instrumental in carrying the state of Pennsylvania for the Republican party in 1860. He called on Lincoln and expressed an interest in the position of Ambassador to Great Britain. When Lincoln informed him that he had already decided on a man for that place, Burleigh told him that he expected something pretty good. "Then Lincoln asked me how I would like an Indian agency. I wanted to know where it was and he said it was out in Dakota Territory. Then I asked him what the salary was and he said 'two thousand dollars.' I told him right then and there that if I took my family out into that frontier country and only got two thousand dollars a year, that I would have to starve or steal."

"Dr. Burleigh," said Lincoln in his dry way, "if I am any judge of human nature, you won't starve."[9] Burleigh served at the Yankton agency, became prominent in territorial politics, and was instrumental in installing his father-in-law as third governor of Dakota Territory.

A brief visit to the files of the Appointments Branch of the Department of the Interior in the National Archives, where one may consult the letters of recommendation of the applicants for appointment as Indian agents, will reveal ample support for any suspicion one might have that the way to get a job as Indian Agent prior to 1900 was to be identified closely with the party in power.

Why the position of Agent was so much sought after does, however, require some explanation. In some instances it was the opportunity afforded a shrewd operator to supplement his salary by running cattle on land close to the reserva-

Indians at beef-slaughter day, Blackfeet agency, Badger Creek

tion, possibly with the assistance of government employees. Contracts for hay, wood, transportation and the like might be shared through the use of "dummy" contractors. The letter books of a trading firm in which Grant's brother, Orville, was a sleeping partner, now in the possession of the North Dakota Historical Society, reveal a few of the ties that bound agent, traders, and contractors together.[10] These outside sources of income might far overshadow the salary paid by the government. Joseph R. Brown, agent to the Minnesota Sioux along the St. Peters River shortly before the Civil War, did not pay for his three-story stone mansion overlooking the river near Granite Falls, Minnesota, or the grand piano and other furnishings that were destroyed during the Sioux uprising in 1862, with his salary as agent. It was commonly said in his day that the position of Agent at St. Peters was worth some $20,000 per year.[11] A study of the Brown papers held by the Minnesota Historical Society provide chapter and verse for some of Brown's later schemes while operating from Brown's Valley, just off the Sisseton-Wahpeton reservation, and make the $20,000 sound credible. Not all agents, however, were as resourceful as Joseph R. Brown.

The importance of the position of Indian Agent in the political spoils system, however, arose not so much from the attractiveness of the position to the individual hoping to fill the post as from the working of politics at the local and/or state level. It was quite fitting that the position of Territorial Governor was, for a considerable period, combined with that of Superintendent of Indian Affairs for each Territory.

On the frontier, government payments were looked upon as a natural resource to be exploited in the same manner as furs, town sites and cheap lands. The Indian Office was roughly equivalent to the Bureau of Reclamation and the Corps of Engineers rolled into one. The dependence of steamboat companies, beef contractors and western mercantile firms upon government contracts is equalled today only in certain defense industries. Indeed, the dependence of frontier business upon the federal government is at odds with the traditional picture of the frontier and raises a question as to the exact nature of the self-reliant individualism of some of the more prominent pioneer figures.

When the Minnesota Sioux were removed to Crow Creek on the Missouri, just below the present capital of South Dakota, it is worth noting that, with political ties oriented to St. Paul, Indian Superintendent Clark Thompson chose to purchase winter supplies in Minnesota rather than at Sioux City, despite the fact that the supplies would have to be hauled by ox teams overland from Mankato late in the season. General Pope, who had to supply a military escort, was suspicious and protested, but finally cooperated.[12]

The position of Agent was also of great importance in local political machines. Late in the century the Republican party leaders in Roberts County, South Dakota, location of the Sisseton Agency, came to demand the right to nominate the agent for that post. When large cash payments were made to the Sissetons in 1890 and 1892, local firms with claims against individual Indians were most anxious that they be permitted to set up a desk close to the scene of payment and, in general, be given preferment in debt collection as against other claimants.[13]

That Indian payments and Indian contracts were important to the communities near them has already been suggested. During the pioneer period this was particularly true. Pioneer areas are traditionally debtor areas. Ready cash had a way of flowing to other sections in payments for land, fencing, farm machinery and seed. Sources of cash, on the other hand, were hard to find. Payments to army troops and payments to Indians were, therefore, depended upon as vital sources of the lifeblood of commerce — good hard money. In 1852, Governor Ramsey of Minnesota Territory visited Washington and picked up Treasury

Crow Indians and cowboys on reservation near Billings

drafts for Sioux money totalling $599,605.00. He deposited the drafts with a New York bank but had $100,000 in gold and $100,000 in notes packed into a pair of iron chests weighing some 200 lbs. each and took them back to St. Paul in person. "I deemed it proper to carry as much money along as could be done safely," he said . . . "for the sake of aiding the territory with currency."[14]

Space will not permit a detailing of the various means or routes by which a dollar in the hand of an Indian was transferred in short order to the hands of non-Indians. Compared with the payroll of a modern business concern, or the cash receipts of today's commercial farmers, the amounts involved were small. But the appreciating dollar of the last half of the nineteenth century was a scarce commodity in all farming areas, and particularly among pioneers. Joseph R. Brown was perhaps only prudent when he advised his son to make sure that an indemnity sum, compensation to the next of kin to two Sisseton Indians killed by Chippewa braves, be paid over at Brown's Valley and not at St. Paul. He advised Sammy to "make arrangements" to get the money.[15]

This discussion opened with the assertion that the reservation system was primarily a transition device. The continuance of the reservation system is an indication that the transition period has not passed. Some like to believe that reservations are islands of the old culture, but cultures are living things and vitality has not been a notable feature of the reservations in this area. What is ultimately preserved of the old Indian culture will be that which can be made to square with the main facts of life, with an adaptation, much as Indian art at one time adjusted to the white man's glass beads or Indian hunters adapted to the white man's horses and guns.

NOTES

[1] Sioux Falls *Argus Leader*, September 25, 1961.

[2] George G. Allanson, "An Interesting Account of the Historic Indian Reservation." *The Sisseton Courier*, July 2, 1942. The treaty referred to is presumably that of July 15, 1830 (7 Stat., 328-332).

[3] Charles Larpenteur, *Forty Years a Fur Trader on the Upper Missouri*, (ed by Milton Quaife), p. 248. Chicago, 1933.

[4] *Annual Report of the Commissioner of Indian Affairs*, 1854, p. 79.

[5] Catholic missionaries have, historically, been less insistent upon industry, sobriety, and thrift as Christian virtues. For that reason, Catholicism called for less of a departure from the Indian's former way of life.

[6] *New York Times*, Aug. 13, 1961, p. 62.

[7] T. S. Williamson and A. L. Riggs, *The Gospel Among the Dakotas*, pp. 393-96.

[8] *Word Carrier* (Indian mission paper, Santee, Nebraska), September, 1877.

[9] Zack T. Sutley, *The Last Frontier*, (New York, 1930), pp. 177-78.

[10] Parkin Papers, North Dakota Historical Society.

[11] "Justice" in *St. Paul Press*, April 17, 1873, p. 1.

[12] *Rebellion Records*, Series I, Vol. XXII, Part 2, p. 671.

[13] See Report of Inspector O'Connell, July 27, 1897, Indian Division, Office of the Secretary of the Interior, National Archives.

[14] *Minnesota History*, XXVII, 321. See also G. A. Patchin, "Banking in Minnesota," *Ibid.*, II, pp., 116, 120.

[15] Joseph R. Brown to Samuel Brown, September 21, 1869, Brown Papers, Minnesota Historical Society.

DREAM'S END

Tragic Retreat

By ROWENA and GORDON D. ALCORN

"Under a buffalo-skin robe, I was sleeping soundly in our tepee beside Chee-Nah my grandmother. . . . Suddenly a rifle shot, then neighing of startled horses roused us. Chee-Nah rose to peer out and a bullet pierced her left shoulder . . . blood streamed from the wound as she pushed me from the tepee crying, 'Suhm-Keen, run to the trees and hide.' I raced up the slope as fast as I could . . . bullets kept whizzing past clipping off leaves and branches all around me. I was very afraid . . . soon some other boys joined me there and we watched trembling at the awful sight below. Our tepees were set afire and our people shot as they tried to run for cover in the timber."

Thus recalled our aged friend Sam Tilden, whose Nez Percé tribal name, Suhm-Keen, means Shirt On. We visited him again last summer (June, 1962), and he was telling us boyhood memories of the historic Battle of the Big Hole on August 9, 1877. Tilden was ten years old when he went along on that tragic retreat. Five non-treaty bands of the Nez Percé nation were fleeing their homeland to seek sanctuary in Canada, "Land of Redcoats."

After they had crossed over the Lolo Trail of the Rockies, the tribesmen hoped they were safe from pursuit by Gen. O. O. Howard's U. S. Army forces. So, exhausted from their arduous trip (encumbered as they were with old men, women and little children) they at last stopped to rest at Big Hole, which they called "Is-Kum-Tse-Talik" (Place of Ground Squirrels).[1]

Scouts should have been sent up the pass to be sure they were not being followed, but in the council of chieftains, Looking Glass vehemently insisted that it was not necessary: "Montana people our friends." This decision was to cost the Nez Percés many lives.

They made camp. Tepee poles were cut, squaws dug camas bulbs and soon roasting pits to cure them were smoldering. They would need as much of this nourishing food as they could prepare for the long trek to Canada. Two camas bulbs and two kous roots could sustain one for a day.

Tilden continued his account of the Battle: "About 4 a.m. before dawn, one of our old men, Nata-Le-Kin, who had poor eyesight, heard the ponies stirring restlessly up on the hillside where most of them were hobbled. It was a chilly night, so he drew his blanket around his shoulders and rode up to investigate the cause of that disturbance. Col. Gibbon's troops were hiding up there ready to attack the sleeping camp, when Nata-Le-Kin appeared. They shot him and the report of the rifle roused our encampment and our warriors rushed from their tepees to do battle. Many of the tepees were set afire by the soldiers, who shot our people as they tried to run for cover in the timber. The first warrior to be killed was Rainbow (Wah-Chum-Yus) who had always told us that if he had to fight before dawn, he would surely be killed."

It was not yet light when the battle started. Five Wounds (Pah-Kah-Tos), lifelong friend of Rainbow, had made a pact with him that they would die on the same day as their fathers had died many years before. When Five Wounds saw that Rainbow was slain, he deliberately walked out into the enemy fire and died. Tilden also saw other great warriors killed: Red Moccasin Tops (Sarpsis-Ilp-Pilp), Shore Crossing (Wah-Lit-Its), Woodpecker (Woo-Kaw-Kaw) and Circling Swan (Wet-Yet-Mas-Lik-Leinen).

In spite of the surprise attack, the Nez Percés were able to drive off the enemy, and even managed to capture the one howitzer hidden in the timber. Then, while a number of warriors held the troops pinned in rifle pits, the other tribesmen buried their dead. Then they hastily fashioned travois from poles of the unburned tepees. On these they placed the wounded and left the sad "Place of Ground Squirrels," and again headed toward Canada. Riding on fast ponies, the fighting men joined the others when they made a camp after traveling "one sun" from Big Hole.

The name of this place they called "Tak-Seen" (The Willows). Here Ollokot's wife, Ai-Hits-Palo-Jam (Fair Land) died of the wounds she had received the day before. She left an infant baby. Husis-Ow-Yeen (Wounded Head), whose Indian name was given to him from the severe head wound received at the battle, had tallied the dead at Big Hole on his buffalo drinking horn: sixty-three had been killed, thirty-two of them men. All the others were women and children. There was much grieving and wailing in the camp that night.

Sam Tilden was born in 1867 when his parents were camped on the Musselshell River during a buffalo-hunting trip. His father was We-Ahch-Chech-Kan (Packing Blankets), his mother Ka-Too-Cham-Miyah (Horse Chewing Grass Noisily). The name of Samuel Tilden was given to young Suhm-Keen by a teacher, Frank Kettenbach of Lewiston, Idaho. English names were frequently given to Indian children by teachers or ministers.

Chee-Nah, Suhm-Keen's grandmother, was the sister of Chief Old Joseph, and she was known as Martha Joseph. The wound she received as the attack at Big Hole started gradually healed during the retreat. She was captured at Bear Paw and taken prisoner with Chief Joseph. She returned to Lapwai where she died after the war, many years later.

Chief Joseph

White Bird, Nez Percé

"During the early summer of 1877," Tilden remembers clearly, "we were camped on the bank of the South Fork of the Clearwater River, not far from the present village of Stites, Idaho." After the Battle of White Bird Canyon on June 17, 1877[2] the Nez Percés moved up onto the Camas Prairie and then down to the South Fork of the Clearwater River (Koos-Koos-Kie). There they made a camp in the sloping meadow directly across from what is now known as Battle Ridge. There, Tilden's family joined the other tribesmen.

On July 11 and 12, a band of twenty-four Nez Percé warriors, led by Yellow Wolf, Ollokot, Wottolen, Peo-Peo-Tholekt, Rainbow, Five Wounds and others, held off the army forces along this high promontory. Meanwhile salvos from the two howitzers landed in the Indian encampment. Finally it was decided that their camp should be moved for safety, and so the Nez Percés headed for Kamiah while the warriors held the soldiers on the ridge. The last to leave was Yellow Wolf, who helped Springtime, Joseph's young wife, to mount her rearing pony, frightened by the roar of the howitzers. With the cradleboard containing her baby, she could not handle the terrified animal. Together, Yellow Wolf and Springtime rode to join the retreating Nez Percés.

Tilden recalls the stormy council of Chiefs — Joseph, Looking Glass, Ollokot, White Bird and Too-Hool-Hool-Zote — after the next attack which came the following day on July 13 at Kamiah Crossing. Chief Joseph suggested that they go back down into the rugged terrain where they could easily elude the soldiers. This was the Salmon River area, which is gashed by awesome canyons. Joseph was overruled by the others who wanted to leave Idaho and go to the "Land of Redcoats," and so preparations were made to leave at once.

Several of the warriors who had fought bravely at White Bird Canyon, the Clearwater Battle and at Kamiah Crossing decided to remain behind at Kamiah with Chief Red Heart and his band, which had just returned from Montana where they were hunting buffalo. These tribesmen were all taken prisoner and

Gen. John Gibbon   Gen. O. O. Howard

were later held for a year at Fort Vancouver. Among them were Halfmoon and an old man, Chief Jacob, who had signed the Treaty of 1855. What a change had taken place in twenty-two short years!

"On the way up over Lolo Trail," Tilden told us, "we had plenty of wild game. I was usually put on night duty to guard the horses. Chief Joseph was my uncle and he asked me to do this."

After the Battle of Big Hole, the Nez Percés were attacked again at Camas Meadows (Kamus-Nim-Takin). This was on August 20. It was while they were still in this area that some of the Nez Percé warriors led by Yellow Wolf and Peo-Peo-Tholekt ran off some of the army animals in a night raid. This was a daring maneuver, especially since the redmen had to stampede them into joining the herd of Indian ponies. However, when it grew daylight, the raiders were chagrined to discover that there were only three horses; the rest were mules. Suhm-Keen (Tilden) laughed when he remembered this incident. "I helped to guard those animals — those mules which they thought were horses in the dark."

On and on the fleeing Nez Percés traveled northward toward Canada. Then at Canyon Creek, Col. Samuel Sturgis' troops tried to corner them on September 13. Only one warrior was killed in this encounter. Tee-Wee-Yow-Nah's pony became terrified by the shooting and bolted, running out into the open where the soldiers found the redman an easy target. Canyon Creek, although not a narrow place, was skillfully defended by the expert marksmanship of the Nez Percés.

"It was growing colder every day as we headed northward," Tilden continued. "On September 29 when we finally arrived in the Bear Paws at the place we called 'Ali-Kos-Pah' (Place of Manure Fires), it was already starting to snow. I helped to gather buffalo chips and before long many fires were burning."[3]

"We are at least two suns ahead of the soldiers and only two suns from the 'Land of Redcoats,' so we can rest here awhile." This was again Chief Looking Glass who had spoken. However, the other chiefs seemed to agree that they might be safe now to remain there at least "one sun."[4]

Several scouts had arrived at the camping spot ahead of the main body of the Nez Percé, and had shot some buffalo. Soon meat was roasting over many fires. The Indians, their hunger appeased and warmed by the buffalo-chip fires, felt at ease now that they were such a short distance from Canada. All night long, the fires were kept aglow by the squaws. To keep warm enough this was necessary, for many of their thick buffalo robes had been destroyed when their tepees had been burned at the Big Hole.

A light snow had fallen during the night and it was bitterly cold as dawn broke. The camp was just stirring when scouts were sent out in different directions as a precautionary measure. "But we were not worried," says Tilden.

"The scouts had been gone just a short while, when suddenly we heard a distant rumbling . . . We all knew that this was not Hein-Mot (real thunder). It was the ominous sound of stampeding buffalo . . . this could mean only one thing! At that very moment one of our scouts appeared on top of the highest ridge. He yelled, then he fired his rifle in the air, at the same time he waved a blanket giving us the signal . . . 'Soldiers coming — soldiers coming.'

"While this scout was still waving the blanket to warn his tribesmen, there suddenly appeared two long lines of cavalry from the ridges; as they raced toward us, they formed two wide arcs to encircle our encampment.

"My mother screamed at me . . . 'Suhm-Keen, grab your packsack and get away to the Redcoats' . . . I ran to my pony and galloped him as fast as he could go. The noise of shooting had stampeded the Indian ponies and they were running away from the encampment . . . As I left the others, ahead I saw another Indian on a pinto pony. He had a long war-bonnet on. This Indian rode toward me and tried to shoot me but missed." (He was no doubt one of the Cheyennes who were helping the soldiers. Some Crow Indians were also at Bears Paw, and it was a great shock to the Nez Percés to see that these Crows, who were supposed to be their friends, had turned against them. The help of these Indians to the troops made the plight of the Nez Percés even more desperate.)

"It was again snowing as I rode on to the north. Toward evening I crossed the Milk River which was almost dry. Here I stopped for the night; my horse was too tired to go on. I had no food, no blankets except the one I used for the horse's saddle-blanket. Along came an Indian, and when we 'threw the signs,' I

Cheyenne police

discovered he was a friendly Cree. He was kind and generous, for he gave me a pair of moccasins and some food. He was a good-looking Indian."

Sometime later, about thirty or forty Nez Percés arrived at the Milk River, and among them, to young Suhm-Keen's joy, were his parents. They had waited until dark, and then slipped away from the camp, and fortunately had located some of their ponies which had run away when the shooting started. Later, more Crees came along and provided these shivering refugees with a few blankets, food and moccasins. Many had arrived barefoot, and it was very cold.

Several days later this bedraggled party slipped over across the border of Canada and at last arrived at the camp of the Sioux Indians. There, Chief Sitting Bull welcomed them and they were treated well. (Sitting Bull rode out to assist the Nez Percés when the word came that the tribesmen needed his help. While he was enroute to the Bears Paw, he met some of the tribesmen who were on foot led by Chief White Bird. When Sitting Bull saw their sad plight, he dismounted and stood there and wailed in sympathy for their lost cause.)

When Chief White Bird arrived with the news that Ollokot was dead, Too-Hool-Hool-Zote was dead, and Looking Glass was dead, they were shocked but almost worse was the dreadful news that three of their bravest warriors had been killed by mistake, by one of their own tribesmen. White Bird told them too that Joseph had surrendered on October 5th, and there was much grieving and wailing among the Nez Percés in the far-off "Land of Redcoats." They all knew that this was the end of all the things they loved.[5]

Tilden's parents remained at the Sioux encampment until 1878, then they crossed into Northern Montana where they lived about two years on a small ranch near the border of Alberta, Canada. The father worked for some white settlers there, milking cows and doing other farm chores. In 1880 they moved onto the Flathead Indian Reservation where they stayed until 1910; they they returned to Lapwai, Idaho.

Gradually more and more Nez Percé tribesmen drifted back into the United States. Some were caught and sent to the Indian Territory where Chief Joseph was being held with all who had surrendered with him at Bears Paw. Chief Joseph was permitted a last visit to the Wallowa Valley, the "Land of Winding Waters," in August, 1899.[6]

Sam Tilden says "I was one of the two first Nez Percé Indians to attend Carlisle Indian College. When I returned from there, I was through school, so I married Amy who was half Nez Percé and half Yakima. We moved back to the Flathead Reservation where I worked as a teamster. We had three boys, Harry, Lawrence and Ralph. In 1914, I became a member of the Flathead Indian Reservation police force, and served on that force for twenty years. During World War I, I was on duty guarding the border between Montana and Canada."

Sam Tilden, a gentle soft-spoken man, lived thirty years of his life in Montana, but when he retired from the police force, he returned to live near Lapwai, Idaho (Valley of Butterflies). His home was between Lapwai and Spalding in a grove of tall locust trees. In the early 1940's Ralph, his eldest son who was deaf, was run down by a train just a few hundred feet from their house. His son Lawrence and family now live in this house, for Sam Tilden has for the past two years made his home in the Orchards Nursing Home at Lewiston, Idaho.

For many years he took part in special Indian celebrations throughout the Northwest. He was active in the Stevens Treaty Centennial at Walla Walla in June, 1955, and was always there for the Chief Joseph Days held each summer at Joseph, Oregon. Although he no longer takes an active part in most of these things, he rode in the Lewiston Centennial Parade in the summer of 1961. He was dressed in his unusually handsome white beaded buckskins.

"I am very proud that my uncle, Chief Joseph, asked me to go back to Washington in 1903 (the last time he made a trip there to plead for the return of the Wallowa country to his people). He told me that I was one of the few people left that he could really trust." (On that trip, James Stewart, Joseph's relative, went along as an interpreter. Tilden speaks perfect English, but there had to be an official interpreter along).

"Chief Joseph wore civilian clothes back there, but always wore moccasins. He never put on shoes of the white man. We went to the White House to meet President Roosevelt . . . you know the 'rough rider.' We had dinner too with Gen. Miles; we ate buffalo meat. Then, Congressman Charles Curtis from Oklahoma took us to the Congress where we shook hands with many people."

The next year, Chief Joseph was dead, many said from grief.

NOTES

[1] Located on State Highway 43 in western Montana, the spot is now marked by a monument maintained by the National Park Service. It is 12 miles west of Wisdom and 21 miles from its junction with U. S. Highway 93. Shallow, grassy trenches and many battle-scarred trees remain as evidence of the historic encounter here.

[2] This was the first battle in the Nez Percé Indian War in which the tribe, driven from their Idaho homeland by broken promises and white duplicity, achieved a complete victory. The Nez Percé split the army detachment of Captain Perry in two and almost wiped out one segment.

[3] This site of the last major Indian battle in the United States is located 16 miles south of Chinook in eastern Montana. It is a little more than 40 miles from the Canadian line, across which Joseph believed he would find refuge for his people. It is now a Montana State Park.

[4] According to some historians, Joseph and his chiefs believed they had actually reached safety in Canada when they arrived in the Bears Paw country of northeastern Montana. "The mistake was discovered when General Miles attacked on September 30," states the Montana Guidebook. "A 4-day battle forced Joseph to make a decision — he must either surrender or abandon the wounded, the old women, and children."

[5] Chief White Bird (Peo-peo-hih-kis-kiok), known as a great medicine man as well as warrior, never returned to the United States. He died about five years after the surrender and is buried near Fort McLeod.

[6] Max Wilson, an attorney who has lived almost all his life in Joseph, Ore., recalls this sad visit by Joseph to Wallowa. Although he was only 14 years old at the time, Wilson followed the famed chief around during the three-day visit. So much had changed during the 22 years which had passed that Joseph realized there was no hope of his people going back to their beloved homeland in Idaho, although he continued to press for permission until his death.

Red Hawk in
Dakota badlands

The Oath (Oglala)

Ghost Dance:
Last Hope of the Sioux

By DOROTHY M. JOHNSON

SITTING BULL, grim and bitter Sioux, brooded on a reservation in Dakota Territory, watching his people starve.

"Our children are dying," they said. "We have nothing to live for any more."

Their countless herds of wild cattle, the buffalo, were gone. The tamer cattle they tried to raise, because the white man demanded it, died of blackleg. Crops had failed. Epidemics of measles, grippe and whooping cough swept disastrously through their camps.

But news of wonder swept the western plains, and Sitting Bull, medicine chief, listened to a rumor of hope for his people: "The good days of the plentiful buffalo herds are coming back again. The son of God has come to earth again, and this time he has come to the Indians alone. The white people will all be destoyed because long ago they killed him!"

Early in 1889 the rumor reached them, running with the wind from tribe to tribe — first the Utes and the Bannocks, then spreading to the Mohave, Caddo, Pawnee, Shoshone, Cheyenne and Arapaho tribes. The news was this:

"There is a new Messiah, and he is an Indian. There is a sacred dance you must learn, and songs you must sing.[1] Soon the Indian dead will live again and the white men will be swallowed up. His name is Wovoka, and he is an Indian like us. He lives in Nevada."

Was it true? It had to be true, for the Sioux needed a miracle.

Sitting Bull listened and waited. In the spring of 1890 he listened to more than a rumor. He had first-hand information from another Sioux leader, Kicking Bear, who had personally visited the new Messiah. Kicking Bear told him:

"The white men will all be swallowed up. God's son in Nevada has said so. Then the good days will come again. But he must hasten that time by learning the sacred dance and singing the holy songs.

"I, Kicking Bear, have learned the dance and the songs. I know the true ceremony of this religion. I can make seven priests."

Sitting Bull believed. He became a priest of the new religion, called the Ghost Dance because some of the dancers were able to go into a hypnotic trance and see the spirits of the dead. He painted his people in the sacred patterns prescribed by Kicking Bear, apostle of Wovoka. And they danced.

The running fire of hope blazed again among the Sioux. It roared into fury. The first Ghost Dance at Sitting Bull's camp was held October 9, 1890. Because of the dancing, Sitting Bull died two months later, and the last resistance of the desperate Sioux crumpled in the bloody snow before the white soldiers' guns at a creek called Wounded Knee.[2]

Then the Sioux were defeated indeed. They never tried again. The Ghost Dance religion had failed them, and it was their last hope.

But the Messiah down in Nevada, who had promised so much, lived on for more than forty years. He was a Paiute named Wovoka; he was also called Jack Wilson. His father before him had been a prophet, a mystic, had promised that the white men would be destroyed but all their improvements would be saved for the Indians.

There were plenty of miracle-promisers throughout the West. Along the Columbia River, 2000 Indians believed the preaching of Smohalla, who promised that all dead Indians would be resurrected and would conquer the whites. Smohalla went into trances in which he did not feel pain. He said, "Wisdom comes to us in dreams." His followers, called Dreamers, included the great Nez Percé leader, Chief Joseph.

Among the tribes on Puget Sound, an Indian named John Slocum came back to life after being dead six hours and started a religion called the Shakers. His followers used some Christian ceremonies but rejected the Bible. They even built some permanent churches.

There were miracles to be related — and miracles were sadly needed. The Sioux needed them worst of all. And so they learned the new Ghost Dance and saw visions and learned to hope again — for a little while.

The Indians of the Plains were open-minded about religion. Did it work? If so, they adopted it. They combined the new with the old, to despair of missionaries. Christianity was newer than their ancient animistic beliefs, and the doctrine of Wovoka, with its strong echoes of Christian beliefs, was newer still. Miracles, as preached by missionaries, were not new at all. Strange things could happen to anybody, and often did before missionaries ever reached them. They believed whatever they wanted to believe.

They wanted to believe in Wovoka. They called him "Our Father" and waited for deliverance and danced to hasten its coming.

Wovoka had his apostles. He himself did not travel far from his own small home area at Walker Lake, Nevada. But seekers for hope heard of him and searched him out — and returned to their people to spread the news of miracles.

One of these was a Cheyenne named Porcupine, who traveled in the fall of 1889 with two companions all the way from the Tongue River Reservation in Montana, searching for the source of the new gospel. These are Porcupine's own words, taken down by an interpreter when he got home:

"I knew nothing about this dance before going. I happened to run across it, that is all. The Fish-Eaters (Paiutes) told me that Christ had appeared on the earth again. They said Christ knew he was coming; that eleven of his children were also coming from a far land. It appeared that Christ had sent for me to go there, and that was why unconsciously I took my journey. It had been fore-ordained.

"Christ had summoned myself and others from all heathen tribes, from two to three or four from each of fifteen or sixteen different tribes. There were more different languages than I ever heard before and I did not understand any of them."

When Porcupine saw the man he identified as Christ, he was surprised to see the man was an Indian. He had always thought the Great Father was a white man.

"I had heard that Christ had been crucified," Porcupine related, "and I looked to see, and I saw a scar on his wrist and one on his face, and he seemed to be the man."

This is what Wovoka, the Messiah, told Porcupine and all the assembled, anxious people of many tribes:

"I am the man who made everything you see around you. I made this earth and everything on it. I have been to heaven and seen my own father and mother. In the beginning, after God made the earth, they sent me back to teach the people, and when I came back on earth the people were afraid of me and treated me badly. This is what they did to me."

He showed them his scars.

"I did not try to defend myself. I found my children were bad, so went back to heaven and left them. I told them that in so many hundred years I would come back to see my children. My father told me the earth was getting old and worn out, and the people getting bad, and that I was to renew everything as it used to be, and make it better."

So Porcupine, who felt he had been drawn mysteriously to the unknown, all-knowing Messiah, learned the sacred dance and taught it to his people, the Cheyennes.

Kicking Bear had gone to look for the Messiah, with two other Indians he did not know; they were mysteriously sent on the same errand, he said. In Nevada they met a man dressed like an Indian, but with long golden hair, who took them up a ladder of clouds and through a hole into the sky. There they met the Great Spirit and his wife. The golden-haired son showed him the marks of his crucifixion. (Wovoka was light for an Indian, but he had heavy black eyebrows and black hair.)

In that land above the sky, Kicking Bear saw a bad spirit, the Devil, who claimed half the people on earth. At first the Great Spirit would not give them up, because he loved them too much, but at last he let the Devil have the whites. The Indians were his chosen people.

Troop C, 8th Cavalry, Big Cheyenne River, 1890-91

The Great Spirit promised to rebuild the old, worn-out earth. He would send a thirty-foot wave of new soil over it to crush the whites — but the Indians, if they danced the spirit dance, would be suspended in the air while the wave surged under them.

Kicking Bear told Sitting Bull, "The Messiah hovered overhead while we were going back to the railroad. He taught us the dance and the songs."

The dance was not easy. The dancers fasted — but the Sioux were starving anyway. They were accustomed to hunger. Here, at last, was hope!

Kicking Bear and his delegation were not the only ones who brought the news to the Sioux. Another group went to see Wovoka. They saw old friends there, men and women long ago dead. On the way back, they killed a buffalo and ate it, but it came to life again, as Wovoka had promised would happen. He had promised, too, to make their return journey short — and one morning when they woke up, they found themselves miles farther along the way than when they had gone to sleep.

Among the prairie tribes the dance of the spirits spread like a grass fire. The Crows rejected it, for less than two years before they had had a prophet of their own, Sword-Bearer, who said bullets could not kill him — but bullets did. So the Crows stood like a bleak island of unbelief, and the prairie fire of the new religion swept past them and burst into a searing flame among the desperate Sioux.

The dance was not the same among all tribes. The Sioux introduced some changes that Wovoka had never preached. In June of that fatal year 1890, they first wore a new costume, which they called a ghost shirt. It was made of buckskin if there was any, or of painted cloth. The shirt was sacred; they believed it would turn away bullets. Both men and women wore the fringed and painted shirt, and both men and women wore a feather tied in the hair. This was an innovation; never before among Plains tribes had women been permitted the dignity of wearing a feather that way.

The Sioux gave up wearing ornaments made of metal, because metal came from the white man. But some of them carried guns in the dance — and that did not fit the peaceful waiting that Wovoka urged.

Neither did the ghost shirts, to ward off bullets. (Bullets were coming soon enough, because the white men were getting scared.) According to Wovoka there was no need for violence. Wovoka preached peace; Wovoka said, "My children, wait!"

Wovoka preached, "Wait, but you must not mourn while you are waiting. You must not kill ponies any more in mourning, or destroy your tepees or gash your flesh. You must not fight. A good time is coming. Be good, love one another, do not quarrel. Live in peace with the whites. Work hard, put away everything of war. And dance to hasten the coming of what I have promised."

Indian camp, Pine Ridge agency, S.D., Jan. 1891

There was nothing wrong with that — except the promise of Paradise on earth: All the dead Indians will come back to life. Nobody will be more than forty years old. The buffalo will come back to life. And the white men will all be swallowed up by the earth. But if you dance, you will be saved.

When the dancing began at his camp on Grand River in October, Sitting Bull made a dramatic gesture. He broke a peace pipe that he had kept for nine long years, ever since he had finally surrendered to the whites and accepted reservation restrictions.

"Why did you break the pipe?" he was asked.

He answered, "I want to die. I want to fight."

At his camp and on other reservations in the Dakotas, thousands of Indians were dancing, and the white agents were worried. One agent, James McLaughlin, sent a force of Indian police, including a captain and a second lieutenant, to arrest the apostle, Kicking Bear. But the police went back without him. The two Indian officers were dazed and glassy-eyed, afraid of Kicking Bear's great medicine power.

"The dancing must stop!" said Agent McLaughlin.

"We will go on dancing," said Sitting Bull. "We have had a message from the spirit world that we must dance or die."

These were two strong, stubborn men, completely opposed, irreconcilable, each sure he was doing the right thing. They had no use for each other, and McLaughlin had no use for the Ghost Dance. "Absurd," he called it over and over in his official reports." "Absurd . . . absurd . . . absurd." But calling the new faith of a desperate people absurd did not make it so.

The Sioux, many of them, dancing to exhaustion, were entering the spirit world for a little while and talking to the dead. Some of them were too hungry, too weak. Their spirits did not come back, and their bodies were buried, but without mourning. The outward tokens of savage grief were important among the Sioux — the cut-off hair of the mourners, the wailing, the gashed flesh and flowing blood, and sacrifices of ponies so the departed spirit would not have to go on foot. But so close was the resurrection, and so potent was Wovoka's warning not to grieve, that these customs were dropped for a little while.

There was even a time set for the resurrection, the coming of Indian heaven on earth: the spring of 1891.

Look now at this man Sitting Bull. He was brave in battle; he counted his first coup on an enemy when he was fourteen years old. He was a great medicine chief, a believer in wonders. After the Battle of the Little Big Horn in 1876, he took his people to Canada, and from there the United States authorities tried in vain for five years to get them back. Then Sitting Bull surrendered and went on a reservation. He was defeated — but he was never conquered.

He had the reputation of being humane, as Indian customs went — he never killed a captive. When there was food, he saw to it that the old people and the

The Ghost Dance (Arapaho)

helpless ones got a share of it. Unswervingly he worked to protect his people, and little thanks he got for it.

Most of the Sioux leaders turned traitor, in his opinion, when in 1889 they ratified an agreement with the government to release 10,000,000 acres of the Standing Rock Reservation for white settlement. When someone asked him how the Indian felt about that agreement, he answered in fury, "Indians! There are no Indians now but me!"

Sitting Bull was bitter against his own people, some of whom had gone over to the white men's side by joining the Indian police.

"The Great Spirit is punishing my people," proclaimed Sitting Bull, "because they gave away their land."

But bitter as he was, he painted the ghost dancers and whirled an eagle feather hypnotically to help them get a glimpse of the spirit world.

The Ghost Dance itself was no frenzied, leaping affair but a slow circling from right to left, hand in hand, bodies swaying, the feet hardly lifting from the ground. There was no sound of drum or rattle as in other Indian dances. But there was always the singing. For many persons, both men and women, there was the frightening, longed-for experience of entering a state of trance.

Sitting Bull, whose medicine was strong, would watch the dancers closely. When he saw one quiver, he would stare into the person's face and twirl an eagle feather, grunting, "*Hu! Hu! Hu!*" until the dancer's eyes glazed and he staggered and fell.

Later, when the person awoke, shuddering, he was helped to the center of the ring to tell what he had seen in the spirit world. A woman saw her dead child, and the experience was so real that she made him a pair of moccasins and carried them thereafter when she danced. Another, momentarily reunited with her mother, sang a song that became a favorite among her people:

> "Mother, come home; mother, come home.
> My little brother goes about always crying.
> Mother, come home; mother, come home."

A hunter who could hunt no more, now that the buffalo herds were gone, saw the great, ghostly herds again in the spirit world and came back to sing:

> "Now they are about to chase the buffalo.
> Grandmother, give me back my bow.
> The father says so. The father says so."

Those who danced the shuffling, dragging dance, day after day, without food or water, could indeed hear the thundering hoofs. Excitement was rising. Wild rumors swept the Sioux reservations — the Ghost Dance was effective! The dead were already on their way back, all the dead Indians, driving immense herds of buffalo and wild horses through the Rocky Mountain valleys! Keep dancing! They are coming!

"Sitting Bull must be arrested," proclaimed Agent McLaughlin. "He must be put in prison where he cannot do any damage."

Another agent brought matters to a head — D. F. Royer, who in October became an agent at the Pine Ridge Reservation. If there was ever a time when an agent needed steady nerves and a level head, that was it. Royer had neither. The Sioux gave him a name that showed what they thought of him: Lakota Kokipa-Koshkala — Young Man Afraid of Indians. In panic, he demanded that the army quiet his ghost-dancing charges.

Time was running out. Short Bull, one of the men who had gone to see the Messiah, announced that the end of the white men could not wait until spring because they were interfering so much with the Indians' religion. Within the next month, the great day would come!

"Gather all in one place," he warned, "and be ready. The Messiah is coming. Troops will surround you, but you must dance anyway. The soldiers' guns will not hurt you, and all the whites will be destroyed."

November 17, President Benjamin Harrison directed the Secretary of War to take over the problem. Troops began to pour into the Sioux Reservations. Infantry and cavalry, they marched and rode — and they included eight troops of the Seventh Cavalry. The Seventh had not forgotten what the Sioux had done to George A. Custer and his men at the Little Big Horn fourteen years before.

Three thousand terrified Indians fled to the Bad Lands, burning their cabins and destroying their own property if they couldn't take it along.

But Sitting Bull, the man who would not give up, did not run. At his camp the Ghost Dance continued.

Colonel William Cody, Buffalo Bill, offered to arrest the stubborn chief and got permission from General Nelson A. Miles. Agent McLaughlin managed to stop him. McLaughlin wanted Sitting Bull put in jail, but he knew that army interference would cause trouble, He had faith in his own Indian police force, and he was sure that advancing winter would stop the dancing anyway. (The winter clothing ration promised to the Sioux and due in August had not yet come and did not come until the middle of that winter.)

McLaughlin received an order from the army: "Arrest Sitting Bull."

There was no time to lose. Sitting Bull was getting ready for a journey. He was going to Pine Ridge, where he expected to meet God.

Forty-three Indian police rode all night to arrest Sitting Bull. From another direction, 100 cavalrymen with a Hotchkiss gun — light artillery — came in. At daybreak, December 15, 1890, they attempted the arrest.

The awakened medicine chief began to dress, while 150 of his frightened followers milled around outside his cabin. Then he changed his mind. He called to his people to help him — and someone fired a shot inside the crowded cabin.

The fight lasted only a few minutes. When it was over, fourteen Indians were dead. Six of them were members of McLaughlin's police force. Included among the other eight were Sitting Bull and his son Crow Foot, seventeen years old. There was worse to come, two weeks later, at a creek called Wounded Knee.

The great medicine chief, the stubborn fighter, Tatanka Iyotanke, Sitting Bull, dead at fifty-six after a lifetime of leadership, did not have the kind of funeral befitting such a man. His body was thrown into a wagon with others on top of it. Later the white men tossed it into a hole in the ground and poured in quicklime.

The fugitives in the Bad Lands were still a menace. Led by Big Foot, they included many of the frightened people who had followed Sitting Bull. The Seventh Cavalry pursued them, demanding unconditional surrender, and got it. The soldiers herded the Indians to Wounded Knee Creek. The military included 470 men with four Hotchkiss guns. Big Foot had 101 warriors with swarms of women and children.

Two weeks from the day of Sitting Bull's death, the encamped Indians — with a white truce flag hoisted — were ordered to deliver up their arms. Big Foot himself had pneumonia. Colonel George A. Forsythe had set up a camp stove in

Gathering dead, Wounded Knee battlefield

a tent where he would receive the sick chief. Trained directly on the camp were the four Hotchkiss guns, with troops posted all around, ready and wary.

A few Indians gave up old guns. Soldiers searched the tepees for more, tearing up packs and frightening the women and children. The tension and the anger of the warriors grew. Almost every one of them wore a ghost shirt.

Among them walked a medicine man named Yellow Bird, promising: "The soldiers can't hurt you. I have made medicine. They will become weak. And their bullets cannot go through the sacred shirts you wear."

A soldier tried to take a blanket off an Indian. Yellow Bird gave a signal — he threw a handful of dust into the air. Another Indian fired at the soldiers. The first volley of return fire from the military wiped out almost half the Indian warriors — then the fight was hand to hand, with knife and war club, revolver and rifle.

And the Hotchkiss guns poured two-pound explosive shells, nearly fifty per minute, into the screaming swarm of women and children.[3]

That was the "battle" of Wounded Knee. Three hundred Indians were cut down, two-thirds of them women and children. Bodies were found two miles away. A rifle bullet could easily catch up with a screaming woman trying to run with her baby. A woman named Blue Whirlwind had fourteen wounds, but she survived. So did her two little boys, both of whom were wounded.[4]

Not all little boys were so lucky. An Indian witness said later that some who had found hiding places came out when the soldiers shouted that they would be safe — and the soldiers butchered them.

One dying woman tore feebly at the ghost shirt that was stained with her life's blood.

'Take it off," she said. "It was no good after all."

Thirty-one soldiers died in the Battle of Wounded Knee; mostly by their own bullets.

Three days later, on New Year's Day, 1891, after a blizzard, troops went out to bury the dead. Four babies were found alive under the snow, wrapped in shawls by their dying mothers. Three of them died.

Bodies were frozen in queer, contorted positions. Big Foot, dead and frozen, was found half-sitting, his stiff hands beckoning, and a strange, grim smile on his cold lips. One woman with a baby in her arms had been killed as she almost touched the flag of truce. Young girls had buried their faces in their hands so as not to see death coming.

There was a mass burial of the Indian bodies, thrown into a long trench like cordwood until it was full, and earth heaped over them. Many of the bodies were thrown in naked, because soldiers stripped off the ghost shirts as souvenirs.

The Seventh Cavalry's terrible defeat at the Little Big Horn was avenged at Wounded Knee. The Ghost Dance had failed the desperate Sioux. The dead In-

Burial of dead after Wounded Knee

dians did not come across the plains from the Rockies, driving the great herds of lost buffalo and fine wild ponies. Sitting Bull, buried in quicklime, would never worry anyone any more.[5]

Wovoka, the Messiah who preached peace but created war, went on working as a farm hand in Nevada. He died forgotten, in 1932, at the age of seventy-eight.

NOTES

[1] *The Ghost-Dance Religion,* James Mooney; Extract from the 14th Annual Report of the Bureau of Ethnology, Government Printing Office, 1896. 1136 pages incl. index. Mooney spent 22 months and traveled 32,000 miles to get this information. He took part in the Ghost Dance among the Arapaho and Cheyenne Indians and met and talked with the Messiah.

[2] *The Last Days of Sitting Bull, Sioux Medicine Chief,* Usher L. Burdick, Baltimore, 1941.

[3] *Indian-Fighting Army,* Fairfax Downey, Charles Scribner's Sons, 1941. This one quotes General E. D. Scott as claiming that most of the Wounded Knee casualties among Indian women and children "must have been from Indian bullets." Another bit of information: Eighteen soldiers got the Medal of Honor for supreme gallantry in the Battle of Wounded Knee. Why?

[4] James Mooney says, "The whole number killed on the field, or who later died from wounds and exposure, was probably very nearly 300." Mooney, as an ethnologist, tried to be impartial and accurate. Fairfax Downey, writing half a century after the affair, says, "The Indian loss, warriors, women, and children, was 145 killed and 33 wounded." It is doubtful whether even the mourning Indians knew the exact figures, and certainly nobody else did. Many bodies were removed from the field before the army went back to count and bury the rest. Downey used one of several estimates made by army officers, and you may be sure the army wasn't claiming any larger number of dead Indians than it had to. The "battle" of Wounded Knee was embarrassing to the army. To the Indians involved, it was worse than that.

[5] For additional bibliography, see: *Death on Horseback,* Paul J. Wellman, J. B. Lippincott Co., 1947; *My People the Sioux,* Luther Standing Bear, edited by E. A. Brininstool, Houghton Mifflin Co., 1928.

Index